Understanding Homosexuality

The Pride and the Prejudice

Roger E. Biery

Edward-William Publishing Company
Austin, Texas

Published in the United States of America
By Edward-William Publishing Company
Number 292, P.O. Box 33280, Austin, Texas 78764

ISBN 0-934411-37-9 (hardcover)
       0-934411-38-7 (paperback)

Library of Congress Cataloging-in-Publication Data

Biery, Roger E., 1955 –
        Understanding homosexuality : the pride and the prejudice / Roger
E. Biery.
        p.   cm.
Includes bibliographical references and index.
ISBN 0-934411-37-9 (hardcover :   alk. paper) : $23.95
ISBN 0-934411-38-7 (softcover : alk. paper) : $15.95
        1. Homosexuality – United States.   2. Gays – United States – Psychology.
I. Title.
HQ76.3.U5B54   1990
306.76′6 – dc20   90-39122
                                                                                CIP

Dedicated to the brave men and women, straight and gay, who strive to protect the rights and dignity of all individuals.

Contents

Preface

This is a book about homosexuality. It is also a book about oppression and human suffering. But ultimately, it is a book about understanding.

You could be reading this book because you are homosexual or think you might be. Ten percent of the population is. This does not necessarily mean you understand homosexuality. You could be reading this book because someone you know and love is gay. You want to learn a little about homosexuality. Gay or straight, you just want to sort through your own feelings. In trying to do so, you may have become frustrated for there is very little readily available and reliable information about homosexuality. You might also feel uncomfortable discussing the subject. Sexuality in general is a very private matter; homosexuality is a particularly awkward topic. Non-gay individuals may be reluctant to ask questions of gay friends and relatives, and gay people may be hesitant to volunteer potentially unwanted information. Even when you find the opportunity to discuss the subject, where do you start? What do you say? Which questions are all right to ask and which ones are too personal?

Understanding Homosexuality: The Pride and the Prejudice attempts to cover what you would discuss in just such a conversation. The book will give you, as the title claims, a sense of understanding by clarifying the myriad facts and the fiction surrounding homosexuality. In addition, the material offers an awareness of and an appreciation for what it means to be gay in the United States. Psychologists call this "consciousness-raising." Finally, it provides practical guidance for overcoming potential barriers and to improve friendships and family relationships.

My research of over one hundred books and countless articles is shared with you in this single volume. It can serve as the source, or only as a starting point for your own knowledge of homosexuality. A wealth of other books, articles, and studies exists on the subject of homosexuality. Many of these are referenced in the bibliography. More than a few of them are intended for psychologists and sociologists. Some assume a basic knowledge of homosexuality which the reader might lack. Others are written for gay people and are sometimes difficult for non-gay readers to understand. *Understanding Homosexuality* assumes no such knowledge and avoids gay jargon. It is a book about the basics, simply presented. Yet it offers a thorough explanation about the condition and consequences of homosexuality. After reading this book, you should be able to read any of the others with much greater understanding.

The struggle for gay civil rights began in the United States in the 1950s. Millions of men and women, straight and gay, have made and continue to make great personal sacrifices in an effort to promote the acceptance of the gay minority in our society. This book is dedicated to these brave men and women. My hope is that it will make a similar contribution to eliminating prejudice.

Acknowledgments

Understanding Homosexuality addresses a complex subject. I accept the blame for its faults and share any praise for its value with those who have contributed. My sincere appreciation and gratitude goes to Rich Gordon, Jeff Johnson, Ralph Lentz, Jeff Levi, Jill Podolsky, Rick Rudy, James Watts, and Ken Yeager. Thank you for your thoughtful review of the many drafts. To Melissa Roberts, whose careful editing turned the "final" manuscript into a better book, thank you for making understanding so much easier. I would also like to thank Steve deSimon and David Schively for their help with the personal computer, and all the organizations and individuals who conducted the research cited throughout. Most of all, I want to thank my life-partner Leonard Bullock, whose love and support served as an inspiration.

Introduction:

A New View

If a little knowledge is dangerous, where is the man who has so much as to be out of danger? *Thomas Henry Huxley*

A grade-school science teacher was telling her class about the work of Copernicus in the sixteenth century. Copernicus was the first astronomer to claim the earth orbited the sun. This theory was met with great opposition since, at the time, people thought the sun revolved around the earth. One young man raised his hand and asked, "How could people have been so naive? Everyone knows the sun rises and sets because the earth rotates. That's obvious." Instead of answering his question directly, the teacher asked the class what it would look like if the sun actually did revolve around the earth. There was a pause before the young man responded, "I guess it would look just the same."

What is obvious to us now was not so obvious to our ancestors in the 1500s. We have the benefit of four more centuries of discovery. Four hundred years in the future, students will be asking the same kind of questions about many of our current beliefs—including those concerning homosexuality.

Knowledge is a precious resource. What we know serves as the very foundation for what we think and ultimately what we do. This is true for everyone. Knowledge is also a dynamic resource. This is true not only for humankind, but for each individual as well. Most people's knowledge of homosexuality is incomplete or inaccurate or both. Given the general stereotypical understanding prevalent in our society, what the individual "knows" has a negative effect on perceptions of homosexuality and gay people.

Dr. Wardell B. Pomeroy, from the Institute for Sex Research at Indiana University, observed, "There is probably more nonsense written about homosexuality, more unwarranted fear of it, and less understanding of it than of any other area of human sexuality." What most people "know" about this emotional subject has been supplied in bits and pieces over time by many sources for a variety of reasons. Even today, there is an incredible lack of readily available and reliable information in the United States about homosexuality. Rarely is the subject ever taught in our society's schools, churches, or homes. So we all must "learn" about homosexuality from what we read in newspapers, see on TV, hear in jokes,

1

and derive from stereotypes. Stories such as these are normally sensational and entertaining, but are seldom enlightening. Can you imagine what your understanding of heterosexuality or even humanity itself would be if these were your only sources?

For example, we all read articles from time to time about men sexually abusing young girls. But we know that not *all* straight people are like that. Everyone understands heterosexuality — even gay people do. Yet most people who read a similar article about a gay man will assume that such behavior is "typical." Why? Because very few people *understand* homosexuality.

The purpose of this book is to provide a complete, accurate, and coherent explanation of homosexuality and related topics. This additional knowledge, combined with the information you currently have, should help you make sense of or *understand* homosexuality.

Homosexuality is an intensely emotional issue, and most Americans have formed some opinion about homosexuality and gay people. Opinions are based on perception, and perception comes from perspective — not necessarily from reality. Your own current perspective might miss some of the reality of homosexuality, creating a misleading perception. Emerson wrote, "People only see what they are prepared to see." An expanded knowledge of homosexuality and gay people may give you a different perspective: a new view. A significant amount of the information contained in the following pages promises to be new to you. And there will be reminders of some relevant facts we all know, but that we sometimes forget or ignore. This different perspective may not change any of your opinions — but then again, it may.

Now, your new perspective requires an awareness of mine. Yes, I am gay. But that should not disqualify me from writing a book about homosexuality any more than being a Christian should disqualify someone from writing a book about religion. Maybe there are no truly objective observers of this emotional topic. But I have neither deliberately distorted nor omitted *any* relevant information. Such an attempt would only destroy the credibility so essential to the purpose of this book. My objectivity, therefore, is just as important as yours. I have also taken a nonjudgmental approach to all aspects of sexuality in general and homosexuality in particular. The privilege to pass judgment has been preserved for you. I will only, and rarely, introduce my opinion where I feel doing so will be helpful. Every such occurrence is clearly indicated.

Naturally, I must write from the perspective of a gay white male. I have tried my best to empathize for your perspective, whether you are straight or gay, male or female, young or old, black or white, Christian or Jew, liberal or conservative. My perspective is not necessarily a limitation, though, because homosexuality has been defined mostly in the context of white males. Of course, this has been a mixed "blessing" for gay men. Similarly, religious matters are considered from a Protestant Christian perspective. This, too, is not really a limitation, because Jewish and Christian beliefs concerning homosexuality have common roots and are nearly identical as a result.

Most of what is presented in the following pages is fact; some is theory. I would have preferred to rely solely on fact, but in many areas theory is all that exists. Nevertheless, every theory offered is backed by solid evidence and extensive research. I avoided the use of anecdotes as evidence and instead cited empirical information, or statistics, as the basis for any general conclusions. Each of the numerous studies mentioned has been conducted by reputable organizations using generally accepted scientific methods.

Please keep in mind, though, that no generalization is universally applicable. This is especially true when considering the almost infinite capacity for human diversity. Recognize also that a "positive" statement about homosexuality should not be taken as a "negative" statement about heterosexuality. They are not opposites, nor are they mutually exclusive in our society.

Understanding Homosexuality is divided into six sections. The chapters in the first section provides a basic understanding of exactly what homosexuality is through a precise definition and a review of the significant studies conducted during the past century. Some of these studies focused on the condition of homosexuality, while others looked for causes and "cures." Section II, "Gay Reality," initially discusses what homosexuality is *not*—in other words, the stereotypes and myths. It then covers gay lifestyles and the gay community, providing some insight into what most gay people are like. Section III on "What is Homophobia?" investigates the causes and effects of prejudice against gay people. In Section IV, "The Church and Homosexuality," Judeo-Christian tradition is examined closely. Biblical passages pertinent to homosexuality are analyzed in detail. Even if you are not particularly religious, you might find this section meaningful for its historical value.

Given the way our culture views homosexuality, being gay becomes a social experience that cannot be understood without an appreciation for the problems faced by gay men and lesbians. These issues are reported in Section V: "Gay in the USA." Some may be relevant to you or a loved one. The consequences of full acceptance and integration of gay citizens, including the history and the status of the Gay Civil Rights Movement, are also examined. Finally, Section VI on "Your Family and Friends" explores what it is like to grow up gay and adopt a gay identity. This is the "coming out" process. The book concludes by offering practical advice on how gay and straight people can better relate to each other.

It is best to read *Understanding Homosexuality* from front to back, as each chapter builds on information from the previous ones. This is especially true for readers who are new to the subject. More knowledgeable readers may find some parts more enlightening than others.

If you have an appetite for more information, the bibliography identifies additional books and other materials. If you make the effort, you *will* understand homosexuality—and that requires first knowing *precisely what homosexuality is.*

Understanding the Definitions

Groups are subject to the truly magical power of words. *Sigmund Freud*

No single definition of "homosexuality" has been universally accepted. In fact, there is no single definition of "sexual orientation" that enjoys universal acceptance either. Most authors of articles and books on homosexuality therefore find it necessary to provide their own definition that encompasses some combination of sexual feelings, drives, fantasies, behaviors, or identities. This author is no exception.

The word *homosexual* was first used in 1869 by Hungarian journalist Dr. Karoly M. Kertbeny. The word *heterosexual* did not exist until a few decades later. Around the turn of the century, this new concept of sexual orientation finally caught on and became commonly used. The prefix *homo* comes from the Greek word for "same," not the Latin word for "man." The suffix sexual has a double meaning: Gender (male or female) and sexual activity. The construct *homosexual* literally means "the same sex," but normally refers to "same-sex sexuality."

Webster's Ninth New Collegiate Dictionary supplies all the definitions in *Understanding Homosexuality*. It defines *homosexual* as "of, relating to, or characterized by a tendency to direct sexual desire toward another of the same sex." It defines *homosexuality* in two ways: "The quality or state of being homosexual" and "erotic activity with another of the same sex." These definitions are at once accurate and misleading because they do not distinguish between same-sex sexual activity and an individual who is homosexual. This important distinction is not always made in discussions of homosexuality. Emphasis is usually placed on the sexual activity or behavior, as this is the only tangible aspect of sexual orientation. It is necessary to recognize, however, that homosexuality, just like heterosexuality, is something one is — not something one does.

Momentarily ignoring the distinction between the words *homosexual* and *homosexuality* reveals there are actually two meanings at issue here. The first would more appropriately be called homo*affectional*. It refers to an emotional and erotic *attraction* to persons of the same gender. Both emotions and eroticism are psychological in nature. The emotion is love; the eroticism is sexual arousal. Neither constitutes behavior. The second meaning could truly be considered homo*sexual*. It refers to the general phenomenon of same-sex sexual activity — the behavior — which can be purely sexual without the presence of emotional or erotic attraction to persons of the same gender. In other words, it is possible for an individual to engage in same-sex sexual activity without being homosexual (emotionally and erotically attracted to persons of the same gender). Sex in prison is a perfect example of this. Conversely, an individual who is homosexual (possessing an emotional and erotic attraction to persons of the same gender) might not engage in same-sex sexual activity. *This is because sexual orientation consists in feelings, not in behavior.* Basically, then, homosexuality, like heterosexuality, is actually a sexual-affectional *orientation*.

4

In addition, this feeling of emotional and erotic attraction must be consistent, not fleeting; predominant or exclusive, not incidental. Homosexuality, therefore, is the "consistent, predominant or exclusive, emotional and erotic attraction to persons of the same gender." Similarly, heterosexuality is the "consistent, predominant or exclusive, emotional and erotic attraction to persons of the opposite gender." If neither of these definitions describes your own sexual orientation, then you may be either asexual (no emotional or erotic attraction to others) or bisexual (emotional and erotic attraction to persons of both genders).

Yes, this is confusing. But *not* knowing the precise meaning of "homosexuality" serves as the foundation for its misunderstanding. It is fundamental to a clear understanding of homosexuality that a distinction be made between feelings and behavior. These two different meanings are frequently used and misused interchangeably. The reason for this distinction will become clear in the first chapter. For now, it may be helpful simply to memorize this definition and keep it mind: *Homosexuality is the consistent, predominant or exclusive, emotional and erotic attraction to persons of the same gender.*

There is an important difference between "homosexual" and "gay" as well. The word *gay* defines those individuals who have a homosexual component to their identity. Its use avoids any possible confusion between *homosexual*, the individual sexual orientation, and *homosexual*, the common means of describing same-sex sexual activity where the participants may or may not be homosexual. Originally believed to be a code word for locating other homosexual people, "gay" was adopted as a deliberate contradiction to the stereotypes. Being gay encompasses a wider social and political consciousness inherent to identifying with the homosexual minority. Once again, this will all become clear later.

The words *homosexual* and *gay* should be used only as adjectives to describe emotional or erotic feelings, sexual acts when accompanied by those feelings, or a professed identity with this minority group. These words should not be used as nouns to substitute for *person*. For example, "He is gay" or "He is a gay man" is preferred over "He is a gay." As with all other minorities, this distinguishing feature, sexual orientation, is only part of a person's total identity. It is impossible to define anyone fully by his or her sexual orientation, straight or gay. Because our society views homosexuality primarily as a male phenomenon, the word *gay* is frequently used only in reference to men. Most gay women prefer the term *lesbian*, as this emphasizes the double minority status of being both homosexual and female. Purely as a matter of convenience in this book, I normally refer to gay men and lesbians simply as *gay people*. Where the differences between gay men and lesbians are substantial or important, a distinction will be made.

Knowing what is meant by these words is only the beginning of a real understanding, for homosexuality is viewed as being much more than "just" a sexual orientation in our society.

5

The Wider Meaning of "Sexual Orientation"

The feelings of homosexual emotional and erotic attraction are *exactly* the same as those for heterosexuality. In fact, homosexuality *in and of itself* is nearly identical to heterosexuality. Interestingly enough, straight people can easily understand homosexual emotional and erotic feelings through a vicarious experience. One need only view homosexuality from a different perspective. If you are a straight woman, you experience the exact same feelings toward men that gay men do. Similarly, if you are a straight man, your feelings toward women are identical to the emotional and erotic attraction lesbians have for one another. The basic difference, then, between heterosexuality and homosexuality is whether these feelings are directed toward an individual of the opposite or of the same gender. Society's perception of and reaction to this difference are what make the issue immensely more complex.

The universal expectation in our society is that men and women are *always* mutually attracted to each other. This serves as the basis for the misunderstanding of homosexuality. Knowing someone is gay should reveal about as much as knowing someone is straight—basically, very little. Yet many folks feel the label homosexual so thoroughly describes a person's place and purpose in life that it is unnecessary to know anything else. The gay identity has actually become so significant that it is viewed as being not just a sexual orientation, but an entire way of life.

That brings up the final distinction which is essential to a clear understanding of homosexuality: The difference between sexual orientation and the many *non*sexual aspects of life regularly associated with sexuality, hetero or homo. To be considered gay, a man or a woman must have a consistent, predominant or exclusive, emotional and erotic attraction to persons of the same gender. As already mentioned, this attraction indicates absolutely nothing about specific, individual behavior. All people, gay or straight, make numerous decisions or value judgments about conducting their lives. Homosexuality is *not* a course of conduct; it is a condition of being. In other words, homosexuality is an orientation, not an implementation or "lifestyle." The condition of homosexuality becomes an essential part of the individual, but not the whole. The consequences of society's beliefs about homosexuality have a *much* greater influence on gay people than their sexual orientation does. The self-repression and social oppression of homosexuality become *the most significant* influential factors on a gay person's total sexual and nonsexual existence. The orientation is discussed in Section I; the implementation, or *how* gay people live, is discussed in Section II, "Gay Reality."

Keeping the Proper Perspective

If you look at life one way, there is always cause for alarm. *Elizabeth Bowen*

Sex is undoubtedly a topic of great interest. It is virtually impossible to get through a single day without being exposed to sexuality in some way through advertisements, news articles, casual conversation, TV pro-

6

grams, radio shows, jokes, or some other means. There is a double standard, however, in the way society views sexuality for gay and straight people. Heterosexuality is so common it has become transparent. Consider how infrequently the word *heterosexual* is used. The word *homosexual*, on the other hand, is used regularly, normally to describe sensational events and controversial subjects. As a result, homosexuality is made to be extraordinary, even though the vast majority of gay people are quite ordinary.

Because heterosexuality is so common, so openly and favorably discussed, gay people know a great deal about it. They know heterosexuality is *not* just about sex. Most gay people never really think about straight sex. They obviously know it exists, but they also recognize it has little effect on them personally. So heterosexuality is not an issue for gay people. Even when most gay people find it necessary, for whatever reason, to consider straight sex, they do not generally find it objectionable in any way.

Conversely, a straight person may know very little about homosexuality. It is primarily for this reason that homosexuality is frequently considered a "lifestyle" in a purely sexual context. Same-sex sexual activity is the facet which becomes the focus. Many straight people even feel that gay men and lesbians must be obsessed with sex: why else would they subject themselves to such negative social consequences? Of course, this occurs while simultaneously denying any prejudice actually exists. Even though sex is a part of homosexuality, it is *not* the proper perspective.

Another analogy with astronomy helps demonstrate the limitations a focus on sexual activity will place on a clear understanding of homosexuality. For centuries it was believed that stars were small points of light in the sky. The invention of the telescope revealed that these "small points of light" (perhaps a thousand) were actually huge suns, much bigger than ours but much farther away. As telescope technology improved, astronomers realized that some "stars" were actually complete galaxies, each containing billions of stars. Every new scientific discovery reminds us that, even though we know a great deal about the universe, there remains so much more to learn. Simplicity in any area of study, including human sexuality, is often replaced with a more complex reality as knowledge increases.

Consider this: Is it that gay people only can think of sex, or that non-gay people who consider homosexuality think only of the sexual aspects? Everyone knows that heterosexuality is not limited to sex. The same is true of homosexuality. Just like heterosexuality, homosexuality is really nonsexuality most of the time. Drs. Alan Bell and Martin S. Weinberg from the Institute for Sex Research at Indiana University point out, "An important lesson to be learned from our data is that homosexual men and women are best understood when they are seen as whole human beings, not just in terms of what they do sexually, despite the connection between sex and other aspects of their lives."

This is the proper perspective. Gay people are not sexual beings, but whole human beings—the same as straight people are. They are influenced by their feelings (emotional and erotic attraction to persons of the same gender) and, as social beings, by society's stereotypical view of their homosexuality (the maligned "gay lifestyle"). To understand homosexuality, it is important to distinguish the *real* difference (the gender of attraction) from the myriad other *perceived* differences (the so-called "lifestyle").

A final word on words is in order here. One of the problems in keeping the proper perspective is that words paint pictures. Too often, the existing pictures are inaccurate. The phrase *sexual orientation* itself only serves to emphasize sexual activity. The same is true of the word *homosexual*. In the early struggle for social acceptance, the word *homophile* was used for this very reason. It minimized the sexual aspect of homosexuality, emphasizing the capacity for love instead. Its use never became accepted by the dominant society, though, which continued to view homosexuality strictly in terms of sexual activity. The word *gay* suffers from a similar problem. Although it connotes happiness, it can also mean one who is "given to social pleasures," which can be taken to mean sex — or worse! By contrast, *straight* has the meaning of "exhibiting no deviation from what is established as usual, normal, or proper." But this may well *not* be true for many facets of a straight person's life, including sexual activity. So the word *straight* is not perfect either, although it is a vast improvement over words like *normal*, which suffer from these same problems and more. Finally, some straight people are offended by the word *straight*.

Unfortunately, I was unable to locate a better alternative than "straight," so I trust that straight readers will not take offense because none is intended. Even the phrase *non-gay*, as strange as it might sound, is not synonymous with *straight*. This will become clear in the following chapter. Imperfect as they may be, these are the only words available in our language. Please keep their limitations in mind.

The above discussion was not meant to be an exercise in semantics, but words can sometimes take on more meaning than intended. The words *homosexual, homosexuality, lesbian,* and *gay,* used frequently throughout this book, are always employed in the context of the consistent, predominant or exclusive, emotional and erotic attraction to persons of the same gender. They should not be encumbered with additional or different meanings as this is not their intended use. I will avoid these words when referring to any same-sex sexuality which is *not* in this context. The author of other books and articles you may read, or statements others make, might not use these words in precisely the same way. Such is the business of being misunderstood. In any event, remembering these considerations will help maintain a proper perspective in *Understanding Homosexuality*.

Section I:

What is Homosexuality?

Chapter 1:

The Search for An Understanding

We are always paid by our suspicion by finding what we suspect.
Henry David Thoreau

It could be said that homosexuality began in the nineteenth century, when the word was used for the first time, but a label does not give birth to something. Same-sex affection and eroticism have existed since the beginning of recorded history — and probably long before that. It is proper, however, to say that the *study* of something begins when it is identified.

To study cultures of the past, historians rely on the literature and laws of the period. In Old Testament biblical times, same-sex sexual activity was thought to be the idolatrous worship of false gods. Around the time of Christ, the story of Sodom and Gomorrah, where the men of these cities wanted "to know" angelic visitors, began to take on a purely sexual meaning. The word *sodomy*, often used in the context of sexual activity between men, came from this story. Even though sodomy was considered sinful by many early Christians, same-sex sexual activity was practiced widely in the Greek and Roman civilizations. During the Crusades and the Inquisition of the Middle Ages, same-sex sexual acts became a "crime against nature" in the eyes of the church. This "crime" was punishable by death. In sixteenth-century England, when King Henry VIII wrested power from the church, he used ecclesiastical law as the basis for English Common Law and declared that the "detestable and abominable vice of buggery" was a felony, also punishable by death. "Buggery" is synonymous with "sodomy." In effect, what was sinful in the eyes of the church became illegal in the eyes of the state. Colonial America, modeling its legal system after English common law, adopted this same view of the "crime against nature" as a capital offense. As each state was added to the Union, this view propagated as a matter of tradition.

All of these prohibitions were created before homosexuality existed as a concept. Historically, then, same-sex sexual activity was viewed as sinful idolatrous worship, heresy, and a "crime against nature." Everyone was thought to be straight, even though heterosexuality did not exist as a concept either. What was sinful to the church and criminal

10

to the state would eventually become a sickness to the science of psychology.

Immediately after sexual orientation was identified in the nineteenth century, homosexuality became an area of scientific study. The most significant of these studies are presented in this chapter. (The history of "homosexuality" prior to its identification is covered in more detail in Chapter 10.) It is not at all surprising that such an emotional and sensitive area of study would generate a great deal of suspicion and potential controversy. That being the case, most of the early "findings" about homosexuality served only to affirm the centuries-old cultural and religious beliefs. After all, anyone who studied sex was morally suspect and viewed as some sort of deviant in the first place. Any nonconformist theory would have been instantly rejected; the scientist's reputation ruined. Yet science is not truly science unless it is totally objective. Conclusions which conform to current social opinions must be examined just as critically as those which do not. Objectivity concerning homosexuality would not exist for nearly seventy-five years after these initial studies.

The kind of controversy caused by any findings not conforming with popular beliefs is demonstrated by Dr. Alfred C. Kinsey's publication of *Sexual Behavior in the Human Male* in 1948. This book reported the results of research conducted on numerous aspects of male sexuality. One of Kinsey's findings was that thirty-seven percent of *all* men had engaged in same-sex sexual activity at least once in their adult lives. The popular belief at the time was that if any man engaged in a single same-sex sexual act, he was homosexual. It is now known that this is not true; many heterosexual men engage in same-sex sexual activity. Still, Kinsey's work was widely criticized. People protested, claiming homosexuality could not be *that* prevalent.

Kinsey's study was challenged for its sociological effects as well. Because most people felt talking about homosexuality would "encourage" it, they advocated censorship. The findings were also denounced for their lack of moral commentary. Dr. Kinsey believed scientists should be completely objective. He did not condemn the behavior he found, he merely reported it. But the criticism continued, much of it directed at the Medical Division of the Rockefeller Foundation, which funded this study. A special congressional committee even held hearings to review the book and its consequences. They "decided" the research was unscientific, its findings insulted the public, and that its effects would weaken American morality and render the nation more susceptible to Communist takeover. This is not a very surprising conclusion when you consider the mood of McCarthyism at the time.

The widely held and deeply rooted negative social attitudes toward homosexuality turned the initial search for an understanding into a search for a cause. It was felt that knowing the cause would lead to a "cure." Society generally does not concern itself with the cause for statistically significant conditions such as heterosexuality. But many felt compelled to find a cause for homosexuality solely because it was different, a variation of the majority's heterosexual "norm."

11

For decades, the emphasis on cause and "cure" would destroy scientific objectivity in the search for any real understanding of homosexuality. Before discussing the studies that shaped society's understanding of homosexuality, it is helpful to examine the damaging effect this built-in bias has on getting the facts straight — so to speak. With an awareness of the these considerations, you will be able to determine for yourself which studies you might read in this book, and elsewhere, are truly meaningful.

Homosexuality: The Problems with Getting It Straight

Get your facts first, then you can distort 'em as you please. *Mark Twain*

Homosexuality is not a purely psychological issue; its study cannot be restricted to any single field of science. Gay people have been studied extensively by the sociologist, the anthropologist, the physiologist, the endocrinologist, the biologist, and so on. From late in the nineteenth century, the lack of knowledge about homosexuality led to a perspective which viewed this variation of sexual orientation as a course of conduct, or behavior, rather than as a condition of being. Because psychology is the primary science for the study of behavior, most of the earlier research was conducted by psychologists. It was also felt that if a "cure" were to be found, it would be found in psychology. All other fields of science offered little, if any, "therapeutic optimism."

To begin, there were very few serious studies of homosexuality. Several reasons exist for this. The stigma associated with homosexuality motivated many individuals to pursue more "socially acceptable" research. There was a perceived lack of need to test current "known" theories. The concept of homosexuality itself was initially difficult to define with accuracy. This will become clear later. There were also the many difficulties inherent to the study of human subjects, especially in biology. Finally, the existence of strong social prejudice made it nearly impossible to locate truly representative study subjects.

What little research was conducted was plagued with problems. Drs. Martin S. Weinberg and Colin J. Williams noted: "The Institute for Sex Research bibliography is replete with examples of work which did not measure up to minimal canons of scientific research." Most of these studies began with the assumption that heterosexuality was the expected development always, and attempted to show "what went wrong" to cause homosexuality. Dr. Sigmund Freud concluded that "one of the tasks implicit in object choice is that it should find its way to the opposite sex." Dr. Irving Bieber put it this way: "We assume that heterosexuality is the biological norm, and that unless interfered with all individuals are heterosexual."

With this approach, homosexual development becomes abnormal by definition. If on the other hand, normal development is defined as the ability to offer and accept love, and to do so sexually as well, then gay people would be considered normal. But the question asked was not, "What causes homosexuality?" Instead, the questions leading to the hy-

12

pothesis for research were: "What goes wrong to cause homosexuality?" or "What could be done to prevent homosexuality?" or "What process could be used to 'cure' homosexuality?"

Clinical psychology is a specialty dealing with the therapeutic *practice* of psychology. This would only serve to fuel the emphasis on finding a "cure." The pure scientist's approach to research and the interpretation of data is not predetermined in this fashion. Clinical psychologists, by the very nature of their work, are involved in concepts of acceptability and desirability, both of which are socially defined. For the psychologist, there is something wrong, or pathological, with anything that is less than ideal. Homosexuality certainly fits this description in our society. Further, psychology is not a precise science, as is physiology. It is relatively easy to locate, isolate, and measure physical variables with complete objectivity. Studies of mental variables tend to be conducted using a trial-and-error process that is replete with subjective evaluation.

Remember, sexual orientation consists in feelings — not in behavior. To study *feelings*, it is necessary to rely on the research subject to supply nearly all of the desired data. Of course, people are inherently unreliable observers of themselves. Everyone tends to reconstruct the past in light of present information. Earlier experiences take on different meaning and significance when viewed retrospectively. Much of society's negative views regarding homosexuality are internalized. These include the current cause theories and the popular stereotypes. In other words, homosexual subjects "learned" about their "problem" *prior* to being studied. The psychological interview normally focused on childhood problems and was guided to an *expected* result. These "conclusions" were reached primarily through the selective emphasis and interpretation of "pertinent" information. Facts not supporting the hypothesis being tested were merely ignored.

For example, research subjects in one study were asked to read information about a woman. Half of the group was later told the woman was lesbian. This half recalled details which were consistent with lesbian stereotypes. The other half, having been told the woman was straight, recalled much different information.

Down's syndrome, or mongolism, serves as another example. In 1958 the "results" of one study claimed that mothers of children born with Down's syndrome had experienced more "shocks" during pregnancy than mothers of perfectly healthy children. This implies that a mother's mental state during pregnancy had a profound effect on her fetal child. A few years later, it was discovered that Down's syndrome was actually caused by an abnormality in the child's chromosomes. Sociologist George W. Brown commented: "The obvious explanation for the original result was that mothers of mongol children had been searching for the reasons to explain their tragedy and were likely to recall shocks or to define quite ordinary events as shocks where mothers of normal children would not. In other words, they assigned a meaning to what happened during pregnancy, *after* the birth of the child, which they would not necessarily have considered noteworthy *prior* to its birth. Such reworking of the past can obviously play havoc with aetiological studies and the example is representative of a number of problems that have to be faced."

This demonstrates the difficulties in determining the cause and the effect of independent variables. For example, consider a theory which proposes that children become gay by identifying with the "wrong" parent. Yet the parent-child relationship is a two-way street. Both parties influence the behavior of the other. Is a boy homosexual because he did not identify with his father, or did he not identify with his father because Dad was repulsed by homosexuality? Or perhaps the father created tension in their relationship due to the boy's perceived lack of "masculine" interests. Which is cause and which is effect?

That brings up another problem. Social attitudes about gender differences have contaminated much of this research. In fact, the very subject of gender is frequently intrusive. For example, femininity and masculinity really have nothing to do with sexual orientation. They are aspects of nonsexual behavior assigned to each gender by social conditioning. Expectations for gender-related behavior range from the degree of aggressiveness or compassion to interests in activities such as sports, the arts, and even vocational pursuits. None of these variables has anything to do with sexual activity or sexual orientation. (This will be explored more in Chapter 3).

There is also the inherent problem of being a "foreigner" in the study of homosexuality. Most studies have been conducted by straight researchers. There are two reasons for this: Most people are straight and gay people are somehow viewed as being less objective. But nonhomosexual people can easily miss the subtle and even obvious aspects of homosexuality. Dr. Alan Bell of the Institute for Sex Research described his concern this way: "I myself feel terribly remote from those who I am in the process of studying, writing from lists reporting significant differences between various samples of individuals I have never met and who have lived out their lives in a social setting I have never known. Because of this, and because of a variety of personal and theoretical biases which keep me uninformed, I am convinced that we have failed to tap important dimensions of the homosexual experience." Gay people, on the other hand, inherently understand this area of study. Individuals of each sexual orientation might be biased in their observations and conclusions equally, but differently. Neither is inherently biased, though. More recent research is conducted by a team of straight and gay men and women.

A number of other problems affected earlier research. Much of it lacked the reliability afforded by large sample sizes. Because these "limited" studies had too few data points, they frequently reached conflicting conclusions. Also, when previous research is verified, consistent methods should be used. This was not always the case with studies of homosexuality. There were frequently no "control" groups used for comparison either. Such standards of measure should always be employed in good scientific research to eliminate independent or irrelevant variables. When control groups were used, they normally consisted of laboratory workers, volunteers, or other unclassified groups. All were *assumed* to be straight, even though ten percent were likely to have been homosexual. Finally, there existed a single cultural influence: What is viewed as unnatural or unacceptable in the United States—including homosexuality—is considered perfectly normal in many other countries.

The single most serious problem was the use of nonrepresentative samples of study subjects. Most of the earlier research was conducted using patients undergoing psychotherapy. They were selected regardless of whether or not their problems related to their *possible* homosexuality (many of these troubled people were, in fact, not really homosexual). In addition, homosexuality was thought to be a homogeneous condition. If an individual had sexual involvement with another person of the same gender, he or she was thought to be *exactly* the same as *everyone* else who also engaged in sexual activity with persons of the same gender. Because it was felt homosexuality was pathological behavior, there was no perceived need to question the use of only psychiatric patients to gain a "general" understanding. Because homosexuality was defined as a sickness, it was assumed that all gay people were as "sick" as those who "properly" sought treatment. Earlier research subjects also included prisoners, military personnel faced with dishonorable discharges for same-sex sexual conduct, and volunteers from homophile organizations. The obvious bias in these nonrepresentative samples went unrecognized until recently.

Consider prison sex as an example. For lack of a better term, the existence of sexual activity in prisons has been labeled "homosexuality." Undoubtedly, some prisoners are homosexual. But same-sex sexuality in prisons is not necessarily homosexuality. For most participants, it is purely a physical release with no emotion and no love. The vast majority of prisoners who participate in same-sex sexual acts consider themselves to be heterosexual. Most of them, probably ninety percent, are. This is amply demonstrated by their heterosexual sex lives after being released from prison. In other words, the "homosexual" rape in prisons is normally perpetrated by heterosexual inmates. In fact, most prisoners really despise homosexuality. Gay men are subjected to severe abuse while in jail. Prison mentality regarding sexuality is "conquer or be conquered." If an inmate is not the active partner, he will end up the passive partner— the "woman." As a result, gay men are frequently raped in prisons— not only by the prisoners but sometimes by the guards. This kind of sexuality is not concerned with mutual pleasure; it is not even derived from emotional or erotic attraction. It is *not* homosexuality.

Yet the most misleading subjects, producing the most damaging "results," were the ever-so-popular psychoanalysis patients. Drs. Bell and Weinberg from the Institute for Sex Research observed: "Another obvious and understandable finding is that clinical samples of homosexual men and women are much more apt to include persons who regret their homosexuality. Unfortunately it is these conflicted people's determination to become heterosexual which has been most evident in the literature and which has prompted clinicians to believe that homosexuality is inevitably problematic for those involved."

15

What if similar samples were used to study heterosexuality? Would convicted rapists, who are apparently straight, make excellent study subjects of heterosexuality? Perhaps divorce lawyers or marriage counselors could provide a list of "typical" heterosexual couples. The bias in these samples is obvious. Dr. Wardell Pomeroy commented on the use of non-representative study subjects: "If my concept of homosexuality were developed from my practice, I would probably concur in thinking of it as an illness. I have seen no homosexual man or woman in that practice who was not troubled, emotionally upset, or neurotic. On the other hand, if my concept of marriage in the United States were based on my practice, I would have to conclude that marriages are all fraught with strife and conflict, and that heterosexuality is an illness." Drs. William Simon and John H. Gagnon recognized this same double standard: "When the heterosexual meets these minimal definitions of mental health, he is exculpated; the homosexual — no matter how good his adjustment in nonsexual areas of life is — remains suspect."

In summary, then, here was a situation where not only was the data limited and error-prone, but it was interpreted subjectively by individuals who did not fully understand the condition being studied, while working under social suspicion and prejudice. This led to some greatly distorted conclusions, which were only convincing if the many shortcomings in the research methods were overlooked. In fact, many studies were mere self-fulfilling prophecies. According to Irving Bieber and the Society of Medical Psychoanalysts, "If we assume that homosexuality is a pathological condition, and our data strongly support this assumption . . ." Each new "study" served to propagate the prejudice on which it was based. And when homosexuality was legitimized as an area of study based on Kinsey's work in 1948 — as the masses of newly self-proclaimed experts tried to help the world understand its ramifications — volume after volume poured out of the labs and onto the streets. The situation during the next twenty years deteriorated to the point of becoming difficult, if not impossible, to separate the wheat from the chaff in an environment where what was "obvious" yesterday would be considered ridiculous tomorrow with today's research. Dr. C. A. Tripp remarked that what resulted was a "fiercely dangerous set of emotions that has proved itself capable of corrupting every channel of enlightenment and of suppressing information that would ultimately be useful to everyone's understanding of himself and the world around him." How ironic that so many researchers were "only trying to help."

Masturbation Insanity

A revealing, and entertaining, example of these problems is found in a subject which closely parallels the social taboo of homosexuality: masturbation. Masturbation was originally called *onania*. This word comes from the story of Onan found in the biblical passage of Genesis 38:6-10. Onan "wasted his seed" instead of using it to impregnate a woman. Wasting seed was not the point of the story, but it was misinterpreted as such for centuries. The original prohibitions against homosexuality were also based on misunderstood biblical passages (to be covered in Section IV on "The Church and Homosexuality").

After having been labeled as sinful, masturbation was then declared a medical and social hazard in 1710 in a treatise titled: *Onania, or the Heinous Sin of Self-Pollution.* It was written by a former minister turned physician. Within fifty years hysterical attitudes were common. In Dr. Tissot's book *Onania, or a Treatise upon the Disorders Produced by Masturbation,* published in 1758, he lists these disorders as consumption, deterioration of eyesight (yes, stop it or you'll go blind), impotence, and insanity. Tissot felt masturbation was a "flagrant crime" and spoke of its victim's deteriorated condition as one "which more justly entitles him to the contempt than the pity of his fellow creatures."

Other evils believed to be caused by masturbation included acne, tainted heredity, seminal weakness, vertigo, epilepsy, hypochondria, loss of memory, shifty eyes, tumors, constipation, hemorrhoids, stupidity, uterine hemorrhaging, bladder disorders, tuberculosis, paralysis, cancer, functional disorders of the heart, spinal irritation, destruction of the central nervous system, schizophrenia, a fondness for eating plaster, palpitation, hysteria, convulsions, emaciation, debility, poor vision, loss of hair, mania, mock piety, disordered childhood growth, perversion of feeling, derangement of thought, nocturnal hallucinations, suicidal and homicidal propensities, "moral leprosy," and even death. Dr. Freud would later add neurosis to this avalanche of evils caused by masturbation.

In a nineteenth-century edition of the *New Orleans Medical and Surgical Journal,* a doctor commented, "In my opinion, neither plague, nor war, nor smallpox, nor a crowd of similar evils, have resulted more disastrously for humanity than the habit of masturbation: it is the destroying element of civilized society." This same view was expressed by another doctor who declared, "Of all the vices and of all the misdeeds which may properly be called crimes against nature, which devour humanity, menace its physical vitality and tend to destroy its intellectual and moral faculties, one of the greatest and most widespread—no one will deny it—is masturbation."

Treatments for this "disorder" included clitordectomy (the removal of the clitoris), the wearing of chastity belts, other means of mechanical restraint, removal of the dorsal nerve in the penis, circumcision, blistering of the inside of the thighs, cauterization of the spine, castration, ovariotomy, colectomy, and lobotomy. Some forms of treatment were less drastic. In 1834 Sylvester Graham wrote that the loss of an ounce of semen was equivalent to the loss of many ounces of blood. Subscribing to Plato's philosophies, Graham advocated that even married men should have sex no more than once a month. He further believed that by eating the proper foods, sexual energy could be controlled. What was this food substance, you ask? Graham crackers, of course. Not to be outdone, John Harvey Kellogg, famous for his Battle Creek Sanatorium, announced special breakfast cereals of corn flakes which would reduce the inclination for this form of "self-abuse." To help stop the epidemic of masturbation, mothers across America began serving these foods to their children. The nation was saved!

17

One doctor finally realized, "Masturbational insanity was now real enough—it was affecting the medical profession." Even as late as the 1940s, the *Boy Scout Handbook* cautioned youth to avoid wasting vital fluids, and the U.S. Navy rejected candidates to its academy in Annapolis for "evidence of masturbation." In 1948, Dr. Kinsey's *Sexual Behavior in the Human Male* revealed that ninety-two percent of all men masturbate by the age of twenty. Yet in the 1959 edition of the *American Handbook of Psychiatry,* masturbation was still listed as a symptom of mental illness. In fact, until 1968, the *Diagnostic and Statistical Manual, Mental Disorders* of the American Psychiatric Association listed masturbation as a form of abnormal behavior. The great irony of all this is that today, masturbation is known to be harmful if and only if the masturbator worries about it!

Everyone looks back on this hysteria over masturbation with some regret, but mostly with laughter. Of course, the people who were hurt by these false beliefs were not laughing then, just as the people who are currently being hurt by false beliefs about homosexuality are not laughing now. Eventually, homosexuality will be understood. But until a complete understanding evolves, gay people and their loved ones will continue to suffer from the injustices brought on by ignorance.

Society's Evolving Understanding of Homosexuality

Nothing is so firmly believed as what we least know. *Montaigne*

Unfortunately, the problems with research concerning homosexuality still exist. Some "scientists" have recently resorted to using medical journals for their research of the "typical" gay person. This cannot be considered ignorance; it is pure deception. Fortunately, most of the newer research does use representative samples of gay men and women. The statement "I have never met a healthy gay person" is now recognized as saying more about the speaker than it does about homosexuality. The new studies have also used methodologies which minimize or eliminate most of the other problems cited above. As a result, they have produced substantially different findings. Nearly all the recent studies have shown that gay people are, not so surprisingly, just like straight people. There are still more questions than answers about homosexuality today, but much more is known.

Among the literally hundreds of studies on homosexuality and related issues, only a handful have any real significance. The others have been disproved or discounted or both. Presented here is a summary of the three major studies, conducted over the last 100 years, which have significantly altered scientific thought or shaped public opinion on homosexuality. Action taken by the American Psychiatric Association to remove homosexuality from its list of mental disorders is also discussed. This chronology of nearly a century of research begins shortly after homosexuality was identified.

18

Out of the Closet and Onto the Couch

A discussion of the studies of homosexuality must begin with Dr. Sigmund Freud. The Austrian psychiatrist's study of homosexuality began late in the nineteenth century and continued until about 1920. During this time Freud published several revisions of his *Three Essays on the Theory of Sexuality* in which he theorized numerous different "causes" for homosexuality. These changed, sometimes substantially, with each revision of his *Essays*. Most of his theories pertained to male homosexuality. Among them were conflict during the "phallic stage" of development, where a child ostensibly identifies with the "wrong" parent; narcissism; castration anxiety; a fixation on the notion of women having a penis; a love for men replacing a hatred of the father; an organic factor favoring passivity; a regression to an early auto-erotic stage; the transfer of distaste for an incestuous attraction to all members of the opposite sex; and certain obstacles to "ordinary" sexual satisfaction. There were even more theories than these, none of which were significant. One would think that with all these possibilities, each based on anecdotal case studies, Freud just might have stumbled onto the real cause. Actually, Freud never really claimed to identify the cause of homosexuality; nor did he ever claim there was a single cause.

A common denominator in many of Freud's theories was that parents *somehow* determined the sexual orientation of their children. One of his more popular theories was that homosexuality was caused by a child identifying with the "wrong" parent during the "phallic stage" of development. Conversely, heterosexuality followed identification with the same-sex parent. A typical Freudian version of how *heterosexual* development should proceed is as follows. All very young children are primarily attached to their mothers. This happens during the "oral stage" from birth until around the age of eighteen months. Next is the "anal stage," where the center of attention moves from the mouth to the anus. This is suggested to occur between the ages of eighteen months and three years. The attachment to the mother continues during this period for all children. Then comes the "phallic stage" between the ages of three or four and six. This is where boys and girls diverge. For boys, the major conflict during the phallic stage is the "Oedipus complex." This term is taken from the Greek play *Oedipus Rex* where a boy accidentally kills his father and enters into an incestuous marriage with his mother. Freud believed every boy relived this drama unconsciously. In doing so, the boy fears his father will discover his desires and punish him by cutting off his penis — the boy's, that is. This is one form of "castration anxiety." The fear of this tragedy convinces the boy to "properly" identify with his father, resolving the conflict.

For a girl, the Oedipus complex, sometimes referred to as the "Electra complex," creates conflict when she discovers she has no penis. Mom is thought to be the cause of this "anatomical tragedy." How a young girl discovers that only males have penises and pins the "blame" on Mom is apparently unknown and unimportant. What *is* important is the "penis envy" which causes it. After renouncing her mother, the girl identifies with her father to the point of desiring a relationship with him. She finally realizes she cannot have her father as a lover and generalizes her sexual feelings for her father to other men.

Something "goes wrong" in this process to "cause" homosexuality. Again, Freud had many theories. This is just an example. If the parents had a weak relationship, the boy would believe that his Oedipal fantasies were being realized. He would eventually feel inadequate in his new "role." This feeling of inadequacy would then be transferred to relationships with all females, making the young man homosexual. Whatever caused this process to go awry did not appear to concern Freud very much. But whatever it was, it "caused" homosexuality. For the girl, Freud theorized that her parental identification might not be transferred back to her mother. When she realizes she is in an incestuous relationship with her father, she will transfer her distaste for this to all men, making the young woman a lesbian. Why this realization of incest and the transfer of distaste for it does not apply to heterosexual children did not seem to be important. Once again, what *is* important is that Freud claimed this "causes" homosexuality.

Of course, you will not remember any of this happening to you since it all occurs unconsciously and you were less than six years old at the time. Many of Freud's theories would actually be quite humorous had they not influenced psychologists and public opinion for the better part of a century, causing feelings of guilt and shame for millions of parents.

In order for this "psychosexual" development to occur, men and women had to possess an innate or constitutional bisexuality. Freud based this belief on the fact that male and female embryos are actually identical at the beginning of fetal development. In time, hormones cause different genitals to develop. Freud applied the physical effect of hormones during fetal development to mental development as well. Freud believed "remnants" of the opposite sex were always present in all individuals, and influenced the psychosexual development which he claimed occurred after birth. He further believed the presence of these "remnants" could unconsciously cause homosexual desires in heterosexual adults and dubbed this effect *latent homosexuality*. (Would those individuals who still subscribe to Freud's theories admit to their own latent homosexuality? Probably not.)

Freud also reasoned that the male was superior by virtue of having a penis. He even believed the male personality was more fully developed and that, consequently, men were more creative. This is why he formulated the concepts of *penis envy* for women and *castration anxiety* for men. Freud actually thought all human motives were sexual in nature.

These unconscious influences constitute the basis for the psychoanalytic approach to psychology. That is why this theory of the cause of homosexuality is known as the *psychoanalytic theory*. Freud's real contribution to psychology was not his theories on homosexuality, but his creation of this psychoanalytic approach to psychology. The psychoanalyst believes that competing unconscious motives influence behavior. This belief has been retained and popularized in the *Freudian slip,* where people make statements which are considered to be motivated by unconscious influences.

Freud's theories on homosexuality are mostly ignored now, despite the numerous other studies which "confirmed" his results. Their damage in stereotyping gay people, however, remains. This is true even though Freud made no moral judgments against homosexuality and, in fact, was supportive of the movement to decriminalize same-sex sexual activity in Austria and Germany. It is also worthy of note that Freud did not feel a homosexual sexual orientation could be changed.

Redefining "Homosexuality"

During the 1940s, a research team from Indiana University studied numerous aspects of male sexuality. Drs. Alfred C. Kinsey, Wardell B. Pomeroy, and Clyde E. Martin (all straight) reported their work in the book *Sexual Behavior in the Human Male*. This is the infamous Kinsey study, cited earlier, which discovered that ninety-two percent of all men masturbate. It was only *incidentally* the first and most detailed study of the occurrence of same-sex sexual behavior in the United States.

Because the team knew their effort would be the most comprehensive and significant study of male sexuality to date, they took painstaking care to assure accuracy. Dr. Kinsey and his associates conducted 5,300 individual interviews. Each subject was asked a set of 350 standard questions. Depending on the answers to these, each could be asked up to 171 additional questions. An interview normally took one and a half to two hours. The interviewers were required to memorize all questions the appropriate order. This would allow them to maintain eye contact, while asking each question in rapid succession. The difficulty of constructing a lie quickly and telling it well while looking someone directly in the eyes virtually assured honest answers. The order in which the questions were asked allowed the subject to become comfortable with the interviewer before getting to the "sensitive" questions. All questions were asked with the assumption that the activity had occurred. For example, instead of asking, "Have you ever masturbated?" this question was phrased, "How old were you when you first masturbated?" Each man could still answer, "I never have," but this approach circumvented the need to "confess" having masturbated. Many answers were also cross-checked and a small percentage of interviews were repeated at a later time for further verification of honesty and accuracy. Lies simply were not tolerated. Dr. Kinsey felt participation was voluntary, but once that choice had been made, the subject was responsible for his answers. Fewer than ten individuals refused to complete the interview.

Kinsey found that thirty-seven percent of all men, during or after adolescence, had engaged in at least one same-sex sexual act to the point of orgasm. Kinsey limited his research primarily to behavior because feelings are an inherently difficult area of study. Yet he found an additional thirteen percent whose same-sex sexual experience did not lead to orgasm, or who only reacted erotically to other males without having any actual sexual contact. In total, then, one-half of all men interviewed had some form of same-sex sexual experience, actual or imagined. Also, about sixty percent of pre-adolescent boys had engaged in same-sex sexual play, most of which involved sexual experimentation in the form of mutual masturbation.

Kinsey said, "These figures are, of course, considerably higher than any which have previously been estimated; but as already shown they must be underestimates, if they are anything other than fact." This is probably an accurate statement. These interviews were conducted on the eve of McCarthyism. Experience with masturbation might not have cast aspersions on a subject's patriotism, but same-sex sexual activity certainly would have.

Kinsey continued: "We ourselves were totally unprepared to find such incidence data when this research was originally undertaken. Over a period of several years we were repeatedly assailed with doubts as to whether we were getting a fair cross section of the total population or whether a selection of cases was biasing the results. It has been our experience, however, that each new group into which we have gone has provided substantially the same data.

"Whether the histories were taken in one large city or another, whether they were taken in large cities, in small towns, or in rural areas, whether they came from one college or from another, a church school or a state university or some private institution, whether they came from one part of the country or from another, the incidence data on the homosexual have been more or less the same."

Kinsey's finding of a thirty-seven percent incidence of same-sex sexual experience appears to coincide with a more recent survey, also conducted by Indiana University, which reported that thirty-nine percent of the respondents felt, "There is an element of homosexuality in everyone." Those individuals who had experienced a same-sex sexual encounter, whether homosexual or heterosexual themselves, would likely feel this way.

Kinsey discovered that the view of homosexuality as an "all or nothing" condition was misleading. His research proved that the presence of heterosexual erotic motivation does not preclude the capacity for homosexual arousal, and vice versa. This meant a single same-sex sexual experience during or after adolescence does not necessarily indicate an individual is homosexual. In other words, homosexuality is not the irreversible event that losing one's virginity is. An isolated same-sex sexual experience could be situational, the result of normal curiosity, or some other anomaly.

Some men had exclusively heterosexual sexual encounters; others had exclusively homosexual sexual encounters; but most men had various mixtures of the two. The division of people into gay and straight was quite artificial because no such dichotomy actually existed. Kinsey observed: "Males do not represent two discrete populations, heterosexual and homosexual. The world is not to be divided into sheep and goats. Not all things are black nor all things white. It is a fundamental of taxonomy that nature rarely deals with discrete categories. Only the human mind invents categories and tries to force facts into separated

22

pigeon-holes. The living world is a continuum in each and every one of its aspects. The sooner we learn this concerning human sexual behavior the sooner we shall reach a sound understanding of the realities of sex."

As a result of these findings, Kinsey introduced a seven-point continuum for rating homosexual-to-heterosexual sexual behavior. This scale is used today to represent sexual feelings, or sexual orientation, as well. A "0" designates exclusive heterosexual sexuality and a "1" designates predominant heterosexual, with only incidental homosexual sexuality. These two ratings classify an individual as heterosexual or straight. Bisexuality is indicated by a rating of "2" to designate predominant heterosexual, with more than incidental homosexual sexuality; a "3" to designate nearly equal heterosexual and homosexual sexuality; and a "4" to designate predominant homosexual, with more than incidental heterosexual sexuality. A "5" is used to designate predominant homosexual, with only incidental heterosexual sexuality, and a "6" designates exclusive homosexual sexuality. These last two ratings classify an individual as homosexual.

Think of sexual orientation as hair color. While the alternatives are generally divided into three categories of blonde, brown and red, one need only walk into any drugstore to realize there are really dozens of colors possible. So even Kinsey's seven categories, while more accurate than two or three, cannot fully characterize the sexual orientation of all individuals.

It is important to understand that a rating of "5" or "6" does not mean the attraction to persons of the same gender is in *addition* to the same type of attraction to persons of the opposite gender. Being homosexual means a substantial or total absence of emotional and erotic attraction to persons of the opposite gender.

Kinsey's data reveal that eight percent of men are "exclusively homosexual," another two percent are "more or less exclusively homosexual," and another three percent have "more of the homosexual than the heterosexual." These percentages, a total of thirteen, represent the Kinsey ratings of "6," "5," and "4" respectively. In a similar study published later in *Sexual Behavior in the Human Female*, Kinsey found lower rates of female sexuality in general and of homosexuality in particular.

A 1970 study by the Kinsey Institute reported a somewhat lower incidence of homosexuality. The major difference between the 1948 and 1970 studies is that the latter one permitted respondents to withhold answers to any question. Considering that a full twenty percent took advantage of this "Fifth Amendment" opportunity, its findings are at best suspect. More recently, a 1985 nationwide poll by the *Los Angeles Times* appeared to confirm Kinsey's original data when ten percent of the respondents identified themselves as being gay or lesbian.

From these findings, sociologists have generally accepted a figure of ten percent, or twenty-four million Americans, as the incidence of homosexuality in the total population — which is more than the number of Americans who golf or bowl or hunt with any regularity. And what if Kinsey were off by an order of magnitude? What if a mere one percent of the population were gay? That would still be more people than in all of Kansas — and Toto, too.

This author sides with Kinsey and consensus, but substitutes "predominant" for Kinsey's phrase of "more or less exclusively" in the definition: homosexuality is the consistent, predominant or exclusive, emotional and erotic attraction to persons of the same gender.

Bisexuality warrants some additional comment at this point. Both heterosexuality and homosexuality are considered "monosexual." Monosexuality is thought to be good, even when "improperly" directed. The bisexual individual, on the other hand, is viewed by both gay and straight people alike as occupying a tenuous position at best — a sort of transitory state on the way from heterosexuality to homosexuality or vice versa. Others view it as some type of corruption of the "pure" sexual orientation. Part, or maybe all, of the problem is that most people cannot fathom a bisexual "relationship." How could a term like monogamy even apply to such a concept? This seems to be blatant defiance of sexual fidelity. But such an argument is a moral one, not a scientific one. A relationship is not prerequisite to determining sexual orientation. Bisexual sexual expression can occur over many years or during a single day.

Further, it is important to distinguish between those who are *functionally* bisexual and those who identify as *bisexual*. An individual in a heterosexual relationship likely identifies as heterosexual. But if the individual engages in a substantial amount of same-sex sexual activity, shouldn't he or she be considered bisexual? What about the sexual partners of bisexual men and women? Do those who identify as bisexual choose partners who are also bisexual, or do they have sexual relationships with same-sex partners who are homosexual and opposite-sex partners who are heterosexual? The answer, potentially, is all of the above. In any event, adequate treatment of this arguably enviable condition is beyond both the scope and intent of this book.

Kinsey's finding that sexual orientation is a continuum, rather than a dichotomy, has profoundly affected the interpretation of data on homosexuality. Many of the individuals being studied were not even homosexual! They were either predominantly heterosexual (a "1") or bisexual (a "2" or maybe a "3"). Their anxieties over occasional same-sex sexual feelings and experiences created an image of torment and misery. The compulsion to "exonerate" these guilt-ridden individuals from being labeled homosexual caused a number of "qualifiers" for homosexuality to emerge. These include real vs. apparent, temporary vs. permanent, and constitutional vs. situational — all serving to confuse the issue of homosexuality further.

For Kinsey, something that was statistically significant, with at least a thirty-seven percent occurrence, could not be psychologically abnormal: "The opinion that homosexual activity in itself provides evidence of a psychopathic personality is materially challenged by these incidence and frequency data." In other words, homosexuality is quite normal for ten percent of the population. Being gay would no longer be considered an anomaly. For the first time in history, gay people were recognized as comprising a sizable minority.

24

The Institute for Sex Research, now the Kinsey Institute for Research in Sex, Gender and Reproduction, rose to prominence as a result of Kinsey's work. It would continue and expand the scope of its activities, while maintaining Dr. Kinsey's important philosophies. These include the protection of confidentiality, the avoidance of commercialism and politics, and the adoption of an objective, nonjudgmental approach to research and reporting. The institute, and Indiana University, where it is located, have become nationally recognized in the study of human sexuality. Many of its other studies, as some of the most comprehensive and credible to date, will be cited frequently throughout this book.

Redefining the "Problem"

In 1952 a group of psychiatrists from the American Psychiatric Association (APA), working under the direction of the U.S. Public Health Service, published the *Diagnostic and Statistical Manual, Mental Disorders* (DSM-I). They undertook this effort because the list of psychiatric disorders in the American Medical Association's *Standard Classified Nomenclature of Disease* had proved inadequate. DSM-I represented an effort by the psychiatric profession to define the jurisdiction of its work. It was created primarily for the classification of chronic mental patients.

DSM-I listed homosexuality in the category of "sociopathic personality disturbances." Those included were defined as "ill primarily in terms of society and of conformity with the prevailing cultural milieu." With this definition, it is impossible to deny the influence of popular opinion. Former APA president Judd Marmor wrote, "In the final analysis, the psychiatric categorization of the homosexual outcome as psychopathological is fundamentally a reflection of society's disapproval of that outcome, and psychiatrists are unwittingly acting as agents of social control in so labeling it." Dr. Charles Silverstein offers another observation about the main problem with this approach: "It is my belief that combining moral beliefs and psychological judgments shows a lack of respect for both; that it minimizes the importance of moral standards in society as well as the potential contributions of psychology."

The influence of the times cannot be ignored when looking back on the significance of this action. The effort to produce DSM-I occurred at the height of the McCarthy era. This was when homosexuality was linked with communism and, as such, was felt to be a threat to the United States. (It is ironic that the Soviets linked homosexuality to the decadent excesses of the American ruling class, similarly claiming that it was a threat to their form of government as well.) Further, Kinsey's *Sexual Behavior in the Human Male,* published only four years earlier, was still under attack.

Disease status was made popular by Freud's work. Prior to being an "illness," homosexuality had been thought sinful and harmful to society based on the biblical story of Sodom and Gomorrah. Psychology merely took over as guarantor of social order when it substituted the concept of illness for that of sin by *redefining* homosexuality as a "social disease." The fundamental flaw of the APA's position was in claiming that a condition should be considered a sickness simply because it was neither observed in nor accepted by the majority. Of course, it is also important to recognize the financial interest some psychiatrists had in considering homosexuality a pathological condition.

At that time, the "ill" individuals did not resist this new definition of their homosexuality for two reasons. First, being "sick" is a little better than being a sinner, as sin implies conscious choice. The "sickness" approach, as the lesser of two evils, might also help eliminate the sodomy laws which made same-sex sexual activity criminal as well. Along with its declaration of homosexuality as a sickness, the APA argued that it was really unfair to make it a criminal offense. Because this psychiatric view maintained that homosexual men and women were not responsible for their sexual orientation, it somewhat relieved personal feelings of guilt—but not the shame. The APA's motives may have been a little misguided and self-serving, but its definition of homosexuality was viewed as an improvement just the same. The second reason for the lack of opposition was that no strong homophile organizations existed to counter the APA's action. A few small groups did not stand a chance against this powerful institution.

In 1968 a revised nomenclature was issued in the *Diagnostic and Statistical Manual of Psychiatric Disorders* (DSM-II). Homosexuality was removed from the category of "sociopathic personality disturbances" and listed as a sexual deviation under the category of "other non-psychotic mental disorders" along with pedophilia, necrophilia, transvestism, transsexuality, fetishism, exhibitionism, voyeurism, and sexual sadism and masochism. This was the same revision which removed masturbation as a mental disorder.

As gay civil rights organizations grew in strength and number, the APA's position became a target for reform. The belief that homosexuality was a mental disorder served as justification for prejudice and for the denial of civil rights. Even if an individual was not under psychiatric care, the mere stigma of being "officially" mentally impaired was sufficient cause for social ridicule and scorn, leading to much personal shame. The worst problem, however, was that this position also protected those clinicians who sought to "cure" homosexuality in their practices.

The stigma of homosexuality became so bad during the APA's 1972 national convention that a gay psychiatrist felt it necessary to wear a mask, concealing his identity, when he participated in a panel discussion on homosexuality. At its 1973 national convention, Dr. Ronald Gold became the first openly gay psychiatrist to participate in panel discussions. In his speech titled "Stop It, You're Making Me Sick," Gold stated, "Your profession of psychiatry, dedicated to making people well, is the cornerstone of a system of oppression that makes people sick."

In December 1973 the thirteen-member board of trustees of the American Psychiatric Association voted unanimously to remove ego-syntonic (or self-accepting) homosexuality from its list of psychosexual disorders in DSM-II. In a statement which appeared in the APA's *Psychiatric News*, the officers defended the deletion of homosexuality from DSM-II by recognizing that "it has been the unscientific inclusion of homosexuality

26

per se in a list of mental disorders which has been the main ideological justification for the denial of the civil rights of individuals whose only crime is that their sexual orientation is to members of the same sex." Never before in history had so many people been "cured" in so little time.

The official statement issued by the board of trustees read in part: "Whereas homosexuality in and of itself implies no impairment in judgment, stability, reliability, or vocational capabilities, therefore, be it resolved that the American Psychiatric Association deplores all public and private discrimination against homosexuals in such areas as employment, housing, public accommodations, and licensing, and declares that no burden of proof of such judgment, capacity, or reliability shall be placed upon homosexuals greater than that imposed on any other persons. Further, the American Psychiatric Association supports and urges the enactment of civil rights legislation at local, state, and federal levels that would insure homosexual citizens the same protections now guaranteed to others; further the American Psychiatric Association supports and urges the repeal of all legislation making criminal offenses of sexual acts performed by consenting adults in private."

In its press release, however, the APA went on to assure that this change "should in no way interfere with or embarrass those dedicated psychiatrists and psychoanalysts who devote themselves to understanding and treating those homosexuals who have been unhappy with their lot." In fact, the APA even created a new category called "sexual orientation disturbance." It applied only to gay people who are "disturbed by, in conflict with, or wish to change their sexual orientation." By having this classification the APA continued to support its members who, in whole or in part, made their living "curing" gay people.

The APA board's decision regarding homosexuality was subject to a referendum vote by its membership. This referendum was petitioned by a few anti-gay members lead by Charles Socarides and Irving Bieber. A majority of fifty-eight percent voted in agreement with the board. Thirty-eight percent voted in favor of the referendum; the remaining four percent abstained.

In 1974 the APA Task Force on Nomenclature and Statistics was formed to prepare a new version of the *Diagnostic and Statistical Manual of Psychiatric Disorders* (DSM-III). In DSM-III "sexual orientation disturbance" was reclassified as "ego-dystonic homosexuality." The diagnostic criteria for "ego-dystonic homosexuality" include:

A. The individual complains that heterosexual arousal is persistently absent or weak and significantly interferes with initiating or maintaining wanted heterosexual relationships.

B. There is a sustained pattern of homosexual arousal that the individual explicitly states has been unwanted and a persistent source of distress.

Considering society's anti-gay beliefs, some struggle in adopting a gay identity is normal and healthy. This distress is a *phase* for nearly every gay man and lesbian. Having a category like "ego-dystonic homosexuality" once again gave psychiatrists a figurative license to "cure" gay people—and made gay people feel the need to be "cured." Some members of the APA argued unsuccessfully against its inclusion. They felt it was arbitrary to include only "ego-dystonic homosexuality" and not include individual categories for every other possible source of "ego-dystonia." (Ego-dystonia is a persistent feeling of distress caused by something.) These psychologists argued that there should be a single category of ego-dystonia, as this was the real problem. Besides, the source of distress for gay people is not homosexuality; it is society's nearly total rejection of homosexuality. So actually, it would more properly be labeled "ego-dystonic anti-gay social oppression." Finally, they argued that "ego-dystonia" should be placed in the category of "Conditions not Attributable to a Mental Disorder that are a Focus of Attention or Treatment." Apparently, none of these arguments persuaded the task force. Thirteen years later, in 1987, the APA removed ego-dystonic homosexuality from its official *Diagnostic and Statistical Manual of Psychiatric Disorders.*

In January 1975 the American Psychological Association, the largest professional organization of psychologists in the United Sates, announced: "The governing body of the American Psychological Association today voted to oppose discrimination of homosexuals and to support the recent action by the American Psychiatric Association which removed homosexuality from that association's list of mental disorders."

The similar action by both groups had a very positive effect, not only on gay people, but on the quality of future research concerning homosexuality. An important lesson had been learned: No longer would unprofessional research on homosexuality, which simply confirmed public opinion, be accepted by the psychiatric profession without scrutiny.

The End of an Era

In 1981 Drs. Alan P. Bell, Martin S. Weinberg and Sue Kiefer Hammersmith (all straight) from Indiana University published *Sexual Preference: Its Development in Men and Women.* The research for this book was the most thorough to date on the cause or causes of homosexuality. Basically, the study attempted to establish correlations among the variables which might contribute to the development of sexual orientation. The variables examined included parental traits and relationships; parent-child relationships and identification; sibling relationships and identification; gender conformity; and social involvement with others during youth.

Scientifically speaking, it is impossible to prove something in the negative. This is analogous to losing your wallet. You can thoroughly check your car, your bedroom, and your office. If you cannot find it, you still have no idea where it is, but you can be reasonably certain that your wallet is not in your car, your bedroom or your office. The same is true for the factors which lead to the development of sexual orientation. Each can be tested to see if some meaningful influence truly exists. If tested well, as in this study, and found to have no significance, it is possible to conclude *reliably* that these factors neither cause nor contribute to the development of sexual orientation.

The factors which were suggested in psychoanalytic theory, such as "dominant" mothers and "weak" or absent fathers, were also tested. The results show that *no* correlation exists between homosexuality and these influences. In other words, the home environment, including parental traits, does *not* determine homosexuality or heterosexuality in children. On the average, the heterosexual control group had nearly identical childhoods to those who were homosexual. This would also explain why most siblings of gay children are heterosexual. (A simple study of "perfectly normal" straight brothers and sisters would have revealed the fallacy in this theory long ago.) Finally, moms and dads everywhere could quit "blaming" themselves. As the study showed, parents do *not* cause homosexuality in their children: "Our findings indicate that boys who grow up with dominant mothers and weak fathers have nearly the same chances of becoming homosexual as they would if they grew up in 'ideal' family settings. . . . For the benefit of readers who are concerned about what parents may do to influence (or whether they are responsible for) their children's sexual preference, we would restate our findings another way. No particular phenomenon of family life can be singled out, on the basis of our findings, as especially consequential for either homosexual or heterosexual development."

Two independent views by leading psychologists reveal the real reasons for "blaming" homosexuality on "dominant" mothers and "weak" fathers. Dr. George Weinberg wrote: "The theory that this configuration is apt to produce a homosexual son provides a strong argument for continuing with the conventional balance of power between man and wife. These days, as women are coming into their own, the balance of power is shifting toward equality. The theory that the combination of an assertive mother and weak father produces homosexual sons kills two birds with one stone. It points to the homosexual as a faulty product and it warns the woman seeking equality that she had better go slow, because if she becomes more assertive than her husband this may cause great harm to her children."

Dr. C. A. Tripp described the reason this way:

The dominant-mother theory has come into such extraordinary prominence as to deserve a special note. For good reasons, sex researchers have never accepted the notion, but it has had quite a run in both armchair psychiatry and low-grade popular sociology — perhaps helped along in recent years by the fashionable tendency to attribute any individual's plight less to factors within himself than to some outside authoritarian oppressor. The dominant mother seemed to fit the shoe. With or without that weak father at her side, she was first credited with causing most male homosexuality. Later, she was implicated as well in the origins of schizophrenia. After that, she was cited as largely responsible for alcoholism, and soon she was named as a major cause of drug addiction. Still later it was "discovered" that her loud ways interfere with the appetite of young children, causing underweight — or else that she tends to force-feed her offspring and is thus responsible for overweight as well. In fact, in the study of not a single negatively defined behavior has she been found either

29

absent or innocent. Apparently she is a hazard to success as well: A recent study of medical students "found" that not only dropouts, but unhappy adults as a group, had "smother mothers." Thus, the whole issue has become ridiculous on its surface; underneath, it is a technical monstrosity. Certainly the mother-son closeness that sometimes occurs in homosexuality is far better interpreted as the product than as the cause of the disposition which supports it.

For those parents who still believe they somehow cause their children to be gay, this concluding thought may help. Before the Institute for Sex Research published this study, it found that forty percent of the population felt "people become homosexuals because of how their parents raised them." Some studies report even higher percentages who subscribe to this belief. If our society *really* felt this way, and if the psychologists *really* believed it too, then why has there been absolutely no training for parents on how to raise straight children? Think about it.

Chapter 2

Causes and "Cures"

The greatest griefs are those we cause ourselves. *Sophocles*

The Indiana University study discussed in Chapter 1 should establish, once and for all, that parents do *not* cause homosexuality in their children either intentionally or negligently. But there is no shortage of other theories on the cause or causes of homosexuality to fill the void left by this unanswered question. This chapter analyzes the six most popular ones.

All of these theories are based in either psychology or biology, or possibly a combination of the two sciences. The psychological theories are potentialist, meaning, that while humans have the capacity for homosexuality, the actual cause could be any number of possible environmental influences. The biological theories are determinist; that is, certain physiological factors are believed to cause homosexuality directly. It is worth noting that no single theory claims to apply in *all* occurrences of homosexuality.

So why is it necessary to examine each of these theories, when all purport to identify some cause and none identify *the* cause? The reason is simple: to break the vicious cycle in the negative belief system surrounding homosexuality. On the one side is a view that homosexuality is the result of "something going wrong somewhere," which makes being gay an undesirable outcome. On the other side, if being gay is considered undesirable, then this attitude serves as a compelling reason to find its cause. Until one-half of this cycle is broken, the negative belief system will remain self-perpetuating. This chapter examines the "cause" side; later chapters explore the "effect" side.

Being Gay is a Choice

Some theories claim homosexuality is a choice, either casual or considered. There is a fundamental flaw to the choice theory however. Yes, behavior does involve conscious choice. But sexual orientation consists in feelings of emotional and erotic attraction, not in behavior. Feelings, including sexual arousal, are simply not a matter of free will. No one, straight or gay, can choose to experience his or her sexual feelings. The only choice is how to respond to those feelings. Perhaps bisexual individuals could choose to behave homosexually. But they too could not choose the feelings which motivate them to do so.

Homosexuality is simply not a choice; it is a discovery. After making this discovery, most homosexual men and women do indeed make a choice to identify as gay. After all, if you're going to be homosexual you may as well be gay. This is part of the coming-out process covered in the final section of the book.

Actually, the choice theory has more of a political basis than a scientific one, and is frequently espoused by the most anti-gay of individuals. It enables them to "protect" the children, who could potentially choose to be homosexual, by claiming certain social sanctions against homosexuality are necessary. They propose certain other social sanctions serving as deterrents to or as punishment for making the "wrong" choice.

But even the most dedicated choice-theory advocates have a difficult time explaining why someone would choose what they also claim is such an abhorrent condition. Why would anyone choose homosexuality? For the wonderful sex? Maybe. But could a straight person really find same-sex sexual expression wonderful? Hardly. To avoid having children? Possibly. But many straight couples have no children — by choice. And many gay couples wish to adopt or have children through surrogate parenthood. Could anyone actually think there are people who make a list of the advantages and disadvantages between homosexuality and heterosexuality, then choose which is better? Naming even a single advantage homosexuality enjoys over heterosexuality is challenging in our anti-gay culture.

It is also interesting to note that many choice theory advocates simultaneously describe homosexuality as a sickness, the result of "improper" conditioning. So which is it: sickness or choice? Homosexuality cannot be both. There is absolutely no evidence to support the choice theory. Evidence to the contrary will be cited throughout this book.

Homosexuality is a Phase

One belief maintains that homosexuality is a fixation in a phase of development preventing heterosexuality and is usually a misunderstanding of the psychoanalytic theory based on its various stages of psychosexual development. It has absolutely no scientific support. Rather, it is founded in optimism, usually that of parents. After all, people go through and get over phases. This means hope — hope for a "cure." Those who claim homosexuality is such an "arrested" phase of development will not usually admit to having gone through it themselves in their own heterosexual development. If homosexuality is indeed a phase, its duration is a lifetime.

Homosexuality is a "Failure" at Heterosexuality

There are those who believe that people are homosexual because they could not be straight. In other words, they tried but they couldn't do it. Of course, this is like saying one cannot like vanilla ice cream if one already likes chocolate. Many gay people do indeed enter opposite-sex relationships. The failure of these relationships, however, does not *cause* homosexuality. The very reason these attempts fail is because the individual is *already* homosexual. So in a way, this theory begs the very question it attempts to answer. Might it also claim that heterosexuality is caused by a "failure" at homosexuality? Obviously not. Do divorced straight people become gay? No. There is absolutely no evidence to support this theory either. Gay people do not "fail" at heterosexuality; they simply have no genuine interest in being successful at it.

As is the case with most false beliefs, there can be incredible harm done by this one as well. Those who believe homosexuality is a "failure" at heterosexuality might also believe the situation can be changed or "cured" with the "right" mate. Many gay people, believing this, have attempted marriage. This form of "therapy" is grossly unfair and painful for both parties. Dr. George Weinberg made this observation: "Poor Miss Right! Often in such cases, the courtship is whirlwind; neither party has time to wait. The girl has wanted marriage, and the man has too, hoping it would help him. I have met a hundred women whose lives were seriously altered for the worse by their marrying homosexual men, often on the advice of therapists who imagined the experience would be good for their patients."

The Social-learning Theory

Another school of thought in psychology is that all behavior is learned. The social-learning theory contends that people are born as "blank books;" the pages are filled exclusively through experiences that are rewarded, reinforcing the behavior, or punished, discouraging any future occurrence. Proponents of this theory are compelled to explain the origins of all behavior, including homosexuality.

But there are two fallacies here. First, homosexuality is *not* behavior. It is an orientation or condition. The individual's implementation of his or her homosexuality is what constitutes behavior—and gay people behave about as differently as straight people do. Second, while it seems only natural that heterosexuality could be learned, considering its almost compulsory status in our society, there exists a corresponding total lack of reinforcement for homosexuality or any same-sex sexual behavior.

At best, this theory too begs the question; at worst, it reverses the cause and effect. Why are only some people interested or even curious about sex with persons of their own gender? Why do some people find same-sex sexual activity enjoyable, while others do not? People who find same-sex sexual experiences rewarding do so *because* they are homosexual.

Most gay people struggle with and deny their homosexuality through adolescence—completely alone. There are very few, if any, gay role models in most social settings. Clearly, none of our social institutions "teach" homosexuality. If anything is taught to children it is that homosexuality is somehow wrong. How someone could ever "learn" homosexu-

33

ality in such an environment is beyond reason. Once again, this belief allows anti-gay forces to justify social controls against gay people, claiming that boys and girls could learn or be "recruited" into homosexuality.

In a sexist society which constantly portrays women as sex objects, one might expect all men to be straight—and all women to become lesbians! There is absolutely no evidence to support this theory and ample evidence to refute it.

The Physiological Origins of Sexual Orientation

Studies of human biology are extremely difficult. For example, consider the problems involved in measuring prenatal hormonal influence. How frequently should measurements be taken? Hourly? Daily? Weekly? Should the fetus itself be injected for samples? Suppose one could get adequate measurements. It would be at least twelve to eighteen years before knowing the results. Then, if one recognized the need to change procedure, another twelve to eighteen years would pass waiting for the new results. Because of these and other problems, biological studies either are not conducted or animals are used as human models. The use of animals, most of which are rodents, as models for human sexuality is problematic at best, and usually very misleading. In addition to these problems unique to biological studies, most of the general problems discussed in the previous chapter apply as well.

Some of the conclusions from these studies are actually quite humorous. One study claimed the existence of male and female "germs" in the fetus, which would later direct the sexual "instinct." In "normal" development, this "germ plasm" of the appropriate gender would destroy the "germ plasm" of the other gender. If this process were incomplete, "traces" of the opposite gender remained, causing homosexuality. Another theory claimed the "sexual center" of the brain is located next to the "visual center." The suggestion was that some disease or malfunction causes the brain to "misinterpret" sexual stimuli. In other words, gay men would see other men, but *think* they were seeing women. Both of these theories were actually published. Fortunately, neither has been accepted.

There are basically only two plausible physiological, or biological, possibilities on the origins of homosexuality: hormonal and genetic.

Hormonal Development

This theory contends that some hormonal imbalance leads to homosexual development in the fetus. Male and female fetuses are identical during the first two to three months of pregnancy; all have *both* the rudimentary male and female sexual organs. Only a chromosomal analysis would reveal the gender. Something must be added to create a male child, and that something is testosterone, a male hormone, or androgen, secreted by the testes. Testosterone promotes development of the male genitalia, while inhibiting development of the rudimentary female genitalia. The ovaries do not excrete female sex hormones, or estrogens, prenatally, so the female develops her genitalia in the absence of sex-related

34

hormones. Neither androgens nor estrogens are exclusively male or female, though; all males and females have both to greater or lesser degrees. From birth to puberty, the sex hormones have little affect on development.

Those who accept this theory believe that since the brain, particularly the hypothalamus, develops at the same time as the genitals, it is influenced prenatally by sex hormones. The hormone theory essentially claims the male develops with some "female" traits as a result of insufficient amounts of testosterone. This, of course, is very stereotypical. It confuses gender role conformity, which is socially determined after birth, with sexual orientation. It also must necessarily conclude that sexual orientation originates from or is controlled by the genitalia. Finally, this theory ignores the reality of the situation: This supposed hormonal imbalance still leads to the development of a perfectly normal penis in homosexual males and a perfectly normal vagina in homosexual females.

The hormone theory was popular in the 1940s and 1950s. Some research has since been conducted, yielding no meaningful or significant conclusions. The results have been contradictory, primarily due to the small sample sizes and the inherent difficulties in studies of this nature, many of which have been performed on rats or other animals. What has been determined, however, is that sex hormones in adults appear to influence sexual drive or libido, rather than sexual orientation. In other words, sex hormones influence the intensity and not the direction of sexual desire. So it could be said that injections of testosterone would make gay men even *more* gay!

Genetic Determination

If you really want to know what causes homosexuality, then ask a gay person. He or she is likely to answer, "I was born this way." Chances are, this is correct. A growing body of evidence suggests that sexual orientation is innate; that homosexuality and heterosexuality are genetic traits, just as hair color and gender are. Some studies report up to 100 percent occurrence of homosexuality in identical twins. Although the results appear convincing, sample sizes have all been too small to draw any definite conclusions at this time. Most such studies do, however, indicate the need for additional research. The science of biology has not evolved the procedures to conduct meaningful research of this nature despite the progress being made in the area of genetics.

It is only reasonable to conclude that at least some component of sexual orientation is indeed genetic. Consider this: A predominantly heterosexual orientation is necessary for the perpetuation of any species. Therefore, it is highly likely that similar, but different, genetic factors lead to a homosexual sexual orientation in some individuals — causing the sexual drive to take a different direction.

There are two factors implicit in evolutionary biology. One establishes those traits that are genetic. The other determines how a particular trait could contribute to survival of the individual or the species. The fact that science *currently* cannot identify how homosexuality could make such a contribution, does *not* mean sexual orientation is not a genetic trait.

In *Sexual Preference, Its Development in Men and Women,* which reports the results of the 1981 Indiana University study, the authors concur that the development of homosexuality is likely to be found in biology. They call for more research which, as psychologists, they would be unable to conduct. Even Freud, in one of his last revisions of *Three Essays on the Theory of Sexuality,* stated he felt the cause of sexual orientation would be biological. For now, at least, being born gay is as much *how* as it is *when.*

"Cures" and Other Care

It's a pity to shoot the pianist when the piano is out of tune. *Rene Coty*

"Cure" in the context of homosexuality means a conversion to heterosexuality. The nature of this "cure" depends, of course, on the apparent cause. Since homosexuality was considered a psychological, rather than a physiological condition for most of the twentieth century, its "cure" has belonged in the domain of psychotherapy.

How many psychiatrists does it take to change a light bulb? Only one, but the light bulb must want to be changed. Of course, a request for sexual "reorientation" should not be considered a truly voluntary desire. Dr. Charles Silverstein summarized the reason why: "To grow up in a family where the word 'homosexual' was whispered, to play in a playground and hear the words 'faggot' and 'queer,' to go to church and hear of 'sin' and then to college and hear of 'illness,' and finally to the counseling center that promises to 'cure,' is hardly to create an environment of freedom and voluntary choice."

Many individuals, psychotherapists included, simply assume that if a person is gay, he or she should want to be "cured." The acceptance of homosexuality is then viewed as being even more neurotic, because the "affliction" is not recognized as such. Application for therapy was simply assumed to be for the purpose of conversion, even if this wish was not expressed. The gay patient's judgment was obviously in turmoil, leaving this essential decision to the psychiatrist. The therapist acts from a position of authority, while the patient operates from a position of vulnerability and confusion. The request, "I need help," is interpreted, "I want to be 'cured' " — and the process begins.

Numerous different techniques have been used to change a homosexual sexual orientation. Sadly, many veteran professionals reverted to the rank of amateur in their zeal for a "cure" for homosexuality, completely losing sight of their oaths of service. Here is a sampling of some of the more dramatic methods: castration, hysterectomy, lobotomy, hypnosis, sedation, and aversion therapy, including electric shock to the genitals and spine. This sounds incredibly similar to the list of "cures" for masturbation, and are analogous to using a tourniquet to cure a nosebleed. Such drastic measures usually caused drastic results, but not the results which were intended. For example, during shock therapy a gay male would be shown pictures of attractive naked men and simultaneously jolted to discourage sexual arousal. But instead of reversing homosexuality, this form of treatment might "teach" the subject to enjoy pain during sex!

Of course, heterosexuality might also be "cured" by some of these same methods. It is easy to understand how ridiculous that would be. Likewise, it is cruel and equally ridiculous to attempt a "cure" for homosexuality through any method. Freud recognized this: "One must remember that normal sexuality also depends upon a restriction in the choice of object; in general, to undertake to convert a fully developed homosexual into a heterosexual is not much more promising than to do the reverse, only that for good practical reasons the latter is never attempted."

Dr. Thomas Szasz, in his book *The Manufacture of Madness,* comments on the reality of attempts to "cure" gay people: "It is a heartless hypocrisy to pretend that physicians, psychiatrists or normal laymen for that matter really care about the welfare of the mentally ill in general, or the homosexual in particular. If they did, they would stop torturing him while claiming to help him."

Typical "Cure" Psychotherapy

Psychoanalysis is the disease it claims to cure. *Karl Kraus*

Psychoanalytic therapy was the method most frequently used to "cure" homosexuality before its futility was realized in the 1970s. Psychotherapy required a great deal of time, money, and motivation. This is how it frequently worked.

The "patient," usually a man, was told that with his help and cooperation he *would* be "cured." Normally, he was informed his homosexuality was an "addiction" and that he would go through some difficulty during "withdrawal." Same-sex sexual expression was described as excess lust. *All* contact with other gay people was to be avoided, or else any "progress" would be eliminated. The patient was kept completely ignorant regarding homosexuality. No positive information was given as he was systematically brainwashed. He was warned that if he were to accept his homosexuality, he would be rejected by his family, friends, and employer. This is not to mention the shame of being a total failure for not even being able to convert. He was convinced that all his problems related to or were caused by his homosexuality. Finally, he was told that any happiness in his life existed despite his homosexuality. All in all, it was not a pretty picture.

Of course, most of these patients had problems which were completely independent of their homosexuality. Dr. Tripp commented: "Not infrequently, a patient is in the throes of a major depression, highly articulate in damning his own lifestyle and unable to site anything of value in it. Often he is in the midst of a broken love affair in which one or both partners are displaying various forms of hysterical behavior, emotional regressions and the like. Of course, the same could be said

37

of the heterosexual patient, except that his situation is one every therapist is familiar with and knows how to keep in perspective."

The purpose of this propaganda was to create motivation for changing sexual orientation. Every person has memories of both pleasant and unpleasant experiences. The unpleasant ones would be highlighted and explored at length. Any pleasant ones, even remotely related to homosexuality, would be discounted. In doing this, the therapist was looking for specific pieces of a puzzle, discarding any information which did not "fit" the purpose at hand.

Therapy continued at great monetary and emotional expense because "progress" was being made. Here is an example provided by Dr. Marny Hall:

> Paul spent almost seven years on Dr. C.'s couch. During that time he discovered a great many childhood traumas. He discovered that his father had been cruel to him, that his older sister had tormented him and that his mother had, during a temporary separation from his father, given the appearance of abandoning him. He dredged up these events and all the pain associated with them. On many days he lay on the couch and wept for the whole session. After such occasions he would leave feeling cleansed and whole and full of new insights. He waited eagerly for his homosexual impulses to disappear, along with his old sense of hurt and bitterness. He was certainly making progress, growing up, learning to accept himself— but, strangely, he felt exactly as before toward men. Dr. C. assured Paul that there was some other buried memory which hadn't been reached yet. The day would soon come. . . .

Is there any harm in this form of treatment? There certainly is. Dr. George Weinberg provides an example. The brother of one man who committed suicide while undergoing therapy called the psychiatrist demanding an explanation. The psychiatrist said smugly that the victim was homosexual. The brother asked, "What's wrong with that?" The psychiatrist responded, "It is a perversion, you know. Homosexuality sometimes runs this course." Is it any wonder why?

Incurable Romantics

There is absolutely no existing evidence to support any claim of "curing" homosexuality. No *real* success would have been ignored. Any failure at conversion, however, was rarely blamed on the procedure. Instead, it was blamed on inadequate screening techniques or the lack of a subject's sincere desire to change. This convenient explanation made it impossible for the practitioners to be wrong—ever. So the attempts continued.

But the purely behavioral approach normally used is terribly inadequate, as it does not recognize the complex nature of human sexuality. The normal "success" was actually the repression of homosexual emotional and erotic feelings, combined with a desperate, day-to-day struggle to prevent sexual expression. Is someone who was simply able to have a single, enjoyable opposite-sex sexual experience to the point of orgasm "cured"? Is someone who gets married "cured?" In cases like these, there is normally something else at stake such as conditional love, employment, or inheritance. When Grandma promises to leave Junior a couple hundred thousand dollars if he "goes straight," Junior might just marry for the money—so to speak. At best, these "conversions" represent a functional bisexuality. Engaging the opposite sex for sexual purposes does not make one heterosexual, just as engaging the same sex for sexual purposes does not make one homosexual. Is someone who is celibate for a period of time "cured"? At best, this represents a temporary nonsexuality. Abstaining from homosexual sexual activity makes a gay person no less homosexual, just as abstaining from heterosexual sexual activity makes a straight person no less heterosexual.

It is rarely determined how these "conversion" cases rated on the Kinsey scale *before and after* the alleged reorientation. Those patients who are accepted for conversion therapy are generally leading heterosexual lifestyles and wish to eliminate homosexual "tendencies." As such, they should at least be classified before therapy as being bisexual, possibly even predominantly heterosexual. Nor is it clear if they were converted in behavior only, or also in thought. These gray areas obscure the dichotomy that conversion advocates would have society believe. Nor is it clear how long the patients remained "converted." Researchers were all too anxious to grab fame and fortune by publishing their "results" immediately. These "optimistic and promising" reports made their way into the popular press, gaining attention and achieving status for the therapist. The popular press is not as enthusiastic about printing a retraction, even if one is offered—which usually is not the case. In all my research, I did not locate a single follow-up study in the journals or in the popular press. Of course, these "scientists" never disclosed the many negative effects their therapy had on patients who were *not* converted.

Dr. C. A. Tripp offered this observation:

A New York psychiatrist [Bieber] who for a number of years has headed a large psychoanalytic research program on homosexuality—a man who has written an important book on the subject in which various percentages of changed cases were reported—did indeed make a definite commitment to exemplify these results. After several delays of several days each, the psychiatrist finally confessed to [Dr. Wardell B.] Pomeroy [of the Institute for Sex Research] that he had only one case which he thought would qualify but that, unfortunately, he was on such bad terms with the patient he did not feel free to call him up. One possible case?—then what about his 358-page book claiming from 19 to 50 percent cures? Like the footprints of the Loch Ness monster, they very often appear, but without the presence of the elusive beast.

Psychologists were not the only ones to offer "cures." A group of so-called ex-gay Christians formed a group called *Exodus* believing that religion held the power to "heal" those "afflicted" with homosexuality.

After eleven years, two of its founders became a loving gay couple and denounced both the organization and its mission.

These ill-conceived attempts at conversion simply compound the real problems of being gay in our society to the point where a neurosis could indeed be induced in an otherwise healthy individual. In fact, there is incredible harm in this false hope of "cure" for everyone involved except the well-paid therapist. The various "treatment" methods, employing punishment in the process or causing punishment in the form of anxiety, invariably made life worse for the patient. There is actually a term for this effect, *iatrogenic disorder,* which describes an illness caused by some form of treatment. The individual, feeling inferior based on his or her homosexuality, is made doubly a failure for being unable to change. "Cure" therapy, therefore, only serves to perpetuate and exaggerate the socially generated feelings of guilt and shame.

Dr. Charles Silverstein noted, "In the seventeenth century, they punished sexual non-conformism with death; in the eighteenth with castration; in the nineteenth with asylums; and now in the twentieth we use psychotherapy or aversion therapy." Gay people can be grateful that all attempts to "cure" homosexuality have failed so miserably. If even one of these techniques had been successful, its use would have continued unchallenged by the ethics of such practice.

This entire discussion on causes and "cures" can be summarized with the statement: The operation was successful, but the patient died. The failure to exorcise homosexuality will cause far more harm than any imaginable good. What is the benefit? So certain people can be accepted by society? And who does that benefit really? Homosexuality simply has and needs no cure.

There is no such thing as being ex-gay or ex-straight. An individual's sexual orientation does not change. Even when a gay person is unable to engage in sexual activity, for whatever reason, he or she is still gay. Remember, homosexuality consists in feelings, not in behavior. Therefore, the word *consistent* is used in defining homosexuality to emphasize the permanence of homosexuality. This consistency is made apparent in a popular gay joke. Two gay men are walking down the street when a beautiful woman passes in the opposite direction. One man turns to the other and says, "You know, at times I wish I were a lesbian." Once gay, always gay.

Lesbian/Gay Affirmative Therapy

The consideration given to a "cure" is quite academic, because most gay people have no desire to change their sexual orientation. Like everyone else, gay people just want to be happy and accepted. Five different surveys have found that approximately nine of every ten gay people do not regret being homosexual and would not change even if that were as simple as "taking a pill." Yet a nearly equal percentage would not "recommend" homosexuality for others. While this may appear to be a contradiction, it is not. In nearly every instance, gay people cited the

40

real problem with homosexuality as social rejection. It is natural for people to prefer their own set of problems, especially once they have learned to deal with them effectively. Most gay people *have* learned to deal with the problems caused by social rejection, but the solutions do not come easily.

Many therapists are simply too eager to "cure" homosexuality instead of the emotional disturbances which frequently accompany sexuality, gay or straight. Studies have shown that nearly half of the population has, at some point in their lives, exhibited symptoms of psychological problems. Homosexuality shares all the "normal" problems with heterosexuality, then, on top of it all, presents myriad unique obstacles to personal fulfillment. Every gay person experiences some, possibly substantial, social prejudice and personal rejection. Actually, any gay man or woman who did *not* experience *some* difficulty adjusting to homosexuality would not be normal! In order for an individual to adjust too easily to homosexuality, it would be necessary for him or her to virtually ignore the views of society. Considering the incredible social prejudice, it is actually more surprising that most gay people manage to lead healthy, happy, and productive lives.

There are three basic reasons why a homosexual sexual orientation does not necessarily cause psychological problems. First, every gay person experiences numerous nonsexual influences. Second, there is an incredible human potential for adaptation. Third, the whole issue is normally considered from a heterosexual perspective. Where straight people see misery, gay people find pleasure.

According to Judd Marmor, former president of the American Psychiatric Association, "If a homosexual is distressed about his orientation, the appropriate diagnosis should be the underlying psychological disorder ... To start creating separate diagnostic categories for the things about which people get disturbed would be a throwback to nineteenth century diagnostic categories with hand-washing manias, an infinite variety of phobias, etc." Drs. Bell and Weinberg wrote, "It would appear that homosexual adults who have come to terms with their homosexuality, who do not regret their sexual orientation, and who can function effectively sexually and socially, are no more distressed psychologically than are heterosexual men and women. Clearly, the therapist who continues to believe that it is by fiat his or her job to change a homosexual client's sexual orientation is ignorant of the true issues involved. What is required, at least initially, is a consideration of why a particular person's homosexuality is problematic and to examine the ways in which his or her lifestyle can be made more satisfying. ... What is required is counselors sensitive to the special difficulties and challenges homosexuals face in their attempt to maintain viable partnerships."

The real situation, then, is one of accepting an identity which is stigmatized in our society. The self-acceptance which accompanies identifying oneself as gay signals an end to the damaging internal repression of feelings. The vast majority of gay people struggle completely alone in coming to terms with their sexuality. Others need help. Fortunately, there are now many therapists who assist their homosexual clients in accepting and adjusting to a gay identity. They do not establish an objective of conversion to heterosexuality or of compliance with the social sanctions prescribed for homosexuality. The goals of this lesbian/gay affirmative therapy are established by the patient and the therapist, not by the parents or any other third party.

Dr. Marny Hall's book, *The Lavender Couch,* helps gay people locate and select responsible counseling services. She points out that the therapist, "to be most effective, must have a bi-focal approach, an ability to move easily from a gay perspective to one where homosexuality is incidental." Instead of "curing" a patient's homosexuality, these therapists help the individual learn to deal with his or her homosexuality. To do this, it is necessary for the therapist to first overcome any personal prejudice. Drs. Masters and Johnson point out that "the therapist as a committed professional does not have the privilege of imposing his or her cultural value systems on the client, regardless of whether the client is homosexually or heterosexually oriented."

Because some of these therapists are gay, they have been accused of being less than objective — as if heterosexuality had some inherent neutrality on this matter. Of course, it is not necessary for the therapist to be gay. There are many lesbian/gay affirmative therapists who are straight. But the problem of being a "foreigner" surfaces again, where a "native" would be much more familiar with the subtleties of being gay. Also, where criticism from the therapist is necessary, it would not be perceived as being anti-gay coming from a gay therapist. This situation is no different than pairing clients and therapists who share the same gender, age, religion or culture. For example, consider an elderly client who is experiencing difficulties with aging. He or she would not likely want to work with a psychiatrist still "wet behind the ears."

Rather than dredging up unpleasant memories, lesbian/gay affirmative therapists focus on and develop the personal strengths which will help the client deal effectively with anti-gay prejudice on a daily basis. This approach is consistent with the therapeutic goal of helping a person achieve "ideal" adaptation. Ideal, not in the form of heterosexuality, but rather as a healthy, happy, and productive gay member of society.

Homosexuality is the consistent, predominant or exclusive, emotional and erotic attraction to persons of the same gender — nothing less and nothing more. It is just like heterosexuality, only different. Our society has created any other "differences" through a history of misunderstanding.

Drs. Masters and Johnson explained, "For many years the oppressive weight of professional ignorance, combined with the intellectually debilitating pressures of public reprobation, has effectively immobilized health-care professionals in their legitimate search for accurate facts about homosexuality. How does one start to separate fact from fiction? How does scientific objectivity grow when public opprobrium still remains unbridled? Literally, so little is actually known of the physiologic and psychosexual aspects of homosexuality that it is uncertain just how ignorant we are about the subject."

Understanding homosexuality does not require understanding its cause. At one level, for example, virtually everyone understands gravity: it's what makes objects fall and keeps us from floating into space. NASA engineers understand gravity, at another level, well enough to calculate complex orbits and trajectories. But physicists have yet to determine what causes gravity.

Homosexuality has the same determining factors as heterosexuality does, whatever they are. The fact that the exact cause of sexual orientation has so far escaped identification is not necessarily bad. But this leaves the whole question wide open to speculation, offering substantial latitude to create numerous different theories. As such, it is possible to choose a "cause" for almost any purpose. The basis for a theory can be anything from legitimate research to assumption, from personal prejudice to political gain. This search for a "cause" continues in the absence of any solid evidence indicating that a homosexual sexual orientation can, or even should be, changed. The most popular theory of parents "causing" homosexuality must be recognized as doing more harm to parents than to their gay children.

It is also important to distinguish between trying to convert someone who is already gay and trying to prevent homosexuality in future generations. In the "nature vs. nurture" debate, science is likely to find that the real cause of sexual orientation is genetic. Prejudice could steer genetic engineering toward "social engineering" in much the same way psychotherapy became a form of social control. *Both* practices are ethically repugnant. This has already been established for psychotherapy. Why is it even necessary to find this kind of solution to a social problem? It is almost as if our society uses its anti-gay prejudice as the sole justification to "cure" homosexuality. As long as society continues to believe homosexuality *is* wrong, it will continue to find ways of solving what *went* wrong — and each new technology will present another opportunity to oppress gay people.

Homosexuality, like heterosexuality, is neither a virtue nor a vice. It is not an accomplishment but a condition. If anyone should care about the cause of homosexuality, it would be gay people. But gay people require no explanation. Their homosexuality is simply a fact of life. Unfortunately, the current environment of social oppression is also a fact of life for these twenty-four million Americans. How much of our nation's precious resources will remain devoted to the "cure" for or prevention of homosexuality when there are so many *real* problems to solve? Until science knows more about sexuality in general, including an understanding of the fundamentals of sexual arousal, it is unlikely anything meaningful will result from knowing the cause of homosexuality. In the meantime, our own society should be careful not to define health and normality in the context of conformity.

Section II:

Gay Reality

Chapter 3:

Stereotypes
and Other Myths

What a man is depends on his character; but what he does, and what we think of what he does, depends on his circumstances. *George Bernard Shaw*

A discussion of gay reality must begin with the stereotypes. After all, the stereotypes depict the way society views homosexuality. The fact that the majority of these beliefs is false makes them no less a part of gay reality. Sociologists know from studying human behavior that when people believe something to be real, that belief has real consequences. Gay people understand this. They know from firsthand experience they will be judged socially based on the gay stereotypes society creates. This awareness exerts a powerful influence on each member of the gay minority. Therefore, to understand homosexuality, it is necessary to understand the gay stereotypes.

This chapter examines the more popular stereotypes. The next two chapters address the reality of gay lifestyles and the gay community. But before discussing the gay stereotypes, it is helpful to understand the reasons for and process of stereotyping.

Understanding Stereotypes

The great enemy of the truth is very often not the lie — deliberate, contrived and dishonest — but the myth — persistent, persuasive and unrealistic. Too often we hold fast to the cliches of our forebears. We subject all facts to a prefabricated set of interpretations. We enjoy the comfort of opinion without the discomfort of thought. *John F. Kennedy*

Society stereotypes a minority to help understand, by filling a void, its otherwise misunderstood members. Lon Nungesser offered an explanation of this in his book *Homosexual Acts, Actors, and Identities*: "The process of generalizing characteristics or motives to a group of people is called stereotyping. According to George Allport (1958), a stereotype is an exaggerated belief associated with a category. Its function is to justify (rationalize) one's conduct in relation to that category. The stereotype acts both as a justificatory device for categorical acceptance or rejection of a group, and as a screening or selective device to maintain simplicity in perception and thinking. Thus, stereotypes in general function to help people classify and process information. . . . [For example,] the term 'homosexual' evokes a certain image and triggers very definite social responses."

Collectively, then, stereotypes offer a description—possibly accurate, possibly not. Individually, stereotypes sometimes take on more meaning and significance than intended. They become distorted or exaggerated, or are taken out of context. In effect, they take on a life of their own, becoming just as misunderstood as the group they represent. When this happens, stereotypes become destructive. This is the situation with homosexuality.

To create stereotypes, society identifies a category of people, then ascribes certain traits to that group. Most of the traits are negative, although some are positive. Naturally, stereotyping is rarely a process which is done fairly and accurately. The next step is to assign *all* of these traits to *every* member of the group. Because most straight people do not really know which stereotypes might have some truth and which ones are completely false, all of them are perceived as being universally applicable. In fact, many homosexual individuals who do not yet identify as gay also accept these stereotypes without exception. This is the very reason adopting a gay identity is so difficult. The vast majority of homosexual individuals are reluctant to identify as gay because they do not fit the "description" offered by the stereotypes.

Even today, there is a clear willingness on the part of society to believe the worst about homosexuality, accompanied by a clear reluctance to believe that which is not. This phenomenon is also inherent to stereotyping. Eric Hoffer observed that when creating stereotypes, "there is a tendency to judge a race, a nation or any distinct group by its least worthy members." To do this, it is only necessary to base a stereotype on a few isolated incidents. This anecdotal approach is regularly used by anti-gay groups and individuals to "describe" homosexuality. The story of a fifty-year-old man who molests a vulnerable twelve-year-old boy is indeed very tragic and emotional. But that does *not* make it representative of homosexuality. If the child had been a girl instead, totally different conclusions would be drawn.

Imagine lumping every negative possibility of men and women having sex together into the "stereotypical heterosexual." That cannot happen because heterosexuality is always kept in the proper perspective; everyone knows that rape, prostitution, incest, child abuse, and so on are independent, even atypical, of heterosexuality. Because homosexuality is rarely analyzed in the proper perspective, however, the anecdotes regularly spawn gay stereotypes. Once again, the reality of the situation must be recognized: It is at best impossible, and ultimately deceptive, to draw general conclusions from isolated incidents.

Lon Nungesser pointed out the relationship between belief systems and stereotypes: "A belief system is a set of beliefs, convictions, or opinions about something or someone and/or about groups of either people or objects. Beliefs become stereotypes when they are overgeneralized

47

and based on too limited a set of experiences." He explained three ways that this can happen. First, the frequency of occurrence of confirming incidents is overestimated. Second, gaps in understanding are filled using information which is consistent with preconceived notions. These preconceived notions are frequently other stereotypes. Third, the only evidence considered is that which supports the stereotypes.

In addition to bringing meaning to the unknown through generalization, stereotypes serve another purpose: social control. Dr. Charles Silverstein provided some insight into how this applies to homosexuality: "The homosexual stereotype was created by the heterosexual world. It is a picture intended to teach a moral or social rule, a summary of the majority's attitude toward a group of outcast rule-breakers. The picture expresses our contempt and anger at people who violate socially approved ways of behaving. The stereotype serves two functions. First, it punishes a deviant group for disobeying the rules. . . . Its [second] major function is to control the behavior of the heterosexual majority. . . . It is a negative role model for others, a role model that shows them that they will be punished if they act in the wrong way." The fact that the "real" man and "faggot" roles represent total opposites shows this to be true. Of course, the gay stereotypes perform their "service" at the expense of gay people.

The control function of stereotypes is demonstrated by society's tendency to lump all sexual variance into a single category of sexual perversion which includes incest, necrophilia, pedophilia, bestiality, nymphomania, voyeurism, and exhibitionism along with homosexuality. It is as if there exists the "coital-intercourse-in-the-missionary-position-on-the-bed-at-night-for-the-purpose-of-procreation-between-husband-and-wife" form of sexual expression—and then there is everything else. Part of this belief is innocent: it is the result of ignorance and a desire for simplicity. Another part is malicious: it is the result of quite intentional deception and a desire for social control.

In effect, then, many straight people view gay people as complete "opposites," solely because the gender of attraction is the opposite of that for heterosexuality. But the reality of the situation is that gay people are not very different from straight people, just as black people are not much different from white people, and just as men are not really that different from women in most respects. None of these are "opposites," they are merely different in some ways. In the case of homosexuality, however, society is constantly made aware of any differences which appear to exist, even though most of these differences are actually *caused* by the very oppression perpetuated by the stereotypes. Some of the studies discussed in the previous section serve as examples of this.

The following pages offer comments on each of the most popular stereotypes about gay people. Most of these stereotypes are either only partially true for a small minority of gay people or they are totally false. Many are inconsistent with the others and some are even completely contrary to reality. In the cases where a stereotype is partially true, the boundaries or limitations will be given to define its meaning more precisely. Of course, it is not necessary to refute every act by every gay person for all time to demonstrate that something is *not* characteristic of homosexuality. That same standard is not used for heterosexuality, or anything else for that matter. Further, any correlation of certain traits with homosexuality should not be construed as being inherent to homosexuality. This phenomenon merely represents the self-fulfilling prophecy, a perfect example being the "white flight" which occurs when white people abandon their homes after a black family moves in next door. The resulting drop in property values is, of course, blamed on the new neighbors. But as we all know, the real cause is stereotypical racist beliefs—which become self-perpetuating by this so-called proof.

A number of these stereotypes are actually true for many people, gay or straight. Because gay and straight people are very similar, many forms of behavior are shared. Normally, though, any undesirable sexual behavior is associated exclusively with homosexuality. Then this undesirable behavior is deemed inherent to being gay. Remember, this is how stereotypes are created. It is important when trying to understand homosexuality that one does *not* compare gay reality with an idealized version of heterosexuality. The proper perspective is reality for both. And keep this truism in mind: Everything and nothing is typical. It is grossly unfair to associate undesirable behavior exclusively with any minority. "Good" people are not all good; "bad" people are not all bad; and every barrel has some rotten apples. The bottom line is that no one has found an absolute correlation between any human attribute, good or bad, and either homosexuality or heterosexuality. Alexander Chase ironically has reminded us, "All generalizations are false, including this one."

The Stereotypical Gay Person

In the book *Gay Men: The Sociology of Male Homosexuality*, Martin Levine offers an excellent summary of the gay male stereotypes:

> To most Americans, gay men are represented by several interrelated stereotypes: the hopeless neurotic, the moral degenerate, the nelly queen, the effete dandy. The first image presents gay men as mentally ill. Strong, domineering mothers and weak, passive fathers supposedly cause hatred for women, resulting in the "pathological" condition. Riddled with anxiety, paranoia, depression, and self-hatred, they are extremely unhappy, often suicidal. If they don't kill themselves, they lash back with vicious tongues. Owing to their neuroses, they are incapable of intimate relationships, leading lonely lives of compulsive promiscuity.
>
> According to the moral degenerate stereotype, gay men are thoroughly and completely debauched. They are sex crazed, and orgasm is their only interest in life. They reputedly solicit indiscriminately, even preying upon young children and adolescent boys. So miserable are their depraved lives that they must seek comfort in alcohol or drugs.
>
> The nelly queen notion depicts gays as men who look and act like women. Supposedly thin and hairless, they walk with swishing gaits, talk with lisping voices, and wear bras and skirts. Naturally,

49

they all work in "feminine" professions—hairdressing, designing, decorating.

As effete dandies, gay men are viewed as exemplars of style and art. Sophisticated and trendy, they inhabit a world of gourmet cuisine, high fashion, and chic night spots. Witty and bright, they dominate artistic, intellectual and literary salons. Their sensitive and creative souls bring about strong interest in ballet, opera, and theater.

Homosexuality is made to be the *exclusive* common denominator for all these traits and more. Most of the stereotypes are discussed here. Some others are analyzed in Chapter 6 as reasons for anti-gay prejudice.

Gay people are all alike. The belief that homosexuality is a homogeneous condition is actually intrinsic to all stereotypical beliefs. It is completely false. In fact, tremendous diversity exists within the gay community, as this minority encompasses many other minorities—yet another factor which makes the gay minority unique. Gay men and lesbians are black and white, poor and rich, short and tall, Christian and Jew, liberal and conservative, kind and cruel, old and young, good and bad. It would be extraordinary if all twenty-four million of these Americans were identical.

Gay people are very different from straight people. Some folks believe that anyone who is gay is so different from *everyone* who is straight, so far removed from this "norm," that it is as if gay people were a different species. As such, being gay becomes more of a human identity than a sexual identity. This stereotype is completely false as well. Gay men and lesbians share the same needs, desires, and problems common to all people. They have some unique needs, desires, and problems as well, resulting from the widespread rejection of homosexuality. In effect, homosexuality is *made* to be a significant aspect in the lives of gay people.

The fact is: There are no homosexuals or heterosexuals—there are just people. Sexual orientation is only one of a number of characteristics which contribute to each individual's total identity. This "dichotomy" between gay and straight is analogous to dividing society into tall and short people, then accusing all short people of "unheightfulness" and a whole host of other imaginary characteristics ascribed to being short. For the most part, the only real difference is height. The rest would be created by definition. Actually, gay people may be ostracized precisely *because* they are not that different from straight people. Rather, they are uncomfortably similar and indistinguishable.

Gay people can be identified easily. Many straight people believe they can recognize gay people by certain mannerisms, speech, dress, or behavior. This amply demonstrates how comprehensive and well-publicized the gay stereotypes really are. According to the Institute for Sex Research, thirty-seven percent of those surveyed felt, "It is easy to tell homosexuals by how they look." During Dr. Kinsey's extensive study on sexual behavior in both men and women, researchers were instructed to guess which subjects they interviewed, in their opinion, had "homosexual backgrounds" before asking any questions about same-sex experi-

50

ences. Their success rate was not very good: fifteen percent for male subjects and only five percent for female subjects — and these individuals were trained and experienced observers. The truth is, gay people even have difficulty recognizing each other away from gay establishments and events. So the adage "it takes one to know one" does not apply to homosexuality.

Most straight people do not "know one" either. A survey conducted for *Newsweek* magazine by Gallup in 1985 revealed that seventy-seven percent of all those polled responded no to the question: "Do you have any friends or acquaintances who are homosexual?" Considering that around ten percent of those questioned were gay and would likely know other gay people, that means close to eighty-six percent of straight people still claim not to know a single gay person.

Still, it seems amazing how much some people pretend to know about homosexuality having never met a gay person. Because ten percent of the population is gay, every straight person does indeed have several gay acquaintances. They simply do not know who is gay and who is not. The reason for this is simple to understand. The "Catch 22" of anti-gay discrimination is that if a gay person is not known to be gay, he or she will not suffer from that discrimination. In essence, gay people are forced to censor themselves by passing as straight.

"Passing" is the concealment of homosexuality. The flamboyant queen or the bull dyke are only the tip of the homosexual iceberg. Most gay people pass as straight to avoid negative reactions and potential victimization or discrimination from prejudiced individuals and social institutions. Passing offers incredible gain and is almost effortless for two simple reasons. First, everyone is assumed to be heterosexual unless he or she is "obviously" gay. Second, thanks to the stereotypes, most straight people believe all gay men and lesbians are "obvious."

Gay people know much more about heterosexuality than straight people know about homosexuality. Because of the predominance of heterosexual socialization and conditioning, a gay person knows how to present himself or herself as heterosexual. To successfully carry off this charade as "heterosexual impersonators," gay people have become skilled at giving answers to questions, directly or indirectly, which do not reveal their homosexuality. These are "lies" of both omission and commission, behavior and word. Surprise or shock are the normal reactions of most straight people upon learning that a friend or relative, or even a public figure like Rock Hudson, is gay; "I didn't know, you seem so — so *normal*" or "You couldn't be gay, you aren't at all effeminate." Stereotypes do not die easily.

The ability to pass is both an asset and a liability. Gay people can live undetected, and therefore, unaffected by prejudice. The personal silence allows the individual gay man or lesbian to avoid the discrimination which continues to exist largely as a result of the collective silence. It reinforces the stereotypes, making gay people partially responsible for the existence of these false beliefs. When people suspected of being gay pass as straight, this gives others the impression there is something to hide, something shameful about homosexuality. And because gay people conceal their homosexuality from family, friends and society, the gay minority remains "invisible." It is unique in this respect. Passing also has a devastating effect on the individual in terms of self-respect and self-esteem. In addition, passing makes it more difficult for gay people to meet each other, form personal relationships, and establish effective political alliances. This is especially true of gay people who live in small towns.

Despite all the disadvantages, though, passing is still viewed as the lesser of two evils. Many gay people who have achieved positions of influence or status are reluctant to risk losing their accomplishments to anti-gay discrimination. Those gay people who are openly gay are still, for the most part, the ones taking risks by tempting intolerance.

The Institute for Sex Research found that approximately sixty percent of all gay people conceal their homosexuality from family and friends; over seventy-five percent do so from employers and co-workers; and nearly eighty-five percent do so from neighbors and distant relatives. Similar results were reported by Jay and Young. Gay people who participate in these studies tend to be more openly gay than those who do not. The "average" gay person is therefore even less likely to come out openly.

Although passing as straight is not really a false identity, it does conceal a widely despised aspect of an individual's total identity. The Institute for Sex Research found that 81 percent of the respondents in one of their surveys agreed with the statement, "I won't associate with these [gay] people if I can help it." Knowing this, one can appreciate why gay people choose to pass. It is common for straight people to consider gay people almost exclusively in the context of homosexuality and on the basis of the stereotypes.

Gay people are found only in big cities. In 1984, when the Democratic National Convention was held in San Francisco, the city's gay civil rights leaders organized a Gay Pride Parade, not as a protest but as a show of support for the party. One of the local television stations was interviewing some of the delegates to get their impressions of the parade. A woman from Iowa responded, "This is wonderful. We don't have homosexuals in Iowa, you know."

This stereotype is based on the fact that nearly every large urban area has a visible gay community. Also in big cities, there are more people, and therefore, there are more gay people. But there is not necessarily a higher percentage of gay people. There are simply enough gay residents to create and maintain a noticeable gay subculture. This visibility gives the impression that a higher *percentage* of gay people might be present. In a small town, there may be no gay organizations, gay bars, or gay businesses. The gay community in a small town may be a circle of friends or a gay "area" where gay people meet. To have access to a "real" gay community, many gay people do indeed move to larger cities. The percentage of gay people in big cities might be slightly higher than ten percent, but the percentage of gay people in a small town is not too much lower.

Gay people dislike all straight people. No, they only dislike the individuals who have taken it upon themselves to dislike the gay minority—

and not because the hate-mongers are heterosexual (or at least most of them are) but precisely because they advocate hate, often disguised as love or concern. Let's face it, most human beings aren't forgiving enough to like someone who wants to lock them up and throw away the key. This topic is examined later in the book.

Gay people have an aversion to or fear the opposite sex. According to the Institute for Sex Research, fifty-six percent of those surveyed felt, "Homosexuals are afraid of the opposite sex." Some people feel this alleged aversion actually causes homosexuality. They believe a dislike of the opposite sex makes it necessary to become gay. Would this then mean that a dislike of one's own gender causes heterosexuality? Probably not. It is a tautological argument at best which results when carried through in a completely different definition of homosexuality. Homosexuality is an emotional and erotic *attraction* to persons of the same gender. It is not an *aversion* to anything.

Many gay men form close friendships with straight women. Friendships between gay men and lesbians are quite common as well. These may be for personal reasons, political activism, or more likely, both. My best friend is a straight woman. There is little "competition" between us and no sexual basis for our friendship. Kathleen even encouraged me to come out more openly. She is totally accepting of homosexuality, has numerous gay friends, goes to gay bars, has had gay roommates, etc. Not surprisingly, society has coined an extremely derogatory term for this kind of woman: the "fag hag." Looking at this term in its component parts, one finds the vicious word *fag* and the grossly unflattering label of *hag*. It would appear that society does not look favorably on such "mixed" friendships. These women apparently do not realize they are supposed to shun gay men like the rest of society does.

Of course, every gay person has openly straight friends. Recall from the section on passing that it was eighty-one percent of *straight* men and women who claimed, "I won't associate with these [gay] people if I can help it." To avoid being "associated" with homosexuality, very few straight men want to form close friendships with gay men. Similarly, most straight men rarely welcome friendships with lesbians. After all, lesbians cannot be considered "sex objects" for them. It must be recognized that *this* is the reason for any apparent lack of friendships between gay and straight people. In other words, it is straight people who have an aversion to gay people, not gay people who have an aversion to the opposite sex.

In fact, a convincing argument could be made that it is actually straight people who have this aversion to the opposite sex. How many straight people form close friendships with members of the opposite sex? The percentage is likely to be quite low. Straight readers might consider how many of their individual friendships, those which are not between couples, are with members of the same sex.

Gay people view straight people as potential sexual partners. This is nearly the opposite of the belief that gay people dislike all straight people, and is simply not true either. This stereotype stems from a belief that gay people are totally indiscriminate about choosing sexual partners; that every individual of the same gender is a "sex object." Straight men are almost paranoid about it, while straight women share the concern only to a limited extent. It stems from the fact that men are accustomed to objectifying sexually. Gay men, socialized as males, suffer from this same mentality as well. Similarly, if a straight woman believes, as some do, that lesbians are "just like men," they may think lesbians also objectify all women sexually.

There are two reasons which make this stereotype completely false. The first is that a gay person is only attracted to his or her "type." Just like straight people, gay men and lesbians have a host of personal attributes desirable in Mr. or Ms. Right. The second reason is that an essential element of this "type" is a homosexual sexual orientation. Gay people understand what it means to be homosexual and seek only mutually satisfying sexual relationships. This implies not only willingness from a partner, but sexual reciprocity as well. They recognize straight people would not be willing partners and would certainly not reciprocate. Therefore, gay people do not view straight people as likely sexual partners. Consider the converse of this situation. Do straight men generally desire sexual relationships with lesbians? No. Gay people know that straight people are simply not interested in gay sexuality, just as they are not interested in straight sexuality. It would be a waste of time at best and possibly harmful: their homosexuality could be exposed or they could be physically attacked.

On rare occasions, a gay person might mistakenly approach a straight person for sexual purposes. This could occur when a gay person is just coming out. He or she may not know any other gay people and is bound to be unaware of a gay community. If this happens, a simple and graceful decline of any such offer is the appropriate response—just as it would be if a similar situation occurred in a heterosexual context. *All* gay people have had to do this. It is socially acceptable for men and women to approach each other sexually. These advances are not generally considered an "invasion of privacy" when they are of a heterosexual nature. It is interesting to observe the reaction when gay people, approached in this way, explain the real reason for their refusal. The explanation is usually met with disbelief and frequently continued coercion. "Oh, you just need the right man (or woman) to make you go straight." This is especially true for lesbians because men are usually more aggressive, sometimes relentless, in their sexual pursuits.

Even if a straight man has never been approached in this way, there is the thought, fear, or hope that he might be. Attractive men and women are generally admired as sexually appealing in an abstract sense by other men and women, gay or straight. If a straight man is not offended by the thought of an "undesirable" woman admiring him in this fashion, then he should not be offended by the thought of a gay man doing the same. How many women, gay and straight, have had to tolerate this behavior from men who ogle or whistle as they walk by? Rest assured that gay people simply do not view unwilling men or women as sexual partners.

54

Gay people are always looking for sexual partners. The Institute for Sex Research found that nearly sixty percent of those surveyed felt, "Homosexuals have unusually strong sex drives." Many people also believe that this "quest" is furtive, and that the goal is always a "quickie." This stereotype about homosexual "hypersexuality" applies mainly to gay men, but is also a characteristic ascribed to lesbians. It exists mainly because most straight people only ever consider homosexuality in a sexual context. For this reason, it is not a case of gay people being obsessed with sex, as much as it is a case of straight people being obsessed with the sexual aspect of homosexuality. Some cite a perceived lack of gay relationships as evidence that gay people *must* always be looking for sexual partners.

There are two main reasons this stereotype is false. First, over half of all gay people are currently in relationships, as monogamous as most marriages. These relationships remain largely unknown largely because they are not recognized by either the church or the state. But the fact that they are neither sanctioned nor documented makes them no less real. Second, the stereotype represents a double standard. Does society assume that a single, straight person must always be looking for sexual partners? Of course, since he or she is straight, the question would probably be phrased as looking for a spouse. Therefore, this stereotype could probably be considered true of *all* single men and women, gay or straight.

Gay people sexually molest children. The Institute for Sex Research found that seventy-one percent of those surveyed agree with the statement: "Homosexuals try to play sexually with children if they cannot get an adult partner." This belief is based on anecdotal reports of child molestation found occasionally in the media. This is sometimes the *only* news coverage given to "homosexuality." Sexual child abuse by adults is clearly a problem. But the problem is not homosexuality; it is a disease called *pedophilia*. Pedophilia is the "sexual perversion in which children are the preferred sexual object." The fact that there are only a few cases involving female pedophiles makes pedophilia almost exclusively a male phenomenon.

This is also a fact: Over ninety percent of sexual offenses involving children are by adult males against young *girls*. As such, they are "heterosexual" in nature. This result has been confirmed in research conducted by the Institute for Sex Research; the American Humane Society; the U.S. Department of Health, Education and Welfare; the National Center on Child Abuse and Neglect; the National Organization for Women; *and* the American Civil Liberties Union. Actually, forty-five percent of all sexual child abuse is by the victim's own father. From this data it would seem fair for gay people to conclude that most pedophiles are heterosexual. But of course, that would *not* be fair — and gay people know it. The problem is pedophilia, not heterosexuality or homosexuality.

That ninety percent of all child molesters are heterosexual should not be surprising. This figure correlates precisely with the percentage of the population that is predominantly or exclusively heterosexual according to Kinsey. It indicates that pedophilia is equally common in both gay and straight men. Further, the Institute for Sex Research found that about half of the *men* involved with *male* children were married at the time. Many of these men knew their victims and had been arrested previously for involvement with young girls. Therefore, pedophilia is sometimes improperly associated with homosexuality even when the gender of the victim happens to be the same. Pedophiles are normally only interested in children, regardless of gender. Pedophilia, therefore, is completely independent of sexual orientation. In other words, homosexuality does not "cause" or represent pedophilia any more than heterosexuality does.

The use of social repugnance to suppress minorities is not unique to homosexuality. In the nineteenth century, when slaves were freed, the specter of black men "on the loose" raping white women was used to "justify" lynchings, even though such occurrences were rare indeed. One South Carolina senator commented that "civilized men" were justified in killing the black male "creature in human form who has deflowered a white woman." As late as 1939, a survey revealed that sixty-four percent of white Southerners believed lynching was justified in such cases. Even today, black men raping white women, infrequent as this is, receive prison sentences three to five times longer than those handed down in other cases.

Considering that twenty-four million Americans are gay, with three-fourths of the half being male over the age of eighteen, why aren't there many millions of cases of same-sex child molestation reported in the press every year, let alone every month? If gay men really fit this hideous stereotype, there would be.

Gay people "recruit" because they cannot reproduce. The Institute for Sex Research reported nearly forty-three percent of those surveyed felt, "[Most] young homosexuals become that way because of older homosexuals." This belief begins with the premise that misery loves company, then reasons that homosexuality is somewhat like a cult—but more like a species—that cannot replenish itself through reproduction. The recruiting is necessary, supposedly, because homosexuality is inherently unappealing to nonhomosexual people and downright appalling to some. It is believed this is done with impressionable children (straight, of course) by seducing them to demonstrate just how wonderful homosexual sex is.

This stereotype is *insultingly* false and completely contrary to reality. First, it totally ignores the wealth of "competing" influences for heterosexuality. Second, with just a little thought, it is easy to see how absolutely absurd the whole idea is. Heterosexual seduction of children usually creates an aversion to the opposite sex or to sexuality in general. Homosexual seduction, on the other hand, is somehow viewed as having just the *opposite* effect. The unwelcomed homosexual sexual advance is claimed to endear its victim to homosexuality, and that once exposed, the child will feel compelled to "convert." People who believe this stereotype also maintain, invariably, that homosexuality is disgusting. What they fail to explain is how something as "undesirable" as homosexuality can be made so irresistible by these "recruiters." They fail to explain it because it defies explanation.

The Institute for Sex Research created fourteen different categories for sexual offenses. Forced same-sex sexual acts were not categorized because, as they noted, "Cases involving real force in homosexual relations are too infrequent to warrant separate classification." The American Psychiatric Association went even further, claiming fears related to being recruited are "unreasonable and utterly without foundation." Gay people do not force or encourage others into homosexuality simply because *they* know there is no need to do so. People are born homosexual, not "recruited."

I personally know of no single gay person who was "recruited" into homosexuality. In the volumes of material I researched, I have yet to read one instance of a gay person who was "recruited." There is absolutely no empirical evidence to support this claim in any of the legitimate studies of homosexuality. Virtually all homosexual boys and girls struggle for years to resist each and every same-sex feeling or desire. They deny this possibility, desperately wanting to be straight. It is a doomed struggle, full of loneliness and anguish. So when someone claims gay people are "recruited," gay people are indeed insulted. Ask your gay friends and relatives if they were "recruited." They will let you know in no uncertain terms.

The truth is, it is *straight* people who try to "recruit" gay people. Gay men and lesbians are constantly encouraged by the dominant society to convert to heterosexuality. Parents do it. Teachers do it. Preachers do it. Doctors do it. They all do it blatantly and without shame. Call it advocating. Call it proselytizing. Call it "recruiting." It's all the same. Does it work? No. It will not work the other way either — and gay people know it.

Yet, when even one gay person encourages another to come out of the closet, cries of protest can be heard everywhere. They are advocating. They are proselytizing. They are "recruiting." This double standard leads to complete censorship: the ultimate form of oppression.

The belief that gay people "recruit" is not just another "harmless" stereotype. This one serves as a foundation for most of the hate and fear that surround homosexuality. It creates a chasm between gay and straight people, motivating heterosexual society to segregate then castigate the gay minority. It is essential in understanding homosexuality to recognize that both this stereotype and the one about gay people molesting children are perpetuated mainly for political reasons by anti-gay activists. The "protection of our children" is a very emotional issue, bringing out the best in people when founded in reality, but the worst in people when founded in myth.

Gay people like to "flaunt" their sexuality. This stereotype is also contrary to reality. Because gay people are an "invisible" minority, any public display of affection including holding hands, kissing or hugging becomes "flaunting."

Of course, straight people do these things regularly. The next time you are in a public place, make it a point to notice the number of straight

57

couples showing affection. Straight people also wear wedding bands, proudly display pictures of spouses and children, and talk about their relationships. The frequency of this activity makes it transparent. But ours is a society unaccustomed to seeing gay couples display or discuss affection. Whenever a gay couple is detected in public, the people nearby invariably do a "double take." Some stare out of curiosity; others glare with contempt.

To avoid feeling uncomfortable, the vast majority of gay men and lesbians pass as straight, camouflaging their existence. Considering the potential for discrimination, and the risk of verbal and physical abuse, few gay men and lesbians would feel safe "flaunting" their homosexuality in most non-gay social settings. Gay men and women recognize the need to be "ambassadors" of homosexuality. "Flaunting" would only serve to aggravate the existing prejudice in society. So actually, the real situation is quite to the contrary.

It is natural for straight people to be surprised, even curious to the point of staring, when seeing gay people display affection. It is unfair, however, to feel offended, repulsed, angered, or wronged. For example, a gay couple was dancing among the straight guests at Disneyland, dreamland for America's children. The couple was removed from the park. Could "Mr. Disney" have wanted children to dream: "When you wish upon a star, it makes no difference who you are" — unless you are gay? This is clearly another double standard which oppresses gay people. Those troubled by seeing a gay couple display affection on occasion should recognize it as a personal problem, and not as a defect of homosexuality.

Gay men are "feminine" and lesbians are "masculine." Many straight people believe that gay men and women are neither. Instead, gay people seem to be a third "gender" which is in-between. In other words, a gay man is not considered to be a "real man" because he has too much "woman" in him. The converse is thought to be the case for lesbians. According to the Institute for Sex Research, sixty-nine percent of those surveyed felt, "Homosexuals act like the opposite sex." There is little doubt that this belief is derived form the dominant mother-weak father theory where a child is suggested to become homosexual through an identity with the "wrong" parent.

Gender is a powerful polarizer. The number *two* has significance in its dualism. It offers simplicity: black and white, bitter and sweet, beautiful and ugly, male and female, straight and gay. Homosexuality is made to fit this nice, neat categorization when the dichotomy is accompanied by distinct expectations for all behavior, including that which is nonsexual in nature.

Femininity and masculinity are regularly confused with sexual orientation. This occurs because very few people are aware of the three completely *independent* components of sexual identity. The first component is gender identity. Gender identity indicates whether or not a man believes he really is a man, or whether or not a woman believes she really is a woman. (Transsexual individuals identify as the opposite gender. This is *not* homosexuality.) The second component is gender role conformity. Gender role conformity involves all aspects of how closely an individual complies with the socialized role for his or her gender. This basically means behaving in either a "masculine" or a "feminine" manner. These roles for men and women are determined by society and taught to all children, straight and gay, by its many institutions. Gender roles encompass behavior related to physical appearance, personality, speech, mannerisms, interests, habits, and so on. (Most of these are non-sexual traits. This is *not* homosexuality either.) The third component is sexual orientation. The majority of people may comply with all three, but this does not make the components related. Each is *completely* independent of the others. Any correlation among them results from other, external influences.

Being born male or female will not, on its own, lead to development of a "man" or a "woman" in any society. Psychologists agree that masculine and feminine traits are cultural constructs which are conditioned from birth. Parents, babysitters, preachers, teachers, textbooks, television programs and commercials, counselors, peers, doctors, and our social institutions all assist in this conditioning.

By some strange logic, our culture in the United States views men as being nearly the "opposite" of women. All possible human traits have been divided between the genders as if they were mutually exclusive. Men possess the more admirable traits of strength, bravery and intelligence. Women possess the more virtuous ideals of sensitivity and compassion. For example, women are said to have intuition because only men are credited with having intelligence. Of course, there are no truly feminine or masculine traits. Good ones should be validated regardless of the individual's gender, and bad ones should be discouraged in both sexes. Men can be sensitive and compassionate, just as women can be strong, brave, and intelligent. Some people, both men and women, sincerely enjoy their respective roles. Many others, however, do not like the masculine-feminine dichotomy. They feel like "victims" of roles which have been defined and imposed without their consent, and maintained by fear and indifference.

In fact, masculinity and femininity have almost become cults. Society has exaggerated and polarized "his" and "hers" to the point where it is nearly impossible for straight men and women to relate to each other in any way *except* sexually. Even in the bedroom, men are expected to perform and women are expected to please. It seems impossible to get away from this typecasting. The day will eventually come when our society recognizes this polarization for the nonsense it is, and for the damage it causes to men and women, gay and straight.

How does all this apply to gay people? It applies in exactly the same way it does to straight men and women. *All* children are assumed to be straight and are socialized with that expectation. As a result, the overwhelming majority of gay men conform to society's view of masculinity and the overwhelming majority of lesbians conform to society's view of femininity. Any belief otherwise is simply a heterosexual "projection" onto homosexuality. For example, because straight men like effeminate women, they think gay men must also value effeminacy in this same way. The converse is true for lesbians who are thought to value masculinity. Therefore, any man who is "effeminate" or any woman who is "masculine" is *thought* to be gay, whether or not this is the case. So if an individual does not totally conform with these gender roles, society inflicts its "punishment" with an accusation of homosexuality.

The labels *sissy* and *tomboy* demonstrate this. Boys who show compassion and sensitivity are branded sissies by their peers and possibly by their parents. Being a sissy is feared for its negative consequences. As such, it becomes a means of behavior control. Girls who are aggressive or competitive are called tomboys. For the girl, though, being a tomboy represents an "improvement" in social status. For a while, at least, it is socially acceptable for all girls to be tomboys. It is interesting to note that our society has found it unnecessary to create a word for the male tomboy-counterpart. In other words, there is no socially acceptable version of the sissy.

Why does our society think it is good for a grown man to demonstrate compassion and sensitivity, but bad when a growing boy does the same? If this "inappropriate" behavior does not change after adolescence, the labels become *faggot* or *dyke* or *fruit* or *lezzie* or *queer* or *homo* or *fairy*. This is true whether or not the individual is actually gay. Homosexual individuals who have yet to adopt a gay identity fear these labels as much, if not more, than straight people do. When a gay identity is finally accepted, these labels are no longer effective as a means of social control for gay people. But they remain very effective means of control for straight people. How ironic. Gay men and lesbians are free to define their own individual behavior, while heterosexual society remains imprisoned by this constraint of its own creation.

So yes, this stereotype is partially true for most gay people. Lesbians are free to be competitive and aggressive. Actually, the feminist movement has helped make this possible for all women, gay or straight. And gay men are free to be compassionate and sensitive. Of course, many straight men are also recognizing the limitations imposed by the traditional "male role" and are doing the same.

That gay people are somewhere in the middle range of the masculine-feminine spectrum does *not* mean gay men are "effeminate" and lesbians are "masculine" however. The same freedom gay people have to choose their own roles also allows them to retain the "appropriate" gender traits to any degree they feel is truly appropriate. Again, this stereotype is just the "projection" of heterosexuality onto homosexuality. For example, gay relationships are thought to have roles analogous to straight relationships: husband and wife. This is thought to be true sexually, as well as in the division of responsibilities, and leads to a belief that gay couples, both male and female, have a "feminine" and a "masculine" partner. Nothing could be further from the truth. In fact, this points out a serious discrepancy with this stereotype: If *all* gay men are supposedly "feminine," must one convert to "masculine" after the relationship is established? For gay people, opposites do *not* necessarily attract. Gay men and lesbians generally couple with other individuals who share their own interests and behavioral traits.

This one has a few corollaries as well. Some folks believe gay men and lesbians vary so dramatically with respect to gender roles that many of them act exactly like the opposite sex and a few, exhibiting extreme manifestations, even desire to become the opposite sex. Therefore, a few comments on transvestites and transsexuals are in order.

Transvestism and transsexuality are neither synonymous with nor characteristic of homosexuality. They are related only by common misconception and stereotypical categorization. In fact, many gay, transsexual, and transvestite individuals all mutually resent the association with one another! The single real connection is political: All are allies in the struggle for equal civil rights.

Gender role conformity is one of the three independent components of sexual identity. One obvious "violation" of gender role conformity is cross-dressing. A component of cross-dressing is to adopt other behavioral traits of the opposite sex as well. This makes the "act" more convincing. The word *act* is intentionally chosen because that is exactly what the gay variety of transvestism is — an act. The dictionary defines *transvestite* as "a person and especially a male who adopts the dress and often the behavior typical of the opposite sex." It also states that this is "especially for the purpose of emotional or sexual gratification," which is true only in the case of the heterosexual variety. An interesting characteristic of transvestism is that it is almost exclusively a male phenomenon. This is true primarily by definition, as it is socially acceptable for women to wear "men's" clothing.

Basically, different men wear women's clothing for different reasons. Three-fourths of male transvestites are *heterosexual*. Conversely, Jay and Young found that ninety-six percent of their gay male respondents had never worn women's clothing. Heterosexual cross-dressing is generally regarded as representing a fetish, which is why there is "emotional or sexual gratification" involved. Female impersonators can be either straight or gay. For them, what may or may not be "real" transvestism is a living. When gay men cross-dress it is called "drag," a form of humor or entertainment: an act. There is no desire to become a woman, no belief of actually being a woman, and no emotional or sexual gratification. Drag is a joke, a way of poking fun at society's gender expectations. Most men and women will laugh at drag queens without ever realizing that their own beliefs are the butt of this joke.

Gender identity is next. This is another one of the three independent components of sexual identity. Gender identity is believed to be established about the time children learn to talk. In other words, it is at this age when a boy understands he is a boy, and a girl understands she is a girl. When gender identity is not properly established, a man believes he is actually a woman while a woman believes she is actually a man. The dictionary defines *transsexual* as "a person with a psychological urge to belong to the opposite sex that may be carried to the point of undergoing surgery to modify the sex organs to mimic the opposite sex." The incidence of male-to-female transsexuality is five times higher than the female-to-male version. There have been an estimated 20,000 total sex-change operations in the United States. But transsexual surgery is not

61

performed casually; it is preceded by years of self-examination and months of formal psychiatric evaluation. This is necessary to ensure the individual is genuinely convinced he has a "woman's brain" in a man's body or vice versa.

The association of transsexuality with homosexuality is doubly erroneous. This belief first associates homosexuality with transvestism. But as shown above, homosexual transvestism is drag, a form of humor or entertainment. The second mistake is to associate transvestism with transsexuality. Remember, though, different men wear women's clothing for different reasons. It is only through this association of transvestism with both homosexuality and transsexuality that homosexuality is ultimately associated with transsexuality via transitivity. The fact is, most transsexuals insist they are *not* homosexual. Many are involved in heterosexual relationships.

But assume for a moment that most transsexuals are gay. It must then be asked if they were only gay before or if they are still gay after a sex change. If they are not still gay, then did the surgery also make them straight? Is a man who becomes a woman and likes men homosexual or heterosexual? How about a man who becomes a woman and likes women? Is she heterosexual or homosexual? What about their sexual partners? Are they homosexual, heterosexual, or also transsexual? A discussion of transsexuality in the context of homosexuality or heterosexuality can become quite confusing.

The whole relationship with homosexuality is quite absurd. Personally, I like *my* penis. No offense to the women reading this, but I cannot imagine enjoying sex without one. I also expect, actually insist, that my lover Leonard keep his penis. So I guess I cannot imagine enjoying sex without *two* of them!

Gay people like "kinky" sex. Most don't, some do. It all depends on one's own personal definition of "kinky." If you believe that oral-genital contact or anal intercourse is "kinky," then yes, gay people *do* like "kinky" sex. But so do millions of straight men and women as well. The problem with a word like "kinky" is that it can have a different meaning for every person who says it, and every person who hears it.

Before describing gay sex, it is helpful to understand the functions of sexual activity. There are three. The first is reproduction. This is obviously not applicable to homosexuality, although gay people are biologically capable of reproduction. The second is emotional expression — in other words, to make love. The third purpose is enjoyment. Sexual activity offers unsurpassed physical pleasure and is undoubtedly number one on the "feels good" list of most people. All three functions are equally valid reasons to engage in sexual activity.

Acknowledging the importance of the last two is fundamental to understanding homosexuality. Emotional expression and physical pleasure have long been eclipsed, sometimes intentionally, by procreation as the *sole* function of sexual activity. But the popularity of reliable methods of pregnancy control demonstrates that procreation is more of a problem with than a purpose for heterosexual sex! The *morality* of using sexual activity for emotional expression and physical pleasure is examined later.

For now, at least, it is sufficient to accept each as valid functions of or purposes for sex.

What gay men and women do sexually is not very different from what most straight people do. The only notable exception is coital intercourse: There are definitely anatomical limitations which prevent two same-sex partners from engaging in coitus. However, this is just one form of heterosexual sexual expression. All of the others used by straight people are also available to gay people. These include mutual masturbation; oral-genital stimulation, specifically fellatio and cunnilingus; oral stimulation of other parts of the body, including kissing; tribadism, the mutual stimulation of each other's genitals by rubbing; and anal intercourse. This list constitutes the main forms of sexual expression for gay people. The estimated percentage of straight people who also practice these noncoital forms of sexual expression ranges from seventy to ninety percent. As far back as 1948, Dr. Kinsey found that sixty percent of all males had participated in heterosexual oral-genital sexual activity as either the active or passive partner. That statistic does not include the percentage of straight people who enjoy the other noncoital forms of sexual expression.

One of the reasons for the prevalence of these "alternate" forms of sexual expression for heterosexuality is the inherent problem of timing orgasms during coitus. The male partner often reaches climax well before his female partner, which must make sexual activity very frustrating for women. These forms of noncoital sex have recently been made even more popular, and socially acceptable, by their inclusion in the numerous "sex manuals" on the market. The result is that a majority of Americans might finally have realized there's nothing wrong with enjoying sex.

The only form of sexual expression which appears, at first glance, to be fairly unique to male homosexuality is anal intercourse. Some straight people go a step further and believe all gay men practice anal intercourse. This is another example of heterosexual "projection" onto homosexuality based upon a singular focus on intercourse. Yet sodomy, as it is often referred to, is practiced by approximately twenty-five percent of straight couples — at least experimentally — and is not an inevitable or necessary part of gay male sex. A related belief is that anal sex for the passive partner is unenjoyable. This is also untrue. The prostate gland, which produces semen, is massaged during anal intercourse, intensifying orgasm for the "passive" male partner.

Another common misbelief is that lesbians use hand-held or strap-on dildos to simulate sexual intercourse. Nothing could be further from the truth. Jay and Young found that only three percent of lesbians use hand-held dildos and none use the strap-on style with any regularity. Once again, this belief results from a heterosexual emphasis on intercourse — including a belief by men, straight *and* gay, that a penis, even if only by proxy, must be present in any sexual act. How vain.

Sexual activity which employs sadism and masochism, or S&M, has also been ascribed to homosexuality as a distinguishing characteristic. Yet *The Spada Report* found that eighty-four percent of gay men have never even experimented with S&M. The study did not report what percentage of gay men actually do practice S&M with any regularity, but it is obviously a minority. Statistics on heterosexual incidence of S&M were not readily available.

In detailed studies conducted from 1957 through 1977, Masters and Johnson determined there was no real difference in sexual expression among homosexual and heterosexual individuals. Any differences they discovered had more to do with gender than with sexual orientation. They observed a performance orientation in heterosexual sexual activity and reported, "The predominant heterosexual behavior pattern was one of purposeful stimulation with obvious goal direction, regardless of which stimulative technique was employed." On the other hand, gay people seemed to prolong and more thoroughly enjoy sexual activity. Much of this is due to an inherent advantage of homosexual sexuality. Each partner knows exactly what maximizes pleasure for his or her own gender. Further, gay people are not concerned with simultaneous orgasms. Gay sex is normally conducted in a "my-turn-your-turn" fashion. This too serves to maximize pleasure.

To some people, these forms of sexual activity are viewed as being "kinky" or "wrong" for both gay and straight people. This opinion is frequently based on a "natural" use of sex and the genitalia. ("Nature" is discussed along with morality in Sections III and IV.) But this opinion is normally a matter of personal taste and *not* some absolute rule of "nature" or universal standard of sexual ethics. People, gay or straight, have every right to govern their own private lives in accordance with their own personal tastes and beliefs. Sexual expression should not be subject to consensus in a free society — although it is. (Sodomy laws are discussed in Chapter 12.)

Gay people are irresponsible. This belief maintains that gay people are either hedonistic or neurotic or both, and therefore are also unstable, unreliable, and, ultimately, irresponsible. The earlier research on homosexuality helped to "prove" this stereotype. More recent studies show this to be totally false. Any irresponsibility found in gay people is identical to and occurs with the same frequency as that found in straight people.

The belief might be fueled still from the fact that gay sexuality does not have a procreative aspect. Some individuals even believe that gay people actually *become* gay to avoid the responsibilities of being parents. Most gay people indeed do not become parents, although some do. But just because most gay people do not have the tremendous responsibilities associated with children does not mean they are irresponsible. Many straight couples have never had or no longer have children in their homes. That does not make them irresponsible people. Further, any time gay people want to have children through adoption or natural birth — usually surrogate parenthood via artificial insemination — these attempts are met with great opposition because "gay people do not make responsible parents." Sometimes, gay people can't win for losing. Although it is rooted in sexuality, this stereotype is extended to incorporate other areas of life, most notably employment. (This is covered in Chapter 12.)

Gay people are unhappy. This is nearly the opposite of the stereotype which portrays gay people as being irresponsible and hedonistic. No one said stereotypes could not be mutually exclusive. The truth is, some people spend much time and energy trying to make this stereotype come true. And they have been successful to some extent. But the vast majority of gay people *are* happy. *The Spada Report* found that eighty percent of all gay men are generally happy. Those who were unhappy gave reasons which were either completely independent of homosexuality or associated with problems of anti-gay prejudice. The Institute for Sex Research found that gay people rated themselves nearly as happy as straight people did. Over eighty percent of the gay people they surveyed were "pretty happy" or "very happy." Only a slightly higher percentage of straight people responded the same way. Similar results were also obtained from a National Institute of Mental Health study as long ago as 1954.

Of course, much of the happiness gay people experience is despite the very belief system which maintains this and the other stereotypes. It is society's oppression which causes any unhappiness related to homosexuality. The prejudice makes it difficult to maximize the enjoyment possible in relationships, career pursuits, and even daily life, making this stereotype nothing more than a self-fulfilling prophecy.

Once again, this belief likely results from the "projection" of a heterosexual perspective onto gay lifestyles. Naturally, straight people would not find gay relationships satisfying. But straight bliss is *not* gay bliss, because happiness cannot be externally and universally prescribed.

A related stereotype is a belief that all gay people are alcoholic. The problems of being gay in our society, combined with the presence and prominence of gay bars, has led many gay people to drink. Some may drink to cope with the additional stress of being closeted, but stress can come from many other areas in life. The gay people who have accepted their homosexuality and can successfully integrate it with the rest of their lives, generally do not suffer from this problem. Others might drink to help eliminate the inhibitions which result from denying a gay identity. According to a study by Marcel T. Saghir and Eli Robbins, thirty percent of both gay men and lesbians have problems with alcoholism. This compares to twenty percent of straight men and only five percent of straight women. The rate of alcoholism in straight women is on the rise, however, as more women pursue stressful careers.

Gay people are lonely. Everyone is lonely at one time or another in life. But this belief goes well beyond occasional loneliness and maintains that gay people are chronically lonely. It is especially thought to be true during old age.

Some people feel that sex is the sole source of pleasure for gay men and lesbians. When this is combined with the stereotype that older people do not have or do not enjoy sexual relationships, it leads to a belief that older gay people must be miserable and lonely. With no sexual outlet, it is assumed they have absolutely nothing to do.

Both of these fundamental beliefs are false. Their sum is doubly false. If older gay people want to have sex, they do — and they enjoy it. Others base this belief on the fact that gay people do not normally have children or grandchildren. Of course, many straight couples do not either. And heterosexuality, even when combined with traditional family life, is no guarantee of security and companionship in old age. Children move away, sometimes to visit only once a year. Married couples divorce and spouses pass away. The same is true for gay couples.

For fear of this stereotype coming true, many gay men and lesbians plan a little better for the possibility of being alone later in life. As a result, an elderly gay person is less likely to experience the problems and trauma of an elderly straight person who is suddenly left alone. During childhood, most gay people feel totally alone in coming to terms with their sexuality. The gay individual learns a certain independence and self-sufficiency. Like bad weather, one learns to live with it. In any event, most gay people *are* happily coupled. Of course, being alone is not synonymous with loneliness. Some people, gay and straight, simply choose to be single and independent. Many gay people also have "extended families" of friends. In fact, the Institute for Sex Research reports that gay people normally have many more close friendships than straight people do. Gay people who are now elderly remember the oppression of the McCarthy era, and some are very cautious about being openly gay. They are not necessarily miserable; they are just not visible.

Many elderly people, gay and straight, live in retirement communities or homes for senior citizens. There are even such facilities exclusively for gay people. These offer companionship, a variety of activities, and support services. The biggest problems faced by most elderly people concern financial matters and health. Difficulties in these areas can compound the problem of loneliness. On the one hand, gay people normally do not have children to provide financial support. But on the other hand, most gay people are better able to prepare for retirement because they do not incur the expense of raising children! Of course, health for senior citizens is really independent of sexual orientation.

The "miserable old faggot" stereotype is simply untrue. According to Drs. Weinberg and Williams from the Institute for Sex Research: "We find no age-related differences in self-acceptance, anxiety, depression, or loneliness. In fact, our data suggest that in some respects our older homosexuals have greater well-being than our younger homosexuals."

Gay people aren't **all bad.** There are some positive stereotypes about gay people which deserve comment as well. These characteristics include sensitivity, compassion, artistic ability, intelligence, imagination, and neatness. As is true for most stereotypes, these admirable traits are normally independent of sexual orientation, with one exception: compassion. Because gay people have been subjected to such intense ostracism and oppression, they have learned the importance of compassion.

With an understanding of what gay people are *not* like, the next two chapters about gay lifestyles and the gay community hopefully will have more meaning.

Chapter 4:

Gay Lifestyles

If a man does not keep pace with his companions, perhaps it is because he hears a different drummer. Let him step to the music which he hears, however measured or far away. *Henry David Thoreau*

There is no such thing as the "gay lifestyle." Still, the phrase is used to embody all aspects of life for all gay people over all time. Apparently, *the* "straight lifestyle" is a heterosexual couple who lives in the suburbs. They have two children, a dog, a station wagon, and a white picket fence. Daddy works and Mommy stays home with the children. Yet less than five percent of American households fit this description.

Most gay people lead lifestyles which are nearly identical to those of most straight people. Gay people work, go out to eat, watch movies, visit family and friends, perform household chores, take vacations, and generally do all the other things straight couples do. Gay men and lesbians like Mom, apple pie, and the boy or girl next-door. All in all, gay lifestyles are pretty normal: ordinary, but far from boring.

Sexual *orientation* is a condition. It is distinct from lifestyle, which is an *implementation*. Every individual's life is influenced by his or her age, religion, race, capabilities, family, social setting, and so on. These influences result in a unique personal perspective, pattern of behavior and, ultimately, a lifestyle. Being gay also has a similar influence. A much more significant influence comes from the prescriptions and proscriptions established in our culture for gay people. Owing to the myriad combinations of circumstances and personalities involved, there are really about as many different gay lifestyles as there are gay people. This seems only reasonable, for gay people come from all geographic regions and socioeconomic levels, practice many different religions, and are of diverse cultural or ethnic backgrounds. About the only commonalities all gay people have are homosexuality and the problems of being gay in America. The creation of *the* gay lifestyle is more a demonstration of society's need for stereotypes than it is a representation of gay reality.

Most of the research on homosexuality has investigated its causes or how gay people differ from straight people. In 1978 Drs. Alan P. Bell and Martin S. Weinberg from the Institute for Sex Research published *Homosexualities: A Study of Diversity Among Men and Women.* This was the most detailed study of gay lifestyles ever conducted. The authors, both straight, comment: "Our hope is that, at the very least, it will become increasingly clear to the reader that there is no such thing as *the* homosexual (or *the* heterosexual, for that matter) and that statements of any kind which are made about human beings on the basis of their sexual orientation must always be highly qualified." In other words, homosexuality is as heterogeneous as heterosexuality.

One of the biggest problems of being gay in our society is that parents, teachers, preachers, and friends do not support gay relationships. Gay "marriages" are not recognized as being valid by the state or the church. This "freedom" from social support leads to a certain emotional immaturity for most gay men and lesbians when compared with straight people in the same age group. This is not inherent to homosexuality but is instead caused by an environment where gay children are deprived of the same learning opportunities straight children experience during adolescence. Gay youth are consistently denied the chance to date and form relationships. Any opposite-sex dating, done in compliance with social expectations, is normally too superficial to explore the depths of a real relationship.

These learning experiences are essential to emotional development. Gay people simply go through them *later* in life. Straight people usually couple in their twenties. Most gay people do not even accept a gay identity until that age. As a result, they normally do not enter serious relationships until their early thirties and possibly into their forties. This emotional immaturity can lead not only to a delay in personal development, but to a different course as well. Without social support and guidance, gay people have been on their own to learn the many important lessons in life. When I came out, for example, I found myself at twenty-six going on sixteen. The exact ages may vary a little for each gay person, but the delayed process is basically the same.

Despite the wide diversity of gay lifestyles, some simple categorization is possible. Drs. Bell and Weinberg developed five behavioral groups. These include Dysfunctional, Asexual, Functional, Open-coupled, and Close-coupled. Should such a study be made, similar categories could be established for heterosexuality, although the percentages assigned to each might be different. To simplify this discussion even further, some related categories are combined reducing the total number to three. The three are Troubled, which combines Dysfunctional and Asexual; Coupled, which combines both Open-coupled and Close-coupled; and the original Functional.

It is important to keep in mind that this categorization was only a "snapshot" made of the participants during the study. People change with time. Nearly all gay people will actually experience behavior associated with all three categories during their lifetimes. The discussion is arranged in what is normally the chronological order.

Coming Out

Ten percent of the population may be born homosexual, but they need to become gay. And in our anti-gay society, becoming gay means trouble for the individual. Remember, being gay involves accepting a gay identity. The process of accepting a gay identity, or coming out, is described in detail in Chapter 16. This section focuses on behavior associated with coming out.

The Asexual and Dysfunctional behavioral styles observed by Drs. Bell and Weinberg, combined here in the Troubled classification, are typical of the coming-out process. The Asexual category is used to describe that period of life, usually the mid-teens to early twenties, when homosexual feelings are denied, resulting in celibacy. Asexuality is the hallmark of denial. A Dysfunctional individual is one who also is unable to accept a gay identity, but engages in same-sex sexual activity anyway. Dysfunctionals rate high in both the number of sexual problems and regret of homosexuality. Both groups experience substantial anxiety, guilt, and shame. Twenty-three percent of the gay men and sixteen percent of the lesbians were rated Asexual, and eighteen percent of the gay men and eight percent of the lesbians were rated Dysfunctional. In total, then, at any point in time, approximately forty percent of homosexual men and twenty-five percent of homosexual women are "Troubled."

Drs. Bell and Weinberg reported: "The Dysfunctionals are the group in our sample which most closely accord with the stereotype of the tormented homosexual. They are troubled people whose lives offer them little gratification, and in fact they seem to have a great deal of difficulty managing their existence . . . . If we had numbered only Dysfunctionals among our respondents, we very likely would have had to conclude that homosexuals in general are conflict-ridden social misfits." Earlier attempts at research did just this.

Before identifying as gay, it is common for *all* gay people to deny any emotional or erotic attraction to persons of the same gender. Children never come to breakfast proclaiming, "Guess what everyone? Last night I became gay!" Coming out is a long and arduous process. No one really wants to be gay, especially in our society where such a "choice" is met with ridicule and scorn. The hideous description of homosexuality offered by the stereotypes is what prevents homosexual men and women from immediately adopting a gay identity. The vast majority of gay people are just not that disgusting. Therefore, homosexual men and women sincerely believe they are not really homosexual — at least for a while. During this time, the individual goes through an adjustment to homosexuality which has a profound influence on lifestyle. Straight people have no reason to go through a similar experience, as there is no need to "adjust" to heterosexuality. Heterosexuality is socially accepted; its behavior patterns are conditioned from birth. Any problems straight people experience sexually are the result of unrelated factors like shyness, physical handicap or appearance, or other personal difficulties. Of course, many gay people share these same limitations to personal fulfillment as well.

During this period of denial, before accepting homosexuality and identifying as gay, troubled homosexual individuals experience numerous problems. These men and women identify as straight as a courtesy to social conformity — and because they do not yet identify as gay. Most at least experiment with heterosexual dating; some even marry and have children. Any homosexual sexual activity experienced during this period is purely sexual. There is no love; no permanent relationships are formed for fear of having to admit one's homosexuality. Most same-sex sexual behavior is therefore conducted furtively and anonymously. The individual is either unaware of the presence of a gay community or consciously avoids it. Because of this, same-sex sexual contacts are sometimes made by "cruising" in public places.

Cruising in Public Places

Cruising involves using speech and behavior to locate a sexual partner. As such, it is not unlike the heterosexual courting ritual of "picking up chicks." Cruising, both the gay and straight varieties, is almost exclusively a male phenomenon.

Gay cruising activity normally takes place in a very secluded public location such as an infrequently used restroom or a hard-to-find area in a park. This "privacy" allows the man, who does not yet identify as gay, to get away from home, family, and friends but still not go totally into public view, where his secret might be discovered. Here is how it works. Those who are not cruising come and go without noticing anything unusual. Men who are cruising wait around, noticing others who are doing the same. They make eye contact and both smile knowingly. One man will then beckon with a nod of the head or a motion of the hand; the other man follows. They go to a private stall or protected area. A few words may be exchanged stating desires, and the sexual activity begins. When finished, the men go their separate ways, saying little or nothing. Both want to remain anonymous. Any name used is likely to be fabricated. More than occasionally, an undercover police officer will "play along" and an arrest is made. This is covered in more detail in Chapter 12 in the section on "Solicitation Laws."

There are many types of men who cruise for same-sex sexual activity in public places. According to one study, fifty-four percent of the men who claimed to cruise at least periodically identified as heterosexual. They were married or leading otherwise heterosexual lifestyles and obviously wanted their same-sex sexual activity to be completely anonymous. Which individuals in this group are truly heterosexual, or are instead actually homosexual or bisexual, is unknown. All three sexual orientations are probably represented. Some would be Dysfunctional homosexual; others would be predominantly heterosexual; while the remainder would be truly bisexual. In any event, none of these men wish to identify as gay. Their behavior creates constant anxiety from the lies to wives or friends, the risk of getting sexually transmitted diseases, and the possibility of arrest and public ruin. But the intensity of their same-sex erotic desires apparently overcomes these anxieties.

70

The study's remaining forty-six percent of men who cruise identify as homosexual, bisexual, or predominantly heterosexual (Kinsey rating of "1"). Possibly they are unaware of the bars and bathhouses in the gay community. Maybe there is no gay community in the area. Of course, some men who cruise in public places are simply too young to get into a gay bar. They have nowhere else to go when trying to meet other gay people their own age. After all, forming a gay youth group would only assist one generation of gay America in "recruiting" the next.

Are there any other reasons a gay man might look for sex in a public place? Not really. "Experienced" gay men, who identify as gay and have access to gay bars and bathhouses (and gay newspapers warning of arrest activity), rarely, if ever, cruise in public places. Cruising is simply too risky. What results is a case of the blind leading the blind. The participants know very little about homosexuality other than their own experience and the stereotypes to which they blindly conform.

As such, cruising locations are the gray area between the gay community and the dominant society. Straight men may occasionally stumble onto the cruising scene and believe, as it is likely to be their only exposure to "homosexuality," that this is the gay community. The anonymous and furtive activity, characteristic of this environment, is felt to typify gay people. The impression leads to a view that all gay men find all their sexual partners this way. Such a belief is really just another stereotype based on nonrepresentative samples: the Dysfunctional phase for homosexual men, and other troubled men who are either predominantly heterosexual or bisexual.

An activity related to cruising is hustling. Yes, the world's oldest profession is by no means limited to heterosexuality. Most hustlers, or prostitutes catering to gay males, do not, however, identify as gay. They are mentioned here only because prostitution, whether straight, bisexual, or gay, must be considered Dysfunctional. Rather than using sexual activity as an expression of love or for physical pleasure, sex becomes a means of income, perhaps the only means available. Most hustlers are runaways, more likely throwaways, from broken homes or have other personal problems. Too young or unqualified to get a "real" job, they are left to their own devices. To them, hustling is a business with little or no operating expense and ample demand for the service provided. The hustler is normally fellated by the "customer." This is usually the extent of the sexual activity. Many hustlers really are straight. Their customers are male primarily because women rarely buy sex. Being a gigolo is not nearly as marketable or profitable. The men who buy this kind of sex could be homosexual, predominantly heterosexual, or bisexual. It's quick and easy—and safer than cruising in public places.

Going Strong

Following the uphill struggle of coming out is a period that Drs. Bell and Weinberg labeled "Functional." This is the behavioral style associated with the stereotypical promiscuous gay person. The parallel classification for straight people is the "swinging single." Functionals rate high in sexual activity and low in regret of homosexuality. Most gay people in this category tend to be younger, having both the energy and the physique to meet sexual partners easily. They might frequent gay bars or bathhouses, but rarely cruise in public places owing to the risks involved. Again, even though being Functional is a brief phase for most gay people, it can be a fairly extended pattern of behavior for some. Approximately twenty percent of the gay men and fifteen percent of the lesbians were placed in this category.

When a gay person finally accepts his or her homosexuality, it is like graduating from the Troubled school. The next "grade" is Functional. As Functionals, gay people learn that homosexuality is *not* the horrible condition they were led to believe it was, and that there are many other gay people just like them. "Oh, all those wasted years of denial." It's like being a kid in a candy store. The feeling is, "Look out world, here I come." This is when a gay man or lesbian makes up for lost time. Repressing earlier homosexual urges creates a reservoir of missed sexual experiences, which releases a flood of promiscuity when the opportunity arises. Drs. William Simon and John H. Gagnon determined: "Sexual contacts during this period are often pursued nearly indiscriminately and with greater vigor than caution. This is very close to that period in the life of the heterosexual called the 'honeymoon,' when coitus is legitimate and is pursued with a substantial amount of energy." Since premarital heterosexual sex has become legitimate, this "honeymoon" effect is not so prominent today.

Promiscuity: Making Up for Lost Time

Promiscuity is often ascribed to gay people as a distinguishing characteristic. Of course, promiscuity is a relative concept. Some people think any sexual activity outside the confines of marriage is promiscuous. For others, anyone who has more sexual partners than they do is promiscuous. The dictionary defines *promiscuous* as "not restricted to one sexual partner." This is an accurate definition. It also states that promiscuous means "indiscriminate." This part is incorrect. Functionals may have many sexual partners, but they are very *discriminating!*

There are a number of reasons why gay people generally have more sexual partners than straight people do. The total rejection of homosexuality has freed this minority to challenge all of society's sexual attitudes. Some gay men even rationalize this sexual freedom as compensation for the injustices of anti-gay discrimination. When a stigmatized minority cannot possibly please the dominant culture, why should any of its members even bother trying? Having "violated" the fundamental issue of sexual orientation, it is only a small step to then depart from the prevailing cultural ideal of premarital celibacy. Of course, gay people are not allowed to get married — and this too helps contribute to the number of sexual partners by discouraging permanent gay relationships.

Society has redefined and relaxed its sexual mores somewhat as well. According to the U. S. Census Bureau, the number of straight couples living together unmarried, or "cohabitating" as they call it, more than doubled during the 1970s. Another study conducted by the Federal government revealed that in the early 1960s, about fifty percent of women engaged in sexual activity before marriage. A more recent study commissioned by the National Institute of Health reports that by the middle of the 1980s, over eighty percent of women had engaged in sexual activity before marriage. The first sexual experience now normally occurs around the age of sixteen for both boys and girls.

Promiscuity, loosely speaking, is actually related more to being male than it is to being gay. Men are taught to "get into bed" as soon as practicable, while women are told to be "good girls" as long as possible. Women are only supposed to engage in sexual activity in the context of a loving relationship, and it is best if they are virgins when they marry. Female chastity and fidelity guarantee the legitimacy of a man's children. Men, on the other hand, are understood to have a need to "sow their wild oats." In essence, male promiscuity is socially acceptable. Men even brag about their sexual exploits, separating physical sexual pleasure from love or companionship, to gain respect from their peers. Studies actually show that for men, the more exploitation and the less love in their sexual adventures, the more positive the feedback from their peers. Sometimes it seems the bragging is just as enjoyable as the sex itself. Whether biologically or socially determined, libido is generally considered stronger (or at least less restrained) in men. As a result, gay men learn to be, or become, promiscuous long before identifying as gay. The double standard of male-female sexuality tends to reduce the incidence of sexual activity for straight men, making them less promiscuous, though not necessarily by choice. Gay men occupy the unique, and arguably envious, position of being on the same side of this double standard.

Many gay men, because of the difficulties attendant to maintaining gay relationships, have learned to fulfill their needs for love and companionship without a primary partner. Most casual sexual contacts are not without affection though. Some "one-night stands" can be very meaningful, just as some relationships can be disastrous. Others choose to avoid a long-term relationship for fear their homosexuality will become apparent to family members and friends. When a person reaches a certain age, having a "roommate" creates suspicion. So, while some gay men might be looking for Mr. Right, others are looking for Mr. Right Now.

In summary of this discussion on Functionals and promiscuity, it is helpful to put gay sexual incidence in perspective. According to averages provided by the Institute for Sex Research, over half of all gay men engage in sexual activity once per week or less; around a third "do it" between two and three times a week; and only less than one in twenty have sex seven or more times weekly. Similar results were reported in two other independent studies by Jay and Young, and Weinberg and Williams. These incidence rates are consistent with those observed for straight people in comparable age groups and, as such, hardly support a homosexual obsession with sex. After all, homosexuality, just like heterosexuality, is really nonsexuality most of the time.

Settling Down

The "Coupled" category includes both Close-coupled and Open-coupled gay men and lesbians as defined by Drs. Bell and Weinberg. The Close-coupled category is used to designate those gay people who are involved in a monogamous relationship. The Open-coupled category is used to designate those gay men and lesbians who are involved in a primary relationship but occasionally engage in sexual activity outside of that relationship. Roughly four of every ten gay men and six of every ten lesbians are coupled. More specifically, fourteen percent of the gay men and thirty-eight percent of the lesbians were rated Close-coupled, and twenty-five percent of the gay men and twenty-four percent of the lesbians were rated Open-coupled. Similar percentages were found in three other independent studies.

Most straight people are astonished to learn that around half of all gay adults are coupled. Their surprise is not too surprising, as individuals who are coupled are generally more content. This is both a cause and effect. As such, they are more likely to lead quiet lives, surrounded by a few close friends, and less likely to show up at a psychiatrist's office or to be arrested for cruising in public places, only to end up in some study of the "typical homosexual." That is why this group of gay people remains largely unknown, despite its significance.

Gay people enter relationships for exactly the same reasons straight people do. Most men and women, gay or straight, have a need for love, companionship, comfort and security. A good relationship can meet all these needs and more. *The Spada Report* found that nearly ninety percent of the gay men it surveyed wanted a primary relationship. Less than one percent of the gay men and lesbians surveyed by Jay and Young had never been in love.

That covers quantity, but how can the quality of a relationship be determined? One way is to ask its participants. In a study which compared answers from both gay and straight couples, the researchers were unable to identify any significant differences between the sexual orientations based on satisfaction, commitment, communication, sharing activities and responsibilities, sexual experimentation, the frequency of sexual activity, and the quality of love. They did, however, discover that gender differences were greater than the differences between being homosexual or heterosexual. This study was reported in *Psychology Today* magazine, where Letitia Anne Peplau commented, "We have learned that gender — the fact of being a man or a woman — often exerts a greater influence on relationships than does sexual orientation." She summarized the findings by stating, "People who cling to the idea that homosexuals are utterly different from the rest of humanity may be surprised we found so few differences." The only notable difference was the extent of monogamy.

Monogamy, or sexual exclusivity, is not necessarily a component of gay relationships. This is the essence of the Open-coupled classification and is identical in this respect to the "open marriage." Is monogamy required for a happy relationship? For many couples, gay *and* straight, the answer is no. Sexual activity with a secondary partner outside of the primary relationship is not infidelity unless its participants have agreed to monogamy. Sexual activity *can* be recreational. Even though there is normally an emotional component, it is not necessary to "make love" when having sex. Sexual expression is only one of the many ingredients in a successful relationship; fidelity should not be so narrowly defined. Love, trust, honesty, loyalty, and commitment are much more important in a relationship than sexual exclusivity. Of course, this sexual freedom can and does destroy many relationships. To minimize the negative effects, most gay couples are usually open and honest about any "extracurricular" sexual adventures. Others "cheat" on their lovers, just as many straight people "cheat" on theirs. One study revealed that forty-two percent of all men surveyed had not always been "faithful" to their wives during marriage. A similar result was obtained in a 1985 survey of 7,500 *Psychology Today* readers conducted by Yale University. This study confirmed that forty-five percent of both straight men and women had "cheated" on their spouse or long-term partner.

While gay relationships are very similar to marriages, they are not identical. Most notably, the husband and wife structure does not apply. Instead, gay couples are happily "married" husbands or happily "married" wives. Gay relationships actually resemble best friendships with the added components of romance and erotic attraction. The rules and roles are unique for each couple. The term *lover* is used, rather than *spouse,* to distinguish between gay and straight relationships. There is, however, one problem with the word *lover.* Many straight people use this word to refer to a person who is having a sexual affair with a married man or woman. This use is *not* the sense of the word in gay vernacular.

Marriage is a significant social institution. There are numerous laws which regulate marriages or address issues in the context of marriage. Elaborate wedding ceremonies are performed and festive receptions are held for friends and families. Numerous resources are available to help make marriages successful. If a particular marriage does not work out, strict legal procedures exist to handle the separation.

Gay relationships, on the other hand, are not this well-defined or formally conducted. Most gay relationships usually just evolve. There is not necessarily less commitment, there is just less structure. For example, a gay couple's anniversary might be the day they met. The belief that gay relationships are more transitory and sexual in nature than the often idealized heterosexual counterpart is easy to understand when considering the difficulties confronting gay couples.

Establishing and maintaining a gay relationship is not an easy task. This is not inherent to homosexuality; it is instead an effect of society's exclusion of gay people from the institutions that sanction and support marriages. Therefore, having several primary relationships in a lifetime is typical for gay men and lesbians. This is analogous to being divorced and remarried. Virtually all couples, straight or gay, enter a relationship wanting it to be successful and permanent. One study found that ninety-five percent of the gay couples questioned felt they would "grow into old age together." This is true even though gay people know the odds are stacked against them.

When a straight couple gets divorced, incompatibility of the partners is normally cited as the reason, rather than some fundamental flaw of marriages in general. Most straight people are brought up to believe love is eternal, and many are surprised to discover it is not. Half of straight couples now marrying will divorce. Gay people are told they are unable to love, and are pleasantly surprised to find out they can. Yet when a gay relationship fails, it is blamed on the many stereotypical beliefs ascribed to homosexuality. There are many reasons why relationships fall apart. Because gay and straight relationships are so similar, they have many problems in common. As with straight couples incompatibility is the main reason gay couples separate. But in addition to all the common problems, gay relationships face a number of other pitfalls.

The Pitfalls Facing a Gay Couple

Poverty is an anomaly to rich people: It is very difficult to make out why people who want dinner do not ring the bell. *Walter Bagehot*

The main difference between gay and straight relationships is the external world in which both exist. Society, quite frankly, has not been interested in supporting gay couples. After all, such support could be construed as "condoning" or, worse yet, "advocating" homosexuality. Presented here is a partial list of social factors which reinforce marriages that are not applicable to gay relationships. As a symptom of this problem, consider that there is no special word for a gay relationship. A culture recognizes something of value to it by giving it a name. While the phrase "domestic partnership" could apply, it is normally employed in a heterosexual context. Gay relationships are not even considered real. As Dr. Betty Berzon so eloquently put it, "Same sex couples? Unnatural, unsanctionable, unconscionable, immoral, sick and immature. Can't work. Won't last. Doesn't count."

To begin, being single is not as acceptable in the straight community as it is in the gay community. In her book *My Son Eric,* Mary Borhek made this comment: "The interesting thing is that at a heterosexual party, which at my age largely means married couples, I am usually a fifth wheel if I am alone, or else I need an escort in order to really be one of the group. At a gay party I seem to be accepted as a whole person, just as I am. It isn't necessary for me to be accompanied by a man. Even though I come alone, I am not conspicuous. Nobody at the party is expecting everyone to be paired off. The gay community has given me acceptance as a single person, which the heterosexual community has somehow not been able to do."

Society is constantly trying to bring straight potential partners together, while simultaneously attempting to deny gay people any opportunity to meet each other. It offers no dances, parties, church or school functions for gay people. When these events are held for "everyone," gay people are excluded. This unwritten rule is enforced nearly every time a couple "invades" the sanctity of heterosexual mating rituals. Friends and families never try to arrange dates with the *right* (gay) partner. The gay community, discussed in the next chapter, does provide similar opportunities for gay people to meet each other. But because gay people are excluded from these social activities during youth, their emotional immaturity shows when they finally do meet the right partner. There is even more to this problem than mere emotional immaturity however.

When two gay people decide to establish a relationship, there are no rules or roles based on centuries of practice and experience to guide them. Because the gay relationships is not the well-developed institution that marriage is, all gay relationship exist under vague terms at best. The gay couple does have one advantage, though: Without prescribed rules and roles, there is more freedom to create truly egalitarian relationships.

Each gay couple normally has two "heads of household." Sometimes there are even two households, with the "unused" home serving to conceal one or both partners' homosexuality. That kind of independence makes separating almost painless. Until only recently in heterosexual relationships, wives were financially dependent on their husbands. As more women enter the workforce and gain equality with men, the two-heads-of-household situation is becoming more of a problem for many straight couples as well. Job transfers, for example, can wreak havok with any relationship when both partners are employed — especially for gay couples. As far as each gay partner's employer knows, an "unmarried" man or woman is more eligible for promotions involving transfers. Should the promotion be turned down? Or should the partner quit his or her job and move away? Obviously, it would be risky to explain one's dilemma to one's boss.

Next, gay people face the problems associated with their socialization. Women are conditioned to be dependent: more cooperative and less competitive. They learn a dependence on others as a means of personal fulfillment. Straight men frequently take it for granted that their wives often supply more than half of the devotion in a marriage. Because of this conditioning, lesbian relationships are generally stable. Conversely, men are conditioned to be independent: more competitive and less cooperative. They are prepared for supremacy, not harmony. This can lead to a general emotional incompetence in men, gay or straight, making gay male relationships especially difficult to maintain.

To add insult to injury, there is no recognition of gay couples by the church or state. Vows are not exchanged formally before friends and family. An official marriage brings a wealth of status and support for straight people. Married men and women are viewed as being more dependable, mature, and moral. Gay couples do not share this same esteem. Of course being officially recognized, it is also necessary for straight couples to officially terminate a marriage. Numerous difficulties are involved in a dissolution or divorce. There is paperwork to be filed, a name-change for the wife, a property settlement, and the possibility of a court hearing. There is also the stigma of being divorced, making it necessary to tell all one's friends and family members "what went wrong." There may be children to help hold the relationship together. Many marriages are maintained through difficult times for this reason alone.

Virtually none of this conjugal support exists to bolster gay relationships. When a gay relationship no longer meets the mutual needs of its participants, it ends. It's that easy — maybe just too easy. No one comes to the rescue. There is very little support from families and straight friends. Families frequently do not share in the joy of a gay relationship. For some families, their joy comes when the relationship ends. To them, it is hope that Johnny or Mary might be "going straight." But because most gay people pass as straight, these relationships remain largely unknown. A lover is described as "only" a friend or roommate. Even when straight acquaintances are aware of and accept the relationship, they may feel at a loss to offer any support. In many locations, there is also a lack of counselors for gay couples. The only available resource for support in most situations is gay friends, often in an extended family.

Rather than reinforcing a marriage-like gay lifestyle, society creates obstacles for gay relationships. Could this be just another self-fulfilling prophecy? Probably. There are numerous additional problems that *successful* gay couples continue to face in our society. Creative means must be used to achieve the many basic necessities that are automatically granted to married couples. Here is just a partial list.

Getting insurance has always been a problem for gay people. Health insurance must be maintained separately by both partners in a gay relationship as most carriers will not extend coverage to a "domestic partner," either gay or straight. These independent policies cannot even complement each other. Auto insurance premiums are also higher for "single" drivers.

Limited legal powers are normally granted by the state to each spouse in a marriage. This is not true of gay couples. Power of attorney must be expressly granted for even the simplest of legal matters. The *durable* power of attorney, or "living will," is especially important. It enables one partner to make medical decisions when the other cannot. Illness always causes hardship, but can cause special problems in a gay relationship. Sometimes the family will not even allow a hospitalized son's or daughter's lover to visit. The hospital may have rules which permit visitation from spouses and immediate family only, instead of allowing the patient to designate his or her own visitors. This is particularly true with critical care or terminally ill patients. Many lovers have been separated in this way, never to see each other alive again.

There are no rules, other than those which may have been established by the individual couple, for use during a disputed property settlement if the relationship ends. Jointly owned property must be divided on the basis of "good will," and good will is notoriously absent during any separation, gay or straight.

The death of a partner is always a possibility, and when it occurs, it is always a tragedy. For gay people, becoming "widowed" is made worse. The problems begin even before the body is buried. A surviving lover is not considered next-of-kin. The family of the deceased might take charge of the funeral, possibly shipping the body out of town without notifying the lover of the arrangements. Their relationship is, of course, not mentioned in the ceremony. Funeral instructions can be expressed in a will, but these are seldom legally binding. Further, the surviving spouse in a legally recognized marriage can sue a third party for malpractice or negligence. This form of justice is not available to gay couples.

A gay couple must also have wills because most state laws automatically convey the deceased's property to the natural family, rather than to the surviving lover. Many people, gay or straight, do not believe they need a will—yet. When wills do exist, some families have been able to successfully challenge their provisions. A will can be contested on the grounds that the deceased was of "unsound mind" or "under undue influence" of his or her lover. The truth is, both reasons are interpreted as meaning homosexuality. Wills are sometimes challenged on technicalities. If the court is influenced by a strong anti-gay prejudice, the will could be annulled. To avoid problems on major investments, such as a house, property can be owned in "joint tenancy," offering rights in survivorship, instead of individually or as "tenants in common." The title is then automatically conveyed to the surviving partner. Finally, if the inheritance does go through uncontested, it is normally taxed at a higher rate; marital deductions are not allowed because the couple was not legally married. For all these reasons, most gay people have their wills carefully drafted by an experienced attorney. Preprinted forms are designed for straight couples, taking into account the law and legal precedence which would not apply to gay couples.

No, gay relationships are not at all "just like" marriages. Society has seen very effectively to that. Overcoming these problems, and more, to lead healthy, happy lives in successful relationships is indeed a testimonial to the determination gay men and lesbians have to defeating prejudice in America.

Chapter 5:

The Gay Community

Birds of a feather gather together. *Robert Burton*

Shortly after I moved to California from the Midwest, a straight friend came to visit me. He wanted to go on a tour of San Francisco. Since I was still a tourist myself, I would have made a terribly inadequate guide. To solve the problem I asked one of my new friends from the Bay Area if he would mind going along with us. He accepted. My new friend was also gay, but we both easily pass as straight. Neither of us were openly gay then. The three of us had a great time taking in the sights of this splendid city. Toward the end of the day I commented, "No tour of San Francisco would be complete without a drive down the Castro." Castro Street is a predominantly gay neighborhood. My friend from the Midwest nervously asked if we should lock the doors as we were about to turn onto Castro Street. I jokingly responded, "No, we won't let you jump out." Amazed to see so many gay men he commented, "Wow! I bet we're the only straight people on this street!" Being in the closet does have its moments.

In any large city, groups of people with common cultural, ethnic, economic, or other "lifestyles" tend to congregate. This is no different for gay people. In fact, the need for gay people to congregate is even greater. Our society has a general indifference toward homosexuality, demonstrated by the appearance of universal heterosexuality. The predominant social values simply do not accommodate the needs of gay people. The "straight" world does not even offer a self-affirming and acceptable lifestyle for the gay minority. Worse yet, society actually frustrates the socialization and happiness of gay people, making gay men and lesbians almost like foreigners in their own country. Any sanctuary from these sanctions is a welcomed reprieve. The place where gay people are likely to find acceptance is in the company of their own kind. They escape, for a while, to find happiness.

As an example of the social restrictions placed on gay people, consider the results from a study conducted by the Institute for Sex Research. It reported that seventy-three percent of those surveyed felt gay people should not be allowed to dance with each other in public places. Nearly half felt gay people should not be allowed to organize groups for social or recreational purposes, and that bars serving homosexual customers should not be permitted to exist. The sociological consequence of discrimination against gay people has been the creation of a gay subculture or "gay community."

A subculture cannot be understood in isolation from the dominant society in which it exists. In other words, the gay community is not a total culture. Rather, it supplies certain elements which are absent in American society: the chance for gay people to be themselves; to enjoy life fully without constantly passing as straight. A gay community provides ways to meet other gay people for personal and political reasons. It offers the networking and communication essential to obtaining accurate information about homosexuality and anti-gay discrimination in the dominant society. It also offers the support to help gay people deal with the problems they face outside of the gay community.

In effect, the "individual closet" has been remodeled by the creation of a "colossal closet," one that incorporates an entire minority. This is the gay community. But a big closet is not what gay people really want. It exists only as a compromise — a tolerance of homosexuality by the dominant culture. It was created by the Gay Liberation Movement of the 1970s, primarily through inspiration from the Black Civil Rights Movement. It is separate, yet far from equal.

The gay community is not necessarily a geographical location. It is a sociological entity comprised of institutions, values, and customs — a sense of unity borne of the gay minority's social predicament. Most large cities do have predominantly gay neighborhoods which could be considered communities as well. Such a visible gay community is not likely to be tolerated in a small town. Of course, city people may be just as anti-gay as rural folks, but in a large city gay people can at least achieve a certain degree of anonymity which is not easily attained in a small town. San Francisco, New York, Chicago, and other large cities also have many residents who hold negative views toward gay people. Small towns may not have any visible signs of this prejudice only because there are no visible signs of homosexuality. The gay community in a small town may be a network of friends, or it might not even exist. Many cities with as few as 50,000 people do have at least one gay bar, but gay men and lesbians in most small towns find it necessary to drive several hours to meet other gay people in a nearby metropolis. Being gay in rural America can be a real struggle. For this reason, many gay people move to larger cities. For many other reasons, however, large numbers of gay people choose not to relocate. They may have family obligations or a well-established career. Possibly they just have an aversion to big-city life. Their happiness is a compromise between their sexuality and other aspects of life.

The previous chapter mentioned some of the institutions, places, and events that are "off limits" to gay people — leaving gay people on their own to provide for their own. In effect, the gay community fills the gaps.

81

The "Night Life"

The oppressive environment surrounding homosexuality not only serves as the impetus for but also defines the boundaries of tolerance guiding formation of the gay community. Gay people basically lead two lives. One is the "straight" life, where the individual passes as heterosexual during the day, especially at work. The other is the gay life, which normally surfaces in the evenings and on the weekends. In other words, gay people only live "gay" part-time. The institutions of the gay community needed to accommodate this phenomenon, at least initially, making the options quite limited. As a result, the first institutions were gay bars and bathhouses. They could remain open late. Some bathhouses stay open all night. There are even after-hours "bars," which do not serve alcoholic beverages. Both businesses could be closed, appearing as ordinary buildings that no one notices during the day. At night they come alive. But no one, except gay people, would be there to notice. Gay bars and bathhouses offered a perfect solution to the problem. This is still the case in many small towns. In larger cities, there are many other institutions in the gay community. Castro Street in San Francisco and Greenwich Village in New York City are always bustling with activity, day or night.

Gay Bars

The gay bar is the major social institution of the gay community. Gay bars are not the "dens of iniquity" or the "meat markets" portrayed in the stereotypes. They are not just drinking establishments as the name implies either. In fact, many patrons drink only sparkling water or sodas. The bars' expanded role serves both social and political needs. They offer a place of refuge to meet friends and to learn of news in the gay community. Topics of interest are discussed in casual conversations. Bulletin boards display notices for groups and events. A stack of gay newsletters sits in the corner by the entrance.

The earliest mention of gay bars appears in eighteenth-century European literature. By 1890—yes, the "gay" nineties—most major American cities had gay bars. In 1975 one study counted over 4,000 gay bars in the United States alone. Bars seemed to legitimize being gay by making homosexuality somewhat public. Before gay bars existed, personal and political contacts were both difficult and risky.

Contrary to popular belief, gay bars vary tremendously in atmosphere and clientele, just as straight bars do. Some cater to businesspeople; others to the blue-collar crowd. Some are discos; others are pubs. Some attract a young crowd; others get an older mix of customers. Some are more like coffeehouses or cafes which are generally preferred by lesbians. Most are frequented by one gender or the other, but there are some "mixed" bars, especially in smaller towns where the lack of a critical mass of gay people precludes this form of specialization. Most welcome both gay and straight patrons. In fact, some of the best discotheques around are gay. So it is not surprising to find many straight couples dancing right along with the gay couples. Many gay men and lesbians do not like bars, but in some areas there are few alternatives for meeting other gay people. A bar is simply one of the few "public" places where gay people can act naturally.

With the emergence of other gay businesses and organizations, bars are becoming less popular now. Even in the early 1970s, when gay bars were at a peak in popularity, the Institute for Sex Research found that nearly two-thirds of gay people averaged less than one visit per month.

Gay Bathhouses

Gay bathhouses are presented here not because they are prevalent in the gay community (there are less than 150 total in the United States and less than one percent of gay men use them with any regularity), but because they are perceived as being "representative" of homosexuality. A gay bathhouse is a licensed fitness club—legally speaking. Although it was not known as such then, the first one likely existed in the Greco-Roman Empire. The "baths" provide a relatively safe (compared to cruising) and pleasant setting for anonymous and recreational sexual activity. They are almost exclusively for men. The men who visit are a mixture of homosexual, bisexual, and predominantly heterosexual. Some are closeted; some are married. The self-identified "non-gay" patrons especially appreciate the anonymity. Many of the gay people are simply too young to get into the bars. Others are too shy to "score" in the bars. A few just like the variety or expediency.

It is important to keep things in perspective here. The Institute for Sex Research found that, even before the AIDS crisis, only around ten percent of gay men visited bathhouses with any regularity. With all the other institutions in the gay community, the baths are really not that popular with the majority of gay people who have no pressing need for anonymity.

A trip to the baths goes like this. You buy your membership, if you don't already have one, then pay your entrance fee. You can get a room or a locker. You get undressed, wrap on a towel, and just walk around. If you rented a room instead, you wait for someone walking by to drop in for a "visit." Partners locate each other through a subtle and polite, often unwritten, set of rules and techniques which include eye contact, body language, and very few words. Newcomers quickly learn these procedures. This is not unlike the cruising which occurs in public places, except that the baths provide protection from the hostile elements. The sex is mutually agreeable. When you are ready to go home, you get dressed, turn in your towel and keys, and leave. That's all there is to it. But this can be more than the promiscuous "one-night stand" implied. Many friendships are formed and some lasting relationships develop.

Gay bathhouses are generally operated as private establishments, requiring membership. This keeps the "innocent victim" from accidentally wandering in. It also helps avoid problems with local law enforcement agencies. Most bathhouses have a series of locked doors to delay police in the event of a raid. Actually, because they are private clubs, most bathhouses operate quite legally. The owners strictly comply with all local health, fire, and zoning regulations. Most baths also provide nonsexual entertainment and recreational facilities including lounges, saunas, hot tubs, swimming pools, body-building equipment, showers, pool tables, a theater and even libraries. Since AIDS, attendance at the baths has tapered off sharply despite the fact that most now distribute free condoms and give advice on safe sexual practices.

The baths are not unlike the institution of prostitution in the dominant culture. There are really only two differences: both partners pay and neither is a prostitute. The baths offer instant and anonymous recreational sex, with no long-term obligation, for only a few dollars. There is no victim. With heterosexuality, men are usually willing partners, while women often are not. Hence the need for prostitution. With male homosexuality, prospective partners may both be willing, but are unable to make contact easily and safely. Hence the need for bathhouses.

Other Institutions of the Gay Community

There are far more other gay organizations than there are bars and baths combined. It's just that their diversity defies broad categorization. Included are numerous organizations and associations. These exist for social, professional, political, and recreational reasons. They represent many special interests including gay doctors, gay lawyers, gay engineers, gay fathers and lesbian mothers, gay Democrats and gay Republicans, gay golfers, gay bowlers, gay mountain climbers, gay square dancers, and gay bridge players. The list is almost endless.

There are gay businesses of almost every type. Some address unique gay needs; others serve everyone. These include stores, repair shops, banks, vacation resorts, financial services, insurance agencies, restaurants, publishing companies, and dating services. Again, the list is almost endless.

There are gay church groups for nearly every mainstream denomination. There are even gay churches and synagogues. The Metropolitan Community Church (MCC) has over 250 parishes located throughout the United States and in several other countries.

There are extended families of lovers and friends, social groups, bookstores that are less like businesses and more like gathering places, clubs, and so on. Many of these are especially appealing to lesbians.

There are political lobbyists, legal organizations, media watch groups, AIDS services, and countless individual and collective activist efforts to fight the daily battles against oppression.

There are gay newspapers and gay magazines, gay directories, gay erotica, gay community centers, and gay youth groups. Most cities have a gay switchboard or information line. Some of these simply play recorded messages of news and events. Others will offer counseling services.

There are gay functions including sporting activities, dances, rodeos, picnics, tours, concerts, plays, parades, rallies, retreats, festivals, parties, and group vacations. The Gay Games, a major Olympic-style sports event, is held every four years. [Gay people do not recognize USOC's claim to "ownership" of this word.] The games were originally called the Gay Olympic Games, but the United States Olympic Committee put an end to that. Apparently, the gay minority would not be able to share this word with other groups like handicapped persons, police, juniors, Explorer Scouts, marathon eaters, and even dogs.

The gay community indeed consists of much more than just bars and bathhouses — and yes, gay people do spend a great deal of time in the gay community and with each other. According to the Institute for Sex Research, gay people who associate with the gay community are less likely to anticipate or fear rejection. They are also less likely to impute society's negative attitudes toward homosexuality into their own lives. Those gay people who are not involved in the gay community are more likely to experience feelings of depression, loneliness, guilt, shame or anxiety, and less likely to have feelings of self-acceptance. Drs. Weinberg and Williams wrote: "Probably our most salient finding pertains to the beneficial effects of a supportive environment. Thus, the homosexual may want to cultivate social relations with other homosexuals and/or utilize the institutions and publications of the homosexual subculture. Through such involvement he most likely will learn that a homosexual identity may not have all the negative consequences that are feared, and perhaps may have more rewards than he has considered. He may, through such association, also learn how to best handle the practical problems of being homosexual, for example, how to handle parents, deal with job discrimination, make the best use of the institutions in the homosexual subculture."

The first two sections of this book have laid the foundation for understanding homosexuality. In summary, homosexuality is the consistent, predominant or exclusive, emotional and erotic attraction to persons of the same gender. No one knows for sure why gay people become gay, but whatever causes homosexuality, gay people remain gay. The many stereotypes and other myths were explored and shown to be largely without basis. Finally, some insight was shared into how this minority of twenty-four million Americans lives, along with an explanation about why gay people live the way they do.

Repeatedly, the most significant difference between heterosexuality and homosexuality was shown to be the environment in which both exist. Gay people are largely on their own to establish their own values, and to implement their own lifestyles. Society has quite literally "written off" the gay minority. Why? To answer that question, an understanding of a condition called *homophobia* is required. But first, straight readers are asked to take a small test.

This test is based on Dr. Martin Rochlin's "Heterosexual Questionnaire." Please try to answer the questions as honestly as possible. Begin.

1. How old were you when you "chose" to experience emotional and erotic attraction to persons of the opposite gender?

2. Before "choosing" these feelings, did you at least consider "choosing" to be attracted to persons of the same gender?

3. Is it possible your heterosexuality is just a "phase"?

4. Is it possible your heterosexuality stems from a fear of others of the same gender?

5. Have you ever experienced problems associated with your heterosexuality?

6. Have you ever sought treatment for these problems or for your heterosexuality?

7. Do you think a heterosexual therapist could be truly objective?

8. If you have never had sexual relations with a person of the same gender, is it possible all you need is the "right lover" to be "cured"?

9. Have you ever attempted to "recruit" gay people to your lifestyle?

10. Why do you think heterosexual men and women place so much emphasis on sex?

11. Have you ever "flaunted" your heterosexuality by:

    A. Inviting friends and relatives to your wedding?

    B. Wearing a wedding ring?

    C. Displaying pictures of your husband or wife?

    D. Holding hands, dancing or kissing in public?

    E. Discussing your personal relationship or activities with others?

    F. Bringing your spouse to social gatherings?

    G. All of the above?

12. Considering the fact that approximately 90 percent of all child molesters are heterosexual, do you think straight people should be allowed to teach in public schools?

13. Do you think the fact that nearly half of new marriages end in separation or divorce demonstrates a lack of responsibility in heterosexual individuals?

14. Have you ever engaged in sexual activity without the intent to reproduce? If so, do you think this is an appropriate use of your genitals?

15. Do you have a negative opinion of gay people? If so, why?

Section III:

What is Homophobia?

Chapter 6:

Understanding Homophobia

He flattered himself on being a man without prejudices; and this pretension itself is a very great prejudice. *Anatole France*

The other day I overheard a little boy, probably only eight years old, call his friend a "faggot." He couldn't possibly have understood what the word meant. But he knew it was bad, that it would insult his friend, and that his father, who was right there, probably would not scold him for saying it. He was right on all three counts.

Gay people have a long history of being victimized — sometimes by names, sometimes by sticks and stones. Nothing stirs compassion more than the innocent victim. But gay people are rarely viewed as victims. Even when gay people are considered victims of some mental illness or demonic possession, they are somehow not considered innocent. They become, therefore, guilty of something, making any victimization or oppression that gay people suffer socially appear "justified." This makes no sense, but that's part of the problem. What causes this seemingly endless spiral, this mobius strip of feelings? Homophobia.

Dr. George Weinberg introduced the term *homophobia* to describe the irrational fear or hatred of gay people. It is not a perfect word, but it's the only one our vocabulary offers. The dictionary defines homophobia as the "irrational fear of homosexuality or homosexuals."

An anxiety about homosexuality and gay people is symptomatic of a mild case of homophobia. When homophobia influences opinion, the result is prejudice; when homophobia influences behavior, the result is discrimination and possibly violence. *No* one is immune from homophobia. Everyone, gay or straight, suffers from it. In other words, homophobia is not a matter of diagnosis; it is a matter of degree. And because homophobia is universal, it becomes transparent — even normal. As a result, most people never question its validity, believing *real* prejudice is arbitrary or unfounded. This chapter identifies and analyzes the reasons often given for homophobia.

Homophobia is rooted in heterosexism, a belief that heterosexuality is intrinsically and totally superior to homosexuality. In this respect, it is the same as racism and sexism. Heterosexism elevates heterosexuality from a sexual orientation to the status of institution that becomes enforced through ideology, theology, and other social institutions. In effect, "straight society" has consciously or unknowingly defined and maintained a view of sexuality which assures it a position of superiority. But homophobia goes *well* beyond heterosexism. This basic feeling of superiority becomes exaggerated, irrational. Most people become unable to even explain *why* they feel the way they do about homosexuality — they just do. When this happens, heterosexism becomes a phobia: homophobia.

The Reasons for Homophobia

An idea isn't responsible for the people who believe it. *Don Marquis*

People can express the exact same belief for a variety of different reasons. Their conviction may also vary. Some beliefs are held casually; others compassionately. Yet people are not born homophobic; it is not innate. Rather, it is an acquired trait. Some people become homophobic because they believe this is consistent with their self-image or other attitudes. A few may have had an unpleasant personal experience with homosexuality or gay people, although this is extremely rare given that eighty percent of Americans claim not to know a single gay person. Most of the time an imaginary reason masks the real cause. Again, most people cannot identify exactly *why* they dislike gay people — they just do. It is simply expected. Homophobia is therefore more habit than sincere hatred.

It is also common to "credit" one's own homophobia to others. People regularly use the alleged needs of others as a justification for *their* personal prejudices. For example, school administrators may claim their homophobia is based on parents' concerns. Parents justify their homophobia as fear for their children's safety — based, of course, on the stereotypes. This is how children start to learn homophobia. Politicians tell the gay community, "I support your civil rights, but if I do something about it I won't get reelected. Now that won't do either of us any good, will it?" Even ministers claim the "church" is not ready to accept gay people into the congregation.

Part of the problem is that straight people feel less defined by their heterosexuality, even taking it for granted, and find disturbing the apparent centrality of homosexuality in a gay person's identity. To the extent this "homo-centric" identity exists, it must be considered an effect of society's homophobia rather than its cause. Similarly, white people rarely consider being Caucasian a significant aspect of their lives, while black people are unable to ignore this distinguishing characteristic that defines their minority status.

It is also helpful to recognize that the fundamental issue with homosexuality is really sexuality. There is guilt, shame, and contempt in our society concerning sexuality in general. The very subject of homosexuality forces sexuality to become a topic that is normally ignored. It is almost impossible to consider homosexuality and not be overcome by an incredible curiosity regarding the sexual aspect and, in fact, to make sexual activity the exclusive focus of attention. Most straight people can, and do, easily and graphically imagine what same-sex sexual expression is like. For straight people, who are intimately familiar with the genitalia of both genders, this vicarious experience is possible whether considering gay men or lesbians. Even if one is too "chaste" to attempt envisioning same-sex sexual expression, it is not too difficult, and deeply disturbing, simply to imagine two men kissing. Kissing is an everyday occurrence everyone experiences. This image, while it should not be, is very repulsive to many straight people. Consider too the nervous giggling or other similar reactions people feel compelled to make in a group whenever the topic of homosexuality is broached. This is especially true in a movie during a gay "scene." It seems some people would rather witness a heterosexual orgy than see two men kissing.

Therefore, before investigating the specific reasons for homophobia, it is necessary to consider how society views all sexuality.

The Sociology of Sexuality

Much of our highly valued cultural heritage has been acquired at the cost of sexuality. *Sigmund Freud*

A 1989 Gallup poll asked American parents the question: "What would you say is the most likely to make you feel uncomfortable [when watching TV with your children]?" Sex was ranked the highest, followed by violence. Apparently killing was OK, "but none of that fornicating stuff."

Much of the general guilt, shame, and contempt concerning sexuality is due to *erotophobia*. Erotophobia involves exaggerated anxieties and fears of all sexual behavior. In the extreme, sexuality can be regarded as a regrettable necessity. Erotophobic beliefs are normally accompanied by extraordinary attempts to place such activities under social regulation making sexuality at once an area of deep personal meaning and heated public controversy. For example, the very concept of deviance and the prevailing gender roles are socially defined and maintained. And everyone — from clergy to doctors and politicians to bureaucrats — apparently wants a hand in dividing behavior into right and wrong. But there is a wide chasm between private behavior and public morality in this area. For example, masturbation was considered "always wrong" by twenty-six percent of those questioned in a study by the Institute for Sex Research, even though Dr. Kinsey's research revealed that nearly everyone masturbates.

Erotophobic training is ingrained in our culture. Virtually everyone is conditioned to view sexuality and the genitalia as "dirty." Children learn to be ashamed of their naked bodies and any sexual abuse of their genitals — especially masturbation. These lessons apparently do not prevent the vast majority of people from masturbating or engaging in other sexual activity; they simply cultivate personal feelings of guilt and shame afterwards. Erotophobia may nurture feelings of jealousy as well, which can lead to contempt for those individuals who are able to enjoy satisfying sex lives. Because all attempts to make certain forms of sex *unpopular* have failed, it becomes necessary to make them *unacceptable* instead.

90

The sexual issues which *are* social include rape, child molestation, sex-for-hire (prostitution), incest, and abortion. Rape and child molestation have victims. Genetic limitations involved in incest lead to birth defects. Abortion is a social issue because it involves debate, not on the morality of death, but on the beginning of life. Most sexual issues, however, are clearly outside the needs of society. These issues include premarital sex, extramarital sex, teenage sex, masturbation, and yes, homosexuality. These are all personal matters. Some are also of concern to the family and even to the church as moral issues, but there is no *social* concern being addressed. Nevertheless, sex is too irresistible for some politicians. When this happens, sexual regulation becomes more like political strategy and less like social policy. The wrong "problem" gets solved, its "solution" creating new, real problems.

Homosexuality: Just Plain "Wrong"

One would think there existed some overwhelming reason or reasons why gay people are held in such contempt in our society. As recently as 1985, the *Los Angeles Times* found that seventy-three percent of their survey audience felt homosexuality was "wrong." Yet this overwhelming majority is usually unable to identify specifically what there is about homosexuality that is wrong, or at least wrong enough to justify homophobia. As such, this attitude is more of a knee-jerk reaction than a considered opinion.

Imaginary fears are always more frightening than reality. So what most homophobic arguments lack in logic, they make up in emotion. Each invokes certain "rules" for acceptable human behavior and typically goes like this: "Homosexuality is wrong, for in order to have sex it is necessary to be married. Because gay people are not married, homosexuality is wrong." This is really a moral premise. Those who believe this do not recognize that our society prevents gay people from marrying while offering no moral alternatives. The argument continues: "Gay marriages aren't allowed because it would destroy the family." This makes homosexuality a threat and ignores the fact that homosexuality has existed in all societies since the beginning of humankind. There is more: "God didn't intend for two people of the same sex to live together. He made Adam and Eve, not Adam and Steve." How people claim to know what God intends is unknown and apparently unimportant. *All* things come from God for *His* reasons, not ours. "It's not natural," whatever that means. "It's a sickness," yet gay people should feel shame. "I don't like it. I don't understand why. I still feel the way to be is heterosexual." Well, the "way to be" is also white, Anglo-Saxon, and Protestant.

Each of these claims, and some others, can be placed into two general categories for justifying homophobia. One is a belief that homosexuality poses some threat to someone or something. Actually, all prejudice claims to be a rational response to some perceived danger or threat. The threats associated with homosexuality range from personal repugnance, which is not really a threat, to a belief that society itself will be destroyed by this phenomenon. The second category is beliefs rooted in Judeo-

Christian religion. The three most common portray homosexuality as being "unnatural," immoral, or sinful. Presented here are the more common reasons people offer to explain homophobic beliefs. The threats are assessed first.

Homosexuality is a threat to children. Children, because they are impressionable and vulnerable, are most frequently cited as the reason homosexuality is threatening. This is really a combination of the "recruiting" and "molesting" stereotypes presented in Chapter 3. Recall from the discussion that the Institute for Sex Research found over forty percent of the population felt, "Young homosexuals become that way because of older homosexuals."

This so-called threat should only exist for straight children, but it assumes *all* children are straight. The fact is, sexual orientation, whether heterosexual or homosexual, emerges during adolescence. In other words, out of every ten children, nine are straight and one is gay. With no basis in the belief that gay people "recruit," there is no conceivable threat. In addition, recall that nearly all pedophiles are heterosexual. So gay adults pose no greater sexual "threat" to children than straight adults do — perhaps even less. Because the evidence does not support either claim, the purported threat of homosexuality must exist elsewhere.

Homosexuality is a threat to society. Homosexuality does disturb the tranquility of conventional social order by "violating" the "uniform" standard of behavior established by the majority. But diversity is always an inconvenience to conformity. This fear maintains that because gay people do not conform to the *sexual* standards in society, they will not conform to any other social values or rules either. Given the premise that many people already believe homosexuality is a neurosis, it is not too terribly difficult for them to imagine gay people must also be sociopathic. After all, the gay minority seems to ignore completely the social sanctions which establish to oppress it.

According to the Institute for Sex Research, forty-nine percent of the people surveyed felt, "Homosexuality is a social corruption that can cause the downfall of a civilization." A Harris Poll in 1969 found that sixty-three percent considered homosexuality harmful to American life. Similar results have been reported by more recent surveys. Another Harris Poll, conducted in 1965, asked people what they considered harmful to the nation. Homosexuality was ranked third behind communism and atheism by eighty-two percent of the men and fifty-eight percent of the women. In the 1950s, many people actually associated homosexuality with communism. Some still do. It is ironic that our society makes this association while the Soviets do the very same thing. They have much more rigid anti-gay controls, claiming homosexuality is both a cause and a symbol of America's decadence.

There are actually many variations on this theme of a "threat" to society. Some people claim sexual variance flourishes when societies are sexually restrictive. They believe sexual "anarchy" leads to political anarchy. It is interesting that others claim just the opposite. They believe sexual oppression leads to political oppression. What is even more interesting is that *both* sides of this issue cite *exactly* the same evidence! The most common example offered is the Roman Empire. The first laws prohibiting same-sex sexual activity appeared around the time of its decline. Some argue this was necessary, owing to the "uncontrollable" increase in such activity, even though same-sex sexuality had been tolerated for centuries. Because the empire thrived during the centuries of sexual tolerance, others blame Rome's decline on rising oppression. But both of these simple conclusions completely ignore all the other considerations including the deterioration of Rome's economy from tax evasion, and attacks by the Goths, Huns, Slavs, Lombards, Saxons, Magyars, Vandals, and Vikings. Rome did not fall; it was conquered.

Other people argue, "What if *everyone* were homosexual? The human species could be wiped out in a few decades!" This is absurd. What would happen if everyone had eight children? A similar fate would await the human species.

There is absolutely no evidence to indicate that the incidence of homosexuality is increased under conditions of acceptance. This belief is actually a reversal of cause and effect. The visibility of homosexuality is what changes, not its incidence. Even when controls were as drastic as torture and death, homosexuality was not eliminated. To believe that homosexuality would "run rampant" is pure nonsense. This is nothing more than a different version of the "recruiting" myth. Although homosexuality and heterosexuality are mutually exclusive for most individuals, they are *not* for society. It is both unnecessary and inappropriate, therefore, to "protect" heterosexuality with the sacrifice of homosexuality.

If it could be empirically established that homosexuality posed a legitimate threat to society, then the government and other social institutions would be justified in having prohibitions and proscriptions against it. But the facts totally contradict the claim. Homosexuality has always existed in both thriving and troubled societies. Dr. Kinsey wrote: "If all persons with any trace of homosexual history, or those who were predominantly homosexual, were eliminated from the population today, there is no reason for believing that the incidence of the homosexual in the next generation would be materially reduced. The homosexual has been a significant part of human sexual activity ever since the dawn of history, primarily because it is an expression of capacities that are basic in the human animal." The *Final Task Force Report on Homosexuality as a Social Issue,* published by the American Psychological Association, summarizes this concern by stating: "There is simply no evidence demonstrating that homosexuality or tolerance of it, is either a symptom or a cause of social decline, decadence, or the fall of civilization. There is considerable evidence to the contrary from history, anthropology and sociology."

It is interesting to note that the distinction between homosexuality and heterosexuality did not even exist until the last half of the nineteenth century. How could something so "obvious" to us now, so "threatening," go undefined for so long, despite its wide existence? Think about it. This belief is normally propagated solely for political purposes. The alleged threat from homosexuality must lie elsewhere.

Homosexuality is a threat to "tradition." Some people claim homosexuality is a "threat" to "traditional" values which, of course, also "threatens" society. The word *traditional* means something different to nearly everyone who uses it. In essence, tradition is the way things were yesterday. For some, it is an "all-or-nothing" ideology. Traditionalists use tradition to justify tradition. And as Mark Twain pointed out: "The less there is to justify a traditional custom, the harder it is to get rid of it." Fearing change and what change might bring, traditionalists become defenders of the status quo — trapped in tradition.

Yet this nostalgia is for a purified past. Do the "traditional" American values include slavery, segregation, internment of U.S. citizens of Japanese descent, and McCarthyism? Probably not. Do "traditional" values *exclude* religious pluralism, labor unions, and women's rights? Probably not. Many aspects of the "good old days" were not so good after all. Social traditions change with the times, being more of a flowing stream than a stagnant pool. Change is simply necessary for progress. Most people, gay and straight, support the traditional values of honesty, integrity, gratitude, compassion, and, especially, tolerance for pluralism. Gay people are, after all, brought up in the same traditions and with the same values as their straight brothers and sisters. The only tradition gay people threaten is homophobia.

Homosexuality is a threat to gender roles. The stereotype of gender role nonconformity was discussed in detail in Chapter 3, but some additional comments are in order here. This alleged nonconformity is perceived by some people as a threat to the *male* role, as men have the most to "lose" coming from a position of superiority. So men tend to be more negative regarding homosexuality, especially toward gay men, and what began as a stereotype becomes the justification for homophobia. This was revealed in an examination of twenty-four independent studies. Sixteen of those studies showed men as being more homophobic than women; five showed no gender differences; and only three indicated that women were more homophobic than men. There appears to be little gender-related difference regarding homophobia toward lesbians. Therefore, in addition to heterosexism feeding homophobia, there is an element of sexism as well. Thus the "dread" of homosexuality is not impressed upon girls nearly as much as it is upon boys.

There are four main reasons for this. First, homosexuality has been largely defined in a male context — as are most things in our society. Second, women are not threatened by a devaluation in their status because they already "enjoy" a position of inferiority. For example, consider the fact that women are accepted more in jobs traditionally held by men. The converse is not true: A female physician is far more socially acceptable than a male nurse. Third, the feminist movement is supported by many lesbians. All women, regardless of sexual orientation, are allies in this struggle against sexist oppression. Fourth, women cannot establish their femininity through hate. Men, on the other hand, can and do establish their masculinity through hate — and many do hate faggots.

When gender roles are challenged, men become anxious. It is their position of dominance which is really being threatened, not by homosexuality per se, but by the stereotypical belief that gay men are "effeminate." Under the code of "male solidarity," men who do not conform totally to the male "role" are thought to degrade themselves while diluting "manliness" for their entire gender. Of course, many straight men also find the male code of behavior undesirable; they are just at a loss to find ways of changing it. There has been no "masculinist" movement to relax the rigidity or at least challenge the male gender role standards.

The incredible fear of being thought homosexual as a result of any display of affection or camaraderie between men has made it necessary to create the concept of "male bonding." Male bonding consists in certain exceptions to the confining rules for masculinity. Because it exists, when "real" men hug and pat each other on the butt, their sexual orientation is not questioned. However, there are still a few "rules" for male bonding. Football players can do just about anything because football is a "manly" sport. But if a man is on the debate team, his manliness will be suspected for simply putting his arm around the shoulders of another man. How ridiculous it all seems.

Think about this: Is it possible for two gay men to "bond"? And can a straight man "bond" with a gay man, or vice versa? If one ponders these questions long enough, it becomes apparent that male bonding is nothing more than a way of eliminating "homosexual suspicion" from perfectly normal displays of friendship and nonsexual affection. The greatest fallacy here is how a few "pansies," outnumbered nine to one, can threaten all those "real" men. No, this is not a valid reason for homophobia.

Homosexuality is a threat to heterosexuality. This is another variation on the theme of "recruiting." The basis for this belief is actually a projection of *homophobia* onto gay men and lesbians. In other words, it is a belief in the existence of something called *heterophobia*. Some straight people want to eliminate homosexuality, so they feel gay people must want to eliminate heterosexuality. This is nonsense. The people who hold this view have just never taken the time to really think it through, or they would realize how absurd it is. Gay people only want pluralism, not monopoly.

Homosexuality is a threat to the institution of marriage. Marriage represents happiness and security for most straight people. Those who believe homosexuality is a "threat" to marriage might also consider gay people a "threat" to their very happiness and security. The fact is: Many gay people simply want to be part of this institutional happiness and security. Gay people do not wish to destroy marriage; they just want to be included.

In countries where same-sex relationships are sanctioned, there has been no significant decline in the rate of heterosexual marriages. The marriage rate decline in this country is based on dissatisfaction with the institution itself as more and more straight people find it too restrictive. According to a study by the National Institute of Health, one-third of the over eight million single women in their twenties have "cohabitated" with men. Can you imagine a straight couple claiming they live together unmarried *because* of the "threat" homosexuality poses to marriage?

It is also "wishful thinking" to blame the current divorce rate on anything which has to do with homosexuality. Divorces do not end marriages, anyway — people do. The divorce is just an official conclusion of a marriage which has already gone sour. People who still like marriage, but get divorced, just get remarried. None of this has anything to do with homosexuality.

Homosexuality is a threat to the family. Today's family is not what it used to be. Instead of mother, father and two children, it's mother, father and four children: his, hers, and theirs. It's a woman and her illegitimate son, a man and his adopted daughter, a divorced woman and her two children, and an older couple with their grandchild. It's a widowed man and his stepson, a divorced lesbian and her son, a gay male couple and their two foster children, and an unmarried couple. People do what they have to do. Actually, the "traditional" family of two children with Mom as full-time housewife and Dad as sole "breadwinner" accounts for less than five percent of American households. Half the men and women getting married today have lived together before the wedding. One in every five births is to unwed mothers. Three in five children born today will live with a single parent by age eighteen. To "blame" this situation on homosexuality is both unfair and unfounded.

Society is changing. That is to be expected. Resistance to this change is also to be expected. Yet I fail to see how a gay male couple living in Sunnyvale, California, in the privacy of their own home, can threaten a family in Miami or even their next-door neighbors for that matter. I *do* understand, though, how a fanatic woman in Miami or a zealous man in Lynchburg can make life difficult for a gay couple.

Gay people have no desire to destroy families. Quite to the contrary, gay people yearn to *form* families of their own. While this may involve *expanding* the definition of "family" from the current, narrow "Mom, Dad and the kids" variety, it hardly involves destroying that which already exists.

Every single threat offered is imaginary: Homosexuality poses no *real* threat to anyone or anything. The so-called threats, therefore, are inadequate as justification for homophobia. The other categorical reason given to justify homophobia is that homosexuality is "wrong." This is believed to arise from some inherent and objectionable "defect" in homosexuality. Basically, this means homosexuality is "unnatural," immoral or sinful.

Homosexuality is "unnatural." Bette Midler once said, "If sex is such a natural phenomenon, how come there are so many books on how to?"   That's a good question. "Nature" is regularly used to explain things people do not understand. "It's natural" is the easy answer to many complicated and otherwise unanswerable questions in life. Other questions are answered in the negative by declaring something is "unnatural."

The word *natural* is frequently used, often abused, and nearly always is subjective. It is *loaded* with meaning. *Webster's Ninth New Collegiate*

Dictionary contains eight senses and three subsenses for a total of eleven definitions of the noun nature. There are fourteen senses and eleven subsenses for a total of twenty-five definitions of the adjective *natural*. And there are four senses and two subsenses for a total of six definitions of the adverb *naturally*. Further, it is interesting to note how many times "nature" is used to define the words *natural* and *naturally,* making it difficult to determine which sense of "nature" is meant. With all these different meanings, it will naturally (with truth to nature — no pun intended) be important to give the sense intended, where known, or this discussion could get very confusing. This will be done parenthetically following each use.

The earliest recorded occurrence of labeling same-sex sexuality "unnatural" is found in Plato's *Laws* written in the fifth century B.C. (I intentionally avoid using the word *homosexual* since the word itself and the very concept of sexual orientation did not exist at the time.) Plato argued there were two reasons for this. The first is that same-sex sexual acts undermine the development of desirable masculine traits. This first belief was likely based on the assumption that such activity reduced men, or at least one of the partners in a male same-sex sexual act, to the lower status of women. The second, more important law was that male sexuality has only one proper use: procreation within marriage. This was because the Greeks believed the physical world had a stable order or structure, and that everything in it had a single, essential, and definable function. Plato maintained these beliefs despite the fact that a growing body of evidence indicates he himself had a consistent, predominant or exclusive, emotional and erotic attraction to persons of his own gender. Using similar reasoning, Aristotle argued that loans were "unnatural" because they violate the true *function* of money.

The emphasis on function was more than a philosophy; it was almost a science. The sciences of biology and physics did not exist then as they do today. Greek thought was dominated by Stoic philosophy. The fundamental Stoic belief was to "live according to nature." "Nature" was understood to be the divinely appointed *order* of the world, and was equated with reason and logic. A Stoic was one who believed people should be free from passion, unmoved by joy or grief. As such, the Stoics valued suppression of *all* emotion. Instead, Plato found pleasure in rational action. He called this *virtuous* pleasure and felt it was much more satisfying than *vicious* pleasure, which was not in accordance with "nature." The only rational, or "natural," function of sexuality was procreation. Physical pleasure and emotional expression were "irrational" and, therefore, "unnatural."

From the time of Christ through the Middle Ages, St. Thomas Aquinas was among the most widely accepted scholastic theologians to discuss same-sex sexual activity in any detail. St. Thomas' philosophies dealt primarily with moral issues, but he based many of his arguments on "nature." In his work *Summa Theologica,* Aquinas listed the "unnatural vices" as masturbation, intercourse with animals, same-sex sexual intercourse, and nonprocreative forms of heterosexual sexual expression. He did not, however, define the "nature" against which these vices exist.

Throughout his writings, Aquinas defined *nature* in numerous, sometimes conflicting ways. In any event, he clearly believed procreation was the only "legitimate" use of sexuality. In effect, he adopted the Stoic philosophy and the Greek ideals of function in his theological interpretation. (St. Thomas is discussed at length in Chapter 10 on "Judeo-Christian Tradition.") Historically, then, sexual "nature" has become synonymous with procreation.

"Nature" as a synonym for "Procreation"

A belief that the sole significance of human sexuality is based on procreation ignores the obvious emotional and pleasurable aspects of sexual activity. As such, it is a minimalist description of human sexuality at best. This mentality has caused some gay men and lesbians to refer jokingly to straight people as "breeders."

But there also seems to be a double standard here between heterosexuality and homosexuality. The emotional and pleasurable part of sex is considered natural (being in accordance with or determined by nature) for heterosexuality, but unnatural (based on an inherent sense of right or wrong) for homosexuality. (Notice the change in meaning. This is common in many discussions based on "nature.") Similarly, the many different forms of sexual expression are considered natural (occurring in conformity with the ordinary course of nature) when they accompany a procreative premise. On their own, however, they somehow become unnatural (having an essential relation with something). For example, some people believe oral sex is "natural" foreplay for intercourse, but "unnatural" as a way of achieving orgasm. The only difference between the two forms of behavior is the situation. Of course, with this convenient double standard, oral sex becomes "natural" for straight people and "unnatural" for gay people.

Because human sexuality has the apparently intended capacity for expressing emotion and feelings of pleasure, it is actually unnatural (possessing or exhibiting the higher qualities of human nature) to restrict sexual activity to procreation alone. Our reproduction is not the result of some natural (implanted or being as if implanted by nature: seemingly inborn) sexual "instinct." Instead, human beings *consciously* choose to procreate. Similarly, many people believe some forms of contraception, like condoms and birth-control pills, are unnatural (touched by the influences of civilization and society) while other forms, like the rhythm method, are natural (having a form or appearance found in nature). Yet it is certainly true that both defeat the natural (occurring in conformance with the ordinary course of nature) "purpose" of sexuality. And conversely, what could be more unnatural (not produced by nature: artificial) than artificial insemination, which is becoming widely accepted in our society.

Personal views on the nature (a creative or controlling force in the universe) of sexual pleasure are independent on whether one subscribes to a divine creation or to evolution as the origin of the species. If the evolutionists are correct, then the emotional expression and physical pleasure associated with sexual activity would enhance the chances of survival for the species. If the creationists are correct, then God gave His children the capacity to express love and to experience joy through sexual activity. In either case, procreation is *not* the reason straight people have sex the vast majority of times they do. Condemning homosexuality because it is not procreative, then, is merely an excuse. Therefore, homosexuality must be "unnatural" for some reason.

The "natural" use of our bodies

This approach to the "natural" basis for homophobia maintains that anatomy is destiny. The very nature (the inherent character or basic constitution of a person or thing) of anatomical design seems to reveal a natural (having a normal or usual character) use for the sex organs. This belief basically claims that because a gender difference exists, it is the only way sexuality should be expressed — as if each individual were a "half" waiting to become a "whole" like two pieces of a puzzle. This gender complementarity theory argues that neither the male nor the female is complete without the other. In the context of procreation this is true. That context aside, though, the argument is unfounded.

In fact, this position could be countered with an equally ridiculous but opposite one in favor of homosexuality when the context is physical pleasure. The fact that each gender more precisely understands its own sensuality, could indicate that the natural (implanted or being as if implanted by nature: seemingly inborn) way to achieve maximum sexual pleasure is with a partner of the same gender. To achieve this degree of enjoyment, other forms of human sexual expression must be learned — including heterosexual coitus. Further, heterosexual sexual expression is inherently problematic when considered in the context of physical pleasure. Attempts to achieve simultaneous orgasm during coitus are frequently prevented by the male's natural (having a specified character by nature) tendency to climax more quickly.

This "natural" use of the body is really a variation on the theme of procreation. Clearly, man and woman must couple for the purpose of procreation. But the fact that the penis "fits" the vagina for this purpose does not invalidate other forms of sexual expression, either heterosexual or homosexual. In other words, heterosexual coitus is not necessarily *exclusively* natural (being in accordance with or determined by nature).

If one defines "sex organs" as the penis and the vagina, then the use of any other part of the body could be considered unnatural (not being in accordance with or not determined by nature). But if one defines "sex organs" as any part of the body which can be sexually stimulated, thus providing pleasure, then everyone has several sex organs. The use of other parts of the body during sex is also both unnatural (not having an essential relation with someone or something — namely procreation) and natural (possessing or exhibiting the higher qualities of human nature — especially emotional expression). The other "sex organs" include the mouth, lips, breasts, ear lobes, anus, fingers, toes, and even

99

the brain — the source of sexual fantasy. The vast majority of straight people do indeed use these other "sex organs" to engage in the alternate forms of sexual expression including fellatio, cunnilingus, masturbation, anal intercourse, and more. One could argue that the function of the anus is to excrete bodily waste, but a similar claim could be made of the penis as well. Considering the reality of the situation (that *all* people engage in sexual activity far more often for emotional expression or physical pleasure than for reproduction), the use of this argument against homosexual sexual expression is at best hypocritical, representing just another double standard. There must be another "nature" which is violated by homosexuality.

Animal "nature"

When animals do something that we like, we call it "natural." When they do something that we don't like, we call it "animalistic." *James D. Weinich*

Many people base their belief that homosexuality is unnatural (not being in accordance with or not determined by nature) on the behavior of animals. Yet same-sex sexual activity has been observed in every species which has been studied for such behavior. Further, this behavior occurs in the presence of available opposite-sex partners; it is not forced or coerced. Therefore, it occurs naturally (being in accordance with or determined by nature). Might anyone conclude, based on this information, that the "homosexuality" observed in other animals is caused by a "dominant" mother and a "weak" father? Probably not. Because psychologists have yet to establish exactly what motivates this particular behavior in animals, it is impossible to determine whether animal "homosexuality" is equivalent to the emotional and erotic attraction toward others of the same gender as found in humans. Animals derive their sexuality based primarily on instinct. They naturally (by nature: by natural character or ability) do not even understand sexuality and reproduction.

Naturally (according to the usual course of things: as might be expected), animals make lousy models for human behavior. But this does not stop some people from doing it anyway. A comparison of man to other animals can be very interesting — misleading, but interesting. Actually, this form of the "natural" argument is also based on procreation. Many animals are restricted to periods of potential fertilization. When the animals are considered "in heat." This is true even in the primates, our closest Darwinian ancestors (provided one believes in evolution). If sexual nature (man's original or natural condition) is only for procreation, then sex would naturally (by nature: by natural character or ability) be limited to such fertile periods. But human beings are sexually responsive constantly. And the natural (being in accordance with or determined by nature) age for unnatural (touched by the influence of civilization and society) marriage would be twelve or thirteen when adolescents become sexually responsive.

So the mating habits of most animals are not at all like those of humans. While animals may experience physical pleasure during sex, they do not "make love." Further, the traditional coupling in humans is rarely found in animals. Should a woman in "heat" be pursued by a pack of men who compete for her? Let's hope not.

It is natural (possessing or exhibiting the higher qualities of human nature) for human beings to exhibit a wealth of unique behavior. A substantial percentage of human behavior is not really natural (having or constituting a classification based on features existing in nature) for other animal species. People cook food, wear clothing, hunt for sport, shave, get circumcised, fly in airplanes (if God intended for man to fly he would have been born with wings), enter monogamouse relationships, and worship gods. Of course, celibacy is unnatural (having a spiritual, intellectual or fictitious existence) too. There must be another reason homosexuality is "unnatural."

The "natural" use of nature

Homosexuality is definitely unnatural (not occurring in conformity with the ordinary course of nature)—and so are blue eyes. Both are also quite natural (being in accordance with or determined by nature). The "natural" arguments against homosexuality often appear convincing, but fall apart under the slightest scrutiny. For example, "It is not natural to be gay, therefore gay people are unnatural." The change in meaning here is significant. Anything which is not *common,* meaning less than a fifty percent incidence, could be considered unnatural (not occurring in conformity with the ordinary course of nature). The fact something is unnatural in the statistical sense, however, does not necessarily make it unnatural in any other sense. It is definitely unnatural (not occurring in conformity with the ordinary course of nature) for *all* people to be gay, but it is perfectly natural (same meaning) for *some*. More precisely, it is just as natural (implanted or being as if implanted by nature: seemingly inborn) for *nine* people to be heterosexual as it is for *one* to be homosexual. So being a member of a minority is no less natural (having a specified character by nature) than being a member of the majority.

It is simply by nature (the physical constitution or drives of an organism) that gay people are attracted to members of the same gender, just as, by nature (same meaning), straight men and women are attracted to members of the opposite gender. If homosexuality does not occur naturally (having a form or appearance found in nature), then it must have been created by someone at sometime. This too is absurd. It is rather ironic that those who argue homosexuality is "unnatural" will not just let it "go away" naturally (without artificial aid). Their action is simply an unnatural (touched by the influences of civilization and society) attempt to control or eliminate some natural (existing in or produced by nature: not artificial) human differences, while exaggerating others. But the limits of nature (the external world in its entirety) are inherently

101

self-imposing, even though the possibilities within those limits are great. As Dr. Kinsey put it, "The only unnatural sex act is one that can't be performed."

The use of "nature" in the context of sexual orientation really indicates the need some people have to find a *purpose* for homosexuality. It is as if Mother Nature, in her infinite wisdom, wastes not a single creature nor any of their distinguishing characteristics. Each only survives as a result of its usefulness. But many things exist in nature without a readily identifiable purpose. Is the "purpose" of heterosexuality procreation? Asked another way, does heterosexual sexuality exist solely for reproduction? What does this philosophy mean for the other aspects of sexual activity: expression of emotion and physical pleasure? These really have no "purpose," as they are merely means to an end. Or are they? In the vast majority of times that straight people engage in sexual activity, emotion and pleasure are the reasons.

So what is the "purpose" of homosexuality? No one knows—yet. Although some theories have been advanced, none are very convincing. What is the purpose of red hair or green eyes? What is the purpose of prejudice and oppression? For that matter, what is the purpose of life itself? Is "purpose" the same thing as "public good"? If so, then except for procreation—which is not in all cases "good" nor is it exclusive to heterosexual individuals—gay people serve the same public good as straight people do. They abide as lawful citizens, fund as taxpayers, invent as engineers, teach as educators, heal as doctors, minister as clergy, and on and on.

Must we find a purpose for everything? And if we must, is it really proper to declare something "unnatural" until we do? The truth is: All sexual *feelings* are natural; all *attitudes* toward sex are socially conditioned. And if the human trait called homosexuality is indeed genetic in nature (pun intended), then it is just as natural (implanted or being as if implanted by nature: seemingly inborn) with just as much "purpose" as heterosexuality. Ironically, those who argue most vehemently against a genetic explanation of homosexuality are the same folks who discount natural (Darwinian) selection entirely in favor of "creationism."

The concepts and words of "nature" are rarely employed with the intent of promoting understanding. They are at best philosophical and always problematic. The use of "unnatural" is just as vague, confusing, and ultimately as meaningless as a term like "un-American." The "natural" argument is an effect of homophobia, not its cause.

The "natural" confusion with morality

Most people have a tendency to equate nature with morality. Things which are natural are considered pure and good. Conversely, things which are unnatural are considered corrupt or evil. This is innocent enough because one of the definitions of *natural* is "based on an inherent sense of right and wrong." But good judgment should not equate what is *common* with right or good. In other words, nonconformity is not the same as immorality. Still, some people seem to confuse what *is,* with what they *think* ought to be.

Nature (the external world in its entirety) is amoral; it is neither immoral nor moral. All things, good and bad, are found in nature. They just exist. The sunshine, the flowers, and a sea breeze are all natural. But so are diseases, earthquakes, and hurricanes. Understanding homosexuality requires diligence to avoid confusing nature with morality and vice versa. There is no doubt, though, that homosexuality indeed raises moral issues.

Homosexuality is immoral.

Sexuality is a bottomless pit of morality, making small steps here prudent. So to treat adequately the subject of homosexuality in the context of morality, some general considerations must be presented first.

Morality deals with what is right and wrong in life. Yet the concepts of right and wrong can be as misleading as the concept of nature. Further, morality involves much more than social convention. In fact, the gap between public morality and private behavior is sometimes quite large. Public morality is normally idealistic, while private behavior is inevitably realistic. Because of this, morality almost seems to invite hypocrisy. As Voltaire put it, "The question of good and evil remains an irremediable chaos for those who seek to fathom it in reality. It is a mere mental sport to the disputants, who are captives that play with their chains." 388.29

Any society must decide what is right and wrong. But social institutions do not necessarily deal with all moral issues adequately or fairly. To do so, some realistic standard is required. Actually, there are two such standards of measure. *Subjective* morality is based on spiritual or personal belief systems. Personal behavior is the jurisdiction for subjective morality. *Objective* morality is based on universally accepted standards for respecting the lives, liberty, and property of others. Social behavior is the jurisdiction of objective morality.

In the absence of objective standards for morality, Adolf Hitler could be considered just as moral as Abraham Lincoln. Each man believed his cause was right. Even in war, killing is considered moral when it is done in defense of people or national interest. The law and other social regulations should be based exclusively on objective morality. In fact, the Fourteenth Amendment was added to the Constitution to emphasize this. It requires "due process of law," which means the government must have a legitimate interest in what it regulates. This interest is explicitly listed as "life, liberty, or property."

For many, there is a temptation to simplify moral issues into purely right, *always,* and purely wrong, *always.* Society creates distinct categories of right and wrong, black and white, good and evil, moral and immoral. But moral issues are not as simple as some people would like to make them. This simplicity usually begins as the justification for an otherwise complex belief. "It's that way because . . . ." This simple justification is frequently based on a few anecdotes and eventually obscures the complexity which exists in reality. When this happens, any information which does not completely conform to the simplified view is discounted or ignored. What was a justification then becomes the very reason some belief is claimed to exist in the first place. As a result, what appears to be a moral argument is really a traditional one.

To make an argument for morality which is simplistic or anecdotal in nature is inadequate, thereby serving an injustice to the diverse people morality is intended to serve. In effect, this sort of approach to morality becomes immoral. Professor Roger L. Shinn of the Union Theological Seminary stated on the need for these objective standards: "The reason is that meanings, including moral meanings, can never be imposed upon life without regard for the specific facts and circumstances that have meaning for people; hence understanding requires empirical evidence."

Finally, it is important to recognize that social consensus on many moral issues simply does not exist. Anyone who claims otherwise does so from a position of simplicity, ignorance, or malice. In many respects, morality is a moving target. Moral opinion *must* be subject to revision based on new information. To give an adequate and fair treatment to moral issues, these many issues and the twin standards of subjective and objective morality must be considered — and considered realistically.

There is no doubt most people do indeed consider homosexuality to be immoral. A Harris poll taken in 1981 revealed that homosexuality was considered morally wrong by seventy-one percent of the population. Because the ten percent of the population which is gay would likely be in the twenty-nine percent of those who did *not* consider homosexuality to be immoral, that means more like seventy-nine percent of all straight people believe homosexuality is immoral. Another survey, conducted by the Institute for Sex Research, confirmed this when it found that seventy-eight percent of the respondents felt sexual acts between two persons of the same sex were "always wrong."

This figure of "eighty percent" keeps popping up. Earlier it was reported that approximately eighty percent of all straight people claimed they did not know a single gay person, and about eighty percent agreed with the statement, "I won't associate with these [gay] people if I can help it." This is not at all surprising. Most straight people, probably eighty percent, have only a stereotypical view of homosexuality. If one thinks that *all* gay people molest children, "recruit" others and are constantly promiscuous, one would also conclude that homosexuality is immoral. Human beings simply have a tendency to criticize and condemn those things they do not understand. This does not make those things immoral, even if the number of people who lack that understanding constitutes a majority. In other words, an opinion is not necessarily a moral one simply because it is passionately, sincerely, and widely held.

Is heterosexuality moral? Most people would likely answer yes. Does that mean heterosexual rape, child molestation, adultery, incest, and promiscuity are moral? No. Is homosexuality moral? Most people would probably answer no, primarily because homosexuality cannot be related to any clearly moral "act," like procreation. Therefore, homosexuality could be considered "inherently immoral." But procreation is not an act:

it is the possible result of the act of heterosexual coitus, which could be committed as rape, child molestation, adultery, or incest. So is heterosexuality moral? That depends. Is homosexuality immoral? That depends too.

The undeniable fact is that both homosexuality and heterosexuality are *amoral*. Sexual orientation is not, in and of itself, an issue of morality. This is because sexual orientation is not a form of behavior or a lifestyle; it is a condition of being. Any sexual act, in and of itself, is also amoral. The morality of sexuality is found in the circumstances, especially the *intent*, and not in the *form* of expression. Like the use of money, the use of sexuality, gay or straight, can be moral or immoral.

This does not mean all gay people are moral, any more than it means all straight people are moral. There are good people, gay and straight, and there are bad people, gay and straight. To prevent simplicity from creeping in, it is important to recognize that the "good" people are not all good, and that the "bad" people are not all bad. A gay man who molests a little boy is definitely immoral by social objective standards and by most personal subjective standards of morality. But he is immoral because he is a pedophile, not because he is homosexual. The same standard applies to a straight man who molests a little girl.

The only situations involving objective sexual immorality are rape, incest (for its genetic ramifications), public sexual indecency, and sexual abuse — especially involving children and women. Everything else which is sexual, is personal. Any ethical judgment passed is also personal — and subjective. What two consenting adults do in private does not violate the objective and universal standard of morality by posing a threat to the lives, liberty, or property of others in society. Adultery could even be placed in this latter category as well. The alleged threats posed by homosexuality are just that — alleged, and nothing more — placing homosexuality clearly outside the bounds of objective social morality.

Heterosexuality has a monopoly on subjective morality if and only if one chooses to define sexual morality as a monogamous heterosexual marriage. But what such a simple definition actually does is merely excuse gay people from the entire concept of morality; it does not make homosexuality immoral. In other words, there is no single road to a moral life. St. Thomas Aquinas understood this: "Because of the diverse conditions of humans, it happens that some acts are virtuous to some people, as appropriate and suitable to them, while the same acts are immoral for others, as inappropriate to them." Being gay is no more intrinsically immoral or evil than being straight is intrinsically moral or good.

Whether a man or a woman loves a man or a woman is not a moral issue, but a personal matter. Is homosexuality immoral? No. Are some gay people immoral? Definitely, just as some straight people are. To help keep the proper perspective on ethical issues, try substituting heterosexuality for homosexuality. In other words, when tempted to claim something related to homosexuality is immoral, will the same claim hold up if the issue is considered in the context of heterosexuality? At times it is necessary to do the converse. What this exercise does is remove the "benefit of the doubt" or double standard that frequently accommodates heterosexuality, and in doing so, zeros in on the real issue at stake. Invariably what is at issue is not sexual orientation at all.

Consider employment issues for example. Should gay people be denied certain jobs? Ask instead, should straight people be denied certain jobs? Different answers? Why? Gay people are a security risk; they could be blackmailed. So could straight people. But gay people could be blackmailed for sexual reasons. So could straight people (adultery, "cohorting" with foreign agents, etc.). But gay people can't control their sexual urges. So the thought process goes, almost like playing both sides of the table in a Ping-Pong game, until an equitable resolution emerges—one that is fair and impartial, and not homophobic.

So, is homophobia itself immoral? No. Everyone is homophobic, acquiring the trait innocently enough through social conditioning. Is discrimination based on homophobia immoral? Definitely. The oppression it causes robs, yes robs, gay people of life (frequently), liberty (regularly), and property (occasionally). If what some people think about right and wrong causes widespread human suffering, then there is clearly something wrong with what some people think is right. Oscar Wilde was right, "Morality is simply the attitude we adopt towards people whom we personally dislike."

Homosexuality is sinful.

Some gay lifestyles are sinful, just as some straight lifestyles are. *All* people are sinners and fall short of the Glory of God. Our salvation is totally in His Grace. Yet homosexuality itself, independent of any particular gay lifestyle, is viewed by many people as a sin which is so horrible, so heinous that it must be punished in this world as much as the next. Religious views clearly are a reason for homophobia. The belief that homosexuality is a sin is deeply rooted in Judeo-Christian tradition.

There are primarily three justifications for this belief. The first basis is interpretation of Scripture, especially the story of Sodom and Gomorrah in the Old Testament, and the Pauline texts in the New Testament. The second is categorizing homosexuality as a "sin against nature" based today primarily on the writings of St. Thomas Aquinas. The third is morality. A recent *US News & World Report* poll indicated that thirty-eight percent of people under the age of thirty, about half of those age thirty to forty-four, and sixty percent of the population over the age of forty-five claimed religion affected their moral attitudes "a great deal." "Threats," "nature," and morality were all discussed earlier independently of religion. Because of the significance of religious influence on homophobia, the next section is dedicated to "The Church and Homosexuality," where all three reasons will be reconsidered in a religious context.

In addition to the "threats" from and the Judeo-Christian perceptions of homosexuality, there are two miscellaneous justifications for homophobia which are rarely cited yet still pertinent to this discussion. These are jealousy or envy, and "reaction formation."

Jealousy or Envy

Puritanism: The haunting fear that someone, somewhere, may be happy. *H. L. Mencken*

As crazy as this might seem, there is actually an element of jealousy or envy in some people's homophobia. Although this may not be the fundamental cause, it can be a significant contributing factor. Many straight people believe the gay minority "has it easy." The stereotypes depict gay people as being completely irresponsible and loving every moment of it. Those who believe this are either unaware of the extent of the gay minority's real oppression, or they feel the oppression is justified because it is a way to "even the score." In either case, the oppressive measures remain while the stereotypes continue. Gay people, then, seem to be ignoring both their "obligation" to get married and support a family, *and* the oppressive measures established to steer them in the "right" direction. No, jealousy and envy do not cause homophobia — they just aggravate it.

Reaction Formation

Me thinks the lady doth protest too much. *William Shakespeare*

Reaction formation is both a cause and effect of homophobia. It is basically "the mechanism of defending against an impulse in oneself by taking a stand against its expression by others." It is therefore a form of hate. Freud introduced this term which was first applied to homophobia by Dr. George Weinberg. Gay-related reaction formation is found mostly in men, because hate is more predominantly instilled in the male of our species.

It is perfectly normal for nearly everyone to have felt, at some time in his or her life, an erotic attraction toward another person of the same gender. According to Dr. Kinsey's research, approximately thirty percent of all men who do not identify as gay, have at one time or another engaged in same-sex sexual activity to the point of orgasm. Another thirteen percent have at least had same-sex erotic feelings or fantasies. This means a total of forty-three percent of straight men have had homoerotic experiences or imagery. Heterosexual individuals are not necessarily incapable of homosexual arousal, and vice versa. One study measured penile responses in heterosexual and homosexual men to stimulus in the form of pictures of naked women and men. Both groups showed some response to the "wrong" stimuli. In other words, most straight men can be and are sexually aroused by other men at times, and most gay men can be and are sexually aroused by women at times. While this may not bother a gay man, it could be deeply troubling for a straight man. The reaction formation is an internal denial of this homoeroticism and an external battle against it. People who exhibit this reaction likely subscribe to the social constructs of "homosexual tendencies" or "latent homosexuality."

Actually, homoeroticism is not necessarily prerequisite to reaction formation. Although some may not admit it, there exists a "what if" sexual element in friendships between straight men and women. This same condition can be potentially threatening if it occurs in a same-sex friendship. The feeling is analogous to the temptation many people feel to jump from a tall building. There seems to be some compelling force which beckons a person to jump, not as a death wish, but more out of curiosity. Most "manly" men would rather disclose being an atheist or a Communist than confess to something as harmless as having masturbated. So for a macho kind of guy to admit he might be capable of having sex with another man, or even contemplate the thought of it, flies totally in the face of masculinity.

Reaction formation is rooted in the false belief that homosexuality and masculinity are mutually exclusive. Men who negatively label gay people are seen as being more masculine. The belief is, "If I am *anti*-gay then I could not possibly *be* gay, and all my friends will know I'm a 'real' man." These fears and anxieties unfortunately serve as justification to physically abuse gay people. The most violently homophobic individuals usually have some form of inner conflict or personal anxiety causing this extreme reaction. Most gay people actually go through a phase of reaction formation in their struggle to resist a gay identity. By doing so, both gay men and lesbians participate in their own victimization.

The Fundamental Cause of Homophobia

Prejudice is the child of ignorance. *William Hazlitt*

There is only one real reason for homophobia: ignorance. Ignorance is the single common denominator in every other reason given above. This includes all the "threats" and the traditional Judeo-Christian belief system for homosexuality, as most people are completely unaware of the history and considerations behind it. Every one of them is merely a rationalization. Of course, this is not a startling revelation because ignorance is really the root of all prejudice — and rationalization is the tribute prejudice pays to reasoning. But in our complex world, it is possible to lose sight of the simplicity which can and does exist. Ignorance creates a void that is filled with stereotypes and other misconceptions. More importantly, all people fear the unknown. Ignorance begets fear; fear begets ignorance. Emerson observed that "Fear defeats more people than any other one thing in the world." As a result, ignorance is *not* bliss for the twenty-four million gay Americans whose lives are affected by it each and every day.

The ignorance about homosexuality has two fundamental and related causes. First, there is a general unwillingness to learn. This is compounded by the lack of an apparent *need* for straight people to learn anything about homosexuality, unless they know someone who is openly gay. But remember, four of every five straight people claim they do not even know a single gay person. The situation is depicted perfectly in the popular joke which asks, "What is the difference between ignorance and apathy?" The punchline is "I don't know and I don't care!" Second, when someone does wish to learn about homosexuality, the lack of readily available and accurate information makes it extremely difficult to do so. It is as if there exists a "conspiracy" of silence and misinformation which regularly censors the facts about homosexuality, making the very topic taboo. Some of this "conspiracy" is innocent, resulting from just not understanding homosexuality. Some of it is quite intentional, though; it is deceptive and it is malicious.

The two fundamental causes are linked in a seemingly endless cycle. Accurate information is available, but some effort is required to locate it. As far as homosexuality is concerned, that effort is seen as unnecessary or inappropriate or both. The unwillingness to learn also occurs in part because, not only is it socially acceptable to dislike gay people, it is almost expected. This peer pressure begins during youth, reaches its peak in adolescence, and continues through all of adult life. In effect, homophobia is contagious. In fact, some fear being labeled homosexual by not being homophobic. The Institute for Sex Research found that sixty-four percent of the respondents in one of their surveys agreed with the statement, "I suppose they [gay people] are all right, but I've never liked them." Seventy-six percent of this same group also claimed they had "no particular love or hate" of gay people. Homophobia can be compassionate or casual. Nevertheless, in the same survey, eighty-one percent believed their attitudes about homosexuality remained consistent over time.

Here are those "eighty percent" figures again. Another survey, conducted for *Newsweek* magazine in 1983, found that approximately seventy-five percent of the straight people surveyed believed homosexuality was not an acceptable "lifestyle." A 1977 survey for the *Medical Aspects of Human Sexuality* journal revealed that sixty-nine percent of the American Psychiatric Association's members still believed homosexuality is a pathological adaptation, despite the official stance of the APA to the contrary and the wealth of psychological studies which prove otherwise. Considering that ten percent of the psychiatrists surveyed were gay, more like seventy-seven percent of the straight psychologists felt this way. After all, psychologists are not immune from homophobia either.

The "eighty percent" figure may be gradually diminishing — at glacial speed. Still, around eighty percent of the straight population does not like homosexuality, does not think it offers an acceptable "lifestyle," believes being gay is a sickness, claims not to know any gay people at all (and don't even care to), thinks homosexuality is immoral, and not too surprisingly, have not changed their anti-gay opinions or attitudes. Perhaps eighty percent flunked the test at the end of Chapter 5. Coincidence? No. Undoubtedly, it is ignorance. Alexander Pope said it best, "Some people will never learn anything, for this reason, because they understand everything too soon."

How could such widespread ignorance occur? Misinformation. The misinformation "campaign," discussed next, is what creates the misunderstanding of homosexuality.

Chapter 7

A Matter
of Misinformation

You've got to be taught to hate and fear.
You've got to be taught from year to year.
It's got to be drummed in your dear little ear.
You've got to be carefully taught.
                    Oscar Hammerstein II (South Pacific)

For centuries the topic of homosexuality, even when it was unknown as such, was never discussed. As Oscar Wilde commented, homosexuality was "the love that dare not speak its name." Today nearly everyone, especially the "eighty percent" group, has something to say about homosexuality. But the picture they paint is not a pretty one. For these four out of every five straight Americans who believe they do not know even a single gay person, homosexuality remains an abstract, impersonal issue. For them, the gay minority remains faceless, nameless. As a result, the vast majority of straight people continue to view gay people as alien: "Not our kind, not like us."

It is impossible to grow up in the United States, gay or straight, without becoming homophobic to some degree. Newborn babies have no value systems; we are all conceived without preconception. By the age of twelve, a value system that serves as a filter to guide both personal behavior and judgment of others is firmly established in most individuals. By this same age, homophobic attitudes become fairly well established.

The conditioning to instill value systems begins at birth. "No" is the key word here. Sometimes intentionally, sometimes not, the conditioning includes homophobia. The lessons, taught by a whole host of social institutions, warn that gay men and lesbians are sick, sinful, criminal, evil, threatening, and more. Virtually every boy and girl is instructed to recognize this endangerment to their well-being, and admonished to avoid it at all costs. And this is just the beginning of a lifetime of anti-gay rhetoric and non-anti-gay silence which permeates our society, making homophobia an inevitable element of an American value system.

Does this sound a little far-fetched, a little like brainwashing? Consider what has occured in the Soviet Union. The Politburo, through "official" news agencies like Tass, has told Russian citizens over and over again about the war-mongering, imperialist Americans. Their propaganda could not have been further from the truth. *We* knew that, but *they* didn't. They believed it. Even Communist Party leaders, who instigated the propaganda, likely began to believe their own rhetoric.

The situation with homosexuality in the United States is much the same. Its periodic, yet steady, and almost always negative treatment, often for political purposes, creates the stereotypes that guide the American conscious on homosexuality. Citizens are told these stories often enough and with such conviction that they naturally start to believe them. As a result, twenty-four million gay citizens are being taught to fear and hate themselves, while everyone else is being taught to fear and hate them too.

The numerous social institutions line up in a parade of misinformation on homosexuality. Each contribution builds on the previous ones, reaffirming and perpetuating the stereotypes and other myths. This homophobic conditioning normally begins with casual conversation and jokes at home and in the workplace. It is fed by sensationalism in the media and the representation of gay people in movies as the "bad guys." Sex education courses and materials in schools make the stereotypes "official." Owing to the intense prejudice, there is almost a total lack of *openly* gay adults to serve as positive role models for gay children.

Some people exploit the situation for personal or political gain, simultaneously feeding from and reinforcing society's homophobia. These abuses are analyzed in the next chapter. The church describes homosexuality as a "sin against nature," creating an aura of righteousness for homophobia (Section IV). Finally, an awareness of discriminatory laws and practices completely legitimizes homophobia (Section V). This seemingly endless spiral of misunderstanding all starts informally, casually.

Casual Conversation

It is not necessary to understand things in order to argue about them.
Pierre de Beaumarchais

The majority of straight people spend little time thinking about or discussing homosexuality. When they do, it is usually in the context of a controversial subject that may or may not be related to homosexuality, such as AIDS, child molestation, or transvestism. Similarly, straight people rarely ever discuss heterosexuality itself. Instead, there is talk about abortion, rape, or child abuse. But everyone understands this is not typical of heterosexuality; it's just controversial.

A conversation about homosexuality may be triggered by a news article. People introduce their personal opinions, which, in the absence of any objection, become accepted as fact. An example may then be offered as "conclusive" evidence. Of course, it is always possible to find an example of something to support any position. This is frequently the only "factual" exposure homosexuality gets. Rarely will anyone ever side with the gay minority, defending gay civil rights, even if he or she is gay or has openly gay acquaintances. This is because homophobia extends its grasp to anyone, gay or straight, who is at all "sympathetic to the enemy."

Then there are the jokes: most of them either too gross or too cruel to put in print. Any "humor" is based on the stereotypes, perpetuating these myths each time a joke is told. This form of casual conversation is everything *but* enlightening.

The Morning Gazette

The man who reads nothing at all is better educated than the man who reads nothing but newspapers. *Thomas Jefferson*

Most Americans get most of their facts on most subjects directly from the media. That is not necessarily bad unless the news is their *exclusive* source. But on the subject of homosexuality, that is normally the situation. There are three main reasons this leads to a misunderstanding of homosexuality. First, journalists are not immune from homophobia. Second, it is difficult to write about a subject as emotional and controversial as homosexuality with genuine detachment and neutrality. Finally, individuals and organizations of the media become *victims* of homophobia when they present any accurate — meaning fair, neutral or positive — gay-related stories. Many news consumers are not at all reluctant to voice their opinions on this matter.

The media has a profound influence on public opinion. The most significant aspect of influence is the content and presentation style of news stories. A more subtle but equally powerful influence comes from being able to determine what is newsworthy. This creates an impression of which social issues are important and which ones are not. The double influence of news coverage and media silence warrants separate examination.

News Coverage

The adage "no news is good news" may well be true for gay news. The public seems to enjoy sensational news, usually bad. The media is a business and not an altruistic service provided for the public good. As a business it must sell its product — news — in a way that will meet the desires of its consumers. But in the absence of any other sources of information, the very nature of news has a tendency to perpetuate society's distorted image of homosexuality. The distortion is immediately evident to the gay minority, but usually escapes the notice of the straight majority.

Of course, there is rarely an intent to distort the news. The influence of homophobia is much more subtle. It may begin during an interview. A straight man interviewing a gay man might be very nervous. He might not totally understand the issue, its history, or its impact. This could result in a hurried meeting, sloppy notes, or biased recollection. The editor might then alter the story. It is even possible that a reporter

112

might write the article with the editor's bias in mind. One professor of journalism tried an experiment. He gave his students a topic, telling half the class the articles they would write were for a liberal paper, the other half for a conservative paper. With no other instructions, most students slanted the same story to reflect the editorial policy of the paper. After all, everyone wants to please his or her boss.

News or feature stories are often simplified for presentation to the diverse audience of the mass media. No special knowledge can be assumed unless the piece is for a trade journal. The effect is to homogenize homosexuality into a "type," forsaking the diversity. Any aspect of the story consistent with this "type" is used and emphasized. The "type" people expect for homosexuality is the stereotype. As a result, most of the information America receives through the media conforms with the stereotypical image of homosexuality. Further, most of the stories about homosexuality are about the sexual aspects, almost to the point of excluding everything else in some publications and broadcasts. After all, this is how the public views homosexuality.

The word *homosexual* is frequently and unnecessarily used to describe a crime when the word *heterosexual* is not similarly used. For example, when a man molests a little boy the article might refer to this as "homosexual molestation." If the victim were a little girl, the article would simply state "child molestation." And even if the second example used the phrase "heterosexual molestation," no one would draw the conclusion, "Those heterosexuals are just terrible. Look at what they did!" Here is another example: Have you ever read an article about a "heterosexual killer"? Of course not. Sexual orientation is not newsworthy in a crime where the victim, or the assailant, is straight.

"Good news" is usually about something bad. Most straight people cannot easily disassociate bad independent qualities from homosexuality. Using the word *homosexual* with "killer" or "molester" actually makes the association for the consumer. On rare occasions this practice is formalized in a style handbook. The converse of this situation is that truly good news may not mention a person's homosexuality. Sometimes this is done as a courtesy to the individual; other times it is intentionally omitted. The general public apparently does not want homosexual "heroes" just yet.

There is another type of association which can be equally misleading. Sometimes two separate articles are grouped together because it is assumed the general topic, homosexuality in this case, is the same. So an article on the Gay Freedom Day parade could end up next to one about a pedophile who molested several children, only some of them being boys, prompting some readers to think, "See, these homos just want their freedom so they can mess with our kids."

Similar effects can result from the use of certain adjectives that are loaded with judgment. A gay bar might be described as "crowded" while a straight pub would be called "popular." Openly gay people can become "admitted homosexuals," or even, "practicing homosexuals." A phrase as often misused as "sexual preference" implies that homosexuality is a choice, making it possible for others to be "recruited." A statement about a religious group "whose members see AIDS as God's rough justice for the sin of homosexuality" implies homosexuality is unquestionably sinful. Even language which seems totally innocent can be very damaging. For example, consider the early coverage of AIDS. In an attempt not to offend the sensibilities of some readers, the media reported the HIV (AIDS) virus was transmitted by "bodily fluids." The only bodily fluids shown to transmit the virus are semen and blood. Yet many people, reading "bodily fluids," thought AIDS could be contracted through sweat, urine or saliva. ("Does this mean *I* could get AIDS from a sneeze or a cough, a bump on an elevator, a public water fountain or a toilet?") Obviously, this served to fuel the hysteria surrounding AIDS.

A headline is frequently enough to convey a distorted meaning. Designed to grab the reader's attention, headlines are usually sensational. "Thousands of Gay Rights Activists March on Nation's Capitol" conveys an entirely different meaning than "Gay Freedom Day Parade Held in Nation's Capitol." Many people will not actually read either article, but the damage is already done with the first headline. The journalist who wrote the first version might quote police in the article: "We had nearly a fourth of our officers working overtime to handle the crowds." Of course, "handling the crowds" is likely to mean traffic or parking problems. A poor choice of words can easily convey an entirely different message.

A picture is worth a thousand words, and it's incredible whose picture is usually taken. After gay parades or rallies where thousands participate, the nightly news or the morning paper often show only the most bizarre individuals present. This is done primarily for attention and amusement as normal routine, which is not necessarily bad. Showing gay people who are just like straight people might make the audience uncomfortable. At a minimum, it would be terribly boring. But this too perpetuates the stereotypes. There are bizarre gay people, just as there are bizarre straight people.

The only difference is perspective and other knowledge of the subject. If a person knew nothing else about sports, he or she might think baseball fans in San Diego are really strange because they all dress up like chickens, or that all basketball fans have rainbow-colored afros. Of course this is not true. But a person with no other information might draw such a conclusion. "Colorful" people are a lot of fun, when everyone else keeps them in perspective.

The media provides our society with a very valuable service. Yet news should never be the sole basis for opinions on any topic. Be assured that for every single negative article about homosexuality, there are nine about heterosexuality. These include mischief, murder, rape, theft, espionage, child molestation, negligence, corruption, and so on. By maintaining the proper perspective, it is easy to recognize these stories are not about homosexuality or heterosexuality at all. They are about people with problems — period.

Media Silence

One of the biggest obstacles facing the gay minority is "invisibility." Gay people often get "bad press," but sometimes they get no press. In effect, crimes *by* gay people are still headlines while crimes *against* them remain largely unreported. For example, neither *Time* nor *Newsweek* even mentioned the historic Gay & Lesbian March on Washington in October 1987. Accurate information about homosexuality is essential to ending the ignorance and the resulting homophobia. Stories about the struggle for gay civil rights would raise public awareness of the issues and would give gay people an opportunity to present the facts for society's consideration. Stories about the oppression gay people face might even create public empathy. "Normal" stories about normal gay people would present realistic role models, helping to eliminate the stereotypes. Unfortunately, these kinds of stories are rarely printed or broadcast. Some publications will not even run gay-related advertisements. All of this is tantamount to censorship.

Does the media have the right to be silent on certain issues? Probably. But doesn't it also have an obligation in a free society to present accurately *all* issues — no matter how emotional or controversial? Most definitely. The broadcast media, unlike the print media, was under regulation by the Federal Communications Commission for years. This was deemed appropriate because the airways are a limited resource. Anyone can publish a newspaper or a magazine, but there exists a limited number of radio and TV stations. Under the FCC's fairness doctrine, radio and TV stations were required to present both sides of a "controversial issue of public importance." The doctrine has since been repealed, but it was in effect long enough, hopefully, to establish a strong tradition of self-regulation. In fact, much of the print media has voluntarily adopted a similar policy. But statements made in the context of news coverage were exempt from the fairness doctrine, which was really an *editorial* policy. The effect was to contribute to the silence on gay civil rights. This "controversial issue" was, and still mostly is, merely avoided in editorial comment, both pro and con. So to the consuming public, the issue of gay civil rights does not exist.

When news on the progress of gay civil rights is presented, it is common to obtain a reaction from the "opposition" as news. This has the effect of presenting an editorial comment in the middle of a news article. The only difference is that this "news" is not technically considered to be an editorial comment. As a result, it appears to have more credibility and is exempt from the practice of editorial fairness. So, extremely homophobic editors can have their cake and eat it too. There is obviously an ample supply of people ready and willing to pull these opposing comments from their repertoire of homophobic rhetoric. As such, their views are rarely news. Would it be appropriate to consult the Ku Klux Klan for an opinion on black civil rights? That would be blatant racism. Would it be appropriate to ask the Moral Majority for a comment on the opening of an abortion clinic? Of course not. Yet similar comments are regularly sought on gay civil rights issues.

Why? Every institution in the media must answer to its consumers first—and its sponsors second. When "good" gay news is presented, there is invariably an outraged response from a minority of extremely homophobic individuals. Fortunately, most publishers and station managers are recognizing this reaction as a knee-jerk response. They are also recognizing that the gay minority is made up of consumers as well. So some media organizations are beginning to adopt a more open position toward homosexuality and gay civil rights issues. The "good" news is being covered more and the "bad" news is only occasionally exploited or sensationalized. Most journalists no longer quote the "opposition" in news articles. Editorial sections and segments are starting to address gay civil rights issues as the "love that dare not speak its name" speaks out.

Ironically, the AIDS crisis has created much of this change. Many talk shows and TV "magazines" are dealing directly with gay issues. Representatives from the gay community are being invited to speak. There are even many programs which specifically address homosexuality itself. Each accurate article or show or editorial column challenges the stereotypes and exposes the audience to the truth about homosexuality. Finally, some media organizations have adopted nondiscrimination employment policies and have gay journalists covering gay news and issues. All the problems have yet to be solved, but change appears to be going in the right direction.

Always the Bad Guy

In the not too distant past, gay people were depicted as the stereotypical pitiful and miserable characters who either went straight or committed suicide. This was true for movies on network television and in commercial cinemas. An episode of *Police Woman* portrayed lesbians as brutal rapists and murderers. *Marcus Welby M.D.* portrayed a "gay person," this time a man, as a science teacher who raped a boy. In the movie *Boys in the Band* there is the line: "Show me a happy homosexual and I'll show you a gay corpse." In *Ode to Billy Joe,* Billy Joe MacCallister jumped off the Tallahatchee Bridge because of his feelings for another man. The movie *Cruising* featured and sensationalized the S&M scene, depicting it as "typical" for all those who watched or even heard about it.

The gay characters in more recent fiction and drama appear fairly normal, but they do not appear very often. It is probably still difficult to find a sponsor who wants its products advertised on "that" kind of show. The movie *Making Love* revealed the story of a married man who struggles with and finally accepts a gay identity. In *Consenting Adult,* a movie made for TV, a young man also struggles to accept his homosexuality. The father dies without telling his son he still loved him. In *Welcome Home, Bobby* and *My Two Loves,* both made for TV, the main characters struggle with their homosexual emotional and erotic feelings. At the end, the audience is left wondering if each is gay or straight or

116

bisexual. But at least these possibly-gay characters were not stereotypical. In *An Early Frost,* the story involves the struggles of a gay man with AIDS. Although these more recent movies are much better than those of the past, the theme is still the same: struggle.

Homosexuality — the struggle — is almost always the plot, and not just an incidental factor. In 1986 that finally changed when NBC portrayed a normal gay character in the TV movie *When the Bough Breaks.* The story was about a police investigation, assisted by a psychiatrist, into organized crime, specifically child abuse and sexual molestation. But it was the police inspector who was gay, and his lover was a doctor. Neither of these men were stereotypical. The psychiatrist, a straight man, was the inspector's friend, *not* his shrink. This was an incredible step forward for gay credibility. Still, there are no happy shows about gay people. Two recent ones for TV — *HeartBeat,* focusing on a lesbian nurse practitioner, and *Hooperman* with a quite normal gay policeman — were taken off the air leaving no regular shows with an openly gay character. Maybe the producers think the American public just isn't ready for that yet. Maybe they're right.

"Nonfiction" Publications

Many nonfiction books, encyclopedias, textbooks, and other course materials are written by individuals who are either uninformed or misinformed about homosexuality. Many of these books were based on and even continue to be based on some of the seriously flawed research discussed in Chapter 1. As a result, there is a substantial amount of fiction in many nonfiction publications. For example, several surveys of psychology textbooks revealed that the subject of homosexuality continues to be treated under the category of "sexual deviance." They discuss homosexuality in the context of sexual dysfunction, behavior disorders, and maladjustment. Much of this is because all textbooks and course materials must be approved by school boards or administrators, who are virtually paranoid about homosexuality. Many public libraries will also not carry books about homosexuality for similar reasons. The same is true for many bookstores — which is not too surprising given a 1985 National Opinion Research Center poll that indicated forty percent of Americans would prohibit books "in favor" of homosexuality (such as this one).

Jan Goodman commented: "When I first realized that I was a lesbian, I didn't know other lesbians, so I went to the library to find some support. I checked the card catalogue. There were no books devoted entirely to lesbianism. However, there were several 'helpful' cross-references: LESBIANISM — see HOMOSEXUALITY, male; PSYCHOLOGY, abnormal; SEXUALITY, deviant; GENDER IDENTITY, improper; also related chapters under ALCOHOLISM; SUICIDE." Although this situation has improved in many libraries, it remains a problem in most. This is true despite the "Library Bill of Rights," an official policy statement of the American Library Association (ALA), which states in part: "In no case should library materials be excluded because of the race or nationality or the social, political or religious views of the authors. Libraries should provide books and other materials presenting all points of view concerning the problems and issues of our times; no library material should be proscribed or removed from libraries because of partisan or doctrinal disapproval." Later in 1977, the ALA found it necessary to reaffirm its position in a more strongly worded resolution that included explicitly the subject of homosexuality.

But wherever you are or wherever you go, it remains difficult to locate accurate information on homosexuality. Most bookstores either do not carry books on homosexuality or the ones they do carry are grossly inaccurate. The latter is especially true for religious bookstores. If it were not for gay bookstores, research for this book or any other on the subject would have been difficult at best. Censoring indeed has a way of becoming self-perpetuating.

Probably the most widely read book to address homosexuality was David Reuben's *Everything you always wanted to know about sex — but were afraid to ask*. This book was so popular that in the first two years alone there were over forty printings. And America gobbled up his homophobic haranguing hook, line, and sinker. With a better understanding of homosexuality, you should be able to judge for yourself just how erroneous and poisonous material like this is.

Reuben opens his chapter titled "Male Homosexuality" with a comment on the "challenge" of anatomical limitations and describes how most gay men approach this with "ingenuity and boundless energy. In the process they often transform themselves into part-time women." Next, he mentions that some men who are "manly in every respect are actually enthusiastic homosexuals . . ." who "are only interested in the endowments of other young men." There is hope though: "If a homosexual who wants to renounce homosexuality finds a psychiatrist who knows how to cure homosexuality, he has every chance of becoming a happy, well-adjusted, heterosexual."

He begins to truly display his ignorance when he discusses sexual activity: "The usual homosexual experience is mutual masturbation . . . Three to five minutes should be enough for the entire operation . . . Generally the circumstances are far from romantic." He then describes how gay people meet in bowling alley men's rooms. In the question-and-answer format of the book he asks himself, "Are all homosexual contacts as impersonal as that?" and answers, "No. Most are much more impersonal . . . Homosexuality seems to have a compelling urgency about it . . . No names, no faces, no emotions. A masturbation machine might do it better . . . There are dozens of variations but they all have this in common: the primary interest is the penis, not the person." Then after describing totally anonymous sexual encounters, he asks himself, "Isn't that kind of dangerous?" and answers, "Homosexuals thrive on danger. It almost seems part of their sexual ritual."

It gets worse: "Those who combine homosexuality with sadistic and masochistic aberrations are among the cruelest people who walk this earth. In ancient times they were employed as professional torturers and executioners. More recently they filled the ranks of Hitler's Gestapo and SS. How does an 'S and M' work? They specialize in luring other

homosexuals to their apartments, trapping them and torturing them . . .
Occasionally the torturer gets carried away, the evening escalates and
ends in mutilation, castration and death. Sadly, that's all part of the
homosexual game." He even describes anal intercourse as "determined
assault by the homosexual penis."

After discussing transvestites he asks, "Aren't homosexuals *afraid*
of being arrested?" and answers, "Maybe they should be, but they aren't.
Lack of fear of the consequences is one of the puzzling characteristics
of homosexual behavior . . . They have a compulsion to flaunt their sex
in public . . . Random and reckless selection of partners is the trademark.
The fact that the stranger is likely to be a policeman, an 'S and M', or
a syphilitic never seems to occur to them. This is the core of homosexuality. But *all* homosexuals aren't like that, are they? Unfortunately, they
are just like that . . ."

Unbelievable — figuratively *and* literally.

Getting an "Education"

I have never let my schooling interfere with my education. *Mark Twain*

Schools, by considering homosexuality to be a "controversial" subject
have become breeding grounds for homophobia. A 1985 Gallup-Phi Delta
Kappa survey discovered that while seventy-five percent of those adults
questioned favored sex education in high schools, less than half felt the
topic of homosexuality should be covered. Another study found that one-
third of sex education teachers indicated their biggest problem was pressure from parents or administrators, especially when dealing with homosexuality, condoms, or abortion. These findings demonstrate the difference between indoctrination and education.

Most sex-ed classes ignore homosexuality, treating gay and lesbian
youth as if they didn't even exist, or superficially cover the topic in a
stereotypical manner. According to the Institute for Sex Research, more
than sixty percent of those who had sex education in school reported
they had been taught absolutely nothing about homosexuality. Among
those whose classes did cover homosexuality, two-thirds remembered being told that it was "always wrong" and *only* one and one-half percent
were told being gay was "not wrong at all." Another study, conducted
in 1979 and reported in the *Journal of Homosexuality,* revealed that
approximately eighty percent of junior and senior high school courses
merely mentioned homosexuality. Only six percent gave adequate coverage. This is changing — gradually. But keep in mind that most adults
today went through this kind of "education."

Sex education courses are mostly human biology and reproduction
courses. They discuss both male and female reproductive systems, sexually transmitted diseases (sometimes as a scare tactic) and the mechan-
ics, not the pleasures, of sexual intercourse — heterosexual, of course.
Other common forms of sexual expression are rarely covered, all of which
are heterosexual as well.

Even when adequate coverage is given to homosexuality, there are usually subtle but serious flaws in the approach taken. For example, most books offer a "homophobic disclaimer." This is an implicit or explicit message informing the reader that while many people experience emotional or erotic attraction to persons of the same gender, these feelings are (or should be) just a phase. Similarly, many books employ the "you" voice throughout, with one exception: the section on homosexuality. The switch to "they" tells the reader "you" could not possibly be one of "them." Whatever the content its treatment, accurate or not, the mere mention of homosexuality is often accompanied by jokes and snickering from the students. And what should a teacher do in response? Some play right along.

The fact is, most sex education courses are virtually worthless in their treatment of human sexuality in general — meaning heterosexuality — and homosexuality in particular. Yet what better institution is there than the schools to take on this important task? The home? A survey of high school students in the early 1980s found that roughly half learned absolutely nothing about sex from their parents. Did the other half receive informed and accurate information? Is the church a good resource? (Imagine a celibate priest trying to explain intercourse to a class of twelve-year-olds!) Should our nation's children keep learning much of what they know about sex from each other, in the streets, and from "pornography" if necessary? A frightening thought, but a fairly accurate assessment.

In the "Surgeon General's Report on Acquired Immune Deficiency Syndrome," Dr. C. Everett Koop pointed out: "There is now no doubt that we need sex education in schools and that it must include information on heterosexual and homosexual relationships. The threat of AIDS should be sufficient to permit a sex education curriculum with a heavy emphasis on prevention of AIDS and other sexually transmitted diseases." What children don't know *can* hurt them. AIDS alone is a compelling reason to put a stop to the "big lie."

It is fairly obvious that schools must teach about sex and cover the subject completely — including homosexuality — and accurately. The "complete and accurate" standard should apply to all official sources of information on human sexuality, including textbooks and teachers. To explain is not to condone. In fact, good instruction in the area of human sexuality *must* be value-neutral. Schools should yield to parents and the church in teaching sexual values. Other subjects which relate to sexuality, such as psychology courses, in compliance with recommendations from the American Psychiatric Association, should stop presenting homosexuality as a sickness, and cover homophobia along with all other forms of irrational fear and prejudice. History or government courses can address the gay civil rights issues and movement. Some school districts have even started to provide sensibility training for teachers, administrators, and counselors on homosexuality and the problems faced by gay youth. *Demystifying Homosexuality* is a good teacher's guide. Books such as *Young, Gay and Proud* and *One Teenager in Ten* should be made available in school libraries. Gay men and lesbians can be invited to address classes in schools where there are no openly gay teachers to serve as role models. Gay-sensitive counselors can be designated. Finally, teachers should be reprimanded and students disciplined for homophobic comments or actions.

All people have a basic human right to know the truth. If for no other reason, reform in this area is a must, for censorship has no place in a free society. And keeping the truth from America's youth is a terrible form of child abuse.

"Looking Up" to the Stereotypes

Children need models rather than critics. *Joseph Joubert*

Some people view gay men and lesbians in any position of influence or prominence as "unwanted" role models. Why is it that gay people, young and old, should have any less of a need for good role models than straight people? Without them, each gay person becomes a pioneer, learning all life's lessons the hard way. And here again, to what extent does society teach homophobia to all people, gay and straight, by the absence of respectable role models who happen to be gay?

There is almost a total void of openly gay role models in the institutions of our society. This is true not only in schools, but in churches, personal and family friendships, and places of work. Where are the gay couples in TV and print advertisements? Where are the gay celebrities? The image of Rock Hudson as a lady's man was shattered when his homosexuality was revealed before dying of AIDS. And where are the gay couples walking down the street hand-in-hand on a beautiful spring day? True, much of this problem is caused by gay people passing as straight. But remember, the reason gay people do this is society's homophobia. Until this vicious cycle is broken, homosexuality will remain in the domain of the stereotypes.

Is it ironic that society is missing all these opportunities to teach its gay citizens an acceptable gay lifestyle, while simultaneously complaining that "the gay lifestyle" is unacceptable? Maybe not. Maybe it's just another self-fulfilling prophecy.

Chapter 8

Intolerance Takes Its Toll

By trying we can easily endure adversity. Another man's I mean.
Mark Twain

The effect of homophobic intolerance is human suffering. The suffering is both external and internal. Externally, it arrives in numerous forms of oppression. Internally, it surfaces as opprobrium which devastates self-esteem. The oppression results from formal and informal social sanctions. Gay people can avoid the oppression only by passing as straight, becoming an "invisible" minority. Yet the ultimate form of oppression is this inability to even speak out in protest. Gay people have become out of sight, out of mind, and unworthy of social consideration — worthless in their own society. Unable to counter the ever-present oppression for fear of the opprobrium public exposure would bring, gay people address the issues alone. Every gay man and lesbian deals with being gay individually on a daily basis. As a result, homosexuality becomes an individual problem — the opprobrium intensified by self-censoring.

Oppression: It's Not Easy Being Gay

No loss by flood and lightning, no destruction of cities and temples by the hostile forces of nature, has deprived man of so many noble lives and impulses as those which his intolerance has destroyed. *Helen Keller*

People have a tendency to dislike or distrust anything unusual or misunderstood. The misunderstanding of homosexuality is especially widespread and deep-rooted. Gay people are different. The consequences of being different are suspicion, fear, rejection, and possibly hatred.

Any society is divided along economic and ethnic lines. Despite this diversity, a dominant group emerges. The dominant group in America is white, Christian and heterosexual. Members of society who do not totally conform to all the characteristics of the dominant group become minorities. In effect, then, "the majority" creates all minorities. Majorities are inherently powerful, especially in a democracy where it is easy for the majority to force its views on any minority. In the United States, we have a Constitution which quite intentionally makes majority dominance difficult through a balance of powers and a guarantee of certain civil rights. Our country was built by diversity, the ability to co-exist being one of our greatest assets. With only a few exceptions, our nation has a respectable record on civil rights and basic human rights for most people, both at home and abroad. Our country is, without a doubt, the most humane nation in the history of humanity. But our record is far from perfect.

The majority which exists on any particular issue is another matter. A situational majority consists of a variety of groups and individuals who might be or may become members of some minority. This varying "teamwork" supports the atmosphere of mutual respect for the rights and needs of others. Sometimes, the combinations seem quite odd indeed. For example, conservative moralists, who adamantly oppose abortion, team with liberal feminists, who favor abortion just as fervently, to fight pornography. The inevitability or even the possibility of changing personal circumstances supports the teamwork and mutual respect as well. Young people will become elderly; the healthy may become ill; a middle-class family could become poor and homeless. Former U.S. Congressman Robert Bauman observed, "Which of us knows with certainty that fate will not cast us into a position in which we will need the understanding and compassion of our fellow men?" Just having a friend who is a member of a minority is usually sufficient cause for an individual to support the civil rights of that minority.

The majority on the issue of homosexuality, however, is nearly constant and virtually omnipotent. *This* majority is ninety percent of the population and consists of whites and blacks, Christians and Jews, the very rich, the very poor, and everyone in between. They share two characteristics: heterosexuality and homophobia. Further, no one who is straight will ever become gay, and approximately eighty percent of all straight Americans claim not to know even a single gay person. As a result, the issues of homosexuality and gay civil rights remain conceptual: abstract, unknown, and unaddressed.

In *The Nature of Prejudice,* Gordon Allport defines prejudice as "an aversive or hostile attitude towards a person who belongs to a group, simply because he belongs to a group, and is therefore presumed to have the objectionable qualities ascribed to the group." This is clearly the situation with the gay minority in the United States today. The vacuum of knowledge about homosexuality in our society has been filled with stereotypes, not truth. The ignorance causes homophobia; the homophobia leads to prejudice; and the prejudice perpetuates the ignorance.

To help break the deadlock on this pattern of prejudice, the Lambda Institute, an organization which counsels social institutions on gay sensibility, uses an analogy they term "The Weed of Bigotry." The weed itself represents prejudice. It is rooted in the beliefs of racism, sexism, anti-Semitism, and homophobia. The weed blossoms as forms of bigotry: mistrust, fear, alienation, discrimination, injustice, hate, and violence. Our society attempts to root out racism, sexism, and anti-Semitism. Homophobia is an exception that not only survives, but thrives, fertilized by a multitude of individuals and social institutions.

The problem with homosexuality, therefore, is not homosexuality. The problem is homophobia. The problem of racism cannot be solved by shipping black people away; it is being solved through education. The problem of sexism cannot be solved by continuing to oppress women; it is being solved through understanding. The problem of anti-Semitism cannot be solved by converting Jews into Christians; it is being solved through respect of individual freedom. Likewise, the problem of homophobia will *not* be solved by eliminating the gay community, by continuing to oppress this minority, or by trying to convert its members to heterosexuality. It will be solved through education, understanding, and respect for individual freedom.

Because our society has not recognized the *real* problem related to homosexuality, the oppression continues in both covert and overt ways. It ranges from subtle job discrimination to physical violence. Where there is no blatant discrimination and opposition, there is frequently only symbolic support in the form of limited tolerance. Homophobia has become a bandwagon with incredible momentum. Maybe might does make right. To make matters worse, gay people are actually expected to understand this treatment as if it were to any extent justifiable. In other words, the gay minority is expected to tolerate the intolerance. There is great irony in this advantage intolerance has over tolerance: Those who really believe in freedom of expression are tolerant of others, even when their views are intolerant. So gay people remain oppressed. As long as homophobia continues to be society's problem, homosexuality will continue to be the gay minority's problem.

Opprobrium: The Internalization of Homophobia

Socialization is the process by which individuals learn to behave in the ways acceptable to others. The dictionary defines *socialize* as "to fit or train for a social environment." In effect, it is the internalization of society's beliefs. This is how every one of us, gay or straight, male or female, learns our respective "role" in society. We all basically become what others expect us to become. We are told what behavior is "appropriate" for our "kind" and where the limits of tolerance are drawn. In the case of homosexuality, these expectations are set by the stereotypes, which hardly lead to feelings of worth and self-esteem.

The internalization of homophobia therefore becomes an opprobrious self-fulfilling prophecy. Its damaging effect is demonstrated by studies where children who are told they are "gifted" perform better in school than those who are informed they are just "average." This occurs even though both groups are nearly identical in capabilities. The prophecy regarding homosexuality is very negative indeed. Gay people are not told they are "gifted." They are not even told they are "average." Instead, gay people are told they are sick, sinful and criminal. They are told they should experience guilt and shame for what they are. There is almost wholesale condemnation of the sexuality which has given so much meaning to their lives.

Drs. Bell and Weinberg from Indiana University stated: "It is taken for granted that homosexual people, lacking others' endorsement of their private identities, raised in a society whose sexual values oppose the usual homosexual life-style, and discriminated against in important areas of their lives, are bound to have extremely ambivalent feelings about their own and others' homosexuality . . . . It is certainly true that homosexuals share with other minority groups a 'legacy of subordination'—a tradition of expecting prejudice and harsh treatment as they go about their daily lives—and this is an important concern for social justice."

Not only is the internalization of homophobia self-fulfilling, it is also self-perpetuating. Gay people laugh at the faggot jokes, conceal their true identities from loved ones, and remain silent when they witness or experience oppression. The daily decisions to behave this way, although motivated by a legitimate concern for personal well-being, have a negative impact on personal attitudes. The negative attitude influences behavior, negatively, which in turn further destroys attitudes, and so it goes in a never-ending downward spiral. Dr. Martin S. Weinberg explains how this can occur: "Every choice [to hide the truth] keeps alive the various beliefs that collectively motivated it . . . . By such acts, committed even before he discovers he is homosexual, he produces the contempt he later comes to feel for himself."

In another study, the Institute for Sex Research found that men who rated themselves high in effeminacy also rated lowest in self-acceptance and highest in depression. But it is important to recognize which is cause and which is effect. When a gay person has little self-acceptance and is depressed about being homosexual, he or she is likely to adopt stereotypical behavior out of despondency. Gay people know they are different and that no matter how smart, or how good, or how beautiful they are, they will never really quite fit in.

The only way to unlearn a lifetime of homophobic conditioning is by living "gay." But internalized homophobia prevents gay people from doing so. This is the old "chicken or egg" question. Which comes first? How does the whole process start? It takes extreme courage for an individual to be different in a society which values conformity. This is the painful "coming out" process which presents its own dilemma: damned if you do; damned if you don't. (Both dilemmas and their respective resolutions are covered in Section VI.)

Because the stereotypes are so negative, gay people experience feelings of unprecedented guilt and shame. That is why the internalization of homophobia becomes an opprobrium. The Reverend Troy Perry of the Metropolitan Community Church refers to this as "oppression sickness." In a society which holds gay people in such contempt, it becomes difficult to live a healthy, happy, productive life. In effect, gay people are not born to fail; they are socially sentenced to fail. And that sentence is sometimes very severe.

Suicide

Eric Rofes, in his appropriately titled book *I Thought People Like That Killed Themselves,* emphasized that gay-related suicides are *not* caused by homosexuality. Instead he pointed out, "To write about suicidal homosexuals without connecting self-destructive tendencies to the oppression which is its root cause is to again blame the victim for the crime visited upon her or him." Or as one gay rights activist put it, "Some may say this man committed suicide. We know he was killed by the society which made him an outcast."

Suicide can be both descriptive of and prescriptive for the lives of some homosexual men and women. After all, this is how the role model, the "miserable and pitiful" homosexual character in the movies, resolves his or her "problem." Social oppression obscures both the purpose and the pleasures of life. Before the Gay Civil Rights Movement, a person was normally identified as being gay through some public scandal, never again to pass as straight. But Rofes cautions that society should not consider suicide a thing of the past for gay people. Indeed, a 1989 *Report of the Secretary's Task Force on Youth Suicide* published by the Department of Health and Human Services cites a "hostile and condemning environment, verbal and physical abuse, and rejection and isolation from families and peers" as reasons that make gay youth more vulnerable to suicide and other self-destructive behavior.

Determining the exact rate of attempted and completed suicides in any group is a difficult task. Many individuals who have attempted suicide will deny it afterwards, motivated to do so by the identical shame which caused the suicide attempt in the first place. Families frequently request that a suicide death not be listed as such, especially if it relates to homosexuality. Some coroners will not classify a death as suicide unless there is a note. Rofes cited one study which indicated notes are left in only about one-third of all suicides. Some suicides are disguised as accidents. Others are considered "unintentional" drug overdoses. Conversely, the deaths of openly gay people are frequently considered suicide, regardless of the circumstances. Because of these difficulties, most suicide studies are of the men and women who have *survived* previous attempts. It is generally believed that homosexual individuals are between two and three times more likely than heterosexual individuals, independently of all other considerations, either to consider or attempt suicide.

In *Living Gay,* Don Clark tells the story of a teenage girl who killed herself by jumping off a bridge:

> No one knew why. Her boyfriend found the answer when the high school principal let him clean out her locker. Scribbled notes in the guise of a story, hidden in the rear flap of her binder told her story. She was gay and she knew it, but her mother had been active in crusading against gay rights. She knew nothing positive about gay people, believed she had been cursed, and dared not disgrace the family. And so she killed herself. Her boyfriend, ironically, was gay also and had not yet found the courage to tell her. They

could have made it through together but they were both too scared to trust one another. The experience turned him into an overnight gay radical, but he curbed his impulse to confront the mother with the reason for the girl's suicide. He felt guilty about it himself and felt he owed his girlfriend the right to her decision about her death even if that decision was made in a cloud of confusion and misunderstanding created with the active help of her mother. That mother mourns her daughter in mystery still, not knowing that she helped to kill her.

Rofes calls for the institutions in our society to be aware of and to address this problem. He specifically mentions the family, friendships, media, schools, churches, law enforcement agencies, counselors and social workers, hospitals, and suicide prevention services. The solution encompasses both long-term suicide prevention and immediate individual suicide intervention. He also encourages the institutions in the gay community to continue their valuable efforts, especially around the holidays, through gay hotlines, counseling, and support of gay friends who lose their lovers.

Most gay-related suicide attempts occur in the late teens or early twenties. This is the time when most gay people struggle with sexual identity. Therefore, awareness of this problem is especially important in the schools and at home. Many gay men and women will not mention homosexuality as the reason for a suicide attempt or suicidal feelings. That is why it is important for counselors to *ask directly* about homosexuality and insist on an honest answer. The question should obviously be phrased to convey acceptance and not condemnation. Any indication of suicidal tendencies should *always* be taken seriously. Young gay people feel so incredibly isolated and alone. Social services must reach out. Addressing this problem directly is the only way to solve it.

As one gay man, whose attempt at suicide was unsuccessful, wrote:

> It is fun but barren to distribute blame — to blame society for stigmatizing homosexuality and to blame myself for not having had the wit, singlehandedly and without advice, to come out. More useful is to recognize that because the lack of role models almost proved fatal to me I should therefore come out now and encourage others to do the same. If I had known gay men and women, if my parents had included openly gay people among their friends, if my literature and history classes in school and college had acknowledged the homosexuality of so many of their heroes instead of denying it altogether or mentioning it coyly or as an example of leprosy overcome, I might not have tried to kill myself. Instead I did the sensible thing and tried to die, for who would want to live, if living meant a charade at best and exile at least?

The Abuses of Severe Homophobia

There is perhaps no phenomenon which contains so much destructive feeling as "moral indignation," which permits envy or hate to be acted out under the guise of virtue. *Erich Fromm*

Anyone can be homophobic without being hateful. Jimmy Carter said, "The issue of homosexuality always makes me nervous . . . I don't have any, you know, personal knowledge about homosexuality." But he also stated, "I oppose all forms of discrimination on the basis of sexual orientation."

Most people simply *use* their homophobia to form various opinions or judgments. Others *abuse* it; they exploit the situation to advance their own causes. For these individuals, homophobia is a golden opportunity for personal or political gain. They apparently love to hate gay people. As a result, they become chronically ignorant, blocking out every channel of enlightenment. After all, prejudice does not like to be proven wrong.

The most homophobic individuals have been characterized by psychologists. They are more likely to be white males, to not know a single gay person, to live in rural areas of the South or Midwest, to be older and less-educated, to subscribe to a conservative religious ideology, to hold traditional views on gender roles which preserve the double standards, to be more negative regarding sexuality in general, to deny any childhood sexual play, to experience guilt about their own sexual activity, to view homosexuality as an illness, and to have negative attitudes toward other minorities.

To the extremely homophobic, the gay minority remains a popular and vulnerable target for both personal and political agendas. Gay men and lesbians are regularly depersonalized, objectified, and finally victimized. Gay people may be the last minority which is not "off limits" to these forms of abuse. In effect, homosexuality is a scapegoat; in fact, a perfect scapegoat. In *The Manufacture of Madness*, Dr. Thomas Szasz wrote, "The homosexual is a scapegoat who evokes no sympathy. Hence, he can only be a victim, never a martyr." Even when homosexuality cannot be blamed for something, the very topic stirs emotion and easily diverts attention from real issues — a sort of "lavender herring." For example, when a newspaper article revealed that a California politician had two illegitimate children, U.S. Congressman William Dannemeyer "defended" the man's reputation by saying, "At least it shows a preference by him for heterosexual lifestyle." Dannemeyer then went off on a tangent denouncing gay political activism.

The Personal Agenda

Boys are brought up to be "real men." Their heroes come from sports, war, law enforcement, and exploration. But with the industrial revolution and increased civilization in the world, most boys grow up to be men who work in offices, marry, and raise families. This new lifestyle is not exactly demonstrative of "manliness." So men must look for other ways to establish their manhood. This could be in terms of salary, golf scores, politics or the type of car driven. Men are also confused. They are expected to hate quiche but like Brie. They are expected to be strong and protective, while simultaneously being gentle and compassionate.

128

The poor "faggot" serves as a perfect scapegoat for the resulting frustration.

Only heterosexual masculinity can be established through hate. Gay men and lesbians do not beat up straight people to show how "gay" they are. Similarly, straight women do not assault anyone to demonstrate how "feminine" they are. Men regularly use their superior strength to achieve or prove something or other. For this reason, wive beating has become a serious social problem in America, and almost ninety percent of all violent crimes are committed by men. It is socially acceptable for men to hate, and hate they do.

A common object of this hate is gay men. One reason for this is that young straight men feel their "manhood" is always in question, perhaps because they regularly question it in others. Gay men are simply identified, defined, then understood to be what "manliness" is not. The existing stereotypes serve this purpose perfectly. Given this "understanding," if a man is not homosexual, he must therefore be "manly." He *proves* he is not homosexual by hating gay men. This is possibly motivated by the reaction formation discussed earlier, but not necessarily.

In a male's late teens or early twenties, this hate often takes the form of physical violence or "fag-bashing." Frequently, these fag-bashers are found innocent on charges of assault and battery, because they claimed their action was a legitimate reaction to or "defense" of an alleged sexual advance. This is known as the "homosexual panic" defense. As maturity and responsibility develop, the attacks become verbal and may not even be made in the presence of a gay person. A good fag joke or a homophobic remark makes the implicit statement, "I'm a *real* man." The saddest part of all this is that it works — even the "homosexual panic" defense. Society may not "approve," but it does little or nothing to stop it.

The Political Agenda

Political extremism involves two prime ingredients: an excessively simple diagnosis of the world's ills and a conviction that there are identifiable villains back of it all. *John W. Gardner*

Preying on people's fear and hate is regularly used to promote other causes. Fear and hate are strong emotions which can elicit equally strong reactions. Homophobia is "made to order" for zealots. It propels them to power. Many causes are furthered and much money is raised against the "threat" of homosexuality. If the attack is not directly on homosexuality, then homosexuality is used as symptom or example of some more fundamental "problem." It is an appeal to people's worst qualities. But again, it works. Here are two examples from recent history.

Adolf Hitler

The great masses of the people will more easily fall victims to a big lie than to a small one. *Adolf Hitler*

Hitler's rise to power offers the most gruesome example of the use of hate for political gain. Dr. Rudiger Lautmann of Frankfurt, West Germany wrote: "This century's most extreme form of antihomosexual repression occurred in Germany between 1933 and 1945, when the Nazis attempted to assure the male domination of society by strictly regulating masculine sexual behavior. Sanctions against homosexual males were tightened to the utmost degree (lesbianism was passed over as being of no consequence) and a kiss or an embrace became a felony. The death penalty was demanded for members of the SS caught in homosexual activity. For the civilian, a record or conviction of homosexuality led to the concentration camp."

Under Hitler's Nazi Germany, nearly eight million people were worked to death, tortured to death, left to die of hunger, or exterminated in gas chambers. Millions more survived, only to suffer for life from memories of the atrocities they witnessed. Jews were not the only group to be victimized, though they were the largest numbering nearly six million fatalities. The others included political opponents, convicted criminals, Jehovah's Witnesses, Gypsies, emigrants, and homosexual men. Because most records were destroyed, it is difficult to determine how many people were actually killed for their homosexuality. Estimates range from under 5,000 to nearly 250,000. If homosexual individuals were easier to identify, however, the number would undoubtedly have been much higher. But the fact that this number is low in comparison to the number of Jewish victims does not make the individual suffering any less. Actually, in Hitler's hierarchy of hate, homosexual men were at the top, followed by Jews and Gypsies. Each despised group wore a small badge to identify its "crime." The badge for homosexual men was a pink triangle. It was a full three inches wide, wider than all the others, making these "deviants" easier to spot. The general fate of homosexual prisoners was to be worked to death. Only the "surplus" were sent to concentration camps for the more "humane" fate of extermination.

Hitler did not necessarily have a genuine hate for homosexual men or for the other minority groups. He actually hated the Russians. But his real hate was not conducive to the cause of promoting his regime and gaining the support of the German people.

Even after the war, the West German government ruled that homosexual men were "legitimately" imprisoned because they were still criminals under German law. As such, they were not eligible for any compensation. As of this writing, in all of Germany there stands but one small stone at Neuengamme commemorating the homosexual victims of the holocaust. Even in America, the land of truth, the homosexual victims are denied mention in most history textbooks. Refusing to acknowledge one form of homophobia is an example of another.

McCarthyism

Following the war, Joe McCarthy's rise to political fame came from his attack on alleged Communists and homosexual men. He may have genuinely hated both groups, but if he sincerely felt all his accusations were legitimate, then he was clearly a psychotic man. In any event, he used the fear and hate of others to propel himself to prominence and power, rallying the nation in frightful display of homophobia. At the height of the hysteria, a U.S. Senate report titled "Employment of Homosexuals and Other Sex Perverts in Government" concluded: "One homosexual can pollute a government office." In 1953 newly inaugurated President Eisenhower issued an executive order barring homosexual men and women from all federal jobs.

McCarthy's demise came when he accused the secretary of the Army of Communist affiliations in 1954. These attacks led to a nationally televised congressional hearing. For thirteen days, millions of Americans were able to see Joe in action. His tactics of evading issues, making irrelevant charges and insinuations, and his general rude manner served to destroy his credibility. In that same year, the Senate voted 67 to 22 to condemn McCarthy for conduct unbecoming of a senator. Harry Truman referred to McCarthy as a "moral pygmy." Because of his "work," many people still associate homosexuality with communism today.

In two textbooks used to research McCarthyism for this book, neither mentioned the attack on homosexual American citizens. Again and again, gay history is censored. Maybe Mark Twain was right: "The very ink with which all history is written is merely fluid prejudice."

This form of hatred is not a thing of the past. It still exists today in the United States. The strategy is the same: Target a despised minority group for political gain. Only the tactics are a little different.

The "Radical Religious Right"

Blessed are those who have been persecuted for the sake of righteousness, for theirs is the kingdom of heaven. *Matthew 5:10*

The "Radical Religious Right" is not an organization. The phrase instead refers to those men and women who hold a particular extremist ideology justified on religious beliefs. The Radical Religious Right could have been discussed in the chapters on the church or in the section on society. But because its views straddle the fence between religion and politics, it represents neither. This ideology is so extreme, it would actually be unfair to associate it with Christianity or include it in mainstream politics. Its members might be preachers, they might be politicians, but they are definitely and extremely homophobic. For this reason, the Radical Religious Right is appropriately discussed here.

President Ronald Reagan's Commission on Civil Rights summarized the problem created by this social phenomenon: "When religious doctrine is wittingly or unwittingly used to place guilt or establish hostility toward another group, then the circumstances are right for an unprecedented explosion of hatred and bigotry that can result in confrontations of serious proportions. Furthermore, when these are perpetrated in a spirit of righteous indignation and fueled by an expectation of media exposure and public tolerance, violence is not surprising." The media exposure is to be expected in a free society, but the public should recognize and no longer tolerate the intolerance of this religious-political extremism.

The Radical Religious Right's reasoning cannot proceed unless it first violates a fundamental principle of our nation: separation of church and state. They may believe in "literal" interpretation of the Bible, but they certainly have a peculiar way of interpreting the Constitution. Their actions involve religious exploitation and political perversion. They do this by disguising their politics as gospel, while ignoring the intent of the Bible for the sake of its words. Their homophobic attack continues to increase in voracity as certain preacher-politicians recognize its fundraising potential. They use gay people as gospel objects and political pawns to intimidate others and achieve their personal goals. Of course, these men and women have every right to practice politics as individuals, but not as clerics or, as some would claim, "representatives" of God.

Reinhold Niebuhr pointed out the problem here by observing that "the tendency to claim God as an ally for our partisan values and ends is . . . the source of all religious fanaticism." These preacher-politicians obviously realize how questionable their political involvement really is by the tactics they use. For example, consider an instruction sheet titled "How to Participate in a Political Party" distributed by supporters of Pat Robertson to delegates at a Republican Party caucus in Iowa. Among its comments were:

> Three (foundational) institutions God established are the family, the church, and civil government. Although the church is crucial — even though it was founded last — the other two are nevertheless also strategic. And God wants *righteous* leaders in all three areas . . . To a degree, keep your positions on issues to yourself. Jesus didn't overwhelm (even his [sic] disciples) with truth . . . Give the impression that you are there to work for the party, not to push an ideology. Come across as being interested in economic issues. Try not to let on that a close group of friends are becoming active in the party together . . . Hide your strength . . . We 'need' (well, we could wisely gain from) the rest of the political party's expertise, work, and fund-raising ability. When you have control of a party, it might not be wise to place 'our' people into any and every position . . . Don't flaunt your Christianity . . . Don't come across as a 'one-issue' person. Be perceived as a person interested in the whole spectrum of issues."

Robertson is the founder of the Christian Broadcast Network, the Freedom Council, and the Committee for Freedom. The latter two are religious-political organizations which promote Christian candidates for elected and appointed offices. The names are misleading, even ironic, as they do little to support anything which even resembles real freedom. In 1986 Robertson announced his intention to consider becoming a candidate for the presidency of the United States. "Of course, you always have to consider what the Lord wants," Robertson said in a *Saturday Evening Post* interview. "If He were to say, 'Run for President' then obviously any man of God would have to obey." By doing this, he portrays *his* political views as *His*.

There are many other institutions of the Radical Religious Right. Most of their names are incredibly misleading and ironic as well. Included are the Liberty Federation (formerly the Moral Majority), the Christian Nation Movement, and the American Coalition for Traditional Values. The title of another, The Coalition for Christians in Government describes their blatant promotion of merging church and state.

The Radical Religious Right promotes a "Christian Nation" which would censor authors and "biblicise" textbooks by removing anything undesirable or unsupportive of their beliefs. For example, they want the "creation theory" taught in conjunction with Darwin's theory on evolution in biology classes. Jerry Falwell advocates, "Biblically sound textbooks must be written for every school child in every course of study." He doesn't stop there: "I hope I live to see the day when, as in the early days of our country, we won't have any public schools. The churches will have taken them over and Christians will be running them."

Members of this movement, seeing Communist under and hedonists in every bed but their own, promote Christian "litmus tests" for prospective candidates, elected or appointed. This is particularly dangerous with respect to judicial appointments, which violates the constitutional ban on religious tests for public office, established to protect a citizen's right to a fair and impartial trial. Some members of the Radical Religious Right even resorted to praying for the demise or resignations of "liberal" justices. They favor the imposition of prayer in public schools as if there is already not enough time in the day to pray, and a child could not already do this on his or her own. They desire favorable tax treatment for those who support Christian schools. They even define the "Christian" way to vote as if their views were part of some divine political platform. Of course, those who do not vote this way are accused of being on "Satan's side of the aisle."

The Radical Religious Right is not *completely* ignorant regarding homosexuality, but they are *dangerously* ignorant. Most of their claims about homosexuality are anecdotal. When they do any research, they do it in all the wrong places. Some have even sunk so low as to get their "general" statistics about homosexuality from arrest records and medical reports. They begin with these nonrepresentative samples, then proceed to "show" that the "typical" homosexual is likely to have been arrested for solicitation or sexually molesting children. Further, the typical homosexual, they claim, is likely to be very promiscuous, regularly engaging in dangerous sexual activity. For example, *The Candidates Biblical Scoreboard* for 1986 published by the Biblical News Service-Christian Voice stated: "In gay baths, homosexuals usually have sex with ten to 30 partners nightly . . . The average homosexual visits a bath two to three times weekly." This would mean that the "average" gay man has between 1,000 and 5,000 sexual partners annually, or from three to thirteen daily! Members of the Radical Religious Right are professionals at deception. Yet these self-appointed "authorities" are easy to identify. Simply checking the bibliography in any of their writings will show how legitimate their research is.

There is actually a great irony in this hateful campaign to ruin lives. In the long run, it will do more good than harm. The only real problem is the toll taken in the meantime. Abraham Lincoln observed, "You may fool all of the people some of the time, you can even fool some of the people all of the time; but you can't fool all of the people all of the time." Eventually, *all* extremists meet with demise. Until then, the activities of the Radical Religious Right keep homosexuality a theological and social issue in America. This gives gay people media attention and exposure, forcing *real* politicians and the American people to deal with homosexuality. Some of the comments by members of the Radical Religious Right about other minority groups are also deeply offensive. Each time this happens, and it happens with predictable regularity, thousands or millions more are alienated. Then, when they say something bad about homosexuality, people consider the source. Jerry Falwell already has one of the lowest popularities of any public figure. The hateful rhetoric backfires, encouraging empathy for gay civil rights. As Edgar Watson Howe put it, "Abuse a man unjustly, and you will make friends for him." The abuse naturally rallies gay organizations as well, fueling the fervor in the struggle to achieve gay equality.

The sad reality of life is that sometimes a problem must be made worse before it gets solved. Actually, the Radical Religious Right will eventually do more good for gay civil rights than most gay people will. Here are two examples: one from the 1970s and the other from the 1980s.

Save Our Children

In 1977 Anita Bryant led an often vicious campaign to repeal an existing ordinance in Dade County, Florida, forbidding discrimination on the basis of sexual orientation. The effort was effectively dubbed *Save Our Children, Incorporated.* Gay people responded, "We *are* your children!" But because the gay minority is "invisible," the campaign received support from many parents of gay children.

Could this have been a case of "love the sinner; hate the sin"? Hardly, especially when cars around Dade County were sporting bumper stickers which read "Kill a queer for Christ" and with Anita referring to gay people as "human garbage."

Her campaign was a skillful one. Example: "The more we let violence and homosexuality become the norm, the more we'll become such a sick nation that the communists won't have to take over — we'll just give up." Notice the words *violence, homosexuality, sick,* and *communists* in the same sentence. She even wrote a book, *The Anita Bryant Story: The Survival of Our Nation's Families and the Threat of Militant Homosexuals.* She did it again: the words *survival, families, threat,* and *militant* are all crammed into the same title with *homosexuals.* It must be a gift.

Jerry Falwell

In his book *Wisdom for Living,* Jerry actually gives a wealth of truly good advice. He tells us that God hates people who sow discord among others, that we should listen to each other, that we should truly love each other and not hurt each other, that we must be compassionate, that the quality of our commitment will be demonstrated by our treatment of the disenfranchised, that we should learn how to help people up not down, and that we should not be judgmental of others.

His most noteworthy advice concerns the "contentious man" as a "busybody," and how to avoid becoming one. He begins by quoting from the Bible, the book of Proverbs, chapter 18:

> The *contentious man* is treated in verses 6-12. Verse 6 says, "A fool's lips enter into contention, and his mouth calleth for strokes." The mouth of the fool continually causes contention and calls for strokes of injustice. Worse than that is the fact that his mouth will eventually cause his destruction if not brought under control (v.7). The contentious man is filled with pride, arrogance, and the bitter spirit of the antisocial man. He allows all this to produce an overflowing of verbiage that is damaging to the character of others. You do not have to pull the trigger on a man to destroy his character. You can assassinate him with your tongue, and that is why Scripture deals so harshly with the busybody. Scripture speaks very strongly against gossip and malicious conversation that hurts and injures other people.
>
> There are three golden gates through which every word about others should pass before we speak those words.
>
> First, is it true? Is it absolutely, irrevocably *true?* Do you know it is true?
>
> Second, if it is true, do we *need* to say it? Some things which are true do not need to be repeated.
>
> Third, if it is true and needful, is it *kind?* Is that statement you are going to make *kind* to others? If it is not true, needful, and kind, you need to close your lips tightly before the words escape. Once the words are out of your mouth you cannot retrieve them. You can apologize; you can ask forgiveness, but the words are out and can never be recaptured.

Of course, he just had to say it: "We must practice what we preach. And in our daily lives the world must see Jesus in us." All this from a man who has claimed, "These so-called gay people would just as soon kill you as look at you" and "[S]ince homosexuals cannot have children of their own, the only way for them to expand their ranks is to recruit your children and mine." The hypocrisy is pathetic.

The Radical Religious Right certainly does damage with its damning demagoguery. Its members *think* they are hurting only gay people, though. To them, that's no real harm done. But they have many more victims, like the father of a gay son: "I am seething. Some religious leaders and other self-styled leaders like Bryant and Falwell are the 'immoral' ones because they preach love and hatred in the same breath. This world has seen its share of wars, starvation, plagues, cruelty, gas chambers and more, mostly perpetrated by the non-Gay world. Yet the demagogues need a scapegoat, the homosexual. Most of the Gays I have met, like my own son, are decent, law-abiding human beings: taxpayers; voters; and, aside from their sexual orientation, no different in their desires and needs from the likes of us. It is an honor to have my son in our family, and if 'family' is the strength of our country, I'll hold mine high up in pride."

Homophobia is the irrational fear or hatred of gay people. To some degree, *everyone* is homophobic—even gay people are. There are many justifications for homophobia, but there is only one reason: ignorance. Homophobia is a disease and it is very contagious. In fact, it is epidemic in our society. As with any prejudice, the treatment is simple. It is only necessary that the "patient" have the will to learn.

Dr. George Weinberg, who coined the term *homophobia* summarized it best: "In the last analysis, the homophobic reaction I have been describing is a form of acute conventionality. Ultimately, it condemns because of difference. It has every basic attribute of an irrational social prejudice." That is why Dr. Weinberg stated, "I would never consider a patient healthy unless he had overcome his prejudice against homosexuality." Everyone *can* overcome homophobia.

The bottom line is that homophobia is more than just a harmless attitude. Homophobia is a destructive force causing untold human suffering. Homophobia is what makes a problem out of homosexuality. As long as gay people remain silent, and as long as straight people continue to fear homosexuality in others, their children and even themselves, homophobia will remain—and the human suffering will continue. Its effect on gay men and lesbians can be devastating, possibly leading to suicide. These twenty-four million Americans suffer the most from homophobia. But gay people are not its only victims. Friends and especially family members suffer, too, merely from knowing that the lives of their loved ones are being diminished each and every day.

Section IV:

The Church and Homosexuality

Chapter 9:

Understanding Scripture

The Reverend Sylvia Pennington recounted her first visit to a predominantly gay church. She is straight.

There were about 200 people there, mostly men. The church was in a semi-circular shape. I took a seat in the back row, as close to an open door as possible, just in case a hasty exit would be needed. I sat down, closed my eyes, and bowed my head. Oh, did I pray! I beseeched God not to let any spirit but His touch me or even get close. I asked the Spirit of God to so fill my mind that none of Satan's devices could insidiously infiltrate there and mess up my thinking. I prayed fervently for grace, truth and protection. The minutes passed quickly, and my anxiety began to ease as I became more aware of the Holy Spirit's presence hovering around, about and within me. I felt the deeply divine sweetness of the very presence of God which has always drawn me like a magnet to church services. Basking in this presence, I suddenly came back to the reality of where I was, and slowly opened my eyes.

The service started. I looked around. Due to the shape of the church I could see most of the faces. Amazing, amazing, amazing! Why they looked like any other group of people at church! They were sensing the same Spirit that I sensed and loving God back as I was. My unbelieving eyes scanned the large male group. There was no doubt about it. They were actually worshipping God. And, God was there—undeniably there! I don't know from what depths of me the tears began to flow, but oh, how they flowed and continued to flow throughout the entire service.

Over and over I cried to God.

"Lord, what are you doing here? Why are you blessing like this? Why are you here? They're all homosexuals, Lord, and they're not even here to change. Oh, dear Jesus, please tell me what you are doing here. This is Sodom, Lord. Why aren't you raining down fire and brimstone? Why are you blessing instead? Why, why, why??!! "

Yes, there are millions of gay Christians and Jews. Yet for hundreds of years, Judeo-Christian religions have not welcomed homosexual members. Understanding why begins with the Bible.

The Bible

> The unfolding of Thy words gives light;
> It gives understanding to the simple.
>
> *Psalms 119:130*

The following pages present many issues pertaining to the Bible and the interpretation of its passages discussing same-sex sexual acts. I am not an expert on the Bible; you may not be either. Actually, I'm not sure anyone is truly expert when it comes to understanding God's Word. Therefore, much of the information in this chapter comes from numerous other sources: ministers, priests, rabbis, theologians, biblical scholars, and knowledgeable laymen. Most of what is presented here is fact; some is analysis. That there are numerous sources for this information is irrelevant. After all, even the devil can quote Scripture. What *is* important is that any legitimate interpretation of the Bible must, at a minimum, accept the facts presented and sincerely consider the analysis offered.

A detailed discussion of the Bible is beyond the scope and intent of this book. But some understanding of the history of the Bible and techniques for its legitimate interpretation are in order.

The History of the Bible

The Bible is unlike any other book. It is a collection of books believed to be written by forty different authors over a period of nearly 1,600 years in different languages, spanning many diverse historical periods and cultures. The Bible is undoubtedly the single most significant book ever written. It is also one of the most difficult books to comprehend.

The Bible did not drop from heaven in the King James or any of the other myriad versions we use today. Its content actually changed many times until evolving into what is now referred to as *the* Bible. Many books originally accepted by the church for inclusion in the Bible were later rejected. The converse is true as well. General agreement on the contents of the New Testament was not reached until over 300 years after the death of Christ. The Protestants and the Catholics still disagree on which books should be included in the Old Testament. Protestants use the same books accepted by the Jews. Catholics use these and several more from the *Apocrypha*. Many different translations, or versions, of the Bible have also existed over the years. Each version was approved by the general consensus of a committee of theologians, not by unanimous agreement on every word in every phrase.

The Old Testament dates back nearly 4,000 years. Many of its stories were passed on orally, sometimes for generations, prior to being written. For example, the Pentateuch, which includes the books of Genesis, Exodus, Leviticus, Numbers and Deuteronomy, is believed to have been written around the tenth century B.C., thousands of years after the fact. Retrospective as they were, none of the "original" manuscripts have survived. The oldest versions which exist are copies of previous copies made hundreds, sometimes thousands of years later. And some of the ones surviving have deteriorated over the years, leaving parts missing or illegible.

Every single edition of the Bible had to be copied by hand. With 600,000 words in the Old Testament alone, one wonders who could copy the entire Old Testament without making a single mistake. Sometimes we cannot even copy an address or phone number correctly. The inevitable errors accumulated over the centuries. The New Testament is more recent; the oldest surviving copies were made "only" two or three centuries after the originals.

Study of the Bible reveals that some New Testament quotations of wording from the Old Testament are different. This is because most New Testament quotations are based on a version of the Old Testament called the *Septuagint.* The Septuagint *was* the Old Testament of the early Christian church. It is believed to have been written between 250 and 150 B.C. in Alexandria, Egypt. That does not mean the exact date is unknown; it means the amount of work required 100 years! Another version of the Old Testament, called the Masoretic Hebrew Bible, serves as the basis for more recent translations. It was written in the fifth century A.D. The oldest surviving copy is believed to date to around 900 A.D.

None of these versions were written in English. The Old Testament was written in Hebrew and Aramaic; the New Testament in Greek. And their translation involves more than merely substituting one word for another because one-to-one correspondence of words simply does not exist between languages. For example, the Greeks had three words for *love* to differentiate between brotherly love, God's unconditional love, and passionate love. In English there is one. On the other hand, there are many instances where Greek is less precise than English. Recall the discussion from Chapter 6 on the numerous meanings of the word *nature* and its derivatives. Translation involves converting thoughts and ideas to new wording which best preserves the original message. It is frequently necessary to use a word or phrase which only approximates the original meaning. In other words, no pun intended, a translation is in part an interpretation.

Each language also has specific rules of grammar, many of which are unique. In all, the Bible has been translated into over 1,200 languages. There are more than a dozen different English versions alone. *The Open Bible,* the New American Standard version, was used for all the quotations in this book.

An example of the difficulty in translating from one language to another can be found in the New Testament. The four Gospel accounts of Christ's life are not identical. This is true even though the story of Christ's life was not passed on orally, as many of the Old Testament stories were. Each account was written around the same time using "eyewitness" information. Jesus spoke Aramaic, but the New Testament was written in Greek, making it necessary to translate His words. Because this was in the days before tape recorders, each speech would also need to be reconstructed from memory or notes.

Translating New Testament Greek is relatively easy compared to translating Old Testament Hebrew. First, the term *Hebrew* actually includes a number of dialects spoken in ancient Palestine. These dialects are part of the Semitic family of languages, much like French, Italian, and Spanish are part of the Latin family of languages today. Aramaic was also a Semitic language. Actually, there was not even *the* Hebrew language. Languages evolve with the societies using them. Each generation adds new words and alters meanings for existing words. Similarly, as some words drop from common usage, their meaning is lost. Just think how much the English language has changed in the twentieth century alone. In the preface to the Revised Standard Version, the publishers comment on the need to change over 300 words from the King James Version because they were used "in a sense substantially different from that which they now convey." Of course, the Hebrew people in biblical times did not produce dictionaries. Language was more for speaking than writing. With this lack of formality, language usage was inconsistent.

In addition, Hebrew was not commonly spoken after the third century B.C. It was only recently revived in Israel, and contemporary Hebrew is distinctly different from its ancient ancestor. Because the "original" Hebrew language was lost, linguists had to reconstruct it from the literature of the period. Most of this reconstruction is based on the Old Testament itself—specifically, the Masoretic Hebrew version written in the fifth century A.D. The Masoretic Hebrew Bible makes use of approximately 8,000 different words, with nearly 2,000 occurring only once. The meaning of each unknown word would be determined from its context. Naturally, this is a very challenging task for the 2,000 words used only once. The translator could not be certain whether an "unknown" word is a copying mistake or truly unknown. Even today, changes are continually being made with the discovery of more literature from the period. This obviously has the potential of significantly altering existing translations.

The most difficult problem with Hebrew, though, is the language itself. During biblical times, the alphabet for Hebrew was composed exclusively of consonants. Therefore the oldest surviving Hebrew texts were written without "points," or what we would call vowels. To make matters worse, there was no punctuation or spacing between words. Because most people did not read or write in those days, this was not a major problem— for them. They studied the Word of God through the teachings of priests, the only people to carry the written Word. The points, word separation, and punctuation were first added to the version known now as the Masoretic Hebrew Bible. Division into chapters and verses did not occur until the Middle Ages. Imagine doing this for the entire Old Testament without making a single mistake. Many point markings have recently been changed to produce more probable interpretations as our culture's understanding of ancient Hebrew continues to evolve.

So, what's in a word? Possibly nothing and maybe everything. The authors of *Understanding Scripture* offer an example: "This situation appears also in 1 Timothy 3:8–13 where there is a discussion about qualifications for deacons. In the middle of the paragraph, verse 11 reads, 'the women (*gune*) likewise must be serious, no slanderers, but temperate, faithful in all things.' The King James translated it, 'Even so must

141

their wives be . . .' The word *gune* that appears here does not tell us whether Paul meant wives, women in general, or women deacons. The only guide to meaning in this case must be the context, and the differences between translations indicate that biblical scholars do not agree as to what Paul had in mind." One translation of the word *gune* would permit women to become deacons; the other would not. So, what's in a word? A lot. It is doubtful the authors of the Bible ever thought their work would be translated thousands of years later into other languages which did not even exist at the time. Had they been able to write in English, imagine how different the Bible might be today.

I point out these issues not to find fault, but to establish an appreciation for the difficulties involved in translating and ultimately interpreting the Bible. These translations are needed to present God's Word in words we can understand today. In the preface to the Revised Standard Version the publishers comment on God's Word by emphasizing, "That Word must not be disguised in phrases that are no longer clear, or hidden under words that have changed or lost their meaning. It must stand forth in language that is direct and plain and meaningful to people today." Along with this *ability* to read the Bible in our native tongue comes a *responsibility* to read God's Word according to His Will. And misinterpreting God's Word, means misinterpreting His Will.

Biblical Interpretation

> Both read the Bible day and night,
> But thou read'st black where I read white.
>
> *William Blake*

Interpretation of the Bible is certainly not infallible. The very existence of literally hundreds of Christian denominations alone, each claiming to represent *the* truth, adequately demonstrates that the process of interpretation is indeed subjective. Only those who have true faith in the Bible's infallibility are willing to keep searching for His truth.

Language, ironically, *can* be a barrier to communication at times. Therefore, great care is required to interpret the Bible accurately, for it contains material of great worth and timeless truth. Its topics are profound, yet its message is often not self-explanatory. Many topics are not even addressed. For those which are, it is frequently necessary to accept only partial answers for now.

"All Scripture is inspired by God and profitable for teaching, for reproof, for correction, for training in righteousness; that the man of God may be adequate, equipped for every good work." (2 Timothy 3:16–17) How the Word was inspired varies. How the words were actually written varies even more. Each author wrote in his own style and was influenced by his environment. (There is no sexism here: All the Bible's authors were men.) As a result, the cultural and political influences in the original Scripture, as well as in its many translations, must be taken into account. Historian John Boswell commented, "It is not readily apparent to modern English speakers with little knowledge of classical languages that the passage of thousands of years obscures, sometimes beyond recovery, the exact meaning of words in the languages of cultures with experiences and lifestyles very different from their own." This external influence exerts itself just as strongly today in our modern interpretation.

Normally, it is impossible to understand the meaning of a passage in the Bible by merely reading it. Walk into any religious bookstore and notice rack after rack of books on the geography, history, cultures, and authors of the Bible. When reading the Bible it is often necessary to "travel" far away and back 2,000 to 4,000 years to help understand what life was like in another place and time. This might involve being part of a Hebrew nation wandering in the desert or being a "radical" advocating some "cult" claiming to be led by the Messiah. Such a journey prevents contaminating an understanding of the *past* with values and knowledge from the *present*. Because this form of anachronism is part of human nature, diligent awareness of its influence is prudent when interpreting the Bible.

No one wrote, no one translated, and no one now reads the Bible in a vacuum of other opinions and beliefs either. These other beliefs have a profound influence on interpretation as well — which is not necessarily bad unless it gets out of control, making one's interpretation more ideology than theology. A good analogy is afforded by the Supreme Court. Here are nine individuals who live in the same time and place, who base their beliefs on the same Constitution, who read the same legal briefs, hear the same testimony, see the same evidence, and yet reach totally opposite conclusions on a regular basis with predictable consistency. It is human nature for existing and complex belief systems, even moods, to have an influence on perspective and perception. For example, a person can read the same biblical passage twice and obtain a different meaning. Different circumstances influence interpretation. People are simply more likely to trust a view which does not conflict with their other existing beliefs. It is therefore *very* important to distinguish all other beliefs from what the Bible does and does not say.

"The sum of Thy word is truth, And every one of Thy righteous ordinances is everlasting." (Psalms 119:160) The Bible always applies to contemporary life even though some circumstances in the Bible are not found today in our society. The Old Testament has over 600 laws. The New Testament has about as many. The book of Deuteronomy suggests that stubborn and rebellious sons should be stoned to death (21:18–21), that blended material of wool and linen should not be worn (22:11), that girls who are not virgins should also be stoned to death (22:18–19), that children born out of wedlock should not be church members (23:2), that interest should not be charged on loans (23:19), and that honeymoons should last one year (24:5). Are we to tell our banks they should not charge interest on mortgage loans? Can you imagine someone telling his or her boss, "See you next year when I get back from my honeymoon!"?

There were good reasons for these laws at the time, and although the laws may no longer apply directly, the *reasons* for them are, more

143

likely than not, still valid. For example, many of the dietary laws in the Old Testament were important for personal health. Pork was infested with the bacteria trichinae, and the wandering Hebrew nation did not have refrigerators or good ovens. The disease trichinosis was a serious threat to the survival of the Jewish nation. Pork is no longer a threat to health, but health is still important today. Yet this is not a purely *biblical* interpretation for it relies on information from other sources. It should, as long as these other sources complement rather than replace an understanding of Scripture. A modern interpretation should consider what the particular passage meant to its original readers and then what it means in *our* time and place.

To do this, there are a number of different "strategies" available, but there is only one which is appropriate. In Romans 8:14 Paul states, "For all who are being led by the Spirit of God, these are the sons of God." A *spiritual* interpretation allows this relationship with God that some other strategies might miss. This does not mean, however, that Scripture should not be read literally. Actually, there is no other way to read Scripture except literally. But some people stop here. They place undue emphasis on individual words and ignore the setting or context of the message. As a result, the real *spiritual* meaning is missed. Some people even claim that this form of interpretation is not really an interpretation at all. Instead, they claim it is what God's Word "clearly" means. What this claim attempts to establish is the absolute authority of *their* interpretation, making any challenge tantamount to heresy. Would they also interpret the parables "literally"? Those who create reality from the symbolic are missing the message in God's Word.

"Literalists" will frequently pull select words or passages from Scripture to justify a belief. While this proof-texting approach is legitimate, it is often abused by reading more into words than intended. A carefully selected phrase from the Bible, if exaggerated or embellished, could justify almost any possible position on nearly any issue. For example, here are two apparently opposite "messages" from the Bible. Micah 4:3 states, "Then they will hammer their swords into plowshares, And their spears into pruning hooks..." Does this mean people should abandon weapons? The "message" in Joel 3:10 is: "Beat your plowshares into swords, And your pruning hooks into spears..." Does this mean people should be armed? Those individuals who abuse the proof-texting method to establish a biblical basis for their own opinions are either ignorant of the context or they consciously corrupt it.

Clearly, then, a text out of context is a pretext. As such, context is the key to unlocking meaning in the Bible. The context of any passage can be found at times by reading several passages before and after it. To understand the context of some passages, though, it is also necessary to reference other Scripture, biblical study guides, or history books.

Before analyzing what the Bible has to say about same-sex sexual acts, one final example will help demonstrate the concepts just discussed.

144

The Story of Onan

Genesis 38:6–10 tells the story of Onan. Er and Onan were the sons of Judah. "Now Judah took a wife for Er his first-born, and her name was Tamar. But Er, Judah's first-born, was evil in the sight of the Lord, so the Lord took his life. Then Judah said to Onan, 'Go in to your brother's wife, and perform your duty as a brother-in-law to her, and raise up offspring for your brother.' And Onan knew that the offspring would not be his; so it came about that when he went in to his brother's wife, he wasted his seed on the ground, in order not to give offspring to his brother. But what he did was displeasing in the sight of the Lord; so He took his life also."

One could stop right here and interpret this "literally" as meaning any man who "wasted his seed" committed a grave sin. Doing so might make this passage applicable to masturbation, coitus interruptus, or other means of birth control—or even male homosexuality. Doing so will also take this text out of its context and miss the point completely. For years this story was interpreted as referring to masturbation. (Recall from Chapter 1 that masturbation was previously called "Onania.")

Deuteronomy 25:5–6 states: "When brothers live together and one of them dies and has no son, the wife of the deceased shall not be married outside the family to a strange man. Her husband's brother shall go in to her and take her to himself as wife and perform the duty of a husband's brother to her. And it shall be that the first-born whom she bears shall assume the name of his dead brother, that his name shall not be blotted out from Israel."

Once again, one could stop here and interpret this as being just another one of those strange laws which for some reason applied to a wandering Hebrew nation, but obviously has no meaning for *our* civilization today. And just as before, this will miss the point entirely.

Even though this law seems strange now, there was good reason for it at the time. The reason is revealed in Numbers 27:8–11 where the Lord is speaking to Moses: "Further, you shall speak to the sons of Israel, saying, 'If a man dies and has no son, then you shall transfer his inheritance to his daughter. And if he has no daughter, then you shall give his inheritance to his brothers. And if he has no brothers, then you shall give his inheritance to his father's brothers. And if his father has no brothers, then you shall give his inheritance to his nearest relative in his own family, and he shall possess it; and it shall be a statutory ordinance to the sons of Israel, just as the Lord commanded Moses.' "

In those days, inheritance was based on secular law just as it is today in the absence of a will. With this understanding of the laws and the culture of the period, the story of Onan now has real meaning to us today. Onan displeased the Lord because he was selfish. As the eldest surviving son of Judah, Onan would inherit both his father's and Er's wealth if his widowed sister-in-law Tamar had no children. Understanding the cultural setting of the period makes the true message rather obvious. The sin is greed, making the passage applicable to *all* of us today. It is important to also note that even though this sin involves a sexual act, the sin itself, greed, is not sexual.

This literal-spiritual approach, taking into account the original meaning of words, will be used while analyzing The Word as it is believed to apply to homosexuality. Of course, most readers have already interpreted parts or even most of The Word, and in this case, those passages the Bible offers concerning same-sex sexual acts. The words which follow are offered to shed light, but only *you* can interpret the Bible for yourself.

The Bible on "Homosexuality"

The concept of sexual orientation did not exist in biblical times. The words used today to describe sexual orientation are products of the nineteenth century. Of course, it is not necessary to have a word for something to observe it and discuss it. As a reminder of this anachronism, every use of the words *homosexuality, bisexuality* and *heterosexuality* will be placed in quotation marks in the following analyses of Scripture. Passages in the Bible describe and discuss "homosexuality" as same-sex sexual acts. Therefore, the intended message will be found in the context, or the circumstances surrounding such an act, and not necessarily in the act itself.

How does one find passages which relate to homosexuality in the Bible? One looks in an index. This implies the passages listed do indeed comment on what we now understand as homosexuality. While an index is helpful, it should not be used as a basis for interpretation. For example, the index in the New American Standard version used for this book missed two references and mentioned one that, although actually applies to this discussion, is not at all a reference to homosexuality.

Please try to keep the above discussion in mind as we turn back our mental clocks 4,000 years, travel to the southern edge of the Dead Sea, and open our Bibles to Genesis chapters 18 and 19.

Sodom and Gomorrah

"Before they lay down, the men of the city, the men of Sodom, surrounded the house, both young and old, all the people from every quarter; and they called to Lot and said to him, 'Where are the men who came to you tonight? Bring them out to us that we might have relations with them.' " (Genesis 19:4–5)

The "men who came to you tonight" were angels sent by God to pass judgment on the people of Sodom and Gomorrah, for their sins had become very grave (Genesis 18:20–21). Lot immediately welcomed the angels as they entered the city of Sodom (Genesis 19:1–3). Sodom was a wealthy city, so its gates were locked at night to prevent free access. Lot was a resident alien in the city. For this reason, his rights were limited and his activities were closely monitored. Any of his guests would have been particularly suspect. This is especially true given that Lot's religion was so foreign to the inhabitants of Sodom.

146

Lot went out to the men of Sodom who surrounded his house and asked them not to act so wickedly toward his guests. He then offered his two virgin daughters to the crowd, presumably for sexual purposes. When the men of Sodom refused Lot's offer, the angels brought Lot back into the house and struck the men around it blind. Then they instructed Lot and his family to leave before the cities were destroyed.

The popular interpretation of this story is that both cities were destroyed because their male residents were "homosexual." This is thought to be the case because the men of the city wanted to "have relations with" the angels, and that phrase is assumed to have a sexual meaning based on Lot's offer of his virgin daughters. But this approach is much too simple. It is seriously flawed for a number of reasons and completely misses the point of the story. Yet assume for a moment that this interpretation is indeed valid.

In Chapter 18, immediately preceding the story of that night, God told Abraham that He might need to destroy the cities of Sodom and Gomorrah. Abraham pleaded with the Lord to save the city on account of its righteous citizens. The conversation concluded with the Lord saying He would not destroy Sodom if there were ten righteous inhabitants (Genesis 18:18−33). If the *sin* is "homosexuality," then the word *righteous* must be interpreted as meaning "heterosexuality." Could anyone really believe that in an entire city *all* but less than ten of the inhabitants, which would be Lot's family plus one other person, were "homosexual"? Of course, the men could have been "bisexual," making the sin any "homosexual" sexual expression of that sexual orientation. Again, assume for a moment that this slight revision of the "homosexual" interpretation is valid.

To analyze the "bisexual" version, it is necessary to leave Sodom and Gomorrah and travel to Gibeah. The story of the city of Gibeah is contained in Judges chapters 19 to 21. It is nearly identical to the story of Sodom that night with only a few differences. The visitors of the host in Gibeah were not angels, but this is not particularly relevant to the story. In Gibeah, just as in Sodom, the men of the city surrounded the house saying, "Bring out the man who came into your house that we may have relations with him." (Judges 19:22) Just as Lot had done, the host went out to the men of Gibeah and asked them not to act so wickedly toward his guests. He then offered his virgin daughter and the visitor's concubine to the crowd. The men of Gibeah refused, but the host seized the concubine anyway, sending her out to them. She was raped and abused repeatedly, and lay dead at the doorway in the morning. Chapters 20 and 21 describe how the Lord destroyed Gibeah with a civil war. If one concludes that the sin of Sodom and Gomorrah is merely the *intention* of "homosexual" sexual expression, then one must similarly conclude that the sin of Gibeah is "heterosexual" sexual expression. But would this sin be "heterosexuality" itself, or would it involve rape? Actually, a purely sexual interpretation of either story completely misses the point.

The New American Standard Version of the Bible substitutes the phrase "have relations with" for the Hebrew verb *yādhá,* which means "to know." If the sentence were translated literally it would read, "Bring them out to us, that we may know them." This is how it appears in the Revised Standard and many other versions. The request "to know" (to learn about) the visitors would have concerned Lot because the angels were there to pass judgment on the inhabitants of Sodom and Gomorrah. Another meaning of the verb *yādhá,* however, was sexual, indicating carnal knowledge. This is why the word is sometimes translated into the phrase "have [sexual] relations with." But the Hebrew verb *yādhá* is thought to be employed in a sexual context in just fifteen of its 942 Old Testament uses. (These include Genesis 4:1,17,25; 19:8; 24:16; 38:26; Numbers 31:17,18,35; Judges 11:39; 19:25; 21:11,12; 1 Samuel 1:19; and 1 Kings 1:4. 14/2&3) *None* of these fifteen passages references same-sex sexual activity. Further, Lot's offer of his virgin daughters does not necessarily indicate the men of Sodom had sexual intentions in wanting "to know" the visitors. This was probably just the most tempting offer Lot could make to appease the hostile crowd. After all, if Lot really thought the men surrounding his house were "homosexual," why would he offer a woman? Although Lot's offer is unimaginable today, it is consistent with the low status of female children at the time.

This brings up another crucial consideration. Men ran everything in those days. Only men were rulers; only men were priests; only men were angels. Every important interaction was between men. If this use of *yādhá* is indeed a reference to carnal knowledge, then it must be interpreted as an *example* of hostility in the form of rape and is only circumstantially between men. The woman in Gibeah was raped. And it is entirely possible that the men in both cities did indeed wish to rape the visitors—because rape had another use in those days. It was common for triumphant warriors to force their defeated enemy to "take the part of a woman," which meant being the passive partner during anal intercourse. This was the ultimate form of insult, humiliation and demoralization, and was used to establish proof of conquest in battle. As such, it was symbolic of domination—an expression of contempt and scorn. If the men of Sodom had intended to degrade the angels in this fashion, they would naturally have refused to accept Lot's offer of his daughters. Even if the angels had been women, the men of Sodom likely would have acted the same way. If rape was intended, this abuse was only *circumstantially* "homosexual." Yet the *sin* would still be rape, just as it was in Gibeah.

The Hebrew people, writing this story a few centuries later, would have viewed same-sex sexual aggression with disgust as a violation of the absolute dignity of the male created in God's image. If *they* thought the story had a purely sexual meaning, they would likely have used the word *shākhabh* instead of *yādhá. Shākhabh* is consistently used throughout the Old Testament to refer specifically and exclusively to sexual activity, both the "homosexual" and the "heterosexual" variety. Its use would have left no doubt. Yet they chose to use the Hebrew word *yādhá.* This word, which is spelled "YD" in ancient Hebrew, has another meaning which was only recently discovered and is completely consistent with the story of Sodom and Gomorrah. It also means "to tame" or "to quiet."

Once again, it is necessary to leave Sodom and Gomorrah to understand this. The story of Sampson and Delilah is given in Judges chapter 16. Delilah has been offered a large sum of money by the Philistines to help them overpower Sampson. Verse 16:9 ends: "So his strength was not discovered." The word *yādhá* here was translated as "discovered," a form of knowledge. But strength cannot be known. The Revised Standard Version states, "So the secret of his strength was not known." By adding the word *secret,* the sentence makes sense but is still not very meaningful. The New English Bible more appropriately states, "And his strength was not tamed."

When this translation is used for the story of Sodom and Gomorrah, the meaning is more clear: "Bring them out to us that we might quiet (or tame) them." Had the men simply wanted "to know" (to learn about) the angels, Lot may have been concerned, but not terribly so. By stating their intentions from the outset as wanting to "quiet" the angels, Lot was properly concerned. The form of this "quieting" may have been sexual, specifically rape, but the *form* of a sin is not its essence. Recall the story of Onan where the sin was greed, not "wasting seed." The men surrounding Lot's house were hostile toward the angelic visitors. Hostility was their sin that night — and it was only symbolic of their many sins.

The two angels were sent by God to pass judgment for the many sins which had *already* occurred. Sodom and Gomorrah were located on a fertile plain near the Jordan River. The area now lies under the southern portion of the Dead Sea. God had given the inhabitants of the area great prosperity, yet they turned away from Him becoming corrupt and greedy, and did not share their wealth with neighbors or travelers. This was particularly important in those days when there were no hotels. Travelers, including the Hebrew nation, were dependent on the hospitality of cities along their route, not only for comfort but for survival. Lot's very salvation was indeed his hospitality toward the angelic visitors (Genesis 19:1–3 and Second Peter 2:6–8).

Had Lot actually turned over his virgin daughters to these men, could anyone honestly believe the Lord would have spared Sodom and Gomorrah? Of course not. Did God spare Gibeah? Hardly. Genesis 19:30–38 reveals the story of how Lot's daughters got him drunk, had sex with him, and bore a son each to preserve the family name. Would God have destroyed two cities for their "homosexuality" just to have the survivors commit incest? Unlikely. Had the angelic visitors been female, would the popular interpretation be different? Probably. Would the sins of Sodom and Gomorrah be any different? Definitely not.

The sins of Sodom and Gomorrah are mentioned throughout the Bible. Some of these references will be cited later in the section on the New Testament. For your own study, the others include: Deuteronomy 32:32; Isaiah 1:9–20, 3:8–9 and 13:19; Jeremiah 49:18 and 50:38–40; Lamentations 4:6; Amos 4:11; and Zephaniah 2:9. Not *one* of these numerous references mentions, either explicitly or implicitly, same-sex sexual acts as the sin of Sodom and Gomorrah. However, the real sins *are* explicitly mentioned. The Reverend Sylvia Pennington counted seventy sins that were specified in both the Old and New Testaments. The only purely sexual sin listed is adultery. These references, which indicate the meaning at the time, are the best and most reliable guide to interpreting the story of Sodom and Gomorrah. Conversely, *none* of the other passages found elsewhere in the Bible, which are commonly believed to address "homosexuality," mentions Sodom or Gomorrah at all. Such a reference, at least once, would seem rather obvious if the real sin were indeed sexual, specifically "homosexual."

The incident with the angels that night was not the cause but merely the occasion of God's judgment. The story of Sodom and Gomorrah is not about homosexuality.

Leviticus: The Holiness Code

The Levites, members of the tribe of Levi, were chosen to assist Jewish priests (Numbers chapters 3 and 8). The laws found in Leviticus are religious in nature and pertain to the Levites. Israel's criminal laws or secular are found in the Book of the Covenant in Exodus verses 20:22 through 23:33, and in Deuteronomy chapters 12 through 26. In the criminal laws, there is no mention of same-sex sexual acts. The Holiness Code, however, which is found in Leviticus chapters 17 through 26, does mention same-sex sexual acts. The Holiness Code prohibits many things, including coitus during menstruation (18:19 and 20:18), garments made of blended fabric (19:19), trimming beards (19:27 and 21:5), tattoos (19:28), taking wives who are widowed, divorced, or prostitutes (21:14), and accepting offerings from people with "defects" (21:17–20). It also contains a number of requirements, most notably the "eye for an eye, tooth for a tooth" form of punishment (24:19–20). When the priesthood changed, the laws could also change (Hebrews 7:11–12). This might explain why some of the laws are repeated.

Our current society ignores most of these laws. While some of them may seem rather odd today, there were very good reasons for them in another time and another place. This is especially true for the laws against same-sex sexual acts:

"You shall not lie with a male as one lies with a female; it is an abomination." (Leviticus 18:22)

"If there is a man who lies with a male as those who lie with a woman, both of them have committed a detestable act; they shall surely be put to death. Their bloodguiltiness is upon them." (Leviticus 20:13)

As the Jews wandered throughout the region, they would come upon other nations and be exposed to foreign cultures. The Jews adopted the language of the Canaanites. No harm done. They were even considered descendants of the Canaanites. Once again, no harm done. However, when the Jews entered a new land, the people around them normally did not practice the same religion. The potential for harm then was great:

"When the Lord your God cuts off before you the nations which you are going in to dispossess, and you dispossess them and dwell in their land, beware that you are not ensnared to follow them, after they are destroyed before you, and that you do not inquire after their gods, saying,

'How do these nations serve their gods, that I may do likewise?' You shall not behave thus toward the Lord your God, for every abominable act which the Lord hates they have done for their gods; for they even burn their sons and daughters in fire to their gods. Whatever I command you, you shall be careful to do; you shall not add to nor take away from it." (Deuteronomy 12:29–32)

What are these "abominable" acts? Just as people today worship God through the study of Scripture, prayer, communion, fellowship, and song, the Canaanites worshiped their gods—but they did so through molten images of silver or gold, burnt offerings, witchcraft, spirits, and *sexual acts* (Deuteronomy 18:9–12). The Canaanites believed their gods were sexual and could be worshiped through sexual acts. This practice is referred to as cult prostitution. The various gods and goddesses were represented by male and female cult prostitutes respectively. Men would "worship" through sexual acts with both male and female cult prostitutes. In other words, "worship services" were both "homosexual" and "heterosexual." The most important deity represented fertility, in this sense applying to agriculture, not to human reproduction. Because there was no understanding of weather in those days, a flood or a drought was thought to represent the displeasure of a fertility god. Further, the Canaanites had no technology to store food for years and their government did not subsidize overproduction of crops as we do today. So fertility quite literally meant survival.

The fertility cult of Asheroth and Baal, a goddess and god couple, flourished among the Canaanites. Some of the Jews started to worship Baal and Asheroth and other like gods or goddesses as mentioned in Numbers 25:1–9, Deuteronomy 4:3, Judges 2:11–12, and Judges 3:5–8.

Cult prostitution, especially between men, would have seemed quite odd to the Hebrew people. They would need to be warned against this form of idolatrous worship. The religious nature of cult prostitution would explain why these two prohibitions against same-sex sexual acts were not mentioned in the criminal laws for Israel contained in Exodus and Deuteronomy, but were instead mentioned in the Holiness Code. For example, between the two "homosexual" passages, in Leviticus 19:4, the Lord spoke to Moses, again saying, "Do not turn to idols or make for yourselves molten gods; I am the Lord your God." Fertility itself is specifically addressed in the context of idolatry in the final chapter of the Holiness Code: "You shall not make for yourselves idols, nor shall you set up for yourselves an image or a sacred pillar, nor shall you place a figured stone in your land and bow down to it; for I am the Lord your God. You shall keep My Sabbaths and reverence My sanctuary; I am the Lord. If you walk in My statutes and keep My commandments so as to carry them out, then I shall give you rains in their season, so the land will yield its produce and the trees of the field will bear their fruit." (Leviticus 26:1–4)

Idolatry is undoubtedly the worst possible sin. In fact, the very first commandment of the Ten Commandments prohibits idolatry (Exodus 20:1–6). Cult prostitution is specifically addressed: " 'You shall not make other gods besides Me; gods of silver or gods of gold, you shall not make for yourselves ... And you shall not go up by steps to My alter, that your nakedness may not be exposed on it.'" (Exodus 20:23–26) "Exposing nakedness" is a euphemism referring here to sexual activity. And in Exodus 34:11–16 God warns His followers not to "play the harlot" with other gods.

Considering the serious consequences of idolatrous worship, it would actually be more surprising if the book of Leviticus did *not* address cult prostitution. Think about it.

For your own study, here is a list of other Old Testament references to cult prostitution: Leviticus 18:30; Deuteronomy 13:12–15, 23:17–18 and 31:16; 1 Kings 14:24, 15:12 and 22:41–53; 2 Kings 17:7–23 and 23:7; Job 36:14; Jeremiah 2:20; Ezekiel 16:17, 20:7 and 20:30–31; Hosea 4:14; and Micah 1:7.

In both of the same-sex passages from Leviticus, the Hebrew word *to'ebah* (sometimes spelled *to'evah* or *to'ebhah),* translated as "abomination," refers to a *detestable idolatrous practice.* If verse 18:22 is read again with this more specific translation, an entirely different meaning is obtained: "You shall not lie with a male as one lies with a female; it is a detestable idolatrous practice." This translation may not be as eloquent, but it is certainly more accurate. Homosexuality, as we know it today, is clearly not this kind of worship. While there are likely no modern religions which still practice cult prostitution as a form of worship, the message here is still the same: God is our Lord and Savior, and there are appropriate ways to worship Him.

If it were the intention of the author of Leviticus to prohibit *all* forms of same-sex sexual expression, the Hebrew words *shākhabh*, which meant sexual intercourse, or *zimah*, denoting secular prostitution, could have been used here, too, just as it could have been used in the story of Sodom and Gomorrah. Instead, the word *to'ebah* was properly chosen to describe the real sin: idolatry. Leviticus does not comment on homosexuality.

Sodom and Gomorrah Revisited

Sodom was a Canaanite city. Sodom's prosperity was dependent on its fertility. The residents worshiped false gods, making idolatry one of their most grievous sins. Because the people of Sodom had their own gods, they would have had no need for God and could demonstrate this by their hostility toward the angelic visitors. One of the differences between Gibeah and Sodom was that the visitors to Gibeah were not angelic. Another difference is that Jewish people inhabited Gibeah. Gibeah's sins did not necessarily include idolatry, for the Jews already worshiped God—in appropriate ways. The Hebrew word *to'ebah,* designating the abomination of idolatry, is used in the following passage from Ezekiel 16:49–50: "Behold, this was the guilt of your sister Sodom: she and her daughters had arrogance, abundant food, and careless ease, but she did not help the poor and needy. Thus they were haughty and committed abominations before Me. Therefore I removed them when I saw it." In other words, they "committed detestable idolatrous practices before Me." (See also Deuteronomy 29:23–26 and Jeremiah 23:13–14.)

Around the third or second century B.C., the story of Sodom and Gomorrah started taking on more of a sexual meaning. This began the process of associating *all* the sins of Sodom and Gomorrah with sexuality. Later, they would be associated with "homosexuality." The Septuagint translation of the Old Testament Hebrew into Greek was made during this time. The Hebrew word *kedshim* (sometimes spelled *kadeshim, gedhshim,* or *gādshim*), referring to male cult prostitutes, appears in the following passages from the Old Testament: Deuteronomy 23:17–18; I Kings 14:24, 15:11–12, 22:43–46; II Kings 23:7; Job 36:14; and Hosea 4:14. This single Hebrew word was translated into six different Greek words in the Septuagint, demonstrating the confusion about whether the sin was sexual or spiritual. Today, versions of the Bible translate the word *kedshim* as "sodomites" in some of these passages and as "cult prostitutes" in others. In each case, "sodomite" does *not* refer to homosexuality; it refers to cult prostitution. Therefore, the sin involved is not sexual. It is spiritual, specifically: idolatry.

The New Testament

One method Christians use to interpret the Old Testament is through the teachings in the New Testament. (Jewish readers might still wish to read this section, for it offers some additional understanding of the history and culture of the period.) We now must turn our mental clocks ahead from the second millennium B.C.) to the first century A.D. and travel to Rome. The Greco-Roman culture dominated the northern region of the Mediterranean. Throughout this area, same-sex sexual activity was common in four different forms. The first was pederasty. Greco-Roman pederasty involved an older male who imparted wisdom and gave gifts to a younger male in exchange for companionship. The typical ages of the "man" and the "youth" are difficult to establish from artifacts of the period, and the ideal model of pederasty was platonic. Still, sexual favors were certainly an aspect of the companionship in many such arrangements. This pederasty might seem odd, even scandalous by today's standards, but it was socially acceptable behavior at the time.

The second type of same-sex sexual activity was male prostitution involving male patrons. Male prostitutes generally were held in disrespect, but not in contempt. Most of them already held a low social status. The young men were not boys. In fact, the rape or sexual abuse of minors was severely punished at the time. Prostitution, by contrast, was so popular then that it was taxed, and a national holiday was held for male prostitutes.

In contrast to the voluntary relationships described above, the third type of same-sex sexual activity involved slavery. Slavery was fairly common at the time, and many slaves were forced into prostitution by their owners. Some of the young men were even castrated to preserve their youthful appearance.

153

The fourth and final type of same-sex sexual activity could be considered what we now understand to be homosexuality: the consistent, predominant or exclusive, emotional and erotic attraction to persons of the same gender. But it would be inappropriate to refer to any of the first three as "homosexuality" for two reasons. First, most of the men who practiced these acts were married. Therefore, a more correct description would be "bisexuality," even though this is not accurate in all cases either. Second, the modern model of homosexuality excludes (stereotypes aside) the three other varieties. Today, our culture abhors pederasty; prostitution is mostly illegal (whether it's gay or straight is only incidental); and slavery, at least for the past one hundred plus years, is considered inhumane.

Once again we must turn back our mental clocks. Consider that we do not have the understanding of human sexuality that we now have; we were Jews and have since accepted Christ as our savior; and in the preceding two centuries, our Hebrew interpretation of the story of Sodom and Gomorrah had started taking on a purely sexual meaning. The Gentiles of the Greco-Roman region do not recognize God. Their religions are very different from ours, and they worship other gods. They also appear to do the same things the Canaanites did sexually. What conclusion might we draw from all this? We would undoubtedly draw the exact same conclusion the early Christians did: idolatry.

A Christian Visit to Sodom and Gomorrah

A full understanding of Sodom and Gomorrah requires one more visit—this time by Christians. Of all the references to these ancient twin cities in the Bible, only two, both in the New Testament (2 Peter 2:4–19 and Jude 7–8), mention the sinful act that night as having a sexual aspect. But even in these, the sin itself is unmistakenly idolatrous. In both, the authority of God is rejected by reviling the angelic visitors.

Take Jude 7–8 for example: "Just as Sodom and Gomorrah and the cities around them, since they in the same way as these indulged in gross immorality and went after strange flesh, are exhibited as an example, in undergoing the punishment of eternal fire. Yet in the same manner these men, also by dreaming, defile the flesh, and reject authority, and revile angelic majesties." The phrase "gross immorality" comes from the Greek word *ekcorneia. Ek* is a prefix denoting completion. The suffix *corneia* literally means to indulge in unlawful lust, which is made unlawful because of its association with *idolatry. Corneia* is used thirty-one other times in the New Testament in reference to unlawful "heterosexual" *idolatrous* lust. The "strange flesh" is referring to angels, not to the fact it was *men* who sought to degrade other men through alleged rape. Ironically, the Greek word for strange used here is *hetera,* meaning different or other. Additional passages which support this merger of sexuality with idolatry include Colossians 3:2–5, 1 Peter 4:3, and Revelations 22:15.

Jesus also commented on the sins of Sodom and Gomorrah. He was, of course, able to keep the proper perspective on the real sins: "And whoever does not receive you, nor heed your words, as you go out of that house or that city, shake off the dust of your feet. Truly I say to you, it will be more tolerable for the land of Sodom and Gomorrah in the day of judgment, than for that city." (Matthew 10:14 – 15) "But whatever city you enter and they do not receive you, go out into its streets and say, 'Even the dust of your city which clings to our feet, we wipe off in protest against you; yet be sure of this, that the kingdom of God has come near.' I say to you, it will be more tolerable in that day for Sodom, than for that city." (Luke 10:10 – 13) These are really the same quotation. The differences involve its recollection and translation from Aramaic to Greek. By His use of the word *receive*, it does not matter in this discussion whether Jesus is referring to hospitality toward individuals, or as acceptance of His disciples and Christianity. In either event, neither interpretation is sexual or "homosexual."

For your own study, here are the other passages in the New Testament which refer to Sodom and Gomorrah: Matthew 11:23 – 24, Luke 17:28 – 29, Romans 9:29, and Revelations 11:8.

The Apostle Paul

Paul is the only New Testament author to comment on what is now believed to be homosexuality. Paul's books in the Bible are actually his letters to others giving advice on specific problems facing establishment of the early Christian church. That is not to say his messages do not apply to us today; it is mentioned merely to point out the context of Paul's teachings.

In the context of context, an important influence on Paul's belief system must be considered. The philosophy of stoicism was popular in the first two centuries A.D. Recall from the discussion in Chapter 6 on "The History of 'Nature' " that the fundamental axiom of stoicism was to "live according to nature." The Stoics were characterized by an indifference to passion or feelings, pleasure or pain. Stoicism maintained that God was "reason." Reason was equated to nature and given definite biological application. The "reason" for male-female sexuality, naturally, was procreation — period. Pleasure, including sexual pleasure, was out. Because no consideration was given to sexual orientation at the time, the only "reasons" for same-sex sexual acts were thought to be either idolatrous practices or a lustful extension of the "heterosexual" sexual desire.

The Stoic philosophy of this period had a definite influence on what is believed to be the earliest existing *purely* sexual, specifically "homosexual," interpretation of the story of Sodom. Stoic philosopher Philo of Alexandria, living from 13 B.C. to 50 A.D., wrote in his work *De Abrahamo*:

> The land of the Sodomites was brimful of innumerable iniquities, particularly such as arise from gluttony and lewdness . . . The

155

inhabitants owed this extreme license to the never-failing lavishness of their sources of wealth ... Incapable of bearing such satiety ... they threw off from their necks the law of nature, and applied themselves to deep drinking of strong liquor and dainty feeding and forbidden forms of intercourse. Not only in their mad lust for women did they violate the marriages of their neighbors, but also men mounted males without respect for the sex nature which the active partner shares with the passive, and so when they tried to beget children they were discovered to be incapable of any but a sterile seed. Yet the discovery availed them not, so much stronger was the force of their lust which mastered them, as little by little they accustomed those who were by nature men to play the part of women, they saddled them with formidable curse of a female disease. For not only did they emasculate their bodies, but they worked a further degeneration in their souls, and, so far as in them lay, were corrupting the whole of mankind.

Apparently, Philo was ahead of his time: His claims were similar to many of the homophobic ones made today. His lack of any real understanding of human sexuality is demonstrated by the belief that male-male intercourse was not procreative owing to "sterile seed." Semen was actually thought to be "life," as the woman's full role in reproduction was unknown. The "forbidden forms of intercourse" were thought to signify idolatrous worship, but this does not seem to concern Philo a great deal.

Paul was influenced similarly by stoicism. His teachings indicate he agreed with Philo's view of Sodom, although Paul did not lose sight of the idolatrous nature of the sins of Sodom. He held an extremely negative opinion of *any* sexual activity and advocated that very little, even none, should be practiced. Paul himself was celibate. He felt the world was coming to an end soon, and that there was therefore no *reason* to procreate. Paul discussed marriage in 1 Corinthians chapter 7. In verses 7–9 he commented on chastity: "Yet I wish that all men were even as I myself am. However, each man has his own gift from God, one in this manner, and another in that. But I say to the unmarried and to widows that it is good for them to remain even as I. But if they do not have self-control, let them marry; for it is better to marry than to burn." The word *burn* means to burn in one's heart with desire rather than to burn in eternity. In the same chapter, verse 29 Paul stated, "But this I say, brethren, the time has been shortened, so that from now on those who have wives should be as though they had none ..."

Paul was also influenced by the Greek spiritual dualism which maintains that a pure love for God requires abandoning earthly loves. This is likely the foundation for his tendency to associate sexuality with idolatry. Such a spiritual dualism is evident in the following passage:

"But I say, walk by the Spirit, and you will not carry out the desire of the flesh. For the flesh sets its desire against the Spirit, and the Spirit against the flesh; for these are in opposition to one another, so that you may not do the things that you please. But if you are led by the Spirit, you are not under the Law. Now the deeds of the flesh are evident, which are: immorality, impurity, sensuality, idolatry, sorcery, enmities, strife, jealousy, outbursts of anger, disputes, dissensions, factions, envying, drunkenness, carousing, and things like these of which I forewarn you just as I have forewarned you that those who practice such things shall not inherit the kingdom of God." (Galatians 5:16–21)

Paul made similar comments in 1 Corinthians 6:15–17 and in 1 Thessalonians 4:3–8.

These influences are important because Paul would frequently speak to his own opinions in the Bible, sometimes making a distinction between his views and *His* views. For example, in 2 Corinthians 11:17 Paul stated, "That which I am speaking, I am not speaking as the Lord would, but as in foolishness, in this confidence of boasting. Since many of you boast according to the flesh, I will also boast." Similarly, in 1 Corinthians 7:25 Paul commented, "Now concerning virgins I have no command of the Lord, but I give an opinion as one who by the mercy of the Lord is trustworthy."

Although Paul felt the acceptance of Christ released Christians from the Law, he believed it was important for the Gentiles to learn the Hebrew laws and traditions found in the Septuagint, the Old Testament of the time. This is explained in Galatians 3:15–29. Paul was obviously concerned about the Gentiles being led away from God. Owing to his Jewish background, he too would have identified any same-sex sexual activity with idolatry. The possibility of such an act being out of love or mutual consent, based on a sexual orientation, would not have occurred to Paul. With this characterization of Paul, the man, his lessons to the Gentiles are better understood in their proper context.

Paul's Message to the Romans

"For this reason God gave them over to degrading passions; for their women exchanged the natural function for that which is unnatural, and in the same way also the men abandoned the natural function of the woman and burned in their desire toward one another, men with men committing indecent acts and receiving in their own persons the due penalty of their error." (Romans 1:26–27)

Paul's use of the words *natural* and *function,* in reference to procreation as the "reason" for sexual activity, clearly demonstrates the influence of Stoic philosophy on his thinking. Paul's use of "exchanged" (*metllaxan*) for women and "abandoned" (*aphentes*) for men is interesting, especially since there was no "homosexuality" or "heterosexuality" in those days. Many people interpret both as meaning the same thing because they are connected by the phrase "and in the same way." As such, they feel Paul is speaking about same-sex sexual acts for both men and women. The phrase "and in the same way," however, could connect references to prostitution, with men being the active partner for *both* male and female prostitutes. In this sense, the women "*exchanged* the natural function" of child-bearing for that of prostitution, and the men "*abandoned* the natural function of the women" by using other men as sexual partners. Even though female same-sex sexuality did exist then, women

157

were not considered to be "sexual." The view of sexuality at the time maintained the need for both an active and a passive partner. With this limited view, it is difficult to imagine how a woman could be "active" without a penis. Had Paul used these words in reverse, stating the men "*exchanged* the natural function" from active to passive partner, and the women "*abandoned* the natural function of the man," or gave up the active partner, then there would be no doubt that this passage applies directly and exclusively to both male and female same-sex sexual acts. But he did not. It is reasonable to conclude, therefore, that Paul is speaking here of female "heterosexual" prostitution and male "homosexual" prostitution. The operative word in both is *prostitution* — idolatrous cult prostitution.

In chapters 1 through 3 of Romans, Paul is asserting that everyone needs the grace of God and should recognize God's sovereignty and holiness. Instead, some people foolishly chose to worship idols. The passages immediately preceding the reference to "homosexuality" in Romans 1:26 – 27 establish the context of idolatry: "For even though they knew God, they did not honor Him as God, or give thanks; but they became futile in their speculations, and their foolish heart was darkened. Professing to be wise, they became fools, and exchanged the glory of the incorruptible God for an image in the form of corruptible man and of birds and four-footed animals and crawling creatures. Therefore, God gave them over in the lusts of their hearts to impurity, that their bodies might be dishonored among them. For they exchanged the truth of God for a lie, and worshiped and served the creature rather than the Creator, who is blessed forever. Amen." (Romans 1:21 – 25)

Paul felt the same-sex lust was God's judgment for the idolatry of those who "worshiped and served the creature." Lust goes well beyond the basic emotional and erotic attraction that characterizes any sexual orientation, carrying it to a self-destructive extreme, in the much same way obsession goes beyond opinion. He wrote: "And just as they did not see fit to acknowledge God any longer, God gave them over to a depraved mind, to do those things which are not proper, being filled with an unrighteousness, wickedness, greed, evil; full of envy, murder, strife, deceit, malice; they are gossips, slanderers, haters of God, insolent, arrogant, boastful, inventors of evil, disobedient to parents, without understanding, untrustworthy, unloving, unmerciful; and, although they know the ordinance of God, that those who practice such things are worthy of death, they not only do the same, but also give hearty approval to those who practice them." (Romans 1:28 – 32)

How many parents have punished crying children by saying, "I'll give you something to cry about," and then giving a good spanking? Crying was not the problem; it was a symptom of some other problem like selfishness or stubbornness. Is God punishing idolatry with homosexuality? No, "degrading passions" and "depraved minds" go well beyond sexual orientation. But the *form* of this punishment was indeed related to the sin of idolatrous cult prostitution.

These verses have been used inappropriately to condemn "homosexual" people for centuries. Yet God does not want His children to judge each other in this way, for that duty is exclusively His. Ironically, Paul's next message cautions against passing this form of judgment: "Therefore you are without excuse, every man of you who passes judgment, for in that you judge another, you condemn yourself; for you who judge practice the same things. And we know that the judgment of God rightly falls on those who practice such things. And do you suppose this, O man, when you pass judgment upon those who practice such things and do the same yourself, that you will escape the judgment of God?" (Romans 2:1–3) Does the phrase "for you who judge practice the same things" mean that judging others is just another form of idolatry?

Paul's Message to the Corinthians and the Ephesians

Paul's message to the residents of the Greek city of Corinth is contained in the two books of Corinthians. In 1 Corinthians 6:9–10 he stated: "Or do you not know that the unrighteous shall not inherit the kingdom of God? Do not be deceived; neither fornicators, nor idolaters, nor adulterers, nor effeminate, nor homosexuals, nor thieves, nor the covetous, nor drunkards, nor revilers, nor swindlers, shall inherit the kingdom of God."

A very similar passage appears in 1 Timothy 1:8–11: "But we know that the Law is good, if one uses it lawfully, realizing the fact that law is not made for a righteous man, but for those who are lawless and rebellious, for the ungodly and sinners, for the unholy and profane, for those who kill their fathers or mothers, for murderers and immoral men and homosexuals and kidnappers and liars and perjurers and whatever else is contrary to sound teaching, according to the glorious gospel of the blessed God, with which I have been entrusted."

(Most biblical scholars now believe 1 Timothy was written after Paul's death. The above passage is included in this discussion of Paul because it was likely based on the one he did write in 1 Corinthians.)

The use of the word *homosexuals* in both passages is clearly anachronistic, but this does not necessarily mean its use is inaccurate. The word *effeminate* is vague at best, and has also been construed to mean homosexuality — based on the stereotypes, of course. Paul may well have intended to include "homosexuality" in this catalog of vices, but this is not clearly indicated in the words he chose to use. The word *homosexuals* comes from the Greek word *àrsenokoitais* (sometimes spelled *àrsenokoitai* or *àrsenokoites*). The word *effeminate* comes from the Greek word *malakois* (sometimes spelled *malakós*). Both words are very obscure. Biblical scholars and theologians are still greatly divided on how to translate each.

The Reverend Sylvia Pennington looked up the translation of these two words in sixteen different versions of the Bible. What the New American Standard version translates as "effeminate" in the verse from 1 Corinthians, some other versions called: weakling, wanton, voluptuous, catamites, and male prostitutes. What appears above in both passages as "homosexuals," some others termed: abusers of themselves with men; them that defile themselves with mankind; bouggerers; liers with mankind;

perverts; sexual perverts; sodomites; homosexual offenders; homosexual perverts; and finally, immoral with women, boys, or men. In a few versions, both words in 1 Corinthians were combined to yield: sexual perverts, homosexual perversion, homosexual pervert, and homosexual. Obviously, these two words do not *clearly* mean anything. The immediate context is of no real value either in determining what is meant. In 1 Timothy reference is made to the laws in the Old Testament where cult prostitution is strongly prohibited. Because idolatry is not explicitly mentioned, it may have been implied by the Greek words *malakóis* and *ársenokoitais*.

Throughout 1 Corinthians, Paul spoke on the divisions and the difficulties in the early church. He was undoubtedly concerned about this, especially given his belief in Greek spiritual dualism. Yet in verse 6:10 he specifically mentioned idolatry, and still refers to *ársenokoitais*. Does this mean *malakóis* should be interpreted as idolatry? Possibly. A few passages later, Paul discussed sexual idolatry in the context of dualism: "Do you not know that your bodies are members of Christ? Shall I then take away the members of Christ and make them members of a harlot? May it never be! Or do you not know that the one who joins himself to a harlot is one body with her? For He says, 'The two will become one flesh.' But the one who joins himself to the Lord is one spirit with Him." (1 Corinthians 6:15–17)

The Greek word *malakóis* literally means "soft." This is how it is translated in Matthew 11:8 and Luke 7:25. Both are references to the type of clothing worn by royalty. This word is also used in Matthew 4:23, 9:35, and 10:1 to denote sickness. It had a variety of other meanings as well, including weak, cowardly, weak-willed, refined, delicate, gentle, liquid, and debauched. In a moral context it meant licentious, loose, or wanting in self-control. Aristotle specifically stated his use of the word to mean "Unrestrained with respect to bodily pleasures." Considering the influence of stoicism and Paul's very negative view of sexual pleasure, this is likely what he meant as well. Not one of these meanings indicates "homosexuality."

In seventeenth-century England when the King James Version was translated, the word *effeminate* meant self-indulgent or voluptuous. This is consistent with Paul's use, but is inconsistent with how our society defines *effeminate* today. In effect, the word stuck while its meaning changed. Therefore, the current translations of wanton or voluptuous appear to be the most accurate. Although gay people, just like straight people, *can* be wanton or voluptuous, these words should not be construed as *meaning* homosexuality any more than they should be construed as *meaning* heterosexuality.

The meaning of the Greek word *ársenokoitais* is even more difficult to ascertain because it did not appear in Greek literature before the Pauline texts. The word is used in a second-century A.D. Greek work, where the context seems to indicate it means "an obsessive corrupter of boys." This could be a reference to what our culture calls *pederasts*. But it is also used later in the sixth century to designate a specific type of sexual activity, most likely anal intercourse. Of course, anal inter-

160

course is not exclusively homosexual, as this latter work comments: "And many even practiced the vice of *ársenokoitais* with their wives." This sentence makes no sense if you substitute the word *homosexuality*. The book of Orthodox Canons calls for more severe punishment when a man engages in *ársenokoitais* with a strange woman than when he does so with another man. And the penalty was harsher still when the woman was his wife.

When *ársenokoitais* is broken into its component parts, some insight is obtained. The suffix *koitais* is a vague word generally denoting base or licentious behavior. The prefix *árseno* simply means male. Putting these components together yields the result "male licentious behavior." What *specifically* does that mean though? The King James Version translates *ársenokoitais* as "them that defile themselves with mankind." This is even more confusing. It sounds terrible, but just what does it mean? Think about this phrase for a moment. It is likely Paul wanted to express what the word literally means: "Male licentious behavior," a disregard for sexual restraints. Considering his dim view of sexuality in general and his belief in Greek spiritual dualism, this is the probable interpretation. But "male licentious behavior" does not mean homosexuality. Straight men can be licentious with women just as gay men can be licentious with other men.

In effect, then, both words really mean the same thing—literally. Figuratively, they could both refer to male prostitution and, therefore, idolatrous practices. This helps explain why Paul used only one of them in 1 Timothy but raises the question: Why did he use both in 1 Corinthians? Possibly he was referring to women with the use of *malakóis* and to men with the use of *ársenokoitais*. But women were not thought to be "sexual" in Paul's day. So what does all fo this have to do with homosexuality? Nothing—and that's the point.

A similar statement to Paul's was made by Jesus in Matthew 15:19: "For out of the heart come evil thoughts, murders, adulteries, fornications, thefts, false witness, slanders." Jesus makes no reference to "homosexuals" or "effeminates." Even Paul, in some of his other catalogs of vices, makes no mention of *malakóis* or *ársenokoitais* or any other Greek word that might have involved same-sex sexuality. (See Romans 13:13, 1 Corinthians 5:10–11, 2 Corinthians 12:20–21, and Galatians 5:19–21.)

If Paul really meant to condemn *all* same-sex sexual acts, independently of any sins, he could have done so. Just as he was familiar with male same-sex sexual practices, he was undoubtedly familiar with the words used then to describe them at the time: *árrenomanes, kínaidos* and *pallakós*. There were also words which could have been used, especially in Romans 1:26, in reference to female same-sex sexuality: *tribades* and *hetairistriai*. These words were all regularly used in other literature of the period to refer to what is currently understood to be homosexuality. They were all available to Paul. Yet he chose not to use any of them.

The fact is, Paul does not address homosexuality. This is not to say, given his views on sexuality in general, that he would have "approved." But this *does* mean that it is both inaccurate and irresponsible to misconstrue Paul's words as meaning anything more than he intended. Paul's beliefs were influenced by stoicism and based on Greek spiritual dualism. Yet we know that men and women, straight and gay, can be both spiritual *and* sexual. In other word's, today's homosexuality is not yesterday's idolatry. Paul was simply surrounded by a culture that valued pederasty, celebrated prostitution, condoned sexual slavery, and, above all, practiced idolatry. It is about these things that Paul speaks, and not of loving same-sex relationships.

Biblical Silence on Homosexuality

> It ain't necessarily so —
> The things that you're liable
> To read in the Bible —
> It ain't necessarily so.
> *Ira Gershwin*

From the above discussion it should be apparent that the Bible is actually silent on the topic of homosexuality, especially when interpreted literally. There are many things which are not discussed in the Bible, but what is important is discussed. Homosexuality is *not* prohibited in the Ten Commandments. Idolatry is. If homosexuality were really such a heinous sin, one that would encompass ten percent of the population, this biblical "no comment" would at least be a serious omission. Jesus never spoke on the topic of homosexuality; no dominical commands concerning same-sex sexual acts or feelings are found in the Bible. For all the association of homosexuality with evil, isn't it at least curious that Jesus was silent on this topic?

The fact that homosexuality was not understood as a sexual orientation during biblical times would *not* have prevented the various authors from discussing it independently of other considerations. There exists in other literature of the period's words which could have been used but were not.

The simple fact is that every single reference to same-sex sexual acts in the Bible is in the context of hostile rape, possibly; "excess lust," likely; adultery, probably; and idolatry, definitely. Yet this overriding context is regularly ignored. Just as in the story of Onan, a sin which *involves* a sexual act does not make the sin itself sexual. Of course, every one of these evils is also mentioned in the Bible, including sexual idolatry, in the context of heterosexuality. But such acts have never been labeled sinful *because* of heterosexuality. Applying these passages to homosexuality extends their meaning well beyond their intent.

Yet most churches ignore the real sins and hold fast to a view of homosexuality as an unforgivable sin to be condemned beyond all hope of salvation. Homosexuality is thought to represent Satan's strongest grip on people. This impression is made even worse by a belief that gay people seem totally unaware of their "demonic possession." Instead of feeling grief and shame, they appear happy and indignant. Of course, this belief equates being saved to being "cured." In effect, the church merely continues to condemn homosexuality today as a matter of Judeo-Christian tradition, without ever considering the history of this tradition. That is the next topic.

Chapter 10

Judeo-Christian Tradition

A precedent embalms a principle. *Benjamin Disraeli*

In *Homosexuality and the Western Christian Tradition,* Dr. Derrick Bailey stated: "It is clearly of the utmost importance that those who are charged with the administration of the law, those who are being pressed to make changes therein, and all who are concerned with the well-being of society and the maintenance of moral standards, should understand how the Western attitude to homosexual practices originated and developed." That attitude is homophobia, and this chapter explores its origin and development in the church and society during the Middle Ages.

The same Bible we read today was not always so "obvious" on its condemnation of same-sex sexuality. (Again, use of the word *homosexuality,* is intentionally avoided, as such use would be anachronistic.) The Middle Ages is that period of European history from roughly 500 to 1500 A.D. Until its beginning and for the first seven centuries of this millennium, same-sex sexual acts were tolerated, even celebrated. Virtually none of the laws through 1250 even mentioned same-sex sexual acts, while other sexual crimes including fornication, adultery, and abortion were prohibited. From 1250 to 1300, same-sex sexual activity went from being completely legal in most of Europe to being punishable by death in all but a few locations. Also by 1300, nearly all "homosexual" literature had disappeared. Why did this happen? There were two related movements at this time, the Crusades and the Inquisition, both of which dramatically altered the way same-sex sexuality would be viewed for centuries to come.

The Dawn of Homophobia

We have just enough religion to make us hate but not enough to make us love one another. *Jonathan Swift*

The original intention of the crusades was to free the Holy Land after it had been conquered by Turkish invaders. The Turks, siding with the Muslims, threatened to invade the Byzantine Empire, which is now Greece and Turkey. Pope Urban II launched the first crusade in 1096. Some 30,000 participants set out from the middle of Europe for the Holy Land. They finally reached their destination two years later, many dying along the way from disease and starvation. In 1099 the Turks and Muslims were defeated, but the Holy Land was not simply liberated. Instead it was settled by these Europeans. Eventually, the Muslims defeated the new settlers and returned to control the Holy Land. During the next 400 years there were dozens of other crusades throughout Europe, the northern Mediterranean coast, and the Holy Land. Some were major efforts; others were relatively insignificant. Individual crusaders were motivated to participate by a combination of religious, economic, and political reasons. The younger sons of feudal lords could not expect to inherit wealth; they viewed the crusades as an opportunity for power and riches. For the peasants, the crusades offered a chance to escape lifelong servitude, even though many of them died or were sold back into slavery. Of course, some did legitimately desire to free the Holy Land as well.

An appeal to emotions based on same-sex rape began with the very first crusade. A forged document, claiming to be from the Byzantine emperor, was circulated to generate popular support. It described how the Muslims would rape mothers and daughters alike, then went on to state: "But what next? We pass on to worse yet. They have degraded by sodomizing them men of every age and rank: boys, adolescents, young men, old men, nobles, servants, and, what is worse and more wicked, clerics and monks, and even—alas for shame! something which from the beginning of time has never been spoken of or heard of—bishops! They have already killed one bishop with this nefarious sin." The practice of demoralizing defeated enemies through anal rape ("sodomizing") was still in use at this time. Despite the difference between *this* kind of sexual abuse and loving sexuality, all same-sex sexual acts soon became universally despised. In the Kingdom of Jerusalem in the Holy Land, the first sodomy law was enacted by the Franks—the French, English, German and Italian settlers. The penalty for sodomy was death by burning.

The Albigensian Crusade, invoked by Pope Innocent III in 1209, led to the beginning of the Inquisition. This combination crusade-inquisition was directed against the Albigensian religious sect in southern France. Twenty-four years later, Pope Gregory IX formally instituted the Inquisition to rid the continent of all heretics.

Originally, a heretic was any individual who had accepted the Roman Catholic religion but did not subscribe to all its beliefs. This was true even though some beliefs, previously accepted by Roman Catholicism, were later declared heretical. When the church changed its views, its medieval members had better change along with it. In time, heretics would include anyone who practiced any other faith. This included Muslims, Jews, and Protestants. Also included were "sodomites" and "buggerers."

The first trials for heresy were relatively civil. Those accused were permitted a defense. Later on, anyone who testified on behalf of a convicted heretic would also be charged with heresy. Torture was used to get accused heretics to "confess." In 1252 Pope Innocent IV actually authorized "torture that does not imperil life or limb." 30 The original, somewhat civilized punishments (including penance, excommunication, fines, imprisonment, flogging, or exile) turned into death sentences by burning, hanging, or stoning.

The Inquisition is among the most hysterical periods in world history. Heresy against the church became treason against the state. Heretics were blamed for every social problem, including drought, disease, and famine. Anyone even suspected of witchcraft, usury, immorality, or blasphemy would be indicted for heresy. At one point, the Spanish Inquisition declared all the inhabitants of the Netherlands to be heretic and condemned them to death.

Just as same-sex sexual acts were associated with Muslim rape, they were also associated with heresy. No two associations could have been more damaging. John Boswell observed, "The widely held belief that both of the greatest threats to Christian Europe's security (the Muslims from without, the heretics from within) were particularly given to homosexual relations contributed greatly to the profoundly negative reaction against gay sexuality visible at many levels of European society during this period."

At the beginning of the Inquisition, early in the thirteenth century, Pope Gregory IX issued the following proclamation regarding same-sex sexual acts: "For if the just Lord will punish those whom the frailty of weakness may in some way excuse, what will the arbiter of eternal salvation and damnation provide for the enemies of nature, who falsify its custom? When these abominable persons—despised by the world, dreaded by the council of heaven, who have become more unclean than animals, more vicious than almost anything alive, who have lost their reason and destroyed the kindness of nature, who are deprived of interior light and do not discriminate one sex from the other—when they come to that terrible judgment, will he [sic] not command that they be tortured in hell with some unimaginable type of pain worse than that given to all other damned souls?" Apparently, Pope Gregory IX was not very fond of "bisexual" and "homosexual" men. This incredibly emotional condemnation is representative of the general hateful attitude of the Middle Ages.

In the middle of the thirteenth century, the following Castilian royal edict was issued: "Although we are reluctant to speak of something which is reckless to consider and reckless to perform, terrible sins are nevertheless sometimes committed, and it happens that one man desires to sin against nature with another. We therefore command that if anyone commit this sin, both be castrated before the whole populace and on the third day after be hung by the legs until dead, and that their bodies never be taken down." A few years later another law appeared: " 'Sodomy' is the sin which men commit by having intercourse with each other, against nature and natural custom. And because from this sin arise many evils in the land where it is perpetrated, and it sorely offends God and gives a bad name not only to those who indulge in it but also to the nation where it occurs, ... For such crimes our Lord sent upon the land guilty of them, famine, plague, and countless other calamities." This law goes on to prescribe the death penalty for participants of sodomy and adds that this same penalty should also apply to anyone, male or female, who has intercourse with an animal. Over the next fifty or so years, same-sex sexual acts were made illegal throughout most of Europe. Civil and ecclesiastical criminal proceedings mentioned sodomy and crimes against nature regularly. It was even common for official terminology to mention "traitors, heretics, and sodomites" together as if all three constituted a single crime.

This is precisely the time St. Thomas Aquinas began writing his *Summa Theologica*. Excerpts from this work are discussed later in this chapter. Anyone who disagreed with the orthodoxy of the church regarding any subject, including same-sex sexual acts, would have been subject to prosecution for heresy. It is not surprising, therefore, that St. Thomas did indeed agree with the "sin against nature" approach to same-sex sexuality. St. Thomas commented on heresy: "It is more wicked to corrupt the faith on which depends the life of the soul than to debase the coinage which provides merely for temporal life; wherefore if coiners and other malefactors are justly doomed to death, much more may heretics be justly slain once they are convicted." 30 Clearly, St. Thomas had no intention of risking a charge of heresy by disagreeing with the church.

The Inquisition continued into the sixteenth-century when Martin Luther began the Protestant Reformation. The Protestants stressed the authority of the Bible and rejected that of the Pope. The Roman Inquisition charged the Protestants with heresy and the Protestant Inquisition charged the Catholics with heresy — all in the name of God. The tension would eventually lead to the Wars of Religion in the seventeenth century. For all their differences, there was at least one area where the Catholics and the Protestants did agree: sodomy. The influence of the times and the writings of St. Thomas on nature are apparent in the following passage from Martin Luther's *Works:* "The heinous conduct of the people of Sodom is extraordinary, in as much as they departed from the natural passion and longing of the male for the female, which was implanted by God, and desired what is altogether contrary to nature. Whence comes this perversity? Undoubtedly from Satan, who, after people have once turned away from the fear of God, so powerfully suppresses nature that he beats out the natural desire and stirs up a desire that is contrary to nature."

The sixteenth century is also when King Henry VIII of England wrested control away from the church by depriving it of judicial power. In 1533 he enacted a statute against the "detestable and abominable Vice of Buggery" as a capital offense. Buggery is to the English what sodomy is to the Americans. The word *buggery* comes from the French word *bougre* which referred to Albigensian heresy. Recall that it was the crusade against the Albigensians which launched the Inquisition. Convicted buggerers were denied the "benefit of clergy" which would have allowed them to avoid the death penalty for first-time offenses.

Not to be outdone by the Europeans, the new Americans held witchhunts during the seventeenth century in Salem, Massachusetts for the "suffering brought upon the country by witchcraft." The original thirteen colonies modeled their legal systems after English Common Law, adopt-

167

ing many of the same statutes. Sodomy was a capital offense in every colony. In Puritan New England, legislators incorporated some language verbatim from the book of Leviticus.

With the Renaissance came religious pluralism, but what a lesson the crusades and the Inquisition had taught. As with most significant lessons, this one came at great expense. Nearly all of the damage has been remedied, with one notable exception: homosexuality. In the nineteenth century, when homosexuality was identified, those who studied it basically "confirmed" existing cultural beliefs. Anything different would have been less drastic than heresy, but still too controversial for most Americans. Even today, because of its controversy, most history textbooks continue to censor any information about the condemnation of homosexuality whether it occurred under Hitler, during McCarthyism, or in the Middle Ages.

The Inquisition is certainly not representative of Christianity. Yet, instead of *truly* learning from the experience, much of this atrocity has been censored or ignored. As John Boswell pointed out: "Moreover, whatever its effect on individual lives, the change in public attitudes had a profound and lasting impact on European institutions and culture as a result of the permanent and official expression it achieved in thirteenth-century laws, literature, and theology, all of which continued to influence Western thought and social patterns long after the disappearance of the particular circumstances which produced them." What the church still embraces from this period is the writings of St. Thomas Aquinas. The theories he advanced provide the very foundation for contemporary religious views on sexual ethics.

St. Thomas Aquinas on Nature and Sexuality

St. Thomas theorized that the sole purpose of sexual acts was procreation. He believed any other use of the sexual organs was lustful and sinful. Same-sex sexual expression is an obvious condition of this general condemnation of sexual pleasure, for such acts can never lead to procreation. Recall as well from Chapter 6 that St. Thomas subscribed to the Stoic philosophy of equating reason to nature. Finally, he was substantially influenced by the Apostle Paul's views on sexuality and Greek spiritual dualism. These beliefs, combined with or based on a quite sincere concern over a charge of heresy, are what made St. Thomas feel "homosexuality," or any nonprocreative sexual activity for that matter, was a "sin against nature." The previous discussion on nature revealed that such a position is at best vague and ultimately misleading. This section explores further the concepts of nature and sexual morality in the context of religion.

St. Thomas believed that all children should be born male because he felt the "result" should resemble the "cause." At the time, people thought semen *was* "life," almost human, for it was the only visible aspect of human sexuality. The woman's full role in reproduction was unknown; she was only thought to "carry" the baby until birth. The "cause" of reproduction was, therefore, exclusively male. Consequently,

St. Thomas reasoned that the birth of a female was the result of some defect. This is consistent with his low opinion of women. St. Thomas said of Eve, "She was not fit to help man except in generation, because another man would have proved more effective help in anything else." With this "understanding" of human reproduction, he would naturally feel that any sexual act which did not "properly" deposit "life" (sperm) in a womb (the incubator), including masturbation, was immoral. Ignorance of human reproduction would continue for several more centuries. In fact, ovaries and their role in reproduction were not discovered until the nineteenth century. The prevailing belief of sperm as "life" helps explain why lesbianism has never really concerned the church until recently.

St. Thomas was a member of a group of theologians, called the Schoolmen, who attempted to apply Greek philosophy to Christian faith. He commented on this approach: "Hence the light of faith does not destroy the natural light of knowledge, which is inborn in us. It is, therefore, impossible that the things which belong to philosophy should be contrary to the things that belong to faith. Otherwise, either one or the other would be false; and since God is the author of both faith and nature, God would be the author of falsehood to us; which is impossible." In this regard, St. Thomas was especially influenced by Aristotle.

St. Thomas can best be understood by reading from his *Summa Theologica*. He began writing this work in 1265 and finished it in 1273. The influence of stoicism is evident in his complete lack of any comment on love and his frequent reference to pleasure and reason. The influence of Paul's teachings and the lack of understanding of human physiology are apparent as well in the following excerpts from *Summa Theologica:*

> It must be said that the more a thing is necessary the more crucial it is that it be regulated by reason and consequently the greater the evil if that order of reason is violated. However as we have already stated sexual acts are very necessary for the common good which is the survival of the race. Therefore concerning them the greatest attention must be paid to the ordering of reason. Consequently if anything is done in connection with them against the order of reason it is a sin. And so without any doubt lust is sin.
>
> To the first objection it must be said that according to Aristotle in the same book *semen is a surplus* which is necessary, he says it is a surplus insofar as it is a residue of the action of the nutrient power yet it is necessary regarding the generative power. The other waste-products of the body are not necessary and therefore it does not matter how they are disposed of provided the decencies of social life are observed. But it is different with the emission of semen which must be done in the way befitting the end for which it is needed . . .
>
> It should be mentioned, as we have already mentioned, that the sin of lechery consists in this—that a person engages in venereal pleasure not in accordance with the right reason. This can happen in two ways: one is respect to the substance of the act in which the

pleasure is sought. The other in which the act is proper but other conditions are not met . . .

To the fifth let me say that as the gloss says that uncleanness stands for lust against nature, while lewdness pertains to corruption of the young which is a form of seduction. Or we can also say that lewdness pertains to those various acts surrounding the sex-act such as kissing, caressing and the like . . .

I answer that as stated above wherever there occurs a special kind of deformity whereby the venereal act is rendered unbecoming, there is a determinate species of lust. This may occur in two ways, by being contrary to the right reason and this is common to all types of lust. Secondly, because in addition it is contrary to the natural order of the venereal act as befits human species and this is why it is called the unnatural vice. It can happen in various ways. First by having orgasm outside of intercourse for the sake of venereal pleasure which pertains to the sin of uncleanness which some call effeminacy. Secondly by copulating with another species which is called bestiality. Thirdly by copulating with the wrong sex, male with male or female with female as St. Paul states (Rom 1:27) and this is the vice of sodomy. Fourthly, by not observing the natural manner of copulation either as to not using the proper organ or as to other monstrous and bestial manners of copulation . . .

St. Thomas' use of the term *effeminacy* refers to masturbation; it is unknown whether his source was 1 Corinthians 6:9–10 or not. He also interprets Romans 1:26–27 as applying to both male and female same-sex sexuality. These two passages were cited in the previous chapter. St. Thomas later establishes a hierarchy for these sins. From lowest to highest it specifies: masturbation, lechery, sodomy (same-sex sexuality), and bestiality.

The lustful man intends not human generation but venereal pleasure. It is possible without those acts from which human generation follow: and it is this which is sought in unnatural acts . . .

And so a sin against nature in which the natural order itself is violated is a sin against God who is the creator of that order. Augustine writes, "Offenses against nature should be abhorred and punished always and in every case. Such as those committed by the people of Sodom which if every nation committed them they would be held just as guilty by the same divine law which never intended that men treat one another in such a fashion. For the fellowship which should exist between God and man would be destroyed when nature which is God's handiwork is made foul by the perversity of lust."

Exactly what St. Thomas meant by his use of "nature" is not clear as he defines it in numerous and often conflicting ways. His definitions include "the order of creation," "the principle of intrinsic motion," and as being "ordained by divine providence to fill some purpose." In his comments on philosophy and faith, he equates philosophy with nature and knowledge, and faith with God. Yet God is also nature, and He could not contradict philosophy. Having several definitions of nature did not

170

appear to concern St. Thomas a great deal: " 'Nature,' in the case of man, may be taken in two senses. On one hand the 'nature' of man is particularly the intellect and reason, since it is in regard to this that man is distinct as a species. On the other hand, 'nature' in man may be taken to mean that which is distinct from the rational, i.e., that which is common to men and other beings, particularly that which is not subject to reason." It is likely this latter definition which applies to same-sex sexual acts: "It must be noted that the nature of man may be spoken of either as that which is peculiar to man, and according to this all sins, insofar as they are against reason, are against nature (as is stated by Damascene); or as that which is common to man and to other animals, according to which certain particular sins are said to be against nature, as intercourse between males (which is specifically called the vice against nature) is contrary to the union of male and female which is natural to all animals." Of course, we now know St. Thomas was wrong: Same-sex sexual activity has been observed in every animal species studied for such behavior.

Whatever he meant by *nature* in the "sin against nature," St. Thomas made it abundantly clear he did not approve of sexuality for any purpose other than procreation — or did he? In reference to pleasure — both a rational pleasure, such as the "contemplation of the truth" and those pleasures man has in common with animals, such as "venereal activity" — he stated: "In the case of both types of pleasure it can happen that what is unnatural simply speaking can be connatural in a certain situation. For it can occur that in a particular individual there can be a breakdown of some natural principle of the species and thus what is contrary to the nature of the species can become by accident natural to this individual." Among his examples of this "accident," St. Thomas specifically mentions same-sex sexual activity. Apparently, this "sin against nature" is quite natural for some people!

There is not a single passage in either the Old or New Testaments which supports the belief that sexual expression is solely for the purpose of procreation. The focus on procreation in the Old Testament is understandable. A small Hebrew tribe in a hostile environment indeed needed children for its very survival. But a statement concerning the importance of procreation should not be misconstrued to mean anything more. For this reason, St. Thomas could not base his views regarding sexuality on Scripture. His reference to Sodom and Romans 1:27 completely ignores the context of hostility and idolatry. Instead, St. Thomas based his views of "unnatural vices" on Greek spiritual dualism and Stoic philosophy. More importantly, though, is the influence of the times. Had St. Thomas felt any differently about same-sex sexual acts, he would have been accused of heresy by the Inquisition.

By the end of the Middle Ages, the real sins of Sodom had been all but forgotten and replaced by this "sin against nature." Father John McNeill, in his book *The Church and the Homosexual,* pointed out the irony here: "For thousands of years in the Christian West the homosexual has been the victim of inhospitable treatment. Condemned by the Church, he has been the victim of persecution, torture, and even death.

In the name of a mistaken understanding of Sodom and Gomorrah, the true crime of Sodom and Gomorrah has been and continues to be repeated every day."

Directly or indirectly, the story of Sodom and Gomorrah has profoundly influenced contemporary thought on homosexuality. Today our culture uses the word *sodomy* broadly in reference to noncoital sexual activity. Yet to most people, "sodomy" *means* homosexuality, not idolatrous cult prostitution as it does in the Bible or anal rape as it did in the Middle Ages. Even *Webster's Ninth New Collegiate Dictionary* comments that the word itself comes from "the homosexual proclivities of the men of the city in Gen 19:1–11," then defines sodomy as "copulation with a member of the same sex or with an animal" and as "noncoital and especially anal or oral copulation with a member of the opposite sex." The influence of St. Thomas is obvious: These two definitions encompass all but one of his "sins against nature."

The confusion of *sodomy* with *idolatry* began in the third and fourth centuries B.C., continued through the time of Christ, and reached its peak during the Middle Ages. And when homosexuality was identified in the nineteenth century, this "understanding" survived and continues today merely as a matter of tradition. In his book *Homosexuality and the Western Christian Tradition,* Dr. Derrick Bailey stated, "I have not carried this general account beyond the end of the Middle Ages because it does not appear that the tradition has undergone any significant alteration since that time." This is the history of the "sin against nature" and the views of the church today on sexuality, homosexuality, and morality.

Sexuality, Homosexuality, and Morality

Fact: A *moral* focus on *biological* reproduction is what created the "homosexual problem." Fact: This "problem" was then "solved" through forced celibacy, as if the "solution" were somehow *more* reproductive than the "problem" itself! But let there be no doubt: Procreation merely serves as a justification for heterosexual sexual expression — and a convenient excuse for homophobia. The very existence of a socially acceptable form of heterosexual sex, coitus, makes straight people almost immune from the kind of scrutiny homosexuality has undergone in being declared "lustful and sinful."

Hypothetically, then, is it "lustful and sinful" for a heterosexual couple who cannot biologically have children, through the natural or human-made condition of either partner, to engage in sexual activity? Should this "reason" for sex also apply to couples where the woman has gone through menopause? Should couples that must rely on artificial means of insemination quit having coital sex? What about the estimated one million men and women who are voluntarily sterilized *annually?* It is incredibly naive to assume that all heterosexual sexual activity is coital and procreative. The average American family has 2.3 children. Does this mean the average American couple engages in coitus only 2.3 times during their entire marriage?

For the procreative argument to be sincerely applied, *every single* heterosexual sexual act would need to be conducted with the genuine intent and high probability of conception, regardless of whether or not the couple is married. Such a standard would rule out all forms of birth control, including the rhythm method. Clearly, this is not the reality of heterosexual sexuality. The current procreative "holier than thou" game has its roots in ancient philosophy and medieval moralism, but those who continue to play it should recognize that their double standard between heterosexuality and homosexuality can boomerang. "Do not judge lest you be judged. For in the way you judge, you will be judged; and by your standard of measure, it will be measured to you." (Matthew 7:1–2)

In fact, a strong argument could be made that procreation is not only not the only reason for sexual activity, but that it is not even the primary reason. Most straight people engage in sexual activity far more often for emotional expression and physical pleasure than they do for procreative purposes—making procreation more of a "risk" or problem than a reason. As a result, the morality of sexuality boils down to one critical question: Is this "joy of sex" a gift from God, or the work of the devil?

Is it the devil who tempts men and women with a consistent, predominant or exclusive, emotional and erotic attraction to persons of the same gender? Maybe. But why does he regularly tempt only ten percent of God's children this way? Is he also tempting the other ninety percent with the identical feelings directed at the opposite gender? Maybe. Are straight people then "giving in" to *their* version of demonic sexual temptation by having sex? Maybe. Are straight people "giving in" by getting married? No. But marriage does not define love for heterosexuality; it defines *morality*. No, the ability to love sexually can only be a gift of human wholeness from God. Why, then, is it necessary to establish a single reason or hierarchy of reasons to justify sexuality? Actually, why does the church even concern itself with the biological and physiological aspects of sexuality, namely procreation and pleasure? Its sole concern should be the use of sexual activity as a means of expressing mutual love, communion, and support—period. This is where the *morality* of sexuality is to be found. When straight people have sex it is called "making love." When gay people have sex it is called "sodomy." The double standard here is blatant. In reality, procreation is not the issue.

Promiscuity is not the issue either. Promiscuity applies equally to heterosexuality and homosexuality. In other words, sexual orientation is amoral. Sexual lifestyles can be either moral or immoral for gay or straight men or women. Ascribing promiscuity exclusively to homosexuality is simply another excuse for homophobia, this one based on the stereotypes. Further, a basis for the promiscuity argument built on marriage, a moral relationship denied all gay people, is merely another double standard.

"Alternate" forms of sexual expression are not at issue here either. The Bible is silent on the topic of oral-genital sexual activity, and with the exception of the disputed translation of the Greek word *arsenokoitais,* there is nothing mentioned about mutually consensual anal intercourse. Yet both of these practices are viewed by most churches as being "unnatural" based primarily on the writings of St. Thomas. And because between eighty and ninety percent of straight people enjoy various "alternate" forms of sexual expression as well, they cannot be considered a sincere, or at least a legitimate, basis for the condemnation of homosexuality either. As a result, this becomes just another example of homophobic double standards.

The reason for homophobia in the church is not procreation, promiscuity, or sexual techniques; it is ignorance about homosexuality. Remember, this is the cause of homophobia. In addition to the ignorance about homosexuality, there is the lack of understanding of "applicable" Scripture and the history of Judeo-Christian tradition. Yes, this is strong criticism, but deeply rooted beliefs are not easily excavated. Just as the story of Onan was used to declare masturbation immoral, the story of Sodom and Gomorrah is used to justify homophobia today. Masturbation is no longer challenged by the church because it is well known, although not commonly stated, that nearly all people have done it, do it now, or will do it later. Our society knows now that masturbation does not cause disease or "waste seed" sinfully. This is as it should be. The ignorance surrounding masturbation is gone, no longer to prevent the truth from being known. But does this also indicate that the morality of sexuality in the church is based on democracy? Is a majority "vote" required before the facts, biblical and secular, can be considered? Unfortunately, this may be so. Father Charles Curran recognized the fallacy here: "The ethicist cannot merely follow the majority opinion, for history constantly reminds us that majority opinions are not necessarily true."

The very longevity of these homophobic beliefs seems to have achieved a certain authority for them. Dr. Derrick Bailey observes, "The Church is discredited, occasionally by an inexcusable error of fact, but far more often by some exaggerated or tendentious assertion which soon comes to be accepted as sober truth." In effect, the church has become trapped in a tradition which has no real biblical foundation, and continues to hate this "sin" while claiming to love the sinner.

Love the Sinner; Hate the Sin

Beware of the false prophets, who come to you in sheep's clothing, but inwardly are ravenous wolves. *Matthew 7:15*

Some folks claim "merely being homosexual" is not sinful, but that doing something about it is. This position has been popularized by the phrase "Love the sinner; hate the sin." Yet this position ignores the fact that sin comes from the heart, as Jesus said: "You have heard that it was said, 'You shall not commit adultery'; but I say to you, that everyone who looks on a woman to lust for her has committed adultery with her already in his heart." (Matthew 5:27-28) "For from within, out of the heart of men, come the evil thoughts, fornications, thefts, murders, adulteries, deeds of coveting and wickedness, as well as deceit, sensuality, envy, slander, pride and foolishness." (Mark 7:21–22) If "doing something about it" sexually is sinful, then the very feeling of emotional and erotic attraction to persons of the same gender is just as sinful.

For the "Love the sinner; hate the sin" position to be valid, it must first create the sin by ascribing a stereotypical promiscuous lifestyle to *all* gay people. In effect, then, *this* kind of "homosexuality," defined in homophobia but not in Scripture, becomes the "hated sin." The Bible is then used to "proof-text" God's disapproval of *this* kind of "homosexuality." Most do this quite innocently; they simply do not understand homosexuality. Unfortunately, others do it maliciously. "For the time will come when they will not endure sound doctrine; but wanting to have their ears tickled, they will accumulate for themselves teachers in accordance to their own desires; and will turn away their ears from the truth, and will turn aside to myths." (2 Timothy 4:3–4)

A few extremely homophobic individuals have even tried to "interpret" the Bible's silence on homosexuality by saying, "God made Adam and Eve; not Adam and Steve." This may be cute, but it's meaningless. What this is really saying is that if God meant to include homosexuality in His kingdom, He would have created it. Well, He did: "All things came into being by Him, and apart from Him nothing came into being that has come into being." (John 1:3)

The Bible does not answer all our questions. But it is ideology, not theology, which attempts to fill the "gaps" by guessing what God intends. Peter did this. He could not understand why Christ should suffer and be killed. As a former Jew, Peter believed that the Messiah should restore the kingdom to Israel and deliver Israel from Rome's rule. So Peter took Christ aside and rebuked Him for describing His crucifixion and resurrection. "But turning around and seeing His disciples, He rebuked Peter, and said, 'Get behind Me, Satan; for you are not setting your mind on God's interests, but man's.'" (Mark 8:33)

Ironically, the Reverend Ralph W. Weltge comments on how homophobia in the church resembles the very idolatry that formed the now-forgotten basis of Judeo-Christian tradition on homosexuality in the first place:

> What is served by this [homophobia], of course, is not the Lord but the self-righteousness of the persecutors. The godly never feel so holy as when they are excoriating sexual sinners. People often legitimate themselves by hating a despised group set up as a counter-image. If your religious identity is unsure then secure it by condemning sinners. If your sexual identity is shaky then shore it up by despising homosexuals. Or, as Peter Berger has put it: "One beats up the Negro to feel white. One spits on homosexuals to feel virile."
>
> In this process the identity of the persecutor is legitimized by the negative identity of the persecuted. The homosexual is a perfect fall guy because his suffering provides a double reward—it makes one both a "man" and a "Christian." But any identity established that way is an idol because it requires human sacrifices as the substance of its cultic practice. Church persecution of the homosexual is idolatry achieved in the very call of duty.

175

The following quotation was taken from an article in the anthology *Homosexuality and Ethics:*

One of the most popular errors in the realm of Christian ethics has been the effort to make love an omnipotent spiritual quality which has the power to sanctify anything that is done in its name. The Inquisition tortured people's bodies in order to save their souls and sought to justify this action in the name of love. For centuries white Christians imposed patterns of paternalism upon blacks as an expression of their love for the sons of Ham. Employers once professed to love their employees too much to let them fall into the evil clutches of labor organizers. Parents tend to dominate their children's lives in the name of this same love. And generations of male chauvinists have counseled their sisters, wives, and daughters to eschew power and find their dignity and security in the love of their menfolk.

It is fashionable to interpret all such claims as sheer hypocrisy, as many of them were. But far more often than we care to admit, acts of exploitation and even brutality have been committed by people who honestly believe they were expressing disinterested love for their victims. It was the recognition of this hard fact of life which led Reinhold Niebuhr to say that we human beings are "never as dangerous as when we act in love." When we are motivated by anger or aggression, he pointed out, we arm our own consciences, alert our critics, and put our intended victims on their guard. But when we act in love, we disarm conscience, critic, and victim in one act and can do our worst unimpeded.

This was very eloquently phrased. It is obvious the author sincerely believes that love should never be used to justify prejudice. Those who do, he points out, are frequently hypocritical. Truer words were never spoken. A few pages earlier this same author said that the church should take a position to support civil rights for gay people. He then stated, "Does the logic of this position require that Christians abandon their historic stand on homosexuality and declare good what they have in the past condemned? Obviously not. What is required is a firm reassertion of the time-honored distinction between toleration on one hand and approval on the other. Or to put it in more familiar religious terms, adherence to the principle that one must *love the sinner while hating the sin.*" [Emphasis added.]

This author's warning that concluded we are "never as dangerous as when we act in love" was actually an argument *against* accepting gay people in the church, demonstrating how completely blinded he became by his own homophobia. (But then, isn't blindness really inherent to all forms of prejudice?) He apparently confuses passionate love with God's unconditional love: " 'God is love' — so runs the argument. Anything that is an expression of love is good. Since same-gender sex is an expression of love, it should be blessed by the church. This is another classic example of question-begging, an effort to define homosexuality into a state of grace. As such it needs very careful examination." After having established this perspective, incorrect as it is, he immediately offers the above discussion on the abuse of brotherly love. The Greeks were indeed wise to have three words for love, as that would have eliminated this author's confusion. In the rest of his article, he encourages the church to engage in the very same forms of discrimination he denounces in society. He is certainly right on one account, though: Passionate love does not "justify" homosexuality any more than it "justifies" heterosexuality.

The Institute for Sex Research found that seventy-eight percent of those surveyed felt homosexual relationships without love were "always wrong." This is not at all surprising. What *is* surprising is that an overwhelming seventy percent felt gay relationships *with* love were "always wrong" as well. Only eleven percent believed that sex between two people of the same gender is "not wrong at all" when they love each other. When one considers that ten percent of the survey sample was probably gay and would likely have felt loving gay relationships were "not wrong at all," that leaves virtually *no* straight people who feel this way. What is at issue here is not love but morality — period. The presence or absence of love in gay relationships has no impact whatsoever on the attitudes of the straight majority toward homosexuality. And the exclusive reason for this is that the church and society have failed to define a moral gay lifestyle similar to marriage. So the *real* problem here is the failure to in fact love the so-called sinners, who become defined as "sinners" by their very exclusion from the majority's moral structure.

This fundamental "oversight" is why many gay people continue to seek brotherly love from the church — not based on their capacity for passionate love — but based instead on God's unconditional love.

God is Love

"Beloved, let us love one another, for love is from God; and everyone who loves is born of God and knows God. The one who does not love does not know God, for God is love." *1 John 4:7–8*

All too often, many Christians and Jews think of religion as what we should *not* do. The Bible is full of the words "shall not." Simply following these many rules for behavior somewhat relieves personal responsibility for understanding the Bible's broader message. By taking such an approach, one runs the risk of missing the forest for the trees. But religion is much more than a moral code Christians and Jews derive from the Bible. It is a relationship with God and fellow humans — for "God is love," and His love is not exclusive, nor is it conditional.

"And one of the scribes came and heard them arguing, and recognizing that He had answered them well, asked Him, 'What commandment is the foremost of all?' Jesus answered, 'The foremost is, "Hear, O Israel! The Lord our God is one Lord; and you shall love the Lord your God with all your heart, and with all your soul, and with all your mind, and with all your strength." The second is this, "You shall love your neighbor as yourself." There is no other commandment greater than these.'" (Mark 12:28–31) "You shall not take vengeance, nor bear any grudge against the sons of your people, but you shall love your neighbor as yourself; I am the Lord." (Leviticus 19:18)

A person who believes in such an unconditional love should ask: Do I love the gay men and lesbians who have been alienated by the church? Do you love the parents, the relatives, and the friends of gay people who are also hurt by homophobia? Do I really love all these neighbors? Do I love, sincerely, my *gay* neighbor?

Chapter 11

Loving Gay Neighbors

There is no fear in love; but perfect love casts out fear, because fear involves punishment, and the one who fears is not perfected in love. *1 John 4:18*

Most churches or synagogues basically give the gay man or lesbian two choices for salvation: Go straight or become celibate. Both mean the same thing: Give up being gay—and a vicious cycle around the real problem is begun. Because an individual cannot change his or her sexual orientation, the church will then "welcome" the gay person under one condition: celibacy. But this not only assumes that a homosexual sexual orientation is accompanied by a capacity for lifetime celibacy, it corrupts the very purpose of celibacy, as Dietrich Bonhoeffer pointed out: "The essence of chastity is not the suppression of lust, but the total orientation of one's life towards a goal." It appears not to matter, however, that celibacy is this special calling and not a form of control or "punishment." That is the condition—simple, black and white, no exceptions—and the vicious cycle is complete.

How convenient. This approach allows the church to ignore the problem of homophobia by "solving" the "problem" of homosexuality, which it defines as a "state of sin." In effect, this form of "acceptance" is like trying to qualify for a loan by proving one does not need the money. All people are sinners and can and seek salvation through the church. But gay people cannot *earn* salvation by sacrificing sexual expression any more than straight people can. So this "Love the sinner; hate the sin" approach serves only as an impasse to progress and reform. If sin comes from the heart, as it does, then there is no difference between hating the sin and hating the sinner.

If you are straight, try to imagine for a moment that you have been told you could *never* love or be loved passionately, that you could not share your life with the person you so loved, and that you would never be saved unless you "gave up" your form of love or became celibate. Imagine how unfair it would seem. Imagine what your reaction would be if your dignity was undermined in this fashion. Imagine what you would think of the institution which made these rules on your "behalf." This is what it is like in the church for gay people.

A survey conducted in Great Britain found that sixty-one percent of the gay people questioned had turned to the church for help in dealing responsibly with their homosexuality. Of those who did seek assistance, eighty-one percent reported they received absolutely no help or comfort. Because the church has almost totally rejected the validity of homosexuality in its approach to the subject, it has lost credibility with much of the gay community. Its wholesale condemnation has created a situation where gay people virtually ignore any criticism coming from the church, even when that criticism is valid. In effect, the church has "cried wolf" about homosexuality so often and with such misunderstanding, that many gay people no longer pay attention.

Given that people can neither change nor repress their sexual orientation, the gay Christian or Jew is left with five choices. The first is to abandon Judeo-Christian religion entirely. The second is to remain a member, passing as straight, while ignoring the church's position on homosexuality. Number three is to remain a member of the church as an openly gay person, trying to promoᴸ change from within. The fourth is to join a different church which accepts gay members, such as the Metropolitan Community Church. Finally, number five is to worship privately. These are the only choices.

According to the Institute for Sex Research, the real effect of traditional Judeo-Christian beliefs on homosexuality is to cause greater guilt, shame, and anxiety for only the first few homosexual sexual experiences. After gaining this personal understanding of just how wrong the church has been in its image of homosexuality, any conflict quickly subsides. The friends and family members of gay people are likely to experience a similar conflict. Their strife will last quite a while longer, but exist to a much lesser degree.

All of this suffering is so unnecessary. Who is served by this traditional condemnation of homosexuality? Certainly not gay people. Certainly not their families and friends. Certainly not the church. Certainly not God. Who? This tradition must be changed — from within.

Changing Tradition

Loyalty to petrified opinion never yet broke a chain or freed a human soul. *Mark Twain*

In his book *The Church and the Homosexual*, Father John McNeill gives three main reasons why the church should reconsider its traditional view of homosexuality: the uncertainty of clear scriptural prohibition; a questionable basis in moral philosophy and moral theology, namely St. Thomas' writings on nature and the purely sexual interpretation of the story of Sodom and Gomorrah; and the emergence of new data which upset many traditional assumptions. He offers a fourth reason, the controversy among psychologists concerning homosexuality, which has since his writing been resolved to establish that homosexuality is not a neurosis or disordered development. As a result, his fourth reason is now really included in the emergence of new data.

The church, both as an institution in our society and as a congregation of individuals, has a responsibility toward its gay members. As Father McNeill points out, "When social structures oppress human dignity and freedom and maintain situations of gross inequality, the persons who share life within these situations also share responsibility for allowing them to continue."

There are two pivotal reasons the church has been able to ignore any challenge of its traditional view on homosexuality. The first is that because homosexuality is so universally despised in the secular world, there has been no great pressure placed on theologians to reconsider the issue. The second is that, by defining the problem as homosexual sexual expression, the requirement of celibacy has conveniently served as its "solution." For these reasons, the church continues to beg the question and avoid the real issue, which is homophobia.

Father Charles Curran warns of three potential flaws inherent to moral theology. First is a tendency to accept, without question, the status quo. Second is the failure to recognize complexity in moral issues. Third is the use of Scripture to justify positions actually based elsewhere. All three apply fully to homosexuality as a moral issue.

Although widely held, the anti-gay position is not universal in the church. Besides, consensus on moral issues should involve much more than merely counting heads. Many priests, ministers, and rabbis are advocating change. Their belief is that the church must provide moral guidance for the implementation of a sexual orientation which cannot be changed. In other words, the church should lead gay people *through* their homosexuality, rather than *away* or *apart* from it. This is the only responsible approach given the reality of the situation. By doing this, the church is not "condoning" or "promoting" homosexuality; it is condoning and promoting a moral lifestyle for those individuals who are gay. In effect, without this approach, the church is missing out on the opportunity to help define a moral gay lifestyle.

There is absolutely no doubt that Judeo-Christian tradition is the root of homophobia in our society today. Lon Nungesser pointed out that, "with the exception of Zoroastrianism [a religion of ancient Persia], antihomosexual prejudice and repression have been limited to cultures under the influence of Judeo-Christianity." There are a few basic steps the church can take to begin reversing this injustice. The first and foremost is for organized religion to reconsider its traditional view with a test of accuracy and fairness. This involves learning the truth about homosexuality. It is very tempting to take what is not understood or what cannot be explained and blame it on the "devil." Replacing ignorance with understanding will remove this temptation. In conjunction with the learning process, each church can demonstrate social leadership by reversing discrimination in its own house. This means truly accepting gay Christians and Jews, including as clergy and rabbis, without a requirement for conversion or celibacy. This new, true acceptance of homosexuality should be conveyed to all members of the church, gay and straight, through revised teachings on sexual morality and the elimination of all double

181

standards. Finally, and this will take time, the church should recognize and support gay relationships.

Learning the Truth About Homosexuality

Ignorance is not innocence but sin. *Robert Browning*

The church is a community in search, not a community in perfection. Cardinal Deardon said, "We must freely acknowledge that the Church must learn and not merely teach what is required in justice." The Reverend Neale Secor agreed: "It probably is the case that, in this particular arena of human conduct [homosexual sexuality], the Christian church has been thrown from its accustomed role of teacher and into that of learner."

God's Word is indeed contained between Genesis and Revelations. But doesn't God continue to reach His children through a wealth of other resources. Can't we safely say that God has yet to have His final Word on any subject? If so, the Bible should not be used as an exclusive source for learning the truth.

Aldous Huxley said, "Facts do not cease to exist because they are ignored." When tradition and facts are in disagreement, tradition should not prevail without first attempting to resolve the conflict. Because the Bible is actually silent on the topic of homosexuality, the church must use knowledge available from other sources, including science, to learn the truth. God has blessed most of His children with a powerful mind possessing the capacity to learn and reason. He has obviously not given men and women this ability simply for it to be ignored. Father Charles Curran stated: "Moral theology must be open to the data and findings of psychology, of psychiatry and of all the sciences about homosexuality. No one should study the morality of homosexuality without such data . . . Moral theology likewise pays special attention to the Christian tradition, but again there exists the questions of knowing exactly what the tradition teaches and of applying this understanding correctly in our contemporary circumstances."

To clear the path for learning the truth, church censorship surrounding the subject of homosexuality must cease. The very complexity of the issues should serve as a caveat against drawing simple conclusions. For centuries, the misinterpretation of the story of Onan was used to condemn masturbation as a sin. This "sin against nature" was also confirmed by St. Thomas and science, even though the Bible is silent on the subject. The "unlearning" occurred when masturbation was first absolved through science and then by the church. The situation with homosexuality will be the same.

This raises the specter of "secular humanism." *Secular humanism* is a term which is at best vague and at worst deceptive. It is used regularly by certain individuals to discredit anyone who disagrees with *their* scriptural interpretation. As such, it is the modern-day equivalent to a charge of heresy. The church has regularly resisted scientific information as some perceived "threat" to beliefs ostensibly based on Scripture. For example, Galileo was tried and convicted by the church for advocating the Copernican theory of the earth revolving around the sun. Yet nowhere does the Bible state the earth is the center of the universe. There really was no conflict between secular knowledge and Scripture. The same is true for homosexuality.

Why is it that most scientists experience no difficulty in accepting both religion *and* the sciences? Albert Einstein said, "Science without religion is lame, religion without science is blind." He also believed, "The cosmic religious experience is the strongest and noblest driving force behind scientific research." Maria Mitchell commented, "Every formula which expresses a law of nature is a hymn of praise to God." The scientists are not alone in this regard either. Martin Luther King, Jr., commented, "Science investigates; religion interprets. Science gives man knowledge which is power; religion gives man wisdom which is control." Ralph Waldo Emerson felt this way as well: "The religion that is afraid of science dishonors God and commits suicide."

There is both hypocrisy and irony in ignoring secular information pertaining to homosexuality. The hypocrisy comes from the fact that secular knowledge is frequently used when it ostensibly agrees with homophobic interpretation of the Bible, and completely ignored when it does not. In addition, when most people are sick, with very few exceptions, they would not think of ignoring advances in medicine, relying solely on prayer for a cure. Why then should the church ignore what science has learned about homosexuality? The irony comes from the fact that traditional Judeo-Christian beliefs about homosexuality are in fact based on secular knowledge (more accurately "*mis*knowledge") of another era, and *not* on Scripture. The understanding of nature and human physiology has expanded substantially in the seven centuries since St. Thomas wrote. It is only appropriate, therefore, that this tradition be broken through an investigation of the new, more accurate information. As Dr. Wardell Pomeroy concluded, "Except for the fact that they were homosexual, they would be considered normal by any definition. To insist that they are abnormal, or sick, or neurotic just because they are homosexual is to engage in circular reasoning which smacks of a blind moralism founded in our Judeo-Christian heritage." Secular knowledge should be used to help understand the Bible, not to replace it. Even St. Thomas himself warned, "Beware of the man of one book."

In Mark 7:5 – 9, with reference to Isaiah 29:13, is the message: "And the Pharisees and the scribes asked Him, 'Why do Your disciples not walk according to the tradition of the elders, but eat their bread with impure hands?' And He said to them, 'Rightly did Isaiah prophesy you of hypocrites, as it is written, "This people honors Me with their lips, But their heart is far away from Me. But in vain do they worship Me, Teaching as doctrines the precepts of men." Neglecting the commandment of God, you hold to the tradition of men.' He was also saying to them, 'You nicely set aside the commandment of God in order to keep your tradition.'" Such is the case with the tradition of homophobia today.

Knowing what the Bible does and does not say about homosexuality is the first step toward loving gay people in the church. But it is not the last. Just as the Bible does not answer *all* our questions, science cannot yet answer all our questions about homosexuality—yet. In the meantime, love, not homophobia, should fill these "gaps."

"Love never fails; but if there are gifts of prophecy, they will be done away; if there are tongues, they will cease; if there is knowledge, it will be done away. For we know in part, and we prophesy in part; but when the perfect comes, the partial will be done away. When I was a child, I used to speak as a child, think as a child, reason as a child; when I became a man, I did away with childish things. For now we see in a mirror dimly, but then face to face; now I know in part, but then I shall know fully just as I also have been fully known. But now abide faith, hope, love, these three; but the greatest of these is love." (1 Corinthians 13:8–13)

Accepting Gay Christians and Jews in the Church

Brethren, let each man remain with God in that condition in which he was called. *1 Corinthians 7:24*

The Reverend Troy Perry founded the Metropolitan Community Church (MCC) in Los Angeles in 1968 when a dozen people attended the first service in his home. The MCC is a nondenominational Christian church for gay people and their straight friends and family members. According to Reverend Perry, "My church was founded because homosexuals simply didn't have any other place to go." By the end of its first year, the MCC's membership had grown to over 500. Enough money was donated to purchase an old movie theater, which served as its first sanctuary. Since then, hundreds more MCCs have opened throughout the United States and abroad. This has not been without some resistance, however, in the form of arson and vandalism at over forty of its churches, and harassment, assault, and even murder of its clergy and parishioners. The MCC is hopefully only a temporary solution to the problem, as Reverend Perry points out that the MCC is "working toward the day when it can close its doors because the other Christian communities with love and understanding will have opened theirs to gay people."

The next step of loving gay neighbors, then, is to welcome gay Christians and Jews through *full* participation in the church. This includes both worship services and church-sponsored social functions for youth or adults. "Do we not all have one father? Has not one God created us? Why do we deal treacherously each against his brother so as to profane the covenant of our fathers?" (Malachi 2:10) "There is neither Jew nor Greek, there is neither slave nor free man, there is neither male nor female; for you are all one in Christ Jesus." (Galatians 3:28) Although "neither straight nor gay" is not specifically mentioned, the message is clear: We are all one in God; we should all be one in His house. God is for us, with us, and in us. An individual's righteousness should not be found in his or her sexual orientation.

Truly accepting gay Christians and Jews will involve a few changes. The church can begin by teaching a revised sexual morality which conforms to the Will of God. Because sin comes from the heart, the morality of sexuality should be based on its loving use, and not on the gender or genders involved. The very action of *defining* homosexuality as immoral prevents an objective consideration of the subject, and provides the foundation for a set of double standards. Single standards help separate the wheat from the chaff in issues of sexual ethics and serve as guideposts when denouncing those forms of heterosexual and homosexual sexual behavior that must be considered immoral: promiscuity, adultery, rape, and child abuse. Sexual acts which are lustful, idolatrous, exploitive, coercive, or selfish should be sinful for both gay and straight individuals alike. Sexuality is a gift from God. While the irresponsible and unloving use of sex may be the work of the devil, there is nothing inherently evil in either heterosexual or homosexual sexual expression.

Sermons should emphasize the *real* sins of Sodom and Gomorrah, inhospitality and idolatry being key among them. This can be accompanied by an explanation of the history of Judeo-Christian tradition on homosexuality and how new, more accurate information has removed the very foundation for these old beliefs. Openly gay members will serve as role models to destroy the myths and stereotypes. Homophobia must be exposed as the form of prejudice it is, for prejudice has no place in the house of the Lord.

Clergy should be prepared to offer responsible individual counseling for both gay people and family members, especially parents. A priest, minister, or rabbi must be *the* person any individual can trust with absolute confidence in personal matters. Where else can people go for help? Possibly the family doctor? Homosexuality is not a medical issue. Maybe a psychiatrist? It is not a psychological issue either. Besides, most families do not have a "family psychiatrist." How about a friend? Perhaps, but there is no assurance that a friend can provide anything more than comfort. The clergy seems a logical source, but it has a very poor track record in this area.

The usual "helpful" response currently offered by clergy to a gay person is: "Oh, you couldn't really be gay. You have a good family; you're a moral and responsible person who attends church regularly; you do well in school; you're kind to other people. No, you couldn't possibly be gay. It's probably just a phase." It is easy to convince a child he or she is not really homosexual when this is something the child wants desperately to believe in the first place. The same story is also given to the parents of a gay child, and they are equally relieved by this "news." Counseling sessions are only effective when they strive to discover the truth, whatever that is. This involves offering support, comfort, and assistance in learning about homosexuality, and how to conduct a gay lifestyle in a responsible and moral fashion. In preparation for this eventuality, clergy should receive training on homosexuality and gay-related issues. Consulting and training by gay people will be helpful in making this change. Responsible books on homosexuality and gay issues are available and can be added to the church library.

A church might publicly condemn discrimination in society for the human suffering it causes, while continuing to practice the very same

185

injustice in its own administration. By denying gay people the opportunity to practice ministry, to participate as laypersons in policy decisions, or to become church staff employees, the church creates a harmful example for its members and society. Professor of Christian Ethics James B. Nelson noted that, "Church assemblies may continue to claim 'prudential grounds' as their main reason for barring gay ordinations for some time to come, but one day perhaps that form of prudence will sound as thin as when it was used to bar women and racial minorities from ministry." Until the church recognizes relationships between gay people, the "go straight or remain chaste" requirement should not serve as an excuse to deny ordination. Of course, this is not a problem in some churches where celibacy is already a requirement for all priests. A gay priest would be no less homosexual simply because he, and hopefully someday she, is celibate.

Finally, the church can officially and formally recognize existing gay groups. Nearly every major denomination has such organizations at a national level, with local chapters in most large cities. These groups stand ready to help when asked.

Episcopalian Bishop Spong sums up this discussion best: "The time has surely come not just to tolerate, or even accept, but to celebrate and welcome the presence among us of our gay and lesbian fellow human beings."

Recognizing Gay Relationships

Marriage has many pains, but celibacy has no pleasures. *Samuel Johnson*

Gay people are forced to say, "I can't," because they are not permitted to say, "I do." So the third and final aspect of loving gay neighbors is the creation of a moral gay lifestyle patterned after marriage and sanctioned by the church. The denial-of-marriage double standard becomes a self-fulfilling prophecy when it is used as the basis for making moral judgments against the so-called gay lifestyle. Those who remain opposed to sanctioned gay relationships may claim it is an abuse of the institution of marriage. But such a stance ignores the history behind this evolving tradition.

Sex was around long before people got married. The original impetus for marriage was secular, not religious; economic, not moral. Marriage assured the legitimacy of heirs and provided a framework for the laws that would govern inheritance. The Old Testament style of marriage was one of polygamy. Women were treated as property then, a practice which continued well into this millennium. Consider the following "traditional" lines from wedding vows: "Who gives this woman to be married to this man?" A man, the father of the bride, responds, "I do," thereby giving his daughter away to another man, her husband-to-be. At the end of the ceremony, we have *man* (the important one) and *wife* (his new "possession"). Some churches have dropped the give-away line completely from modern ceremonies; others have changed the response to a less sexist "We do" or "Her mother and I do." And many now conclude the ceremony by presenting the couple as "husband and wife." Still, the "tradition" is hardly one which instills pride in this institution.

The first Christian marriage was recorded in the fourth century A.D. Yet marriage was not given the status of sacrament in the church until the fifteenth century, and priests were not a required part of the sacrament until over one hundred years later. This was when the Council of Trent first mandated a Christian ceremony to validate marriage, primarily in response to the Protestant Reformation. Even then, the main reason for marriage was economic, the arrangement selected by the bride's and groom's families for them. As the Puritans were arriving on this continent, the vast majority of commoners they left behind were living together, begetting children, without the benefit of clergy. With no wealth to pass on, there was no compelling reason for them to get married.

This brief review of the history of marriage was offered not to poke holes in marriages, but merely to point out the fallacies involved in claiming that "tradition" prohibits inclusion of gay people in this important institution. In fact, through the sixteenth century many same-sex couples did indeed get married in the church. So a focus on marriage is counterproductive. The focus should be on defining morality for gay relationships. And one obvious alternative is marriage.

Father Charles Curran commented on the basic approach of using marriage to define morality for gay people and offered a caveat: "There must be the context of a loving relationship striving for permanency. Here, too, one must take account of the fact that social pressures work against a more permanent type of relationship between homosexual partners." There is a another caveat here as well: Establishing an acceptable format for gay relationships that will endure for centuries will not be an easy task. A union between two people is much more than a ceremony; it involves detailed regulation through secular law. This was amply demonstrated in Chapter 4 by "The Pitfalls Facing a Gay Couple." Our homophobic society may not be very cooperative, at least for a while. But the process of change must start somewhere. Because traditional religious views have led society to view homosexuality as immoral, the church is the appropriate place for the process of reform to begin.

Some may also raise the issue of procreation as an argument against sanctioning gay relationships. This is exactly what St. Thomas did in his discussion on nature, which started the whole problem in the first place. Yet having children is not a prerequisite for marriage, nor is it even an expectation for many heterosexual couples. And some gay people do have children through previous marriages or other means. The point is that the quality of a marriage between two people is determined by their love for one another, not by their reproductive capability or gender-difference.

Until gay "unions" are officially sanctioned by the church, those relationships which exist currently should be recognized as being both meaningful and legitimate. Recognition includes allowing gay couples to take communion and attend church functions together.

The gay Christian or Jew learns the same moral outlook that any other Christian or Jew does concerning sexuality. A gay relationship, sanctioned by the church, is simply a recognition of this fact. It is ironic that this omission has actually had the effect of "sanctioning" promiscuity. Isolated acts of same-sex sexual expression have historically been considered less sinful by the church than living within a loving and permanent gay relationship. How blind we become to reality when trapped in tradition.

Each religion has, at some point in its history, had to fight oppression by secular forces and other religions. Under separation of church and state, our society has achieved religious pluralism where the right to practice any religion is respected. Sexual orientation is no different. Gay people respect the needs and desires of straight people. They live and let live. All they ask is for the same respect in return. "Therefore, however you want people to treat you, so treat them, for this is the Law and the Prophets." (Matthew 7:12)

Dr. Derrick Bailey offered an excellent summary of Judeo-Christian tradition on homosexuality:

> The most prominent feature in the tradition proves on examination to be the most vulnerable. It has always been accepted without question that God declared his judgment upon homosexual practices once and for all time by the destruction of the cities of the Plain. But Sodom and Gomorrah, as we have seen, actually have nothing to do with such practices; the interpretation of the Sodom story generally received by Western Christendom turns out to be nothing more than a post-Exilic Jewish reinterpretation devised and exploited by patriotic rigorists for polemical purposes. Thus disappears the assumption that an act of Divine retribution in the remote past has relieved us of the responsibility for making an assessment of homosexual acts in terms of theological and moral principles. It is no longer permissible to take refuge in the contention that God himself [sic] pronounced these acts detestable and abominable above every other sexual sin, nor to explain natural catastrophes and human disasters as his [sic] vengeance upon those who indulge in them. It is much hoped that we shall soon hear the last of Sodom and Gomorrah in connection with homosexual practices — though doubtless the term "sodomy" will always remain as a reminder of the unfortunate consequences which have attended the reinterpretation of an ancient story in the interests of propaganda.

"For nothing will be impossible with God." is the message found in Luke 1:37. What does this mean regarding homosexuality? For years I prayed, even begged God to make me straight. I no longer interpret that passage as meaning I will become straight someday. My prayers and ultimate conclusion are not unique. The same prayer has been repeated by millions of other gay Christians and Jews. A similar prayer has been said by many parents, relatives, and friends of gay people. Why homosexuality? Only God knows. He created it for His reasons, not ours. And if and when He decides to change things, it will also be for His reasons, not ours. The *Serenity Prayer* reads: "God, grant me the

188

serenity to accept the things I cannot change, the courage to change the things I can, and the wisdom to know the difference." This is truly good advice for everyone, gay or straight.

Malcolm Boyd, an Episcopal priest, observed:

They stand inside your church, Lord, and know a wholeness that can benefit it. Long ago they learned that they must regard the lilies of the field, putting their trust in you.

Pressured to hide their identities and gifts, they have served you with an unyielding, fierce love inside the same church that condemned them.

Taught that they must feel self-loathing, nevertheless they learned integrity and dignity, and how to look into your face and laugh with grateful joy, Lord.

Victims of a long and continuing torture, they asserted a stubborn faith in the justice of your kingdom.

Negativism was drummed into them as thoroughly as if they were sheet metal. They learned what it is to be hated. Yet, despite real rejection, they insisted on attesting to the fullness and beauty of all human creation, including theirs, in your image.

They are alive and well and standing inside your church. Bless them, Lord, to your service.

We should all strive to ensure that those who suffer might be comforted, and that those who are comfortable might be disturbed by the suffering of others.

Section V:

Gay in the USA

Chapter 12

The Pursuit of Happiness

We hold these truths to be self-evident, that all men are created equal; that they are endowed by their Creator with certain unalienable rights; that among these, are life, liberty and the pursuit of happiness. The Declaration of Independence

Those who have liberty often take it for granted; those who do not must constantly struggle to achieve equality. Such is the case for the gay minority in the United States. A social minority exists, not because there is a difference, but because the majority makes that difference relevant. Gay men and lesbians so far have been defined by a society which at worst persecutes them and at best tolerates their existence. As a result, it's not easy being gay in America.

Throughout recorded history "homosexuality" has had many different meanings. Accordingly, having a consistent, predominant or exclusive, emotional or erotic attraction to persons of the same gender has fallen in and out of social grace. There have been periods of acceptance in many societies, but *never* in the United States. If one's perspective is purely "American," it is difficult to appreciate the wide acceptance of homosexuality in the rest of the world. Dr. Alfred C. Kinsey pointed out: "In our American culture there are no types of sexual activity which are as frequently condemned because they depart from the mores and the publicly pretended custom as homosexual activities. There are practically no European groups, unless it be England, and few if any cultures elsewhere in the world which have become as disturbed over male homosexuality as we have here in the United States." Dr. Wardell Pomeroy offered a similar observation: "It is difficult for those who are not acquainted with cultures other than our own to understand fully how inhibited and rigid we are when it comes to sex. Anthropologists tell us that we are almost unique in the proscriptions, the anxieties, and the rigidities which we have developed in this area." He cited a study which found that in 193 different cultures, only fourteen percent rejected male homosexuality and only eleven percent rejected female homosexuality. Of all the societies studied by anthropologist Clellan Ford and psychologist Frank Beach, only 76 made reference to homosexuality. Forty-nine of those seventy-six, or sixty-four percent, considered homosexuality to be both normal and socially acceptable. Even Native Americans accepted same-sex sexuality well before the new Americans brought European culture and Judeo-Christian tradition to the North American continent.

Yet in our free society—the land of liberty—homosexuality has been associated with sin, crime, and sickness. Same-sex sexual acts were illegal in all of the original colonies, and in many states they still are. Punishment for homosexual "crimes" have included penance, fines, imprisonment, and even death. When the Pilgrims were setting foot on the new continent, they brought with them a custom of burning at the stake those men and women accused of committing "sodomy." The fires were started using small sticks of wood, or "faggots." Needless to say, but maybe not, the word *faggot* is derived from this practice. Its origin, probably unknown to most of those who use the word, is certainly understood by those who are its victim. Gay people have been arrested by civil servants, attacked on the streets by total strangers without protection or recourse, fired from jobs, condemned in the churches by righteous Christians and Jews, and denied public accommodations and services. They have been evicted from their homes, had their children taken away from them, and subjected to "cures" which included lobotomy, castration, and shock therapy. Today our society might be somewhat more civilized and subtle in its hostility toward gay people, but this minority is still oppressed in numerous ways.

The label *homosexual* has become as much of a social status as it is a sexual orientation. The nature of prejudice and discrimination faced by gay people today takes on myriad forms. The most insidious is a social "invisibility" which often ignores the gay minority's needs and even its existence. Gay men and lesbians remain hidden, passing as straight, to escape the oppression which surrounds them. The "invisibility" also serves to internalize the oppression, making it an individual problem rather than a social problem—and this kind of self-censuring is the ultimate form of oppression.

Understanding homosexuality requires an appreciation of what being gay is like in our society today. Without this insight, it is only natural to view gay civil rights as a frivolous enterprise. The issues of the Gay Civil Rights Movement are anything but frivolous. The gay minority continues to suffer from numerous instances of injustice and denials of basic civil liberties. It would be impossible to discuss every problem. Presented here instead are the major issues of concern to America's twenty-four million gay men and lesbians. Although women's issues are *important* to lesbians, they are not *unique* to lesbians. For this reason, and because most Americans already have an appreciation for women's issues, these will not be covered here. Specifically, the gay civil rights issues include: the victimization of gay people and the "homosexual panic" defense; sodomy and solicitation laws; employment discrimination; child custody, visitation, and adoption; insurance discrimination; the recognition of gay relationships; immigration and naturalization; and equal access to public accommodations and services. Indeed, homosexuality is much more than "just what people do in bed."

The Victimization of Gay People

On May 25, 1985, in Kalamazoo, Michigan a thirty-two-year-old gay man was sitting under a railroad trestle near a stream. He was joined by two teenage youths who had been drinking. The youths beat this man for nearly ten minutes, kicking him in the face and hitting him over the head with a log. The man attempted to defend himself, but did not fight back. The assailants left their victim lying in a pool of blood to attend a party. After about an hour at the party, one of the assailants returned to the scene with his cousin and a sledgehammer. When they arrived, the man was still there. He was making a gurgling sound caused by the blood in his throat. The original assailant raised the sledgehammer and drove it into the man's skull, not once, but *three* times. The victim was survived by his lover of eight years.

This is "fag-bashing." Also known by the euphemisms "gay-bashing" or "queer-bashing," "fag-bashing" was mentioned in Chapter 8 in the section on "The Abuses of Homophobia." The majority of the assailants are in their late teens or early twenties. Most of this senseless violence is perpetrated by these young men almost as a rite of passage into "manhood." It is at this age when young men first start to deal with many issues, including their own sexuality. Both the assailants and their victims are normally male, but lesbians are victims as well. In effect, gay people serve as a convenient and vulnerable target for whatever "manly" insecurities are experienced by men in our society.

The usual pattern of fag-bashing involves multiple assailants against a lone victim, indicating that such incidents are premeditated. According to available statistics, in only three percent of the reported cases are the victims and assailants equal in number; the average ratio is four to one. Some of these groups are gangs from the inner city; others are cliques of "nice" middle-class teenagers from the suburbs. A group assures that the odds of "success" are quite high, so that a lone assailant might never be defeated by some "sissy faggot" acting in self-defense. "Real" men must be victorious.

Fag-bashers will prowl gay areas or neighborhoods to assault gay men verbally, physically, and sometimes fatally. Typically, they ridicule their victims verbally first as if, by this action, the assailants give themselves permission to continue their assault. It is not uncommon, in fact, for a group of teenagers to consider fag-bashing an acceptable form of evening entertainment. And the results are frequently hideous. The authors of an article on gay-related violence observed: "That intense rage is present in nearly all homicide cases with homosexual victims . . . A striking feature of most murders in this sample is their gruesome, often vicious nature. Seldom is a homosexual victim simply shot. He is more apt to be stabbed a dozen times, mutilated, *and* strangled."

A typical incident, like the one in Kalamazoo, might start like this. A gay man is walking down a deserted street late at night, possibly on his way home from a gay bar. A car with four teenagers pulls alongside him. One of the young men yells, "Hey, faggot. You wanna suck my dick? You'd love that, wouldn't you?" What would *you* do? Would you

194

run? Maybe. Would you respond in anger? Probably not. Would you ignore them? Most likely. Would they just forget it and drive on? You certainly hope so, because you are scared. You think, "What will I do if they keep harassing me? What will I do if they stop and get out of the car?" Your adrenaline starts to flow as your heart pounds in panic. I know. This very incident happened to me.

In another case a young assailant, after physically attacking a gay man, had the nerve to phone a gay hotline to ask if he may have gotten AIDS.

Sadly, most law enforcement agencies consider anti-gay violence a problem unworthy of maintaining official statistics. Several civil liberties organizations and gay civil rights groups therefore have taken surveys of their own to point out the seriousness of this issue. Although these studies used relatively small sample sizes, the results have been reasonably consistent — and shocking. Three independent studies found that over eighty percent of gay men and lesbians reported incidents of verbal abuse. Nearly half reported threats of violence. Over one-third mentioned being chased, with slightly more than one-fourth actually experiencing physical assault. One of every five gay men and lesbians have had personal property vandalized. In 1986 alone, just forty-one organizations representing major cities in only twenty-seven states reported eighty homicides.

The respondents in most of these studies were primarily white, highly educated people in their thirties — a group which normally is much less likely to be victimized. The National Gay and Lesbian Task Force reported a victimization rate of seven times the national average. The Justice Department listed gay people as the most frequent victims of hate crimes. Sometimes straight men and women, who are mistakenly identified as gay, are also victimized.

The locations where this physical or verbal abuse takes place are not limited to gay areas or neighborhoods. Frequently cited were junior and senior high schools, homes, and the workplace. And this abuse is not limited to the typical fag-basher characterized above. Roughly one-half mentioned some form of abuse, physical, or verbal, by the police. Owing to the genuine risk involved, the vast majority of the gay minority passes as straight regularly to avoid potential victimization. Understandably, gay people do not "flaunt" their homosexuality.

The victimization of gay men and women is only half of the problem. Prosecuting these crimes is the other half.

The "Homosexual Panic" Defense

A fox should not be one of the jury at a goose's trial. *Thomas Fuller*

In the Michigan case cited above, the assailants defended their actions by claiming that sexual advances were made by the gay man. This is the essence of the "homosexual panic" defense. Character witnesses called by the prosecution testified it was highly unlikely that the victim would have made any sexual advances. But even if the alleged advance

195

had occurred, there would appear to be little chance for the defendants to claim legitimate "self-defense." The assistant prosecutor commented, "This body was horribly mangled . . . The face was unrecognizable as a human face." Several witnesses also testified that the assailants had bragged about "killing a fag." The most incriminating evidence against this defense was that one of the original assailants, accompanied by his cousin, returned to the scene with a sledgehammer to "finish off" his victim. No reasonable person could ever consider such action justifiable. But because homophobia has a way of overcoming reason, it worked. The primary assailant was found innocent of *all* charges: first-degree murder, second-degree murder, aggravated assault, and manslaughter. The judge in the case stated, "This is the first time in almost 12 years on the bench that I felt I would strongly have differed from the jury. I would have found first-degree murder."

Basically, the homosexual panic defense claims the defendant felt threatened by an alleged sexual advance. He then claims his "natural" response was self-defense — violent and brutal self-defense. This is analogous to the claim that a woman "deserved" to be raped by the way she acted or dressed. The story of events leading up to the assault is normally just that — a story, exaggerated or fabricated. It originates in the homophobia of the defendant and relies on the homophobia of the judge or jury for its success. In many ways it is similar as well to the purported fear of black men raping white women so often used to justify lynchings. Even if the alleged sexual advance were real, the violent nature of the response is well beyond any necessary and sufficient means of self-defense. Common sense alone dictates that any such advance, when outnumbered two-to-one, would have been verbal and not physical. An appropriate response would be a corresponding verbal, "No thanks, I'm straight" or "Get lost, I'm straight" or "Go to hell faggot, I'm straight." The operative phrase is "I'm straight" — enough said. And that would be the end of it. Instead, the defendants will claim, "He got what he deserved."

When an advance does occur, it is normally encouraged or even initiated by the defendant. Fag-bashing incidents nearly always take place late at night in secluded locations, mostly in gay cruising areas. Could anyone really believe that the multiple assailants were merely strolling along, minding their own business, when out of nowhere comes this gay man to rape them? Fag-bashing just doesn't happen that way. These are simply *not* cases of rape, even when the circumstances are dramatically exaggerated. Actually, just the opposite is true. The overwhelming number of male-male rapes reported are committed by heterosexual assailants against homosexual victims. The alleged sexual advance by the gay man is only used as an excuse to do what was intended all along: fag-bashing.

Because the homosexual panic defense relies on a homophobic jury, lawyers for the defense will regularly exclude jurors they suspect of being gay or merely "sympathetic" toward the gay minority before the trial even begins. The belief is that these jurors would be sympathetic toward the victim, rather than toward the defendant. How unfair. But at least

196

this part of the homosexual panic defense may be changing. Prior to 1986, there was no need to justify the exclusion of any prospective juror. A 1986 Supreme Court decision permits challenges to exclusions, making it necessary for the lawyer to offer some legitimate reason. The case involved racial exclusion, so only time will tell if this ruling will be applied to trials for fag-bashing.

Getting Away with Murder

The lack of consequences for the accused fag-basher serves to de-criminalize the victimization of gay people. In other words, it keeps fag-gots "fair game" for abuse and makes many gay people reluctant to report these crimes fearing the publicity will precipitate more violence. Marcel T. Saghir and Eli Robbins found that only forty-three percent of the gay people victimized in their survey reported the crime to the police. Other sources cite even lower rates.

Fag-bashing is similar to rape in other ways. Rape is also an act of violence. Many rape victims never go to the police. Failing to report the crime can lead some women to begin questioning their own innocence. The victim also feels degraded; self-worth is devastated. Both forms of assault are nightmarish experiences which are best left in the past. Yet, neither will ever be totally forgotten by its victim.

Social worker Craig Anderson described the experience:

> At the time of the assault, the issue of power is inherent in the victim's terror. His fear for his life, and his recognition of powerlessness in the face of a life-and-death situation, can prove overwhelming. The feelings of being violated and devalued, coupled with a sense of having lost the ability to control his circumstance, his body, or his own life, can also have an emotionally immobilizing effect on the victim . . . In the rare instances when a victim is able and willing to report the assault, he is usually greeted with disbelief or outright hostility by the police, who are the first line of formal intervention. This hostility may be di-rected at the victim's homosexuality. Even if he is not gay, the police may take it for granted that he is, the same assumption made by the assailant; or they may assume that his victimization was deserved and brought about by his own behavior. The victim is further humiliated and may be deterred from seeking additional assistance, whether medi-cal, psychological, or judicial.

Another perspective on this issue is afforded through the hypotheti-cal heterosexual panic defense for "breeder-bashing." Neither this of-fense nor its defense exists, but what would happen if they did? Virtually every gay man and lesbian has been approached sexually by a straight woman or man. When a straight woman "comes on" to a gay man, should he assault her in "self-defense"? When a straight man tries to "hit on" a lesbian "chick," should she douse him with mace, kick him several times in the groin, and go get her sledgehammer?

The solution to the social problem of anti-gay victimization is straight-forward. It begins by recognizing that *all* acts of aggression must be

197

condemned, not condoned. At a minimum, statistics that call attention to the problem and its magnitude must be maintained. There should be increased penalties for any act of violence motivated by hate, because such acts are clearly premeditated and unprovoked. Many states already have such provisions for other minority groups, and gay people should clearly be placed under this umbrella of protection. Civil lawsuits by the victim, or his or her surviving lover, should be permitted as well. Police departments can add sexual orientation to their nondiscrimination policies, designate a liaison to the gay community, and provide training for officers on gay lifestyles. Similar education in the schools, especially for teenage males, will help decrease homophobic attacks. Victims should be encouraged through various means to report these crimes. Prosecution must be rigorous, with training provided for countering the "homosexual panic" defense. Any attempts to stack a jury should be considered unconstitutional as a way of preventing a fair trial. Finally, the gay community should continue its awareness and victim support programs.

One of the main reasons gay people are reluctant to report these crimes is that many states have sodomy laws and most states have solicitation laws. In effect, these laws almost give gay people a "criminal status."

Sodomy and Solicitation Laws

It would be difficult, if not impossible, to make homosexuality itself illegal. To do this, it would be necessary to define what "homosexuality" meant *legally*. The consistent, predominant or exclusive, emotional and erotic attraction to persons of the same gender accurately defines homosexuality, but it would be blatantly unconstitutional to think someone would be guilty of something as a result of feelings. Even though some individuals might believe such *feelings* do constitute a "crime," an accurate means, within the constitutional guidelines for self-incrimination, would be necessary to detect these feelings. Therefore, being gay is not a crime. Instead, same-sex sexual acts or the proposition of same-sex sexual acts are what is made criminal. This approach, not too surprisingly, is identical to that of the church, where the "sin" is not homosexuality itself, but its sexual expression. That is why these laws are frequently referred to as "morals charges" — an appropriate phrase. The "crime" itself is victimless; the laws preventing the "crime" only enforce a particular ideology of personal morality. In effect, sodomy and solicitation laws turn private acts into public crimes. Although they are treated together here and are even sometimes related, these laws can be and are enforced independently of each other. Because they belong under state jurisdiction, this discussion will necessarily be in general terms.

Sodomy Goes Secular

To prevent a gay couple from making love, society has made laws: sodomy laws. As recently as 1961, all fifty states had sodomy laws. As of this writing twenty-four states and the District of Columbia still have sodomy laws. The laws in nineteen of those twenty-four states apply equally to both gay and straight sexual practices. Even in Nevada, where prostitution is legal, sodomy, the homosexual variety only, is illegal. The commission of sodomy can be a misdemeanor or a felony. Punishment ranges from a $200 fine to twenty years in prison, as if prisons are the place to "reform" such behavior.

Normally, sodomy laws prohibit some frequently unspecified sexual act or acts. Some states use the word *buggery;* others use an assortment of vague phrases: crime against nature, unnatural intercourse, lascivious act, carnal copulation, sexual perversion, sexual misconduct, sexual psychopaths, perverted sexual practices, and deviate sexual conduct. The one thing they all have in common is that none prohibits coitus. Still, those versions that apply "equally" to both sexual orientations are invariably enforced exclusively against gay people. The mere availability of coital sex makes straight couples exempt from scrutiny. This approach is, once again, identical to the one taken by the church. (Is there a pattern emerging here?) In effect, then, these laws apply equally to both gay and straight people about as much as city ordinances against sleeping on park benches apply equally to both the poor and the rich. The only difference is that certain vagrancy laws at least represent some legitimate social interest.

In his book *The Gay Mystique,* Peter Fisher explained how these laws are deeply offensive: "By their very existence, they tell all homosexuals that no matter how decent and moral a life they try to lead, society considers them criminals and undesirables, second-class citizens with limited rights. No homosexual can respect these laws, and some gay people find it difficult to maintain respect for the political system which created them, the society which continues to allow them to exist, and those who choose to enforce them on a discriminatory basis."

Sodomy laws are not only victimless and offensive, they are basically worthless. Most gay and straight people are totally unaware such a law exists in their own states. When its existence is known, the law is completely disregarded. This serves to create a lack of respect in the gay community, and even in the dominant society, for the institutions of government, the law, and law enforcement agencies. Any law which prohibits popular, widely practiced, and private behavior cannot be considered good government.

The difficulties in enforcing sodomy laws are rather obvious. Because sexuality is a very private matter, very few gay people have ever been arrested on sodomy charges. Therefore, other laws have been enacted to "enforce" society's homophobia.

Solicitation — Loosely Speaking

How many straight men have said something to the effect of, "Hey baby, how would you like to come over to my place and see my etchings?" How many women, straight and gay, have been deeply offended and insulted by such an advance, even though this behavior is considered socially acceptable for men? Maybe this is not the most ideal behavior possible, but it is far from being illegal. A similar statement by a gay man could subject him to arrest and prosecution, potentially resulting in a fine or imprisonment or both.

Solicitation laws are much more complex than sodomy laws. Nearly all states have solicitation laws to prohibit individuals from offering bribes, inciting riots, or committing other crimes which pose a genuine threat to social order. This type of solicitation should not be confused with prostitution, nor should it be confused with laws that prohibit rape or child molestation. When solicitation laws apply to sex, it is only necessary to violate some purported "standard of decency" of an "innocent" bystander. In states with sodomy laws, the solicitation crime can be the proposition to commit a sexual "crime." But again, this is not necessary.

Solicitation is inherently an unfinished event; it is an offer to do something without necessarily completing, or making good, on that offer. As such, it occurs at the juncture of intent and behavior. A sexual advance typically involves many nonsexual forms of behavior, such as speech or body language. Even if no "offer" is made, some men have been arrested for simply hanging around or "loitering to solicit," because they are believed to have the intent of making such an offer. Sometimes a sexual offer is made by indicating or displaying the genitals, or literally, getting caught with one's pants down. Even when this occurs in a restroom, the act can be construed as "lewd and lascivious" behavior — another basis for criminal prosecution. In at least one case, two men merely holding hands were charged with lewd and lascivious behavior. Where there are no sodomy laws or laws specifically prohibiting solicitation, it is possible to *make* this activity illegal. One method is for an undercover officer to offer money, when none was requested, in order to misconstrue the situation as prostitution. Gay men have even been arrested for solicitation based on charges of "disorderly conduct" or "vagrancy." All of these laws are similar in both their nature and their use. They are all therefore discussed here under the general category of "solicitation laws."

The normal justification for solicitation laws is the purported "innocent" bystander who might be offended. Yet practically no solicitation cases on record were brought by "innocent" bystanders. Nearly all involve an undercover police decoy. The officer selected is usually young and attractive. He goes to a public location where cruising is thought to take place. The officer may make certain remarks or gestures, or wear distinctive clothing, with the *intent* of giving the impression a sexual offer would be favorably received. The "etiquette" of cruising calls for an invitation to be made *only* when receptive impressions are conveyed. Considering the potential for fag-bashing, gay men are not likely to make advances to a complete stranger in a public place without at least some indication of receptiveness. When an offer is made, the police officer will suggest going to another location where an arrest can be made in private. This protects his cover, allowing several arrests to be made at a single location.

For charges to be legitimate, the intent to commit this "crime" must originate in the defendant. Otherwise, the police would be guilty of en-

200

trapment. Entrapment, broadly defined, is action which fosters rather than prevents crime. It is practically impossible to determine where an idea originates, but the police officer would undoubtedly have more credibility during trial testimony. After all, some juries, based on their homophobia, even acquit murderers. Although technically such actions might not constitute entrapment, they are certainly questionable as good police practice.

Sometimes solicitation arrests are conducted on a mass scale. This was the case at a Michigan roadside rest stop in 1986. Police videotaped *all* the individuals who used this rest stop for any reason during a ten-day period; every license plate number was recorded. During this time, there were no citizen complaints, no innocent bystander victims. Several days after filming, the police arrested forty-one men, charging most with "gross indecency." In Michigan this is a felony punishable by up to five years in prison and a $2,500 fine. Then the police released the names, occupations, places of employment, and home addresses to the *media!* Unbelievable. Twenty-eight, or seventy percent, of the forty-one men arrested were married.

Here is another example. The following excerpt is from a letter written by a gay man's father.

> Four years ago, our son, aged eighteen, was stalked in the park in Florida by a cop. The police story was that he was loitering for the purpose of prostitution and robbery. He was supposed to have approached the cop and invited him up to a nearby hotel room, having settled on a price. Five dollars. He was supposed to have lunged at the cop, going for the genitals. The cop said that he flashed a badge and that my son flashed a knife, a switchblade. They fought and my son was killed. We got a call in New York to come down for the body. If all this was true, why was our kid carved like a turkey ... Our son never had a knife. Especially a switchblade. Sure, he used to look for boys. But he never hurt anyone. That [Anita] Bryant witch and her mob helped kill him. She spread enough hate to kill lots of kids. Gave the crazies an excuse to witch hunt. We overheard a detective at the morgue say that our kid's death was no great loss ... There are probably lots of parents like us, who lost our kids to the "law." And what can we do. What can we prove.

While it is easy to be critical of the homosexual, bisexual, and predominantly heterosexual men who attempt to use public places in search of sexual partners, it is important to keep in mind all the places where they cannot meet. Most arrests on charges of solicitation are made in small towns where there are no gay bars or bathhouses. Some of these "criminals" are just too young to get into a bar. Of course, straight people can and do regularly meet sexual partners in public places. The only difference is that such behavior is socially acceptable.

Sexual *activity* conducted in public places is a different matter. But the use of solicitation laws as a means of prevention is both homophobic and ineffective. Yet here again is a double standard. Straight people caught practicing "autoeroticism" in the back seats of their cars at the thousands of "lovers lanes" from coast to coast are merely told, "Go home if you want to do that."

A "License" to Quell

There is no doubt: Both sodomy and solicitation laws serve as literal license to quell by providing society a framework for "legitimate" discrimination against and harassment of gay people. After all, we are a nation of laws, not men/women. And these laws are the epitome of double standards and self-fulfilling prophecies.

Recall that many gay people are reluctant to report crimes when they are victimized. The "criminal status" of gay people in states with sodomy laws is one of the primary reasons. In addition, the mere existence of sodomy laws has been used by the courts to deny the freedom of association on the grounds that people who meet at gay functions or in gay groups might have sex with one another, thereby violating "the law." In one case, a judge ruled it was illegal for bars to serve gay people in order to "prevent the congregation at liquor establishments of persons likely to prey upon the public by attempting to recruit other persons for acts which have been declared illegal by the legislature." Of course, that would be like saying people cannot drive cars because they might speed. Putting it in a heterosexual context, it would be like saying straight men and women cannot be members of the same organizations because someone might get raped. Just as with the courts, the legislative and executive branches of government can use the mere existence of sodomy laws as "justification" to deny funds for public education of safe sexual practices that would help prevent the spread of AIDS, to ban sex education courses in the schools from addressing homosexuality, or to pass a law allowing forms of discrimination in the workplace or in public accommodations and services.

In effect, then, sodomy laws are more like resolutions granting all three branches of government—legislative, judicial, and executive— the *excuse* to exercise homophobia. But this excuse is inexcusable. Justice Pashman, in a decision by the New Jersey Supreme Court, said it best: "Private personal acts between two consenting adults are not to be lightly meddled with by the State. The right of personal autonomy is fundamental to a free society. Persons who view fornication as opprobrious conduct may seek strenuously to dissuade people from engaging in it. However, they may not inhibit such conduct through the coercive power of the criminal law."

Legalizing private, consensual sexual acts between two adults does not mean that a majority of society must like or "approve" of such behavior. Legalization means repealing the sodomy laws that are ineffective, unconstitutional, and a total waste of taxpayers' dollars. To this end, gay civil rights organizations have been joined by numerous other groups, including the American Bar Association, American Psychological Association, American Medical Association, American Law Institute, International Congress of Criminal Law, American Law Committee, National Commission on Reform of the Federal Criminal Laws, National Legal

Aid and Defense Association, American Civil Liberties Union, National Institute of Mental Health, American Mental Health Foundation, American Public Health Association, National Organization for Women, and the American Psychiatric Association. With such a comprehensive list calling for repeal, one is left wondering who still supports sodomy laws?

Solicitation laws are equally oppressive, but in a rather insidious way. After going through all the trouble and expense to make an arrest, solicitation charges are, more often than not, either dropped or reduced. Authorities probably figure they will be unable to prosecute successfully based on the numerous constitutional issues raised. (These are discussed in Chapter 14.) On the other hand, the unconstitutionality of these laws may be irrelevant because this form of "justice" often bypasses the judicial system in practice.

Newspaper reports of the arrest inform a man's friends, family and employer of his "homosexual tendencies." Some men arrested on these charges end up losing their jobs. Where permitted by law, companies regularly ask all prospective employees if they have ever been arrested on any charge, regardless of guilt or innocence. This might make it difficult to get a new job. Some locations require individuals convicted of "sex crimes" to register as sex offenders, making it nearly impossible to get a new job. Then there are the "fines" involved. The defendant has attorney fees and possible court costs. Because there is no victim to press charges, some men arrested are blackmailed by officials who recognize this golden opportunity for personal gain. This is especially true considering that the majority of men arrested for solicitation are married or otherwise leading predominantly heterosexual lives. And once a man is identified as being gay, even if he isn't, the chance of verbal or physical assault by total strangers is increased.

On the rare occasion that a solicitation case does go to trial, a phenomenon similar to fag-bashing's homosexual panic defense occurs during jury selection. But this time, it is the attorneys for the prosecution who attempt to screen out jurors suspected of being gay or "sympathetic," all but eliminating the possibility of a fair trial. In an atmosphere that is less than compassionate toward homosexuality, the best a man charged with solicitation can hope for is a hung jury.

The punitive process can lead to ruined lives, possibly ending in suicide. Clearly, the human suffering involved goes well beyond any conceivable benefit society could ever hope to achieve.

Earning a Living

So much of what we call management consists in making it difficult for people to work. *Peter Drucker*

The workplace mirrors society. The work environment, however, affords a much greater opportunity to discriminate against gay people. In society, the gay minority is not accepted, but it is at least tolerated. Society *must* put up with diversity to some degree. Even when the civil rights of a minority are not assured, the minority itself cannot just be "eliminated." This is not the case in the workplace.

One's job is one's livelihood. Fear of losing that job is one of the main reasons the vast majority of gay people choose to conceal their homosexuality, passing as straight—and for good reason. Many psychologists and sociologists observe that if gay people were as "obvious" as black people are, there would be millions of gay men and lesbians out of work.

Because the gay minority is afforded little protection from employment discrimination, the workplace is frequently targeted for attack by homophobic activists. The "justification" is generally for the safety of others, especially children. The fear of the spread of AIDS has provided an opportunity to discriminate against gay people as well, mostly in the food service and health care industries. Discrimination in the workplace is damaging enough on its own, but it can establish a harmful precedent affecting other areas of gay people's lives.

The double standards and self-fulfilling prophecies of employment discrimination begin with the jobs that are considered "off-limits." Five special areas are then examined more closely. These include teaching school, military service, security clearances, occupational licensing, and the private sector.

The Off-Limits Opportunities

Based on a stereotypical belief that gay people are irresponsible, and that they sexually molest children and "recruit" others, it naturally follows that they might be "inappropriate" for some jobs—making certain career opportunities "off limits." According to the Institute for Sex Research, over two-thirds of those surveyed felt gay people should not be allowed to work in the following capacities: court judge, schoolteacher, minister, medical doctor, or government official. What career pursuits did they feel gay people should be permitted to pursue? The respondents overwhelmingly "approved" a not-so-surprising list which includes beautician, artist, musician, and florist. This is, of course, much more than just a "harmless" opinion. A significant proportion of those who hold this negative view of homosexuality and gay people are managers who do the hiring.

Some people claim certain jobs should be off-limits to gay men and lesbians based on popular opinion of this despised minority, apparently failing to recognize they are an integral part of that opinion. This position is at best tautological, for it is really a use of prejudice to justify prejudice. Such an argument could never be successfully advanced to discriminate against black people, handicapped persons, straight women, Jews, or any minority for that matter.

Many homophobic attitudes at work are based simply on a belief that straight workers may feel "uncomfortable" when working with gay employees, or that morale and productivity will suffer. Co-workers frequently imagine potentially threatening behavior from gay employees based on the stereotypes. According to the Institute for Sex Research, thirty-eight percent of those surveyed felt, "Homosexuals tend to corrupt their fellow workers sexually."

Similarly, some people will claim homosexuality does not "belong" in the workplace, as if sexual orientation could be left at home. They either forget or do not realize how often they bring their heterosexuality to the office. Gay people are constantly exposed to heterosexual "lifestyles" at work as straight people "flaunt" their sexuality. There is clearly a double standard here. For example, it is acceptable for a man to ask a women for a date at work, while a man asking another man or a woman asking another woman the same question is considered "inappropriate" behavior for the office. Even though the gay version of the question would unlikely get asked, the fact it could seems to be enough to justify the discrimination.

In James A. Doyle's book *The Male Experience,* he describes "How to Tell a Businessman from a Businesswoman." The thought process used to create the following sexist double standards is no different from homophobic stereotyping:

A businessman is aggressive; a businesswoman is pushy.

A businessman is good with details; a businesswoman is picky.

He loses his temper because he's so involved in his job; she's a bitch.

He follows through; she doesn't know when to quit.

He's confident; she's conceited.

His judgments are her prejudices.

He is a man of the world; she's been around.

If he drinks because of job pressure; she's a lush.

He's never afraid to say what he thinks; she's always shooting off her mouth.

The homophobic thought process creating similar differences between gay and straight employees completely ignores the reality of the situation: These "problems" currently do not exist in the workforce which is already ten percent gay. Gay people can be found in virtually *every* occupation and capacity. This is amply demonstrated by the numerous gay organizations for lawyers, doctors, nurses, psychiatrists, public health workers, historians, political scientists, librarians, social workers, clergy, public employees, teachers, consultants, engineers, linguists, scientists, and pilots. The list goes on and on. If gay people are so "obviously" inappropriate for certain jobs, why is it that this becomes obvious only after discovering an employee is gay? Is this incidental factor enough to turn a good employee into a bad one overnight? These imaginary "problems" with homosexuality, based on homophobia, are what leads to discrimination — creating very real problems for both employees and employers.

The most "off-limits" career pursuit for gay people is teaching. Despite the wealth of evidence to the contrary, there are those who continue to claim gay people should not work with children in any capacity, especially teaching, which is a particular problem for lesbians, as many of the jobs open to women involve children. This form of discrimination not only denies gay youth the benefit of respectable gay role models, it

205

alerts them to the anguish they will experience in our society for the rest of their lives. Naturally, these sanctions against gay adults also teach homophobia to straight youth. This situation warrants a closer look.

Teacher, Teacher I Declare — Dykes and Faggots Everywhere

If Leonardo daVinci were alive today, many people would not want him teaching a science class. Why? Because he was homosexual.

The worst fear any society has is the corruption of its youth. This evokes incredible, often irrational reactions. A 1977 study by the Institute for Sex Research found that seventy-four percent of those surveyed agreed with the statement: "Homosexuals are dangerous as teachers or youth leaders because they try to get sexually involved with children." This fear of "attack" or molestation is totally unsupported by the evidence. Recall from the discussion of stereotypes in Chapter 3, that approximately ninety percent of all pedophiles are *heterosexual*. Therefore, young girls are nine times more likely to be abused sexually by male teachers than young boys are. Society should indeed protect *all* children from any sexual aggression, heterosexual or homosexual. The single standard is simple: Pedophiles should not be permitted to teach in school.

Similarly, there is no basis for a belief that gay teachers would "advocate" homosexuality. The First Amendment guarantee to freedom of speech protects those teachers who might "advocate" socialism or school prayer, but for some reason "advocating" homosexuality is not viewed as an issue of constitutional liberty. Actually, what is interpreted as "advocacy" in the case of homosexuality is frequently the mere absence of negative attitudes and beliefs. Of course, straight people have tried unsuccessfully to "advocate" heterosexuality, even trying to "recruit" gay people, for nearly a century. But no amount of social tolerance or social oppression is going to change the fact that ten percent of the population, including students, is gay. In opposing California's Proposition 6, which would have barred gay men and lesbians from teaching positions, Governor Ronald Reagan quoted a woman who had gone to parochial school: "If teachers had such power over children, I would have been a nun years ago." He was right.

The American Federation of Teachers announced its opposition to this form of discrimination in 1970 when its Executive Council declared: "The American Federation of Teachers protests any personnel actions taken against any teacher merely because he or she practices homosexual behavior in private life." In a 1974 resolution the National Education Association similarly stated that "personnel policies must guarantee that no person be employed, retained, paid, dismissed, or demoted because of... sexual orientation." These organizations apparently recognize that any restriction on gay teachers sends a warning to the gay students about the oppression they can expect in life, and a message to the straight students that this form of discrimination is perfectly acceptable.

More Than an Adventure — It's a Job

Sgt. Leonard Matlovich served in the U.S. Air Force for thirteen years. He completed three separate tours of duty to Southeast Asia and consistently received the highest possible ratings from his commanding officers. His awards included the Bronze Star Medal and the Purple Heart. Despite all this, and despite the fact that *all* his sexual activity occurred in private with consenting adults off the base, when Sergeant Matlovich informed one of his commanding officers of his homosexuality, he was discharged from the service. His tombstone reads: "When I was in the military they gave me a medal for killing two men and a discharge for loving one." The case of Sergeant Matlovich was well publicized, but it is far from unique. An average of 1,700 members of the military are discharged from service each year based on a homosexual sexual orientation, according to the Department of Defense.

The military has a history of prejudice in its treatment of most minorities, which is not unlike the history of most other social institutions. The only difference is that the military, to a significant extent, is exempt from the provisions of the Constitution, making reform difficult. Even the courts seem to uphold this constitutional "immunity." In one case the court ruled: "Armies cannot be maintained and commanded, and wars cannot be won by the judicial process. Supervision and control over the selection, appointment and dismissal of officers are not judicial functions. Dismissals of officers are not limited or controlled by the Bill of Rights." With only a little imagination, a similar argument could be made that private companies and even the government itself might conduct business more efficiently if it were not for that darn judicial process or Bill of Rights. Such an attitude is completely inconsistent with the principles of democracy.

In another case the assistant chief of naval personnel argued, "An officer or senior enlisted person who exhibits homosexual tendencies will be unable to maintain the necessary respect and trust from the great majority of naval personnel who despise/detest homosexuality, and this would most certainly degrade the individual's ability to successfully perform his duties of supervision and command." Such circular reasoning is nothing new to the military, which has used it before to justify discrimination against other minorities, specifically black people and women. In a 1951 edition of the *Annals of the American Academy of Political and Social Science,* an article titled "The Case Against Army Segregation" stated, "Integration would lower morale and impair efficiency. Whites just will not serve with blacks, and even if they would, it is not possible to train and use Negroes in highly skilled jobs." The same style of argument was used in opposition to the Women's Armed Services Integration Act of 1948, and more recently in countering attempts to admit women to military academies where it was believed that some men might not have respect for female commanding officers.

Discharge from the service is the military's preferred way of handling the "homosexual problem." But this is coming under stronger attack. Considering that approximately ninety percent of all discharges are honorable, anything less carries great stigma. Dishonorable, undesirable, and even general discharges can make it virtually impossible for the individual to get another job. Essential veteran benefits can also be denied. Because of this, gay people who do not receive honorable discharges are compelled to appeal in the courts. To avoid these suits, the military recently has begun granting honorable discharges to most gay people. Many men and women who previously were given less-than-honorable discharges for homosexuality have appealed, seeking an upgrade through either military or civilian courts. Civilian court reviews of military discharges are normally on procedural grounds, creating a lack of legal precedents to guide the military's policies pertaining to homosexuality. Without legal precedents, the military can quickly and easily change its ways. So while the current practice of granting honorable discharges to gay people may appear gracious, it is really quite self-serving. The military simply wants to avoid problems. Besides, this approach misses the point. Gay military personnel do not want early honorable discharges; they want to continue their careers of service to their country.

The navy appears to understand this. Revised naval regulations state it is no longer mandatory to discharge gay people. The new policy makes it "necessary" for the navy to show that a gay person is "unfit" for military service before a discharge can be issued. But with homophobia as strong as ever, this position has had very little real effect on the number of discharges. Navy regulations still claim, "The presence of such a member [gay person] in a military establishment seriously impairs combat readiness, efficiency, security, and morale." Some additional reasons offered by the navy and other branches of the military which are claimed to make a gay person "unfit" include maintaining discipline, protecting recruitment, fostering mutual trust and confidence among servicemembers, insuring integrity of the system of rank and command, maintaining the acceptability of military service, facilitating assignment and worldwide deployment of servicemembers who frequently must live and work under close conditions affording minimal privacy, reducing tensions and hostilities, and preventing breaches of security.

Anyone would agree that these issues are very important, but interestingly enough, it is not necessary for the navy to establish a relationship between these issues and homosexuality. This is because the military employs different standards of justice from what the rest of society uses. Military justice is based on a "preponderance of evidence," *not* the standard of innocent until proven guilty beyond a reasonable doubt. For example, an argument which addresses combat readiness but fails to establish a clear relationship with homosexuality could be quite adequate. In fact, the "burden of proof" frequently is placed on the defendant to show that these issues are *not* related to homosexuality. Most gay people feel, "Why even bother?" The most convincing argument would simply fall on deaf ears.

Naval regulations go one step further by creating a classification system to permit "flexibility in handling" gay personnel. Class I is "servicemen who have committed homosexual offenses involving force, fraud, intimidation, or the seduction of a minor." Class II is "servicemen who have willfully engaged in, or attempted to perform, homosexual acts which do not fall under the Class I category." Class III is "servicemen who exhibit, profess, or admit homosexual tendencies or associate with known homosexual others." Incredible. A type of discharge is recommended for each of the navy's classes. Although it is allowable, in no classification is the recommendation for an honorable discharge.

The army has an interesting policy as well. They define *homosexual acts* as "bodily contact between persons of the same sex" or "any proposal, solicitation, or attempt to perform such an act." Their policy continues by stating: "Members who have been involved in homosexual acts in an apparent isolated episode stemming solely from immaturity, curiosity, or intoxication normally will not be processed for discharge because of homosexual acts." The ignorance is nothing short of incredible.

These policies and procedures leave gay people two choices: join the forces, serving their country and risk getting "caught," or avoid the military entirely. The latter is obviously preferred by the military. Such treatment of gay people is not only unnecessary and discriminatory, it is actually quite ineffective. On the average, most gay people do not identify as gay until the late teens or early twenties. Many gay men and lesbians therefore enter the military with a sincere belief in their own heterosexuality.

In any event, the military's practice completely misses the point: *Homophobia* is what causes problems, not homosexuality. Returning to the navy's "issues," it is homophobia which causes problems in recruitment by deterring gay people. It is homophobia which perpetuates the prejudice that impairs combat readiness and efficiency, creates lack of respect from subordinates, causes tension and hostilities, reduces morale, and so on. Finally, it is homophobia which creates a security risk by making gay people targets for blackmail attempts.

More than being denied an opportunity for direct work and pay, gay people are denied an opportunity to acquire valuable skills and useful experience. And failure to find gainful employment based on a lack of skills or a less-than-honorable discharge can place a financial burden on the rest of society. There is great damage indeed, and for no good reason. Many of America's allies run their militaries very effectively and efficiently *without* homophobic discriminatory policies and practices.

How long will the military's homophobia continue, even in contradiction to its own findings? As long ago as 1957, a navy study refuted the notion that gay people posed any security threat. More recently, a 1989 report by the Defense Department's own Personnel Security Research and Education Center concluded that "the preponderance of the evidence presented in this study indicates that homosexuals show preservice suitability-related adjustment that is as good [as] or better than [that of] the average heterosexual."

What is required is a single standard applying equally to men and women, gay and straight. Judd Marmor, former president of the American Psychiatric Association, commented, "If *individual* homosexual women or men prove to be unsuited to military life by virtue of specific actions that would apply equally to heterosexuals, those individuals should be separated from the service. As a *class,* however, there is no sound psychiatric basis for treating homosexual men and women any differently from other people in the armed services. In actuality innumerable gay men and women have served in the armed forces with distinction and have received honorable discharges. The fact that they were undetected as homosexuals merely indicates that their sex life, no less than that of heterosexuals, was a private matter, as indeed it should be."

Probably worse than the direct consequences of its discriminatory practices is the poor example the military offers for other government agencies and private industry. In fact, it has led to the creation of a whole new form of discrimination: the denial of security clearances.

Clearance Sales — Selling Out To Prejudice

President Dwight D. Eisenhower, formerly General Eisenhower, issued an executive order directing the Department of Defense to create the Defense Industrial Security Clearance Office (DISCO). DISCO is responsible for screening applicants to grant or deny security clearances for employees in the *private sector* working on sensitive government contracts. The standard used for security clearances was that approval should be "clearly consistent with the national interest." There are numerous criteria, all explicit, used to deny clearances to gay people. Included are emotional instability, mental disorders, moral turpitude and "reckless" behavior which might make an applicant subject to blackmail. The *DIS Manual for Personnel Security Investigations* lists homosexuality along with bestiality, voyeurism, necrophilia, pedophilia, nymphomania, sadism and masochism, then disassociates all of these with heterosexuality by stating that "normally DIS does not investigate allegations of heterosexual conduct between consenting adults."

Unfortunately, society still seems to agree with this blatant homophobia. According to the Institute for Sex Research, fifty-nine percent of those surveyed felt, "Homosexuals are a high security risk for government jobs." This is true despite the fact that nearly everyone who has been found guilty of spying recently is heterosexual. It would seem reasonable that this might be true for ninety percent of all cases, but my research uncovered no recent cases involving gay people. More extensive research by the National Gay Rights Advocates found absolutely no cases of gay-related blackmail — period. Even the government itself, through testimony in 1985 by the FBI and the Defense Intelligence Agency before the Senate, was unable to produce evidence supporting the homosexual blackmail theory.

The reasoning behind this position is really a "Catch 22." Judge Peckham of the Ninth Circuit Court of Appeals described this perfectly in a dissenting opinion he issued in 1974: "Of course, any homosexual with a security clearance will fear disclosure — if not to his family and friends, at least to the government — as long as the Department of Defense continues to revoke security clearances on a mere finding of homosexuality. However, the Department of Defense easily can cure the danger to national security allegedly posed by all homosexuals. It can abandon its arbitrary system of revoking security clearances solely on a finding of homosexuality and, thus, end homosexuals' fears that public exposure will cost them their security classifications." This purported threat is actually just another self-fulfilling prophecy of homophobia.

Recognizing the inherent fallacy here, a new charge is emerging. In *Padula v. Webster* the D.C. Circuit Court issued a 1987 ruling which read in part: "It is not irrational for the [FBI] to conclude that . . . the general public opprobrium toward homosexuals exposes many homosexuals, even 'open' homosexuals, to the risk of possible blackmail to protect *their partners,* if not themselves." [Emphasis added.] Where will it all end?

For many of the same reasons mentioned above regarding exclusionary practices in the military, the government no longer considers homosexuality itself a "sexual perversion" for the purpose of granting security clearances. Most gay people who are openly gay are now able to get security clearances with little or no difficulty. The onus is with the government to establish that an applicant is either subject to blackmail or has a history of "reckless" behavior. But because this is a very subjective process, and again for many of the same reasons, gay people continue to be denied clearances based on factors which *relate* to homosexuality. This is particularly true when extremely homophobic individuals serve on the review board.

For example, here is the question which should be asked: "Is there anything in your past or present which would make you subject to blackmail?" Instead, the review board may ask a gay applicant about the nature, frequency and circumstances, including time and place, of his or her homosexual sexual activity. A double standard exists because straight candidates normally are not asked such questions. If *any* of these highly personal questions are answered with *any* degree of inaccuracy, even by omission, denial can be ruled. Can you accurately recall every time you had sex, where you were, who your partner was, and what you did? This type of interrogation will likely continue until the government, by statute or judicial decision on the merits of a case, prohibits it as a form of discrimination. Even when a clearance is granted, and it usually will be if a denial is protested, the time spent in court is time spent away from the job. The individual loses valuable experience and state-of-the-art knowledge. The whole process is also very expensive — for the individual *and* for the taxpayer.

It is unfortunate, but not surprising, that some homophobic companies welcome this practice. They do not say to the government, "Hey, you can't deny her clearance because she's lesbian. We need her on the project." They instead say to the gay employee, "Sorry, there's nothing we can do." It is a great excuse which gives homophobic individuals the opportunity to create problems for both gay employees and their employers.

A License ... To Kill

Occupational licenses are analogous to security clearances for certain careers. Most states have strict licensing standards for the various professions. A license is required to practice that profession in that state. Frequently, there is a requirement for "good moral character." If members of the licensing board are homophobic, as many are, a gay person is likely to be judged on the basis of the stereotypes. The stereotypes are hardly demonstrative of "good moral character." Openly gay candidates may be subjected to additional scrutiny leading to delays, at a minimum, and potentially the unreasonable denial of this essential license. Most licensing agencies no longer discriminate solely on the basis of sexual orientation, but this practice is rarely formal. To set an example, the American Psychological Association added sexual orientation to its list of prohibited discriminations in their statement of policy regarding equal employment opportunities.

Privacy and the Private Sector

A 1977 Gallup poll indicated that only slightly more than half of those questioned favored equal employment opportunities for gay men and women. A 1985 *Los Angeles Times* survey confirmed this result by reporting that only half said they would hire an openly gay person. But the position that certain jobs should be "off-limits" for gay people is just part of the problem in the private sector. According to *The Cox Report on the American Corporation,* approximately one-half of both top and middle managers surveyed felt homosexuality has a "very negative" effect on promotion possibilities. Another fourth felt homosexuality has a "somewhat negative" effect. In total, then, nearly seventy-five percent of managers feel homosexuality is a liability at the office. The potential for discrimination is obvious.

Other minority groups share this "potential" of discrimination in the workplace. Black people have civil rights; they just can't get jobs as easily as white people do. Similarly, the average woman earns less than the average man. Women can get jobs; they just aren't paid as well. And this occurs despite the fact that discrimination against black people and women is now illegal nationwide. The same is not true for gay people. In fact, the discrimination against gay people is quite legal in most situations.

Based on the pervasiveness of homophobic beliefs, gay people have ample reason to be concerned. The Institute for Sex Research found that only fourteen percent of gay employees are open about their homosexuality to their employers. This contributes to the problem because the secrecy leads most employers to believe they have very few gay employees. As a result, homophobic discrimination is a problem which is rarely even mentioned, let alone addressed in most organizations.

Unlike the military, the vast majority of American corporations do not have formal discriminatory policies. But strong and well-established informal practices of discrimination clearly exist.

Some companies claim they do not practice discrimination, making a written nondiscrimination policy unnecessary. Even if this were true, it would not serve as a good reason *not* to have such a policy. All companies regularly formalize informal practices through written policy. Yet a nondiscrimination policy regarding sexual orientation meets with both active and passive resistance in nearly all companies. Even if such discrimination does not exist today, it may tomorrow. This position is analogous to claiming that automotive insurance is unnecessary because one has never had an accident. Other companies claim they do not want to "cater" to gay people. This is similar to society's view that to permit is to "condone" or "promote." Once again, this view misses the point, which is the numerous problems caused by homophobia. These problems are addressed below.

Many companies claim sexual orientation itself is not an issue. They state that a person's "private life" is not important at work. But homosexuality, like heterosexuality, is not just what people do in bed. Again, straight people regularly "flaunt" their sexuality at work, while gay people dare not even mention theirs. What is missing is a single standard of conduct that applies *equally* to gay and straight employees. Of course, this is really the very definition of discrimination. A set of standards for acceptable heterosexual behavior may not be written, but it certainly exists.

Not having a written nondiscrimination policy encompassing sexual orientation allows homophobic individuals to treat gay people unfairly with impunity. As a result, homosexuality remains an ambiguous subject at best for both management and gay employees. The very lack of such a policy demonstrates that the fear of discrimination is justified.

In certain areas of employment, discrimination against gay people is already prohibited by law. The Civil Services Reform Act of 1978 specifically prohibits discrimination on the basis of private matters, including sexual orientation. This protects approximately ninety-five percent of the federal government's civilian workforce. Similarly, many cities and states have legislation or executive orders prohibiting homophobic discrimination by government agencies, and by companies serving as contractors to or receiving services from the government. Only two states and a small number of cities have passed ordinances prohibiting discrimination based on sexual orientation by private employers.

A few companies, recognizing that *all* employees are their most valuable resource, have voluntarily adopted nondiscrimination policies. Relief from the tension and burden of passing as straight has a powerful influence on improving employee loyalty and job satisfaction. It is ironic that the companies which care enough about their gay employees to adopt a written nondiscrimination policy are probably the *least* likely to need one.

Problems, Problems, and More Problems

There are even more problems caused by homophobic beliefs than those mentioned already. Anti-gay discrimination harms both employees and employers. And the consequences of discrimination have real costs to any organization. These costs are difficult to quantify, but because ten percent of the workforce is gay, they are not trivial.

The potential for discrimination, real or perceived, profoundly influences a gay person's attitude toward his or her job. Fear of homophobic reactions such as termination, demotion, harassment, or alienation necessitates secrecy on the job. This causes tremendous stress which consumes productive energy and undermines enthusiasm. Everyone experiences stress from a number of areas on and off the job. The unnecessary and additional stress created by a homophobic work environment can be the proverbial straw that breaks the camel's back, leading in turn to increased medical costs and lost work time. Stress can be experienced as well by prejudiced co-workers who are not made to confront and conquer their own homophobia. The effect is to reduce both the quantity and the quality of work all around. Stress costs *real* money.

Many gay employees feel it is better to avoid office conversations and social functions, even though these activities serve as the foundation for good camaraderie and effective communications. Gay people who are in the closet fear being asked personal questions like, "So, do you have a girlfriend (or boyfriend)?" or "Hey, would you and a date like to come over to the house tomorrow evening for dinner?" These normally harmless questions can be devastating for gay people.

Some gay employees risk the security of the closet, coming out openly at work, only to experience a completely different set of problems. The openly gay employee is frequently made to feel awkward, and might even suffer repercussions for "flaunting." At least *one* person, possibly an influential manager, is bound to be offended by having to work with a "faggot" or a "dyke." To avoid being patronized, rejected or pitied, many openly gay men and lesbians seek to avoid work associates. Both predicaments—the "closet case" and the "flaunting faggot"—have the same negative effect on teamwork. Both sets of problems also have the same basic cause: a homophobic environment lacking mutual respect and trust.

Many gay men and lesbians overcompensate for feelings of inferiority by working harder and longer. They do this to gain the respect of co-workers who reject them for their sexuality. This does not ensure acceptance, however, for performance is not the only criteria for success in most companies. If these extraordinary efforts are not rewarded by promotions and salary increases, the individual is tempted to think, "The hell with it. I'll never make vice-resident in this place. Why even bother?" No organization would consciously encourage such feelings, but it happens regularly. Gay people know there are very few single (read "gay or heterosexual nonconformist") executives. Specifically, *The Cox Report* found that only four percent of top managers and eight percent of middle managers are single.

The real or perceived discrimination begins to take its toll in the form of reduced morale, company loyalty, job security, and job satisfaction for the gay employee. As a result, turnover can become a problem as well. This is especially true when a gay person has been "found out."

He or she may feel it necessary to find a new job with new co-workers to resume passing, possibly at a company that has a nondiscrimination policy.

Finally, if a gay employee is unjustly denied a promotion or fired by an obviously homophobic supervisor, he or she may have no other recourse except to file a civil lawsuit. Many suits are lost, but many are won. The cost to employers is both tangible, in the form of damages and legal fees, and intangible through the loss of employee morale and company reputation. This alone is a compelling reason for many companies to adopt nondiscrimination policies and practices. It makes good business sense to avoid as many problems as possible.

All these costs add up, which is why more and more employers are taking action.

Controlling Homophobia in the Workplace

Nondiscrimination policies and practices covering sexual orientation may not *eliminate* homophobia in the workplace, but they will *control* the homophobic behavior that is so costly to employers and gay employees. Gay people are not asking for special treatment, just equal treatment; there is no need for affirmative action. In fact, affirmative action will not work. Many gay people would still not disclose their homosexuality, even if a nondiscrimination policy existed. For this reason alone, it would be impossible to count gay employees accurately. Conversely, because homosexuality is difficult to "verify," let alone define precisely, an affirmative action policy would lend itself to abuse by straight people who might be willing to "admit" to being gay just to improve their opportunities at work.

The first step of nondiscrimination is very simple. It requires merely adding the phrase *sexual orientation* to the existing nondiscrimination policy. The second step is more difficult, but not terribly so. It involves adopting nondiscrimination *practices*.

Basically, nondiscrimination practices allow gay people to do anything and everything straight people are allowed to do, in effect eliminating any formal or informal double standards. This means not only allowing but actually encouraging gay couples to attend company functions. It means permitting gay employees to place pictures of lovers on their desks without fear of harassment or retribution. It means leaving notices which announce gay events posted on any bulletin board provided for general notices. Most importantly, it means communicating these changes to all *straight* employees as well. This can be done through example, casual conversations, reprimands for homophobic behavior, company meetings, memorandums, and sensibility training classes or handbooks. Gay employees should be willing to offer assistance if needed. There are even organizations, like the Lambda Institute in San Francisco, which provide training classes and materials. The task is *not* a monumental one. All employers regularly use all of these same methods to communicate all company policies and practices to all employees. All that is required is to add a single additional agenda item where appropriate.

215

Some progressive companies are actually restructuring their benefit programs to eliminate past inequities. They feel employees should be compensated for the tasks performed, and not according to family status. With respect to salaries, this is increasingly true in nearly all places of employment. But total compensation includes benefits as well. And because benefits typically constitute over one-third of employee compensation, this is a significant issue. Benefit equity would not favor a gay employee over a straight one, nor would it profit the single employee at the expense of the married one. It would merely eliminate the current advantage married employees have over their single co-workers.

For example, the ability to name lovers as beneficiaries on life insurance policies, to have health insurance coverage for dependent lovers and to receive bereavement benefits are all important to employees in domestic partnerships, both gay and straight. The excuse that these relationships are "unofficial" is just that — an excuse. How many employers look at marriage licenses anyway? An employee's word is good enough, especially under a "cafeteria" plan where the individual selects his or her personalized benefits from a list of those available. Some insurance companies may not be very cooperative, but that is another issue and should not serve as an excuse either. If a company's current insurance provider is unwilling to provide for *all* its employees, then a new provider seems to be in order.

In summary, sexual orientation is a personal matter and does not affect work performance, but homophobia clearly does. Gay workers have incredible potential which is being underutilized. If anything, being gay could have a very positive effect at work. Many gay people possess a greater ambition caused by a desire to be accepted as worthy individuals. Gay people understand no one will respect them *because* they are gay, but they can expect to achieve respect through performance. Gay people also tend to be more empathetic and compassionate as a result of the oppression they have experienced over the years. Finally, gay people are often more entrepreneurial, not irresponsible, by being in a position to take additional risks.

The bottom line is: What is right will prevail, for gay people cannot afford, quite literally, to lose the struggle for equal employment opportunities.

Child Custody, Visitation, and Adoption

Child custody and visitation may not seem like gay civil rights issues, but they are. It is common for most gay people to enter into heterosexual relationships. Nearly every gay person has at least dated a member of the opposite sex at some point in his or her life. Three independent studies found that nearly one-fourth of both gay men and lesbians have even married. Gay people normally marry before accepting a gay identity and, on occasion, the "homosexual tendencies" are discussed before the wedding. Both partners apparently believed the general social impression that "it" is just a passing phase that will go away. Others simply follow the traditional social pattern of marriage and family without giving the situation considered thought. They seek the happiness society claims will always be found in such a relationship. *The heterosexual lifestyle is an irresistible utopia:* marriage, 2.3 children, a house in the suburbs with a white picket fence, a station wagon, and the ever-lovable dog. In fact, marriage is often represented as the only possible way to live. Although homosexual individuals who find themselves in this situation should technically be classified as bisexual, their erotic and emotional attraction may be exclusively homosexual.

Many of these "mixed" marriages involve children. Child custody is primarily of concern to women, as women are awarded custody of any children during most divorces or separations. Correspondingly, visitation rights go to the ex-husband.

Joy Schulenburg, in her book *Gay Parenting,* presents the situation a gay male or lesbian parent going through divorce or separation will face:

If you have decided that you do indeed want either sole or joint custody of your child or children, you must next ask yourself if you are prepared to fight for it. This means a lot more than simply hiring a competent attorney and paying her or him to handle it for you. For the homosexual parent it probably means having your life-style, your relationships, your children and your activities scrutinized by strangers, some of whom will probably be most unsympathetic. After the scrutiny, the information and conjectures gleaned will be paraded in a public courtroom. You will be asked all manner of personal questions, some relevant to your parenting ability, some asked out of ignorance, bigotry or prurience. You and your children may undergo a battery of psychological tests and, above all, you will be out of your closet for good if the subject of homosexuality is allowed as admissible evidence in court. It is important to decide whether you have the stamina to cope with a struggle that could be drawn out over many months or even years. This means a realistic examination of yourself, your support systems and your environment.

Many individuals, gay or straight, might not endure this ordeal.

The issue of gay parents is a particularly complex and emotional one. The standard used in awarding custody is to determine what is in the "child's best interest." It is therefore not necessary to prove or establish that one parent is "unfit." A homophobic judge may merely decide that it is in the "child's best interest" to be with the heterosexual parent for any reason — including homophobia. Also, it is natural for society's sympathy in cases like these to be directed toward the "innocent" party, who is identified as the straight partner. He or she is viewed as a victim of deception; someone who was used. But keep in mind that the gay partner is also a victim, whose suffering has been and will continue to be greater in our society. Actually, both individuals are victims. For the straight partner, the realization is a bitter pill to swallow. For the gay partner, a rough road lies ahead.

There are three reasons generally offered why it may not be in a "child's best interest" to be placed with a gay parent. The first is that the child might be stigmatized. This concern is not a result of homosexuality itself, but is instead based on society's homophobia. In the final analysis, it is just another example of the use of prejudice to justify prejudice. If a child is to be stigmatized for having a gay parent, that will not change if custody is denied. There are numerous other stigmatized minorities in our society. It would be unconscionable to consider taking children away from black parents in racially mixed marriages. The situation with homosexuality is no different. Blanket denial of custody to gay parents only serves to validate homophobia; it does not help the child. Ironically, many children of gay parents report a very positive effect: They tend not to socialize with other children who are prejudiced. In other words, they become more mature judges of character, less tolerant of intolerance. As one judge put it, "If defendant retains custody, it may be that because the community is intolerant of her differences, these girls may sometimes have to bear themselves with greater than ordinary fortitude. But this does not necessarily portend that their moral welfare or safety will be jeopardized. It is just as reasonable to expect that they will emerge better equipped to search out their own standards of right and wrong, better able to perceive that the majority is not always correct in its moral judgments, and better able to understand the importance of conforming their beliefs to the requirements of reason and tested knowledge, not the constraints of currently popular sentiments or prejudice."

The second belief is that because parents are such important role models, a child might develop "improper" gender role behavior or, worse yet, may grow up to become gay. First of all, gender role conformity is independent of sexual orientation. Even if the parent does exhibit some "improper" gender role behavior, there are numerous other influences which socialize children. All people, gay and straight, recognize the importance of adopting socially acceptable behavior. In addition, this improperly assumes as well that *total* gender role conformity is an appropriate goal for behavior in the first place. As for the concern about the child's sexual orientation, a child is either gay or straight; more specifically, ten percent are gay and ninety percent are straight. There is zero evidence to support this "parental recruiting" myth. The sexual orientation of children with lesbian mothers was studied at California State University in 1975. The study found that "the incidence of lesbian, gay or bisexual children in this sample is no larger than in the general population." Straight children cannot be converted to homosexuality just as gay children cannot be converted to heterosexuality. Gay parents are well aware of this fact. The only real difference between gay and straight parents is that if a child thinks he or she might be gay, a gay parent is less likely to rush the child off to a therapist to be "cured."

The third belief is that heterosexual households are inherently "superior." This may be true. The study from California State University points out, however: "The difficulties in being a lesbian mother do not appear to be inherent in the role, but rather come from society's attitudes and discriminatory behavior." In addition to using prejudice to justify prejudice, this claim of superiority seems to introduce the issue of morality. Although sexual orientation is amoral, some individuals continue to feel heterosexuality has a monopoly on morality. They simply equate what they dislike or cannot understand with immorality. Of course, all children are exposed to a number of things which some parents and "interested" third parties dislike. These influences include peer behavior, TV news and drama, movies, music, books, and so on. In other words, they get a good dose of real life on a daily basis. Discovering homosexuality exists and that either Mommy or Daddy is gay bothers children infinitely less than it seems to bother others.

Even when custody or visitation rights are granted, the court will frequently place restrictions on a gay parent. These might involve visible expressions of homosexuality through openly gay relationships or association with other gay people, socially or politically. Sometimes these require that a heterosexual adult must always be present or that a gay lover must always be absent during visits. Apparently, this prevents the child from seeing something he or she should not see — especially in the bedroom. How ridiculous. When *you* were young, did you know what your parents did in bed? Did you even care? In one case, a judge ordered a gay father to take the HIV (AIDS virus) antibody test before his two daughters could visit him. Even if the father had been infected by the virus, he could not possibly transmit it to his daughters through casual contact. This request was based fully on homophobia, probably with the intent of finding the father in contempt of court for refusing to follow the order, which he did. To deprive a child of a parent's full love is far more damaging than any imaginary "protection" he or she might receive.

The remaining component of social issues involving children is that of adoption. Many couples, gay or straight, who for various reasons cannot biologically have children, choose to adopt or become foster parents. Although this has met with great opposition when the couple is gay, the American Psychiatric Association passed a resolution in 1976 declaring that the sexual orientation of the natural or adoptive parent should not be the sole or even a primary consideration in child custody or placement. In fact, gay couples are often considered ideal foster parents for gay children for those children who do identify as gay. Both the APA and the National Association of Social Workers favor this policy. Foster parents are assigned temporary responsibility for and care of children until they can be adopted. Foster children generally go from home to home and suffer from many problems as a result of being denied a stable environment. In the hierarchy of demand, these are not the most "desirable" children available for adoption, so they remain in the foster system. But they are far from being criminals. Instead, they are victims, who *especially* need love. Fortunately, many gay couples are willing and able to offer the love these children need as either foster or adoptive parents.

Insurance Discrimination

Gay people have always had difficulty getting life and health insurance coverage. This was true well before AIDS. Since the AIDS crisis began, many gay men have experienced even more problems getting insurance. AIDS has merely legitimized this tradition. It seems the insurance industry would like to categorically consider *all* gay men as "high risks." Of course, some insurance companies would like to consider the elderly, overweight people, smokers, and individuals with a history or heritage of disease as also being at "high risk" for one thing or another. Our society would be outraged, however, at any attempt to disqualify these latter categories. For example, men are more likely to get heart attacks, but that does not mean all men will. Similarly, the fact gay men are more likely at the present time to contract AIDS does not mean all gay men will. It all boils down to this: Insurance companies must never be allowed to pick and choose which diseases they like, and which they don't, for doing so flies in the face of the very concept of insurance.

Nevertheless, to achieve this exclusionary objective, some companies have resorted to "red-lining" as a screening device for individual policies. That is, they try to detect homosexuality through demographics like address, occupation, or the gender of a "roommate" or beneficiary. Others are pursuing action to disqualify certain "high risk" individuals from group coverage. They threaten the cancellation of group life and health coverage if any or any more employees develop AIDS. This would have the effect of causing employers to discriminate against gay men. In companies which are self-insured, the economic impact is direct and so might be the discrimination. A growing number of insurance companies want applicants to take the HIV antibody blood test, despite the fact this test has no real diagnostic capability. Such a policy could set a dangerous precedent, not only for AIDS as it spreads into the "general" population, but for other diseases as well.

When AIDS-related claims are made, some companies attempt to deny benefits for two reasons. First, they claim the disease was a "pre-existing condition" owing to the long incubation period, and is therefore excluded from coverage. Second, they argue that treatments are "experimental," as there is no cure, and are therefore not covered by the policy. The effect is to place the burden of care on the individual and the taxpayer.

AIDS aside, gay couples invariably need to maintain separate health insurance policies, as most carriers do not permit a lover in a domestic partnership to be named as a dependent. Further, these separate policies cannot be used to complement each other in the event of a catastrophic illness. Even insurance provided by the government, such as Social Security, suffers the same problems relating to benefits for the gay "spouse." For the same reason, gay people are unable to name lovers as beneficiaries on life insurance policies. To purchase life insurance, it is necessary to have an "insurable interest" in the other party. Insurance companies do not consider gay relationships as meeting this requirement. One way around this problem for life insurance is to take out a policy naming the estate as beneficiary. The estate can then be left to the lover in a will, or the policy can be changed later naming the lover as beneficiary.

The effect of this discrimination goes well beyond higher rates or denial of coverage. Many gay people are reluctant to make their homosexuality known to their doctors. They fear, quite appropriately, that this information could be discovered and used against them in employment or insurance eligibility. As a result, the quality of health care for gay men could be compromised. For example, straight men are not checked, normally, for the presence of sexually transmitted diseases in the anus. Gay men who are passive during anal intercourse should be. If not discovered early, a disease like syphilis could progress to an advanced stage, causing serious complications.

The gay community is not alone in its recognition of this problem: "The ACLU opposes the differential treatment of persons applying for insurance by carriers of health and life insurance on the basis of race, sex, *sexual orientation,* marital status, location of residence, national origin, alienage or immigrant status." The two leading insurance trade organizations, the Health Insurance Association of America and the American Council of Life Insurance, both oppose the use of sexual orientation in underwriting. Of course, this position is not binding on the member companies, many of which will continue to discriminate until required to do otherwise.

"Unmarried" Gay Couples

Marriage laws establish and regulate social contracts. Nearly all specify a union between a man and a woman. In those few states where the gender is unspecified, same-sex couples are excluded by precedence or prejudice. The extent of the prejudice was revealed in a 1989 *Time/* Cable News Network survey in which sixty-nine percent of the respondents answered no to the question, "Do you think marriages between same-sex couples should be recognized by law?"
Such universal exclusion prevents gay couples from achieving the many benefits and legal protections afforded by marriage, and serves as the basis for an array of problems that were discussed at length in Chapter 4. A few churches have already taken the lead in eliminating this serious social omission. But because gay marriages are something which, realistically, will not be blessed any time soon, it is a long-range goal for the Gay Civil Rights Movement at this time.

Immigration and Naturalization

The United States is the "melting pot" of the world. Yet this diversity continues to exclude gay people seeking to become American citizens. Of course, the "melting pot" does not really include the twenty-four million men and women who are already here either. So why should the foreign "faggots" be treated any differently.

There are three main areas where the Immigration and Naturalization Service (INS) discriminates against gay people: exclusion from entry (even for tourists), deportation (when "caught"), and naturalization to establish citizenship. The reasoning it offers is purely stereotypical. Long after the APA determined gay men and lesbians were okay in their book, INS regulations giving gay people a "psychopathic personality" that is lacking "good moral character" sit on the shelves collecting dust.

This is despite the fact that the Public Health Service, which determines such requirements for the INS, also no longer classifies gay people as being suspect in any way. In an oblique display of homophobia (and possibly racism) the INS began screening for AIDS in 1987, prompting more than a dozen organizations to threaten a boycott in protest of this policy during the Sixth International Conference on AIDS hosted in the United States. As of this writing, the matter remains unresolved.

These problems continue to exist in large part because the INS is substantially immune from constitutional scrutiny, for the situations they address concern individuals who are *not* currently U.S. citizens. While this is technically true, it should not be allowed to serve as an excuse to ignore our nation's fundamental beliefs. Remember, except for Native Americans, we were all foreigners at one time.

Public Accommodations and Services

There are numerous other areas of discrimination which come under the category of public accommodations and services. Countless gay people have experienced difficulty renting apartments or hotel rooms. Their homosexuality is obvious when a single bedroom or bed is involved. Many leases prohibit "roommates," while allowing for spouses, providing a loophole to evict gay tenants. Some gay youth are "evicted" from their parents' homes, only to experience difficulty getting responsible care and placement from social service organizations. ("Johnny thinks he might be gay, so let's place him in a good Christian family to straighten him out.") Counseling services, especially suicide prevention, rarely address gay issues and seldom provide training for staff members on gay lifestyles. A study in Oregon found that eighty percent of the doctors surveyed would prefer not to have any gay patients. This may not be a major problem, as half of those who will take gay patients are probably gay themselves. Most gay people prefer gay doctors anyway. Nevertheless, in the event a rare specialist is required, this homophobic attitude could be deadly. At best, it is a violation of the Hippocratic Oath.

In a rather incredible display of homophobia, Delta Airlines actually attempted to convince a civil court that a straight life was worth more than a gay life. A Delta jet crashed in 1985, killing all 137 people on board. A lawsuit was filed by the parents of a gay male passenger. The airlines claimed the value of the man's life was lessened by the possibility of him contracting AIDS! The legal ramifications of "possibility" would be immense if the court accepted such an argument. Delta made its claim without a shred of evidence that the man had AIDS or any health problems, or that he even tested positive for exposure to the virus. The only "evidence" was that he was indeed gay. Fortunately, for everyone, Delta lost.

The discrimination is most blatant when children are involved. I know many gay male or lesbian couples that would make fine adoptive parents. Yet there exists a scant six such cases on record. I also find it ironic that the Radical Religious Right, among others, can fight abortion (ostensibly for heterosexual women) and adoption by gay people in virtually the same breath. Gay and lesbian couples lose. Adoption agencies lose. But most importantly, an unloved child somewhere loses too. Indeed, homophobia has many victims.

Chapter 13

AIDS, Homophobia, and Other Forms of "Social Disease"

There are only two ways to think about AIDS: One human being at a time, or the mounting wave of statistics. Either way, AIDS is horrifying. *U. S. Congressman Henry Waxman*

AIDS is *not* a gay civil rights issue. It is a global health problem of great urgency. But since AIDS has affected primarily gay men *so far,* society's response to the disease has been both inadequate and inappropriate. Therefore, it serves as a perfect, and painful, example of why misunderstanding homosexuality is so harmful—and not just to gay people.

At the time of this writing, society's understanding of AIDS is changing rapidly. Not until this disease is defeated will the story of AIDS become fully understood. The following material should be read with this "time limitation" in mind.

AIDS is a syndrome, not a single disease. It is believed to be caused by a retrovirus that disarms the body's defense system, rendering it severely weakened or completely inactive. Another disease associated with AIDS is AIDS-related complex or ARC. Finally, there is the asymptomatic condition of being infected by the virus—a state that generally leads to ARC and then on to AIDS. All three are grouped here under the single label AIDS.

AIDS, at least in the United States, can be and thus far has been, more often than not, transmitted by morally controversial behavior. Other health problems, such as cancer and heart disease, are based on personal behavior to some degree as well, but their victims receive less judgment and more compassion than do those with AIDS. Among the practices known to transmit AIDS are unprotected sexual activity, especially anal intercourse more common among gay men than straight couples, and the sharing of needles during intravenous drug abuse. Blood and semen share basic characteristics which permit the transfer of retroviruses like the one believed to cause AIDS. In this respect AIDS is similar to hepatitis, which also cannot be transmitted casually. Although cases in the

224

United States may have occurred as early as 1969, based on retroactive diagnosis, the epidemic was not officially recognized until 1981. It is conservatively estimated that in the first ten years of the epidemic, AIDS-related illnesses will have killed more Americans than the Vietnam and Korean wars combined—and millions more will have been infected by the virus.

There are actually two epidemics at issue here. One is new: a disease that kills. This one is AIDS. The other is quite ancient: widespread and irrational fear, bordering on panic at times. This could be labeled "AFRAIDS." The public anxiety and even hysteria surrounding AIDS has been nothing short of incredible. Much of the anxiety results from the horrible manifestation of the disease itself. The primary reason for the hysteria, however, is precisely because AIDS, from the very beginning, was considered a social issue rather than a medical one.

AFRAIDS: Acute Fear Reaction to AIDS

The political significance of AIDS cannot be understated. According to *Scientific American* magazine in an article on the social dimensions of AIDS, "No other disease in modern times has engendered such frustration, resentment and anxiety or demanded more compassion, intelligence, selflessness and integrity on the part of health professionals"—and others charged with the public welfare.

Some actions demonstrated obvious bigotry. California Assemblyman John Doolittle once commented, "If it were only the offbeat populations—homosexuals and IV drug users—that get AIDS, no one would care about it. I am concerned because we know it is spreading through the heterosexual population." He means no one *like him* would care. Another politician, this one a candidate for mayor of Houston, stated during his campaign that one way to deal with AIDS would be to "shoot the queers." Others were somewhat more diplomatic in exercising their homophobia. For example, in 1985 Health and Human Services Director Margaret Heckler said, "We must conquer AIDS before it affects the heterosexual population and the general population . . . We have a very strong public interest in stopping AIDS before it spreads outside the risk groups, before it becomes an overwhelming problem."

These examples highlight how homophobia and other forms of prejudice would prevent an effective response to this medical crisis.

While the majority of Americans continued to ignore the issue, clinging to a belief that AIDS would not cross the "boundaries" of the gay male and IV drug abuser communities, others began fearing widespread contagion. One way AIDS was capable of reaching the "general" population was through the nation's blood supply. So there was a great sigh of relief from many health care officials, and the public at large, when the ELISA (enzyme-linked immunosorbent assay) test was approved by the Food and Drug Administration in March of 1985. So much for *that* avenue leading to Main Street USA.

The other fear was having casual contact with those already infected. Although extensive research had shown that the human immunodeficiency virus (HIV) could not be transmitted casually, many individuals chose either to disbelieve this medical finding or to irrationally believe otherwise. It is true that, scientifically speaking, nothing can be proved negative. But there had not been a *single* instance in the tens of thousands of AIDS cases occurring through casual contact. Conversely, the tens of thousands of health care workers and family members close to people with AIDS *had* not been infected through casual contact. In fact, in a study of 1,500 health care workers exposed to HIV through needle pricks or open wounds, only one tested positive to the virus. And in a Centers for Disease Control study, no cases involving skin or mucous membrane exposure had transmitted the virus. To claim this was "insufficient" evidence was an insufficient argument.

The epidemiological evidence simply did not support transmission of HIV via casual contact. If AIDS were indeed spread through casual contact or other similar means like insect bites, it would have followed the pattern of diseases which *are* spread by these means. The most prominent historical example of such diseases is the bubonic plague, or Black Death, which killed an estimated twenty-five to fifty million men, women, and children in Europe during the fourteenth century. This same pattern of widespread infection did not occur with AIDS. The surgeon general commented, "The first cases of AIDS were reported in 1981. We would know by now if AIDS were passed by casual, non-sexual contact." This is because AIDS is an infectious disease, requiring direct blood contact, rather than a contagious disease passed on, for example, by a sneeze. Yet despite the wealth of evidence to the contrary, a 1986 CBS poll (five years into the epidemic) revealed that one-third of Americans still believed AIDS could be contracted through kissing or drinking from the same glass.

The U.S. Justice Department added momentum to the AIDS hysteria bandwagon by ruling that even though people with AIDS were protected from job discrimination under federal handicap laws, it would still be legal, in their opinion, to fire any individual an employer felt could pose a threat to other employees. Employers did not need scientific reasons. They did not even need good reasons. They only needed reasons, and homophobia is a "good" one. In its opinion, the Justice Department stated that employers were not prohibited from making "incorrect, and even irrational decisions so long as their decisions were not based on handicap." How convenient. This distinction between contagion and handicap was nothing less than a specific instruction on how to avoid the law, serving to nullify any protection available to people diagnosed with AIDS or infected by the virus. A US Circuit Court of Appeals in 1987 ruled unanimously that people with AIDS were indeed protected by federal handicap laws. Ultimately, and only after a Supreme Court ruling reaffirming nondiscrimination for persons with infectious diseases, did the Justice Department reverse its opinion. But the bandwagon had picked up speed.

The one group that should have been expected to maintain an unbiased perspective — health care professionals — allowed their homophobia to overcome rational thinking as well. People with AIDS were shown little or no respect in many hospitals, often being turned away. One hospital in Florida bought a one-way ticket to San Francisco for a man with AIDS, further endangering his life at a time of critical need. After people with AIDS were admitted to hospitals, some nurses and doctors would refuse to work with them, despite the evidence that simple, routine precautions prevented infection by the virus. Paramedics would withhold first aid from people merely *suspected* of having AIDS. Almost none of the 19,000 nursing homes, traditional providers of long-term health care, accepted people who had AIDS. Similarly, many hospice organizations denied their valuable service to those individuals who eventually needed it. It got so bad that the American Medical Association found it necessary to reaffirm the Hippocratic Oath, for it had become a "hypocritic oath" instead.

While there was little or no sympathy for the faggot or the junkie, nearly everyone had sympathy for the poor "innocent victims" of AIDS — that is, all others! This appeared to mean that AIDS was felt to be deserved somehow by some people, but not by others. Of course, this was not a medical opinion, it was a theological one.

The Theology of Disease

The fear-mongers of the Radical Religious Right were the worst offenders. It is important to distinguish between those individuals who, out of ignorance, were genuinely afraid and those who exploited the fear to advance their own causes. Many conservative moralists fell into the latter category. They had a field day with this unfortunate crisis. For them, it was a godsend — not only literally, but figuratively as well. AIDS was irresistible: A *lethal* sexually transmitted disease. The Radical Religious Right preys on the fears of people — and AIDS was "made to order." These groups, historically homophobic, had an "I-told-you-so" tone in their rhetoric in the early days of AIDS. Seeming to take such great joy in this epidemic of human suffering, AIDS became their "proof" that homosexuality was harmful to society — a position held for centuries. Actually, the only thing AIDS confirmed is some people's lack of genuine compassion and love, not only for the victims of AIDS but for its other victims as well. Lovers, friends, parents, brothers and sisters, aunts and uncles, and grandparents all suffer too. Their suffering may be different, but it is just as real.

Yet no amount of suffering has stopped the hateful campaign of the Radical Religious Right. In his *Liberty Report,* Jerry Falwell commented, "AIDS is God's judgment on a society that does not live by His rules." Apparently, though, Falwell did not trust God's aim: "If the Reagan administration does not put its full weight against this, what is now a gay plague in this country, I feel that a year from now, President Ronald Reagan, personally, will be blamed for allowing this awful disease to break out among the *innocent* American public." [Emphasis added.] Jimmy Swaggart claimed, "Homosexuality . . . came out of the bathroom, into the bathhouse and now into the blood bank, and we have AIDS." Presidential candidate Pat Robertson commented, "We have a bankruptcy of

227

morality and AIDS is the consequence." And members of the Ku Klux Klan marched with signs reading: "Praise God for AIDS."

But is was not only the Radical Religious Right which believed God's wrath was the "cause" of AIDS. In a 1987 Gallup poll, sixty percent of evangelicals surveyed agreed with the statement, "I sometimes think that AIDS is a punishment for the decline in moral standards." But thirty-six percent of non-evangelicals also agreed. Overall, forty-two percent of those surveyed felt, "Most people with AIDS have only themselves to blame." One individual even defaced a poster of a gay organization at Stanford University by writing: "AIDS—America's Ideal Death Sentence."

Were these same people likely to feel that society should try to cure AIDS or prevent its occurrence when doing so might condone certain "sinful" practices? An officer of the Moral Majority commented: "If the medical community thinks that a new drug is what is needed to combat these diseases, it is deluding itself. There is a price to pay for immorality and immoral behavior." In a similar vein, the Roman Catholic Archdiocese of Los Angeles issued a statement against the use of condoms as a preventative measure: "In the issue of AIDS, such use implies either heterosexual promiscuity or homosexual activity. The church approves of neither." Such a view seemed to claim that all gay people, but only the promiscuous straight ones, might "deserve" to die for their sexual "sins." The church has never been in the business of helping those who drift outside its teachings, but this particular archdiocese had misplaced its priorities in a big way.

What do hemophiliacs do to "deserve" AIDS? What do some babies do to "deserve" AIDS? What terrible deed have some straight men and women, who are not IV drug abusers, done to "deserve" AIDS? For that matter, what is being "punished" by cancer? Is Alzheimer's Disease "punishment" for living too long? Are heart attacks "punishment" for gluttony? What sin is being "punished" when we all get colds and flus? Conversely, why are there so many perfectly healthy murderers and rapists running around? A more revealing question is: Why are some people so driven to find meaning or purpose in disease and suffering? The theology of disease is totally unfounded and crumbles under the slightest scrutiny. *No* one deserves to die like this. Then why? Why only certain people? Why now? These are questions for the scientists, not for the theologians. Yet they are regularly asked whenever anyone dies.

I am reminded of my neighbor. David died from a brain tumor at the age of sixteen. He was a beautiful person. Why so young? When meaningful answers evade us we rationalize about God acting in mysterious ways. Was his death God's work at all? Is AIDS God's work? Maybe it is. Maybe He is just testing us—*all* of us. If so, how are you responding?

Why Gay Men?

Theology failed to explain the apparent focus of AIDS on gay men, but science did—eventually. Many diseases are spread by contact, casual or intimate. Included are colds, skin rashes, influenza, and so on. All of these can be spread through sexual contact as well. They are not classified as sexually transmitted diseases (STD), however, because other modes of transmission are possible. Sexual activity is simply the closest form of contact possible between two individuals. Sexual intimacy allows fragile disease-causing agents like germs, bacteria, and viruses to be transferred from one partner to the other. Sharing needles is also a form of intimate contact, but the question being addressed ("Why gay men?") implies a sexual context.

The answer was actually very simple: certain aspects of gay male sexual activity are more conducive to the transmission of the AIDS virus.

Consider the fact that women are more likely than men to contract the HIV virus during heterosexual sex. There is a basic physiological explanation for this. A sexually transmitted virus can enter the female's bloodstream through the thin walls of the uterus during coitus. A small tear in the skin tissue is required normally for this to occur, and more pronounced abrasions, especially sores from syphilis or herpes, greatly increase the likelihood, or efficiency, of exposure. If the male partner is infectious with AIDS, his semen, deposited in the vagina, could transmit the HIV virus. As the active partner, a virus transmitted sexually would need to enter the male's bloodstream through the urethra. This is not as easily accomplished, as the exchange of fluids *into* the small opening of the urethra is limited. In some cases a single unprotected sexual act is sufficient to transmit HIV for either men or women, while other situations demonstrate repeated unprotected sexual contact with no exposure to the uninfected partner. The heterosexual coitus scenario indicates relatively easy transmission from male to female, but not vice versa.

Anal intercourse, more popular with gay men but by no means exclusive to male homosexuality, is more accommodating to HIV. To begin, evidence shows that HIV need not enter the bloodstream because it can directly infect rectal cells. Next is the unique ability gay men have to alternate between the active and passive roles during anal intercourse. The virus is passed from the active partner through his semen into the bloodstream of the passive partner during unprotected anal intercourse. If *this* passive partner is infected by the virus and later becomes the active partner with another man, the virus could be transferred once again. Because AIDS does not appear to be a simple infectious disease, cofactors of some form or another are also highly suspected. Certain other aspects of gay male sexuality might introduce these cofactors. For example, many gay men use a drug called amyl or butyl nitrate, commonly known as "poppers," during sexual activity. Poppers enhance the intensity of sexual feelings by dilating the blood vessels. This dilation increases the likelihood a virus will be absorbed into the bloodstream. Poppers are also believed to damage the immune system directly.

That explains why gay men are more susceptible, but it only partially explains why AIDS is so prominent in the gay male community. There are two additional reasons why this is true. First, the smaller size and closer integration of the gay community makes the likelihood of transmitting diseases sexually greater than in the straight community, especially because gay men do, on the average, have more sexual partners than straight people. The second, and more significant, reason is homophobia: During the initial years of the AIDS crisis, the federal government failed to make gay men aware of safer sexual practices, which allowed the virus to establish a stronghold.

Basically, safer sexual practices are those which prevent semen from entering a partner's bloodstream. This can be accomplished by using a condom, or by avoiding anal intercourse and certain other forms of sexual activity. There are plenty of alternatives available. (More information on specific and up-to-date safer sexual techniques can now be obtained from a local health agency or through the gay community. Safer sex is the only way, short of abstinence, to avoid spreading AIDS sexually as of this writing.)

Is abstinence better than safer sex? Only the individual can decide what constitutes an acceptable level of risk. An analogy with driving is helpful. Driving has become almost a necessity in our society, and it *can* be very dangerous. But it can be *safe* as well if precautions are taken. Wearing seatbelts and driving defensively reduce, but do not eliminate, the risk of death or serious injury. The only difference is that people *know* they were not in a fatal accident ten years ago. The same is not true of AIDS.

Before leaving this topic, it is important to put the situation of gay men and AIDS in perspective. The fact that around seventy percent of people with AIDS in the infancy of the epidemic were gay men did not mean a majority of gay men were infected. In fact, it was estimated that less than ten percent of gay men in the US had been infected by HIV. So a better question to ask might be, "Why gay men—*first?*"

The AIDS Boomerang

AIDS, the disease, is caused by a virus; AIDS, the epidemic, was caused by prejudice. And the history of AIDS in America will demonstrate, for generations to come, how damaging prejudice can be. AFRAIDS positioned AIDS as a gay disease that would preclude a prompt and effective response. This casual at best, hostile at worst, attitude about AIDS was tantamount to tossing a boomerang that would return with a vengeance.

Originally, AIDS was named GRID for "gay-related immune deficiency," even though many non-gay people had been diagnosed as well. This served to define the disease as a "gay problem," shaping both the perceptions and politics of the crisis. Americans have always been reluctant to address any issue pertaining to sexuality, especially homosexuality. Having defined the disease as a "gay problem," elected and appointed officials could all but ignore the entire issue as a "special interest" of the gay community. The stigma associated AIDS also had the adverse effect of causing underreporting by people attempting to protect the present or posthumous reputations of others. This "courtesy" helped permit the relentless virus to spread "unknowingly" into the "general" population.

From the beginning in this country, there appeared to be more interest in determining who discovered the virus first, the Americans or the French, than in solving the crisis. Dr. Luc Montagnier from the Pasteur Institute in Paris isolated and identified the culprit as a lentivirus in 1983. But the majority of U.S. scientists ignored the news. Then one year later Dr. Robert Gallo from the National Cancer Institute in Bethesda, after having once abandoned his search, declared the cause of AIDS to be a member of the human T-cell leukemia virus (HTLV) family he had discovered years earlier. Each gave it a different name. Montagnier called his *lymphadenopathy-associated virus* (LAV). Gallo named his *HTLV-III*. Although his announcement came a year later, Gallo was able to capture most of the credit because he was the original discoverer of the HTLV family. It soon became clear, however, that these were the same virus, a lentivirus and not an HTLV, apparently making Montagnier the true discoverer. In the ensuing controversy, medical science seemed to replace its humanitarian motive with the quest for national prestige and Nobel Prize eligibility. The conflict subsided when the name was changed to *human immunodeficiency virus* (HIV) in 1986, and Montagnier and Gallo were named "co-discoverers." So add nationalism to the types of prejudice that prevent progress.

Society's homophobia had the effect of causing *social* solutions to precede *medical* ones. For example, federal funding was virtually nonexistent in the first two years of the epidemic. In fact, more money was spent in one week on a single aspirin-poisoning incident than during the first three years of AIDS. Two years later, in 1985, U.S. Congressman Henry Waxman was still trying to get the Department of Health and Human Services to pay attention to AIDS by charging, "Every day there are deaths that are a monument to your irresponsibility." In that same year a *Los Angeles Times* survey reported that thirty-nine percent of the respondents would want increased funding for research if AIDS affected primarily heterosexual men and women. By this time, four years into the AIDS epidemic, less money had been spent per victim on AIDS than on either Legionnaires' Disease or toxic shock syndrome.

The neglect was so bad that many started to claim NIH no longer stood for the National Institute of Health, but instead meant "Not Interested in Homosexuals." The surgeon general did not issue his report on AIDS until 1986—five years after the first US cases. That same year the federal government finally got around to seeking bids for studies on ways to prevent AIDS through education about safer sexual practices. The pamphlet *Understanding AIDS* was mailed to 107 million households in May 1988, seven years into the crisis and only after a year of heated debate in Congress. And by the time President Ronald Reagan delivered his first speech about AIDS, over 50,000 people had died or been diagnosed. Of course, this later activity was also well *after* society realized AIDS had infected the "general" population. The government's "too little, too late" response demonstrated that fag-bashing is not the only way homophobia kills.

Discrimination against people with AIDS continued to drive the disease underground. This is why every agency or task force that has studied AIDS (including the President's Commission on AIDS, the National Academy of Sciences, the American Medical Association, and the American Public Health Association) has recommended strong nondiscrimination laws to rectify the situation. The National Academy of Sciences (NAS) published a report in November 1986 calling the government's response "woefully inadequate." The President's Commission on AIDS published its report two years later which cited a catalog of failures, many of them the same as those offered by the NAS, and recommended over 600 steps that could and should be taken. Year after year, report after report, these warnings continued to fall on deaf political ears.

The gay community struggled to raise awareness in Washington and in all fifty states. It educated the nation, changed its own behavior by itself, cared for the sick, and conducted privately funded medical research to accelerate finding a cure. No one wanted to stop this killer more than those hit hardest by it. But that was precisely the problem. The majority, thinking they were immune from immunodeficiency, were not quite ready to put forth the effort necessary to defeat AIDS.

Much of the neglect was caused by the media. What is important is newsworthy, but the converse is also true: News coverage determines which social issues are important and therefore worthy of public consideration. What made AIDS newsworthy was not gay men dying, but straight people being diagnosed. For example, the very first AIDS story to appear in the *Wall Street Journal* carried the headline: "New, Often-Fatal Illness in Homosexuals Turns Up in Women, Heterosexual Males." The boomerang had returned.

What was fairly obvious, at least to some, by this point was that sex would serve as the primary avenue for AIDS into the gay male community, with needle-sharing coming in a distant second. Just the opposite would be the case, at least in the United States, for the heterosexual population. The vast majority of those infections would result from sharing needles, and sexual transmission (during anal and to a lesser extent vaginal intercourse) would be secondary.

Nevertheless, even when it became abundantly clear that the virus did not discriminate based on sexual orientation, a hierarchy of risk groups was quickly established to prevent widespread panic. Gay men were at the top of the list, followed by IV drug abusers, Haitians, and blood product recipients, especially hemophiliacs. Later, after much protest, Haitians were dropped from the list. Later still, "prostitutes and sexual partners of the above" were both added at the end. Then "children born to infected mothers" achieved official recognition. "Gay men" was changed to "promiscuous gay or bisexual men." People needed to check regularly to see if they too had made "the list." By the time it was realized that people of color were nearly twice as likely to be infected as white people were, the list had fallen out of vogue. This disproportionate exposure apparently was considered unimportant. Racism was added to the list of prejudices contributing to the view of AIDS as "somebody else's problem."

Now AIDS is everyone's problem, for AIDS always has had nothing to do with *being* anybody and everything to do with high risk *behavior*. Congressman Henry Waxman made this observation one year into the epidemic: "There is no doubt in my mind that, if the same disease had appeared among Americans of Norwegian descent, or among tennis players, rather than gay males, the response of both the government and the medical community would have been different." He was right.

When AIDS finally got the attention of *all* Americans, the solution expanded beyond the initial priority of containment in the now-defunct high risk groups. Resources were poured into other means of prevention, and research activity accelerated in a race to find both a vaccine and a cure. This three-pronged approach of containment, prevention and research are each examined successively in the following discussion.

"The Test"

During the course of the AIDS epidemic, various tests will go in and out of use as new, improved ones come along. Some, like the original ELISA test, were inexpensive ways to detect for the presence of HIV antibodies. Others, generally more expensive and thereby restricting their use to laboratory research or confirmation of less-reliable antibody tests, can actually spot the culprit virus. All are treated here as "the test."

"The test" was created not as a diagnostic tool but as a screening tool for donated blood, making the impetus for the test one of containment in the initial "high risk" groups. While containment was a worthy goal in itself, it was far from adequate *by* itself. Still, numerous officials touted "the test" as *the* means to "control" the spread of AIDS. After all, it was the only tool available. When all one has is a hammer, every problem is a nail.

Recognizing the potential for abuse, the first test packets were labeled: "It is inappropriate to use this test as screen for AIDS or as a screen for members of groups at increased risk for AIDS in the general population." Many would eventually ignore this warning and abuse AIDS testing in numerous ways.

Before "the test" became available, an exclusionary policy was adopted which deferred, indefinitely, all men having had sex with another man during the last ten years, along with members of other high risk groups, from donating blood. This practice continues at this printing because detectable AIDS antibodies may take up to ten years to develop. The version of "the test" that detects the actual virus could be used to plug this gaping hole, but it remains too expensive as a screening device. Now consider the effect this exclusionary policy might have on blood donations. According to Alfred C. Kinsey, nearly fifty percent of *all* men have had at least some same-sex sexual contact in their lives; that is, they rate on the scale from "1" through "6" (See Chapter 1). While not all may have had their "experience" during the previous ten years, a substantial percentage of them have been declared ineligible as blood donors. As a result, there developed a noticeable shortage in the nation's blood supply.

233

It is important to emphasize that "the test" does *not* diagnose AIDS, nor is its predictive value fully known. In other words, there has been no determination that HIV exposure will lead to development of AIDS in all cases. And there is no current medical intervention available for those who test positive. These reasons, combined with the very real threat of discrimination, motivated gay civil rights leaders to caution everyone, gay or straight, against taking "the test." They instead encouraged all individuals who have not been in a monogamous relationship for five to ten years, especially those in the high risk groups, to follow safer sex and other risk reduction guidelines. This advice applied independently of either positive or negative test result. Further, taking it once is inadequate for those individuals who are sexually active with more than one partner. A single test is also inadequate if one partner of a monogamous couple already carries the virus or if either shares IV drug needles.

The decision to take "the test" would need to be one that was fully informed and personally made. A positive result could have devastating psychological effects, possibly contributing to the development of AIDS. If taken, it would need to be done anonymously. Confidentiality is poor protection against discrimination in an environment where there is no guarantee that confidentiality will be maintained. Changes in legislation, signed releases on employment or insurance applications, court subpoenas, or accidental disclosure could all destroy confidentiality.

With all its shortcomings, but to no one's surprise, "the test" continued to be misused as it provided a perfect opportunity to exercise homophobia by denying civil rights to gay people. For example, some orders of the Catholic church began using "the test" as a screen for ordination into the priesthood!

Because presumption that *all* gay men carried the virus would have been blatantly homophobic, some folks "only" called for the *testing* of all gay men. This somehow seemed less like prejudice and more like precaution. What would happen to those individuals who tested positive was not well-defined. With no medical intervention available, though, some people began talking of quarantine. Given that quarantine would be impossible logistically, this draconian suggestion could only be the result of a homophobic thought process. Surgeon General C. Everett Koop attempted to put this issue to bed by claiming, "Quarantine has no role in the management of AIDS because AIDS is not spread by casual contact." Maybe it did not occur to the quarantine advocates that only a fraction of the resources their approach would consume might be sufficient to discover a treatment and a vaccine. On the other hand, maybe this did occur to them.

During the public debate, and once again to no one's surprise, the military undertook massive testing of all existing personnel and potential recruits. Discharges based on positive results were permitted for the "convenience of the government." Its action was ostensibly for the protection of other military personnel. Yet real protection would *only* be provided if military personnel engaged in unsafe sexual contact with each other, shared IV drug needles, or received infected blood transfusions. The military offers the last case as its real reason, especially during wartime, when the extraordinarily rare direct person-to-person transfusion might be required, because "surely" the other two activities never occur in *our* military forces. Being captured, shot at, showered with napalm, or bombarded by the enemy seem to be acceptable risks for servicemembers—but even the slightest possibility of exposure to AIDS was entirely out of the question.

It was rather obvious what the military was up to. "The test" was designed for use on donated blood, not on blood donors. The military could quite easily have used it in this, its intended, fashion. Instead, they chose massive testing. So to be truly effective, this massive testing would need to continue at regular intervals and at massive expense. During the first year of testing, only about one-fourth of all active-duty forces had been tested. Officials optimistically estimated the first round of testing would take three years to complete. During the three-year testing cycle, numerous individuals who "passed" year one could become infected by year three, making the entire undertaking rather worthless as a way of protecting the blood supply—and only slightly better as a means of detecting homosexuality and IV drug abuse. And how many person-to-person blood transfusions were performed in the interim? Zero. At best, this misguided approach might disqualify someone as a blood donor; it should not disqualify someone *period*.

Admiral Watkins, as a member of the Joint Chiefs of Staff, originally supported military testing for AIDS. As chairman of the President's Commission on AIDS, he would revise his thinking to cite such discrimination as "the most significant obstacle to progress."

To the general public, though, unaware of the serious shortcomings, massive testing appeared to be prudent precaution: "If it's 'necessary' for the military, why isn't it equally necessary for the public at large?" This irresponsible action only cultivated hysteria and homophobia. The surgeon general, recognizing the problem, attempted to squelch public concern by rationalizing the military's action in his report on AIDS. Defending this irrational waste of taxpayers' money was a dirty job, but someone in the government had to do it.

An Ounce of Prevention

While AIDS remained uncontained and incurable, it continued to be preventable. Education would need to be the foundation for preventing the spread of AIDS. But instead, officials called for a stop to all behavior which was thought to "cause" AIDS. Gay men were advised to quit having sex, and IV drug abusers were cautioned against taking drugs. Not only were these simplistic approaches naive, they completely missed the reality of AIDS. People continued having sex, some of it unsafe, and most IV drug abusers remained addicted, using shared needles, while the illusion of testing as a means of containment focused attention away from truly effective measures. As a result, the gay community was left almost entirely on its own to provide education on safer sexual practices for *all* people, gay and straight, and to warn against sharing IV drug needles. In opposition to these measures, many public officials, believing that descriptions of safer sexual practices and life-saving advice on drug abuse might offend the sensitivity of certain citizens, advocated a watered-down approach to education. Apparently, a "good" person's sensitivity was infinitely more important than the lives of a few faggots and junkies.

As of this writing, safer sex education is beginning to make its way into homes across the nation. In 1988, when the Senate approved more money for education than the total spent in the first seven years of the epidemic, Senator Edward Kennedy commented, "Finally we have declared war on the virus and not on the victims."

Still, clean needles are not being made available in most cities. Continuing the prohibition against the availability of sterile hypodermic needles basically requires IV drug abusers to reuse and share old needles, exposing them to the risk of contracting AIDS. This irresponsibility is tantamount to murder. The ACLU stated its position as follows: "Because it is known that the use of contaminated drug paraphernalia is the cause of the spread of AIDS/ARC among intravenous drug users, and because the ACLU views drug addiction as an illness and not as criminal behavior, the ACLU endorses the concept of legalization and distribution at low or no cost of sterile drug paraphernalia among I-V drug abuser populations." People are not going to *start* taking IV drugs simply because clean needles are made available, any more than they are going to *stop* taking drugs because needles are withheld. The financial side of this issue also makes sense. Thousands of needles could be given away for the same cost of caring for a single AIDS patient. Most significantly, IV drug abusers do not live on an island. They have sexual partners and children. Ironically, this avenue for AIDS into the straight community remains open.

Safer sex education, to be effective, requires precise knowledge of how America has sex. The most recent study is Kinsey's, now over forty years old! In 1989 the Public Health Service proposed conducting a survey of sexual behavior in the United States. Twenty thousand people would be asked some 300 questions about their own sexual behavior. The "guardians of purity" on the right were outraged, and the proposal became mired in controversy. Congressman William Dannemeyer and Senator Jesse Helmes protested that the survey, anonymous and voluntarily, would be an "invasion of privacy." This conclusion comes from two men have been disturbing gay people's privacy for years. What are they afraid of? Might this survey confirm that ten percent of the population is indeed gay or lesbian? Would it reveal what most people already know: That people *do* masturbate? Would it shock the populace to find out how many of them are having sex outside of marriage? And as for oral sex—is the thought unmentionable? Professor Moses at Stanford University's Medical School commented, "Mr. Dannemeyer and Mr. Helmes may know all they need to know about sex, but there's a great lack of hard information in the scientific community."

So the story went: Uncle Sam continued to stick his head in the sand, and more people, gay and straight, continued to become infected and die. This neglect was particularly devastating owing to the ten-year average, but as long as fifteen-year, latency between infection and diagnosis. The virus was indeed spreading rapidly—and invisibly. People were becoming infected, and infecting others, unknowingly. In actuality, then, the relatively "few" officially diagnosed cases were just the tip of a gigantic, swelling iceberg. It was time to find a vaccine and a cure.

Gay Guinea Pigs

People with AIDS were, and to some extent still are, treated like human "guinea pigs." Patients would learn of promising treatments and become hopeful, only to be informed that a potential life-saving or life-prolonging drug could not be made available to them. About half of those who got lucky enough to participate in a study quickly had their luck turn sour as they became doomed scientific "controls." In other words, they would *not* be given the promising medicine. Instead they were injected with or told to swallow a placebo, simply fake medicine. The tests would be administered "double blind." That is, neither the patient nor the doctor would be informed of the true contents of the container. In roughly half of the trial sample, then, selected at random, the substance figuratively marked "hope" would be, in actuality, saline solution or sugar pills. Each sample would be coded for identification at a later date when the "control" groups' possible lack of improvement or earlier deaths might show the medicine *had* indeed been effective.

Control groups are always necessary in properly conducted scientific research. It is not necessary, however, to have *new* control groups when historical information is readily available on numerous patients who received no medication. Comparative controls, where one drug's effectiveness is judged against another's, could also be used. In medical experimentation, it has been established that up to one-third of a "control" group will respond positively to a placebo. This is believed to be a psychological effect on physical health. If an experimental drug is not effective in substantially more than one-third of its trials, a "standard" control group, so to speak, its real value would be questionable.

Placebos are great for testing something that might cure acne or grow hair, but their use in life-threatening situations is unconscionable. A physician's first and foremost responsibility in a life-and-death situation is to provide the best possible care for his or her patient. Certainly, there are possible "side effects" with experimental drugs. But the "side effect" of not doing anything about AIDS is certain death. If for no other reason, experimental drugs should be dispensed to anyone who wants them, for they are accompanied by hope. Hope, for reasons not yet fully understood, *does* help. And at this time, an AIDS patient's only hope may well be hope.

The various circumstances coming together made conflict inevitable. Possibly for the first time in history, an organized minority, threatened with a deadly disease, was rapidly losing money, hope, and patience. Insurance companies, long a nemesis of the gay community, were targeted for their unwillingness to pay for AIDS therapies. Citing exemptions for "pre-existing conditions," based on the long incubation period, or "experimental drugs," several refused to make payments, bankrupting many a person with AIDS. In the absence of *the* cure, every possible therapy is experimental. So when a drug is good enough for a doctor to approve, that should serve as sufficient reason for an insurance company to pay up.

The FDA, with its typical seven-year approval cycle, labeled the "Foot Dragging Administration" by some, became another target for reform. The FDA traditionally has allowed only those drugs which demonstrate effectiveness to be used in widespread experiments. Their job is to protect the public by weighing a prospective drug's potential value against any possible harm. But do they have to do it so slowly? AIDS activists and scientists alike began advocating a new standard of allowing any nontoxic drug to be used experimentally — and not necessarily in a project supervised by the agency. As a result, the FDA relaxed its rules a little. Nevertheless, policies governing experimental drugs are likely to remain a heated issue during the course of AIDS.

The denial of medical treatment for early intervention or compassionate use disgusted San Francisco Mayor Art Agnos so much that he lashed out, "There is something severely wrong with a federal policy that requires people to go to death's door before they find a welcome mat."

The decision to take an experimental drug, which is distinctly different from a decision to participate in a controlled experiment, must remain with the individual facing risk or death, not with a doctor or some government agency on the patient's "behalf." If *you* had AIDS, would *you* want a placebo?

... and miles to go before we sleep."

In Haiti, in 1983, seventy-one percent of AIDS and ARC cases were contained in the same high risk groups established in the United States during 1987. Three years later in Haiti, the original "high risk" groups accounted for only eleven percent of the diagnosed cases. This same pattern could occur in the United States if enough drug-abusing and/or sexually active straight Americans continue to ignore the warnings about AIDS. Government statistics show the rate of STD infection, a good indicator of possible exposure to HIV, rising in the non-gay, non-drug-using populations at the same time it continues to decline in the gay male community. As early as 1986 military screening in New York City had revealed an almost equal ratio of exposure to HIV in male and female applicants.

The epilogue on the AIDS epidemic may attempt to blame the gay community for this crisis. In fact, AIDS already has had a negative effect on society's attitude toward gay people. In a 1985 Gallup poll, nearly forty percent of those questioned indicated that AIDS had "changed [their] opinion about homosexuals for the worse." Of course, this would mean that gay men must have some sort of kamikaze mentality. Could anyone really believe gay men would visit this suffering upon themselves just to strike out at an oppressive society? Nonsense. It bears repeating: AIDS, the disease, is caused by a virus. AIDS, the epidemic, was caused by a society that ignored the problem for too many years. An ounce of prevention would have been well-worth the pound of cure we must now face — together.

Everyone can and must help defeat AIDS. Each individual has the means, and therefore the responsibility, to protect himself or herself. To avoid infection by the virus *all* people at risk, male or female, gay or straight, should continue using safer sexual practices and generally stay in good health. Consider yourself at risk sexually, gay or straight, if you have not been in a completely monogamous relationship for the past ten years. But because between forty and fifty percent of all marriages are not completely monogamous, only a minority of the population is totally isolated from exposure.

The best possible universal advice is this: Simultaneously assume you have *not* been exposed to HIV to protect yourself, and that you *have* been exposed to protect your partner(s). Safer sex really works. Many long-term partners of AIDS patients show no signs of exposure to the virus. Until clean needles are made available, any shared needles used to inject drugs can and must be cleaned using chlorine bleach and water. (Contact an AIDS organization or a local health agency for more information.) The screening of all blood products should continue. There should be increased counseling and support services for people living with AIDS. So far, most of these services have been provided by the gay community and conscientious non-gay volunteers in some 400, and growing, AIDS-related service organizations. Experimental drugs should be made available for compassionate use. Finally, funds for research and public education should be increased drastically.

The National Academy of Sciences, in agreement with the surgeon general, called for "perhaps the most wide-ranging and intensive efforts ever made against an infectious disease." Everyone, the most homophobic people included, should want the equivalent of a medical "Manhattan Project" against AIDS for its sound economics. As the surgeon general put it, "Although AIDS may never touch you personally, the societal impact certainly will." Even if only for the "innocent" victims, this disease *will* be defeated. The US indeed has both the resources and the technology to conquer this disease; all we need is more national will to find the way.

When this medical crisis is over, and both a cure and a vaccine have been found, future generations will look back with shame on how a generation responded. Randy Shilts, author of *And the Band Played On,* summed up the early history of the epidemic: "The bitter truth was that AIDS did not just happen to America — it was allowed to happen by an array of institutions, all of which failed to perform their appropriate tasks to safeguard the public health. This failure of the system leaves a legacy of unnecessary suffering that will haunt the Western world for decades to come." One would hope that the lessons learned will preclude prejudice from ever causing a similar crisis again.

It should be apparent from the many issues presented here and in the previous chapter that gay civil rights is *much* more than a frivolous enterprise affecting more than just the gay community. It should also be apparent that the *real* problems are caused not by homosexuality, but by homophobia. Gay people are not merely defending a "lifestyle"; in many cases they are fighting for their very lives. Sure, most gay people can avoid most of the discrimination most of the time. But they need to do it every day, and most do it by passing as straight. Others confront the issues head-on through social and political activism in the Gay Civil Rights Movement. And history has shown us, repeatedly, that the only way to eliminate the traps is to assure liberty and justice for all.

Chapter 14:

Liberty and Justice for All

Those who feed the flames of intolerance, set fire to their own house.
Harold Stassen

During the 1984 Democratic National Convention in San Francisco, a visitor asked local columnist Herb Caen why his city has so many gay residents. Herb responded, "Just lucky, I guess." Apparently, he saw the value to both gay and straight people of a society where *all* citizens enjoyed full participation in life, liberty, and the pursuit of happiness free from prejudice, fear, and hate.

Gay people comprise the largest minority in the United States that pay equal taxes while being denied the assurance of equal civil rights. The gay minority cannot even enjoy "separate but equal" status, because separate services are never really provided. Today, most straight people are able to control their homophobia, intellectually, while continuing to feel repugnance, emotionally. The result is tolerance. But tolerance is terribly insufficient.

The difference between tolerance and acceptance is quite significant. Tolerance merely permits an objectionable practice to continue. In effect, then, tolerance is a "gift" extended to an "inferior" group — and therein lies the problem. As long as society continues to perceive homosexuality as "inferior," it will continue to condone the various unjust forms of oppression. In other words, the road to private hell is paved by social tolerance. Frank Moore Colby pointed out that "tolerance is composed of nine parts apathy to one of brotherly love." The AIDS crisis serves as a painful reminder of this. Tolerance can co-exist with hostility; acceptance cannot. Acceptance, therefore, is basically the recognition of full equality.

Acceptance for the gay minority will not come when the majority realizes homosexuality is not much different from heterosexuality. It will only come when the few differences are recognized and no longer condemned. Earlier attempts to integrate black people were really geared toward making them "just like white people" in the way they talked, looked, dressed, and acted. Black people are *not* just like white people. Women are *not* just like men. Gay people are *not* just like straight people. As Sister Boom-Boom, a flamboyant and controversial gay rights activist commented, "The freedom to be like everyone else, is no freedom at

241

all." Acceptance means legitimizing and validating homosexuality through official recognition and the elimination of any and all social sanctions which prevent gay people from living "gay."

At a minimum, gay people seek a casual indifference by society regarding homosexuality. There is incredible irony, however, in that to make homosexuality irrelevant, it is necessary first to make it an issue. In fact, homosexuality is a very important aspect in the lives of gay people only because it can *not* be taken for granted. In a word, then, acceptance really does mean equality—and equality means granting equal civil rights to America's gay citizens.

Gay Civil Rights

Citizenship is man's basic right for it is nothing less than the right to have rights. Remove this priceless possession and there remains a stateless person, disgraced and degraded in the eyes of his countrymen. *Chief Justice Earl Warren*

Everyone has rights. This is true even when those rights are somehow denied. The phrase *gay civil rights* is actually a misnomer. Gay people do not seek special treatment, only equal treatment. They simply desire an end to both public and private discrimination, accompanied by a beginning of equal protection under the law. Only then will gay people be able to participate fully and equally in the social, political, and economic liberties and opportunities available to the majority. Finally, gay people seek dignity. They want the ability to work and live freely as *members* of society, not secretly as social outcasts; no longer do they want to be second-class citizens. The rights gay men and lesbians are currently denied are called *gay civil rights*. While the phrase may not be accurate technically, it adequately describes the problem.

There is no dilemma in claiming that gay people, who are different, deserve the identical treatment in our society. Most of the differences between gay and straight people are socially determined anyway. The United States is indeed a "melting pot" of people from around the world. We enjoy a wonderful mix of cultures which enriches our society and everyone in it. Because conformity leads to mediocrity, diversity is actually one of our nation's greatest assets. The camaraderie which exists is both cause and effect of the mutual respect so essential to our form of government. It is the very foundation of an egalitarian society. Our form of government may be the best in the world, but its abuse by homophobic individuals clearly causes problems of concern to gay Americans.

Many politicians and appointed officials have apparently forgotten the very reason the United States became a sovereign nation: to escape the oppression of England's King George III. The Declaration of Independence is very clear on the principles which woud make our nation great: "We hold these truths to be self-evident, that all men are created equal; that they are endowed by their Creator with certain unalienable rights; that among these, are life, liberty, and the pursuit of happiness." *All*—that means *no* exceptions. In George Orwell's *Animal Farm,* all creatures are equal — some are just more equal than others. Unfortunately, the same is really true in our society today. Erich Fromm pointed out the reason why: "Men are born equal but they are also born different."

In any nation, the people's behavior must be regulated by the government to protect the civil rights of *all* citizens. In the United States, the government's behavior is also regulated, by the Constitution which both grants *and limits* the powers vested in the government. In the *Federalist Papers,* Alexander Hamilton warned that the Constitution must provide protection against "serious oppressions of the minor party in the community." The Constitution is also very clear on those civil rights that belong to *all* citizens. These encompass freedoms of thought and expression including speech, press, religion, and peaceful assembly; prohibitions against the establishment of religion; security from unwarranted intrusion; the right to a fair trial; bans against cruel and unusual punishment; guarantees of due process and equal protection under the law; and safeguards for life, liberty, and property. Others, most notably the right to privacy, have been implied in the Constitution based on judicial interpretation. Gay people are regularly denied each and every one of these constitutional liberties. This is the core of gay civil rights.

For example, consider the restrictions on First Amendment rights for gay people. In a work environment that regularly fires gay people, is a lesbian able to display in her office a sign supporting a gay candidate? If homosexuality is considered sufficient cause to evict a tenant, can a gay man circulate a petition in support of a gay civil rights measure arund his apartment complex? Can his lesbian neighbor feel safe enough to even sign it? Can gay people in the military write a pro-gay letter to the editor at the local newspaper or march in the local gay pride parade? Can the lesbian or gay man with a security clearance join a gay civil rights group, or merely contribute money? That some gay people do these things does *not* protect the rights of the individual. In other words, there is no such thing as "group rights" in the Constitution. Rather, the constitutional collection of freedoms and protections apply to all citizens — as individuals — equally.

Our society is greatly distressed, and rightfully so, when in some countries the very act of political dissent is made a basis for the diagnosis of psychiatric illness. This frequently has occurred in the Soviet Union. But aren't we really doing the same thing here in the United States? For gay people to be tolerated, are they expected to be silent? Richard Mohr in his book *Gays/Justice: A Study of Ethics, Society and Law* offers some food for thought: "As an invisible minority, gays cannot fight for the right to be open about being gay, unless gays are already open about it; and gays cannot reasonably be open about being gay, until gays have the right to be openly gay. One would hope that once society was made aware of this paradox, if society had any sense of decency and fair play, it would on its own move to establish civil rights for gays."

One Nation Under God

There are those in the United States who would like to rewrite this line from the Pledge of Allegiance. The Radical Religious Right might prefer it read: A nation under one God. At least, that is how these "literalists" seem to interpret it. Then there are those who recognize how wrong this would be.

One of the fundamental principles of our society's form of government is the separation of church and state. The First Amendment reads in part: "Congress shall make no law respecting an establishment of religion, or prohibiting the free exercise thereof." This second phrase prevents the government from interfering with the practice of religion. The first phrase prevents organized religion, or the church, from interfering with the government. Together these restrictions assure that a dominant religion is unable to influence the government to a point which would interfere with the practice of other religions, thereby eroding the very concept of religious freedom. The separation of church and state is the very reason religious institutions are not taxed. A tax could unfairly interfere with the practice of religion. It was Chief Justice John Marshall who so rightly claimed, "The power to tax involves the power to destroy." Conversely, because churches do not pay taxes, they have no voice in how the government's money is spent.

The separation of church and state, however, must be contrasted with the *inseparable* religion and politics. Individual Christians, Jews, Muslims, Mormons, Buddhists, Jehovah's Witnesses, and Gnostics must vote their religious conscience. In fact, prohibiting political debate based on religious beliefs would violate the First Amendment guarantee of free exercise of religion. Rather, the separation principle simply means that *all* laws must have some legitimate interest to the state. In other words, every *moral* claim based on religion (and no single religion has a monopoly on morality) must also have a *social* claim to justify regulation by the state.

What if this were not the case? What if religious doctrine were a legitimate basis for secular law? In addition to sodomy laws, Judaism and Christianity might want adultery, greed, haughtiness, and idolatry to be illegal and punishable. The already overloaded courts would crumble under the new caseload. The Mormons would want polygamy legalized. The Methodists might want to bring back prohibition. Each of the hundreds of religions would want something or other made legal or illegal. Even the various Christian denominations have yet to converge on "the" way. Jesse Jackson and Jerry Falwell agree that the country must change its "wicked ways," partially through the force of law, but they cannot agree what those are. This political Pandora's box is what prompted Thomas Jefferson to say, "Our civil liberties have no dependence on our religious opinions" and call for the government to "erect a wall of separation between church and state."

The long and painful history of the church and homosexuality boils down to basically one issue today: morality. Now, our society correctly believes that what is legal is moral, and that what is immoral should be illegal, based on social reasoning. In the case of homosexuality, though, this whole relationship of morality and law has gone full circle. Society, assisted by the church, has created a situation where what is not explicitly legal becomes immoral. This is why sodomy and solicitation laws are so damaging, even when unenforced. From a constitutional perspective, homosexuality should be treated using the *same* standards society employs for heterosexuality. Those acts which are clearly immoral, for social reasons, should be illegal. Any other expressions of sexuality should be perfectly legal for *all*. Clearly, reform in this area is long overdue.

The Avenues of Reform: Legislation and Litigation

I would remind you that extremism in the defense of liberty is no vice. And let me remind you also that moderation in the pursuit of justice is no virtue. *Barry Goldwater*

Social reform will undoubtedly have a profound effect on the oppressed, but it will barely be noticed by the oppressors. There is really no need to give up anything, except possibly for a self-applied sense of superiority. For gay people, social reform will release positive energy which is now being diverted to self-preservation. Social reform will also release the negative energy which is regularly used to "ride herd" on conformity for the sake of conformity. How many of our precious social resources will we, as a society, continue to waste trying to solve the wrong problem? This is why gay people are so thoroughly convinced that once society recognizes the *real* problem of homophobia, gay civil rights will prevail. The gay minority has so much to gain; society has absolutely nothing to lose. History will indeed be on the gay side of this issue.

There are two basic and related problems preventing the gay minority from obtaining equal civil rights. The first is the present situation of inequality. That means change is required to eliminate the inequities, and change is always resisted. Which brings up the second reason: The government and the majority are doing basically nothing to change the situation. The result is a stubborn momentum for the status quo. The Gay Civil Rights Movement attempts to break the deadlock by getting society to act, and act responsibly, on the issues. Before discussing the activities of the movement itself, it is helpful to understand the current response to the gay civil rights issues by both elected and appointed officials in the government.

Elected Officials

Telling American lawmakers that they are hard on homosexuals seems to me like telling inquisitors that they are hard on heretics. *Dr. Thomas Szasz from* The Manufacture of Madness

The best advice I ever read regarding the stock market has a very interesting parallel with law. It recommends investors consider *selling* stock, in terms of *buying* it. In other words, if you are contemplating selling a certain stock because you think its price may have reached a peak, ask yourself if you would instead buy more, given the cash to do so. If you would buy more, chances are you think it's a good choice of stock, and you should hold on to your existing shares. If you would *not* buy more, then you are really betting it's a bad choice. Therefore, you would be better off selling your existing shares, even if that means selling them at a loss. By keeping them, you will probably just lose more money.

How does this all relate to law? Well, a majority of Americans would hopefully be at least a little upset if their legislative and executive representatives tried to pass even more laws oppressing gay people. But this same majority seems to feel it is perfectly acceptable to keep existing oppressive laws on the books. Think about it.

Homosexuality and gay civil rights become issues in politics mainly because they serve as a point of disagreement between the two parties. Because both parties actually agree on so many subjects, it is sometimes necessary to "create" issues. Homosexuality seems to fit the bill. Republicans claim homosexuality is a matter of law and order—a "threat" to society; Democrats see it as an issue of liberty and justice.

It is absolutely amazing how the former party has changed. The Republican Party formed in 1854 primarily around a single issue: slavery. Its first presidential candidate was John C. Fremont. His campaign slogan was "Free Soil, Free Speech, Free Men, and Fremont." The first Republican president, Abraham Lincoln, under pressure from the party, signed the Emancipation Proclamation in 1862 freeing America's black citizens. Lincoln said of his new party, "Republicans are for both the man and the dollar, but in the case of conflict, the man before the dollar." In the case of gay civil rights, there is no conflict. How ironic it all seems. Why the change? Obviously, it is not the result of any single reason, but the Radical Religious Right has quite strongly influenced the Republican Party recently.

Most gay people could be located on the liberal end of the political spectrum. After all, because the liberals are even nice to whales, they are bound to accept homosexuality. So most gay people are Democrats. In fact, for the first time, the 1980 Democratic Party platform supported gay civil rights: "We must affirm the dignity of all people and the right of each individual to have equal access to and participation in the institutions and services of our society, including actions to protect all groups from discrimination based on race, color, religion, national origin, sex or sexual orientation . . . Appropriate legislative and administrative actions to achieve these goals should be undertaken." And many Democratic politicians actively support gay civil rights. For example, Senator Edward M. Kennedy said, "I believe our party's platform should commit itself to the issuance of an executive order prohibiting discrimination based on sexual orientation in government programs, and the enactment of legislation protecting the civil rights of those who have historically been stigmatized on the basis of sexual orientation."

Gay people are not single-issue voters. They worry about preventing nuclear war, keeping our national defense strong and capable, reducing pollution, allowing American industry to remain competitive abroad, keeping the tax base solvent and the burden equitably distributed, improving the school system, maintaining the quality while controlling the cost of health care and, of course, promoting civil rights for *all* Americans. A significant number (albeit a minority) of gay people simply believe the Republican Party offers a better overall "plan" for America, despite its poor record lately on civil rights. They feel remaining in the party will help to promote change from within. They also recognize that much of the support from the Democratic Party offers more symbolism than substance, demonstrating a phenomenon that might be labeled "latent" homophobia. Unfortunately, maybe there really is not that much difference between the two parties on the issue of gay civil rights after all.

The 1964 Civil Rights Amendment

The law which would virtually assure equal civil rights for gay people is sitting idle in the US Congress. In 1975 the National Gay and Lesbian Task Force worked with Bella Abzug's office and twenty-four congressional cosponsors to introduce a bill which would amend the 1964 and 1968 Civil Rights Acts to add the phrase "affectional or sexual orientation" to the list of protected classes which currently includes race, color, religion, sex, national origin, and pregnancy. This is a nondiscrimination law which does not constitute preferential treatment. The inclusion of sexual orientation would protect heterosexual men and women as well. This is similar to "race" prohibiting discrimination against white people and "religion" offering protection for Christians. Although these last two examples of protection are largely unnecessary, they would do no *harm* to the majority in either case. Of course, the very reason for nondiscrimination policies is protection for the minorities that really need it.

Any nondiscrimination legislation must be accompanied by a means of enforcement. This also already exists. The Equal Employment Opportunity Commission was formed to create the specific regulations and guidelines necessary to enforce the Civil Rights Act's policy of nondiscrimination.

Therefore, everything is in place to offer protection for gay people from discrimination on a *national* level. Such a law would serve as a weapon against oppression, a way of creating a "fair fight." Although society cannot legislate attitudes, this law would serve as a catalyst to encourage straight people to confront their own homophobia. Numerous organizations support this legislation, including the American Bar Association, the American Civil Liberties Union, the National Organization for Women, the YWCA, the National Education Association, and the American Federation of Teachers. And it now has over seventy cosponsors. But there it sits, stuck in committee, while the oppression continues in our free society. Only two states, Wisconsin and Massachusetts, along with a handful of cities ban discrimination based on sexual orientation through similar legislation. This is a sad comment indeed.

247

The only threat this law might pose is to the reelection of the politicians who support it. But even that is changing. Gay people comprise ten percent of the voters in this country. While gay people may not be optimistic about reform, most do register and vote. Gay people cannot afford to be apathetic. For them, voting is more than a right, it is a responsibility. A survey of readers of *The Advocate,* a gay magazine, found that eighty-three percent of the gay people polled had voted in the previous election. Many elected officials recognize the gay community as a substantial voting bloc, especially because most races are won by narrow margins.

They have also realized it is prudent politics to add the relatives and friends of gay people who are similarly concerned with gay civil rights. Just look at the numbers. Every gay person has two parents. On the average, each gay person has 1.3 brothers or sisters, who, chances are, are married. Their siblings also have children, so add three or four nieces and nephews. Similarly, the parents of gay children each have brothers and sisters who likely married, for a total of approximately six aunts and uncles. Each has, on the average, 2.3 children, adding seven first cousins. The total so far is about twenty relatives for each gay person. Of course, there is some overlap because two of these relatives are probably gay as well. Anyway, next add sixteen second cousins and four grandparents. The total is up to forty now. Because one-fourth of gay people were or are married, their spouses, children, and in-laws should be included in the totals — provided they're not bitter about the break-up. Then there are the countless friends and coworkers each gay person has. Considering the above exercise, it is safe to say that *every* American knows not only one, but several gay people. In fact, climb any family tree just a few branches, and you'll find a few fruits. So when a politician attacks "those gays," everyone knows that some friend or relative somewhere is being threatened, making the "gay constituency" much greater than ten percent of the voting population. This also demonstrates why coming out is such a high priority with the Gay Civil Rights Movement.

Is support of the amendment to the Civil Rights Act a threat to reelection then? Apparently not. The more than seventy cosponsors, mostly Democrats, in the House of Representatives have been consistently reelected term after term. Would Congress pass a law stating that anti-gay discrimination is legal? Probably not. Yet by *not* passing this amendment, that is exactly what they are doing. Eventually, this piece of legislation will be recognized as a good "stock" to buy for both parties. But eventually may be a long time. It took twenty-two years to achieve a majority for the original act. Progress can be so painfully slow.

Appointed Judges

He that judges without informing himself to the utmost that he is capable, cannot acquit himself of judging amiss. *John Locke*

In a legal system based on case law, such as the one we have in the United States, the courts make interpretive judgments on statutory regulations. Written legislation serves mainly to provide guidance, the applicability of each law being determined by the judicial process. In a trial, the defendant may be found not guilty of a particular law. He may be found guilty under extenuating circumstances which reduce the severity of the sentence. Or the law itself may be found in conflict with another law or with some provision of the Constitution. This last situation is what holds the most hope for gay civil rights.

It is generally easier to obtain social reform through the courts, even though most judges are older, straight, Christian, white males. Homosexuality is too much of a political "hot potato" at this time. Judges are not directly responsible to a homophobic constituency in the way elected representatives are. Actually, most judges are appointed to life terms specifically to avoid any direct obligation to the voting public. This is fundamental to the balance of powers in our nation. Judges interpret only the law, and not public opinion. This also helps make ours a nation of laws, and not one of men. Still, because judges are either appointed by elected officials or are elected themselves, their outlook tends to reflect the predominant social views of the period and region. Conservative lawyers likely feel they have been served well by their opinions over the years. In fact, it is these same opinions which often make them "qualified" for appointment to the position of judge. Further, judges and jurors are not immune from homophobia. Anti-gay rulings can therefore result from habit or homophobia, or more likely, both.

The infrequency and inconsistency of judicial rulings demonstrates the degree to which personal prejudice, in the absence of sound legal precedent, influences litigation. So to some extent, judicial decisions tend to follow rather than lead social attitudes. For example, Supreme Court Justice William H. Rehnquist, in a summary affirmation of a Court of Appeals' opinion, commented that a gay group's right to organize at a Midwestern universit was "akin to whether those suffering from measles have a constitutional right, in violation of quarantine regulations, to associate together and with others who do not presently have measles, in order to urge repeal of a state law providing that measles sufferers be quarantined. The very act of assemblage under these circumstances undercuts a significant interest in the State." It is obvious Justice Rehnquist believes not only that homosexuality is a "disease," but that it is contagious. This ruling came three full years after the American Psychiatric Association declared: "It has been the unscientific inclusion of homosexuality per se in a list of mental disorders which has been the main ideological justification for the denial of the civil rights of individuals whose only crime is that their sexual orientation is to members of the same sex." Apparently, the APA's findings had still not found their way to Justice Rehnquist as much as ten years later when he ruled on another case analyzed below.

The Supreme Court has considered only a handful of cases addressing issues related to homosexuality and gay civil rights. With one notable exception, its actions have been essentially procedural. In other words, the Court has managed to avoid ruling on the merits in these cases. Unfortunately, procedural devices such as summary affirmation do not establish a binding precedent. This procedural screening is required to select from the over 4,000 petitions for review submitted to the Supreme Court every year, and the Court can accept only about 150 cases for full hearings and written opinions on merit. In effect, the Court selects only those current issues it wishes to address. It is surprising, though, that the Court would continually decline cases involving gay issues which are so important to such a large segment of American society. Considering its recent conservative trend, it may b just as well the Court has *not*. But in 1985 the Court agreed to hear the case of *Bowers v. Hardwick* — a challenge to Georgia's sodomy statute.

The Supreme Court on Sodomy

The case of *Bowers v. Hardwick* began in 1982, when Michael Hardwick was cited for publicly carrying an opened bottle of beer, a misdemeanor offense. Hardwick paid the fine. But owing to an administrative error, this did not show up on the records. A warrant was issued for his arrest. The same officer who cited Hardwick for "drinking in public" went to Hardwick's home to serve the warrant. When the officer arrived, he was directed to the bedroom by a guest. He entered the bedroom to find Hardwick in bed, with another man, engaging in oral sex. Both men were arrested on sodomy charges. Georgia's 170-year-old sodomy law makes "any sexual act involving the sex organs of one person and the mouth or anus of another" punishable by up to twenty years in prison.

Hardwick spent twelve hours in jail before being released. The authorities kept moving him from cell to cell, each time informing the other prisoners about the sodomy charge. Hardwick recalls his feelings: "I kept thinking I was about to get gang-banged, and I was scared to death." The district attorney declined to prosecute, but Hardwick filed suit against Georgia's Attorney General Michael Bowers anyway, asking for the law to be declared unconstitutional. Ultimately, the US Court of Appeals for the Eleventh Circuit sided with Hardwick. This decision was appealed by Bowers to the Supreme Court, which accepted the case on its merits. Of course, it was accepted with the opportunity to reverse the lower court's decision — and that is exactly what happened. Not too surprisingly, Justice Rehnquist ruled *with* the majority.

Hardwick based his defense on the "right to privacy." The right to privacy is not explicit in the Constitution. Instead, it is considered implicit based on principles found elsewhere in the original document and its amendments. The right to privacy was first officially recognized in a Supreme Court ruling in 1965. In the case of *Griswold v. Connecticut,* the Court invalidated a Connecticut statute forbidding the use of contraceptives in a marriage on grounds that the law violated the constitutional right to privacy. There have been numerous cases since then affirming this constitutional right which recognizes the home as a sanctuary for relationships and intimate emotions and their expression. In another ruling, the Supreme Court extended the right to privacy to the individual, stating, "the Fourth Amendment protects people, not places."

The Court essentially ignored the constitutional right to privacy and ruled five to four against Hardwick for a number of *other* reasons. The majority was able to do this by *redefining* the issue before the Court as "whether the Federal Constitution confers a fundamental right upon homosexuals to engage in sodomy." Justice Harry A. Blackmun pointed out the fallacy in this redefinition when commenting in a dissenting opinion: "Rather, this case is about 'the most comprehensive of rights and the right most valued by civilized men,' namely, 'the right to be let alone.'" He also pointed out that Hardwick's homosexuality was irrelevant because the Georgia sodomy law "involves an unconstitutional intrusion into his privacy and his right of intimate association does not depend in any way on his sexual orientation."

With the issue before the Court carefully redefined, the majority was able to discount most of Hardwick's arguments by declaring "none of the rights announced in those cases bears any resemblance to the *claimed* constitutional right of homosexuals to engage in acts of sodomy that is asserted in this case." [Emphasis added.] Stated later in its opinion: "It is obvious to us that neither of these formulations would extend a fundamental right to homosexuals to engage in acts of consensual sodomy." Of course, the Constitution does not provide an explicit fundamental right to engage in consensual heterosexual sodomy either. (Remember, sodomy in this case involves the sex organs of one person and the mouth or anus of another.) This was a fairly blatant display of homophobia by the majority, but it got even worse.

In his opinion for the majority, Justice Byron R. White pointed out, "Sodomy was a criminal offense at common law and was forbidden by the laws of the original thirteen states when they ratified the Bill of Rights." He appears to be rather unknowledgeable about the history of these laws. The first "US" versions of sodomy laws were adopted by the original thirteen colonies before the United States declared its sovereignty. More significantly, this was also before the separation between church and state was established in the Bill of Rights and later amendments. These laws were based on English Common Law enacted in the sixteenth century (discussed in Chapter 10). As a result, sodomy laws date back not just 300 years, but over 3,000 years. All of this activity occurred without *any* understanding of homosexuality, as the concepts of sexual orientation and homosexuality did not even exist until late in the nineteenth century — long after the Bill of Rights was passed as well.

In a concurring opinion, Chief Justice Warren E. Burger recognized this history, but defended it anyway: "Condemnation of those practices is firmly rooted in Judeao-Christian [sic] moral and ethical standards . . . To hold that the act of homosexual sodomy is somehow protected as a fundamental right would be to cast aside millennia of moral teaching." In his dissenting opinion, Justice Blackmun stated, "Like Justice Holmes, [quoting from *Lochner v. New York* in 1905] I believe that 'it is revolting to have no better reason for a rule of law than that so it was laid down in the time of Henry IV. It is still more revolting if the grounds

251

upon which it was laid down have vanished long since, and the rule simply persists from blind imitation of the past.'"

At best, the majority's historical view ignored the fact that other minorities, most notably black people and women, enjoyed no civil rights when the Constitution was written. Subsequent constitutional amendments only granted suffrage to these minority groups. One would think Justice Sandra Day O'Connor, the only woman on the Supreme Court, would have been especially cognizant of this fact. But she also seemed to ignore it and ruled with the majority.

What is worse, though, is that this opinion completely ignored the very provisions of the Bill of Rights and the Fourteenth Amendment. The majority actually recognized this when in White's opinion he commented, "Respondent [Hardwick] does not defend the judgment below based on the Ninth Amendment, the Equal Protection Clause [of the Fourteenth Amendment] or the Eighth Amendment." Justice Blackmun pointed out the fallacy of this claim by stating, "the procedural posture of the case requires that we affirm the Court of Appeals' judgment if there is any ground on which respondent may be entitled to relief . . . The Court's cramped reading of the issue before it makes for a short opinion, but it does little to make for a persuasive one."

In an attack of "constitutional amnesia" the majority ignored, or at least rationalized, certain of its provisions in determining the constitutionality of the Georgia law. Each would be sufficient on its own; all together they present a compelling argument for Hardwick. The First Amendment prohibits establishment of religion. As a "morals charge," sodomy laws clearly have a religious basis. The very word itself comes from the Bible. Other laws may have religious roots but, to be constitutional, they must be based on social needs. That is why the Fourteenth Amendment contains the Due Process Clause, which requires that any law must represent a legitimate state interest, and the Equal Protection Clause, which declares that laws should not be enacted or enforced in a discriminatory fashion. Sodomy laws and their enforcement clearly violate both of these clauses.

The Eighth Amendment prohibits cruel or unusual punishment. What is the proper punishment for sodomy, anyway? Is a $200 fine sufficient to deter this heinous crime against nature and civilization? Is twenty years in prison, the penalty in this case, a bit stiff for a "roll in the gay hay"? In a concurring opinion Justice Lewis F. Powell discounted this issue entirely by claiming, "respondent [Hardwick] has not been tried, much less convicted and sentenced." The fact that a law was not enforced in a particular instance does not determine its constitutionality.

The majority ignored, as well, the Ninth Amendment: "The enumeration in the Constitution, of certain rights, shall not be construed to deny or disparage others retained by the people." And then the Tenth: "The powers not delegated to the United States by the Constitution, nor prohibited by it to the States, are reserved to the States respectively, or to the people." But again, with the way the majority *redefined* the issue, Justice White was able to claim, "There should be, therefore, great resistance to expand the substantive reach of those Clauses, particularly if it requires *redefining* the category of rights deemed to be fundamental." [Emphasis added.] How about that for the pot calling the kettle black? The majority "expanded" the issue before the Court as a "fundamental right to engage in consensual sodomy," then declared this expanded version unconstitutional. The *real* issue, the right to privacy, required no such expanded reach of the Constitution.

In his next argument, Justice White actually begged the whole question before the Court, when he argued that because sodomy is illegal, it is exempt from the right to privacy: "Plainly enough, otherwise illegal conduct is not always immunized whenever it occurs in the home. Victimless crimes, such as the possession and use of illegal drugs do not escape the law when they are committed at home. *Stanley [Stanley v. Georgia* in 1969 on pornography] itself recognized that its holdings offered no protection for the possession in the home of drugs, firearms or stolen goods. And if respondent's [Hardwick's] submission is limited to the voluntary sexual conduct between consenting adults, it would be difficult, except by fiat, to limit the claimed right to homosexual conduct while leaving exposed to prosecution adultery, incest, and other sexual crimes even though they are committed in the home." Only the most homophobic individuals would accept such a tautological argument. Each of these analogies is either ridiculous or insulting or both. Drugs are illegal because they are inherently dangerous to the individual, and potentially to society. Firearms are only illegal when improperly registered. Stolen property was obviously wrongfully deprived of another individual. Finally, instead of comparing homosexual sodomy to heterosexual sodomy, and with no explanation, the majority chose to compare it to adultery and incest. This ignorance is unbelievable, bordering on unforgivable.

And here's the clincher, again quoting Justice White: "Even if the conduct at issue here is not a fundamental right, respondent [Hardwick] asserts that there must be a rational basis for the law and that there is none in this case other than the presumed belief of a majority of the electorate in Georgia that homosexual sodomy is immoral and unacceptable. This is said to be an inadequate rationale to support the law ... We do not agree." That's an interesting concept. If all laws are passed by majority votes, as they must be, and if majority views are in all cases valid, then by this reasoning *all* laws are constitutional! Court adjourned — forever.

Clearly all the "reasons" given by the Court's majority were mere excuses for a decision based solely on homophobia. In a footnote written by Justice White, he ignored the law itself and focused on instead the fact it was being challenged by a gay man: "We express no opinion on the constitutionality of the Georgia statute as applied to other [heterosexual] acts of sodomy." The law clearly applies to *both* gay and straight people despite the fact Attorney General Bowers, in testimony, told the Supreme Court the state of Georgia had no intention of applying this law to married couples. Of course, married couples is not even synonymous with heterosexuality anyway. By the way the court redefined the issue, without *any* doubt, it aimed its decision *solely* at gay people. And by striking at the very essence of the difference between gay and straight people, the Court ruled that gay people are excluded from the provisions of the Constitution. This is equivalent to claiming Jewish people can be Jewish as long as they don't practice religion.

To add insult to injury, the Supreme Court announced its decision the day after Gay Freedom Day. Four days later, on Independence Day, gay citizens were left questioning the nation's commitment to liberty and justice for all. The question was made even more poignant with the televising of festivities for the Statue of Liberty's 100th anniversary. The US is the only nation in the world which regularly says "welcome home" to complete strangers—unless of course they're gay. If you are straight, try to imagine the demoralizing effect this had on the nation's gay citizens. Gay people listened to hundreds of speeches telling them how wonderful their country is, while having been told a few days earlier they are excluded from it all. Civil rights are wonderful, but they have no civil rights. Freedom is essential, but they have no freedom. Liberty is precious, but they have no liberty. Justice is fundamental, but there is no justice for gay people. America seems to want gay people back in the closet, and the Supreme Court has ruled that the closet is unprotected by the Constitution.

A century from now, people will read of this decision the same way our generation reads about the Court's treatment of black people in 1857. In the case of *Dred Scott v. Sandford,* the Court ruled that freed black people were not citizens protected by the Constitution. Instead, the Court believed all black people belonged to a degraded class of residents when the Constitution was written and, therefore, enjoyed no rights of citizenship. The majority was then able to rule that the Fifth Amendment actually protected *citizens,* white people, from being deprived of their property, black people, without due process of law.

In his dissenting opinion in *Bowers v. Hardwick,* Justice Blackmun stated, "I can only hope that here, too, the Court will reconsider its analysis and conclude that depriving individuals of the right to choose how to conduct their intimate relationships poses a far greater threat to the values most deeply rooted in our Nation's history than tolerance of conformity could ever do."

The Gay Civil Rights Movement

The immorality of surrender to prejudice ranks second only to the immorality of prejudice itself. *Franklin E. Kameny*

James Baldwin pointed out: "People wouldn't have to spend so much time being defensive—if they weren't *endlessly* being *condemned*." To date, gay people have been defined by a society which does not understand homosexuality. When this power resides elsewhere, some amount of struggle is required to get it back. The stereotypes, the myths, the double standards, the self-fulfilling prophecies, the false "threats" and their resulting social sanctions put drastic limits on how gay people can live. But life goes on. Gay people cannot simply "halt" their lives and wait for these issues to be resolved.

The Gay Civil Rights Movement is the struggle to achieve equality, freeing gay people from the oppressive standards of a homophobic culture. In isolation if necessary, the gay minority will adopt its own set of standards. Gay people will live constructive and satisfying lives with or without the "approval" of others, while continuing to promote social reform. Because change does not occur on its own, some pressure must be applied. Woodrow Wilson observed: "If you want to make enemies, try to change something." But homosexuality already has its enemies. The Gay Civil Rights Movement was therefore created out of necessity, not out of desire, and it will continue until the oppression which fuels it is exhausted. Gay people will simply no longer excuse their enemies; they will no longer tolerate the intolerance; and they will no longer patronize their own persecution.

The Homophile Movement of the Fifties

The struggle for gay equality began in the 1950s when it was termed the Homophile Movement. In addition to the oppression, especially from McCarthyism, there was another important reason the movement organized at this time. In 1948 Dr. Alfred C. Kinsey published *Sexual Behavior in the Human Male,* which found that there were millions of gay men, and presumably lesbians, in the United States. Gay people were no longer considered an anomaly; they were finally considered a significant *minority*. This gave every gay person the reassurance of being part of a larger group, no longer to face oppression alone. The movement began in major metropolitan areas, made possible primarily by a critical mass of gay people, and gradually spread through the rest of the country.

There were two prominent organizations during this time: the Mattachine Society, an association of gay groups for men, and the Daughters of Bilitis for lesbians. Both were cautious and secretive, which made it inherently difficult to raise awareness and effect change. Any confrontational activity would have been "suicidal" for two related reasons. First, it would likely encourage a negative response from local law enforcement agencies, which would expose the participants. With little, if any, public sympathy at that time, the exposure would have resulted in lost jobs and ruined lives. Second, fearing this possibility, gay people were reluctant to participate. As evidence of this fear, it is noteworthy that many of the individuals participating used false names. These pioneers had no desire to be martyrs as well.

With ignorance as the enemy, education, rather than confrontation, became the strategy. The tactics consisted almost exclusively of quiet, behind-the-scenes education to raise awareness. But it was difficult to find publishers who would risk their reputations for gay freedom of speech. Recall the controversy surrounding the publication of Dr. Kinsey's *Sexual Behavior in the Human Male.* By word of mouth, though, the movement was kept alive.

The very survival of these organizations would ultimately cripple their effectiveness. Gay people felt safest when they went unnoticed.

Most minorities have everything to gain by speaking out; gay people had everything to lose. It was a very frustrating period indeed.

Gay men and lesbians had also not yet learned the importance of working together. They did not even share the same issues. In effect, the problems were divided into "his" and "hers." Gay men were more the victims of police harassment and employment discrimination. The lesbian's oppression resulted more then from her gender than from her sexual orientation. Lesbians therefore viewed men, gay or straight, as being the source of their oppression. This was indeed an accurate observation. Gay men, conditioned in tradition, were not immune from sexism. In fact, some gay men at the time were the epitome of male chauvinism, maybe because they did not have the same "need" for women that straight men do. Similarly, many lesbians were "separatist," having no apparent need for men. Gay men and lesbians each selfishly focused all their own energies on their own problems. This division would exist through the early 1970s when women began to achieve equality with men, and lesbians began to experience the "luxury" of being oppressed for their homosexuality.

In summary, their small numbers were relatively powerless against the ominous forces of McCarthyism and society's extremely homophobic views. By the end of 1959 there were fewer than a half-dozen national homophile organizations. By 1968 there were nearly forty.

To help cope with the oppressive environment, gay people began poking fun at the various stereotypes. This evolved into a form of humor known as camp. Although camp is not unique to gay people, especially gay men, it remains associated with homosexuality to this day.

Camp humor

No one is laughable who laughs at himself. *Seneca*

Camp, or any form of humor for that matter, is difficult to define. The dictionary defines it as "something so outrageously artificial, affected, inappropriate, or out-of-date as to be considered amusing." Vito Russo, in an article titled "Camp," defines it as "a way of deflating the pomp and making the most of the circumstance at the same time, for camp is also a sensibility best understood by select groups who are privy to a special view from their rarified position."

Camp begins by passing as straight, which is very easy to do. This element of irony is combined with something outrageous and surprising in the form of exaggerated "compliance" with a stereotype, normally feminine behavior for gay men, thus revealing the "little secret." The result is camp. It is an action which simultaneously defies and ridicules society's homophobic stereotypes and sexist gender roles. Camp is therefore a mockery of the serious predicament facing the gay minority. When properly done, camp can be about as therapeutic as it is humorous.

To truly appreciate camp humor it helps to see the world from the perspective of a misunderstood and oppressed minority. But here are some fairly obvious examples. Gay men sometimes act "nelly," which is feminine-appearing behavior that mocks the gender roles. In effect, it is drag without the dress. When gay men act nelly, they usually call each other Mary — it's part of the act. Then there's "Miss Thing": a guy in drag who looks nothing at all like a real woman. He might be nearly bald and have a beard. The image is so bizarre others cannot help but laugh. Finally, there is the classic story about two cardinals in the Catholic church. One cardinal was bearing incense during mass. The incense is lighted and carried in a small container on a chain. The second cardinal leaned over as the first approached and whispered, "The hat's divine and your coat is lovely. But dear, your purse is on fire!" That's camp.

The Gay Liberation Movement of the Seventies

The Homophile Movement continued until it erupted into the Gay Liberation Movement. To a large extent, this was due to the rise of civil rights activism in general. The counterculture activism encompassed free speech, feminism, black civil rights, and the hippie "love" movement, with its exploration of unconventional relationships and sexual techniques. Just as the movement of the fifties reflected the political quiescence of the times, the movement of the 1970s reflected the political activism of a period marked by anti-racist, anti-imperialist, feminist, anti-war, and anti-establishment sentiments.

The Stonewall Rebellion, in New York City in June of 1969, marked the beginning of the Gay Liberation Movement. The Stonewall, like most other gay bars around the country, had been raided on numerous occasions. Patrons were hustled outside then released. Gay people were getting rather tired of this form of harassment and for the *first* time fought back. The patrons in the street, now joined by many others, started throwing anything and everything they could find at the police. The police retreated into the Stonewall. The *Village Voice,* a newspaper in Greenwich Village, reported in part, "Vengeance vented against the source of repression — gay bars, busts, kids victimized and exploited by the mafia and cops." Because of the low status of gay people, it was very common for the Mafia to own and operate gay bars — and the Mafia had effective means of providing protection. Except for police raids, gay people felt safe in gay bars. The ownership of gay bars by organized crime was just another effect of the tremendous oppression of the period. Today, most gay bars are owned and operated by gay people.

The two-day rebellion became known as "The Hairpin Drop Heard Around the World." Dropping a hairpin was a sign that one was gay. For the first time in history, it was okay to be gay.

The Gay Activists Alliance (GAA) formed in New York City just six months after the Stonewall Rebellion, and would soon became a prominent gay civil rights organization. By the end of 1973, the GAA was communicating with over 1,100 other gay groups nationally, giving assistance and guidance. It offered a compromise between the conservative strategy of the earlier Homophile Movement and the radical tactics of some other newly formed gay groups. The GAA's approach was to inform gay people they were members of an influential political minority. Its slogan was to come "out of the closets and into the streets." The members were militant, but not violent. Training sessions were held in the techniques of conducting peaceful demonstrations. One GAA document read: "DON'T provoke, by action or word, any violent actions under any circumstance except in self-defense." According to its constitution, the GAA could not provide legal assistance for anyone who knowingly provoked, advocated, or instigated any form of violence unless in self-defense. Despite all these precautions, much of the money the GAA, and other organizations like it, raised was still needed to post bail and defend those who were arrested.

The tactics of the GAA and similar gay groups were borrowed from other minority organizations, especially those of the Black Civil Rights Movement. These included the creation of gay media and the utilization of nongay media through news articles and appearances on TV and radio talk shows. To be successful, any civil rights movement must work effectively with the media. There was, of course, a significant amount of civil disobedience which included the staging of newsworthy events like rallies, parades, protest marches, confrontations with politicians and social institutions, sit-ins, picket lines, and boycotts. Boycotts can be particularly effective as they do not require the participants to identify with the cause or, in other words, come out of the closet. Staging public demonstrations would force elected and appointed officials to deal with gay civil rights issues. Gay groups would also distribute information at nongay public events, hold press conferences, and call attention to instances of abuse and injustice. They persuaded gay public figures to announce their homosexuality openly, worked to get gay civil rights legislation introduced, and offered financial and legal assistance in discrimination lawsuits. Finally, they represented the gay community as a large voting bloc through the registration of voters, contributions to and volunteer work for candidates, support of political action committees, and petition and letter writing campaigns. It was a very busy time.

These activities may be a little more dramatic than lobbying and litigation, but they are far from violent. Radical gay organizations, such as the Gay Liberation Front (GLF), represented a small minority of gay people. Their actions were viewed as counterproductive by most gay civil rights leaders. The GLF insisted on using exclusively their own tactics and would not support other activities. Radicals seem to reject any diversity which conforms to tradition, making the freedom to be different more of a requirement. Most gay people felt then, and still do, that violence will not work in a social movement. It discourages public support and sympathy. In fact, it rallies the opposition. Violence reduces the number of people who will participate, and it is impossible to maintain for any length of time. Most importantly, violence begets violence. It simply has no place in a peaceful society.

The National Gay Task Force was formed in 1973. The name was changed to the National Gay and Lesbian Task Force (NGLTF) in 1986. NGLTF's role was one of national coordination of local gay groups, media relations, and lobbying activity. The NGLTF was the first gay civil rights group to have a full-time, paid staff instead of part-time volunteers. Its structure was modeled after that of the American Civil Liberties Union. One of the most significant milestones in the struggle for gay civil rights also occurred in 1973. This was the year the American Psychiatric Association removed homosexuality from its list of mental disorders. The NGLTF, instrumental in this decision through lobbying efforts directed at the APA, emerged as the leading national gay civil rights organization.

The Gay Liberation Movement faded away with the counter-culture movement just as the economic crisis of the mid-1970s forced most Americans to alter their priorities. The movement also suffered from some infighting—not between gay men and lesbians this time, but between "liberals" and "conservatives." Some gay people blamed oppression on the bizarre "flamboyant types," who in turn blamed oppression on the cautious "closet cases" for not coming out openly to fight the stereotypes based on the "flamboyant types." And around and around it went. Gay people have now recognized this animosity for the discrimination it is. There is much better cooperation today. The movement's new focus is on the real cause of oppression: homophobia.

The gay men and lesbians who participated in the Homophile and Gay Liberation movements can be very proud of their accomplishments. The annual National Gay Pride Week is a celebration of their success, with rallies and parades held in cities across the nation. Culminating National Gay Pride Week is Gay Freedom Day, which falls on the last Sunday in June in remembrance of the Stonewall Rebellion. In a way, it is the gay "Fourth of July."

Gay Pride

"Two! Four! Six! Eight!
Gay is just as good as straight!"

Gay Pride is not a pride in one's homosexuality, because there is no real accomplishment; homosexual people are born that way. Rather, Gay Pride is a recognition of a fundamental right to live freely as gay men and lesbians. This involves expressing feelings of love for each other and demonstrating anger at an oppressive homophobic society. It is a pride symbolic of the ability to transcend society's prescription for a miserable existence, and instead live happy, healthy, and productive lives. In effect, Gay Pride is a therapeutic act of self-affirmation and liberation which can and does occur independently of external ostracism and that is why Gay Pride is replacing camp humor in the gay community. It is a pride which screams, "I'm just as good as anyone else, and considering all the problems of being gay in America, damnit—I'm better!"

The Gay Pride immediately following the Stonewall Rebellion was reflected in a flier passed out at a subsequent protest: "Do You Think Homosexuals Are Revolting? You Bet Your Sweet Ass We Are." Oppression creates a certain psychology in the oppressed. Being gay denies an individual the chance to be normal, as defined by the dominant culture.

259

A belief in personal dignity is the first step toward release from the bonds of oppression. Instead of being defeated victims, gay people become survivors. This is Gay Pride.

Gay Pride emerged during the Gay Liberation Movement when gay people achieved recognition as a minority. Most minorities desire to maintain an identity; gay people needed to establish one. It was indeed a time for coming out of the closets and going into the streets. Probably the most significant accomplishment of the Gay Liberation Movement was the creation of a visible and accessible gay community. A limited social tolerance for this gay community was also achieved. That tolerance is what exists today. It applies solely in major cities, and then only under certain circumstances. In effect, the claims of gay people have been recognized but not satisfied. Recognition alone is obviously insufficient, for it does nothing to prevent the suffering from oppression on a daily basis by millions of gay men and lesbians. As a recognized minority, gay people are now demanding acceptance in the form of equal civil rights. That is the goal of the current Gay Civil Rights Movement.

The Movement in the "Gay Nineties"

To achieve its objectives, the Gay Civil Rights Movement will continue to work, as long as necessary, within the "system" — mostly through lobbying and litigation. Militancy is still viewed as being counterproductive. The gay minority wishes to show it is numerous rather than dangerous, especially when the current efforts for reform are meeting with some success. The importance of visibility is demonstrated by the emerging tradition of National Coming-Out Day each October.

The problems which plagued the previous attempts to obtain equal civil rights have been mostly resolved. Although the issues are still somewhat different, gay men and lesbians have realized their potential combined strength and are working effectively together. For example, lesbian organizations did not hesitate a moment to offer their resources in the battle against AIDS. Most importantly, more and more gay people are getting involved in the movement as demonstrated by the "March on Washington" in October 1987. The crowd of over 650,000 gay and straight men and women was the largest civil rights protest in the history of the United States.

There are three main reasons gay people participate in political activism. First and foremost, involvement is a sincere reaction to the injustice and oppression. Every violation of gay civil rights produces at least one more dedicated activist. Second, it is therapeutic and self-affirming. The participants learn homosexuality is not a sickness, but homophobia is. Third, involvement offers a chance to meet other gay people who share similar interests and backgrounds. To be successful, any organization must offer a common denominator for its members. Simply sharing the same sexual orientation is not enough. Nearly all gay political organizations are therefore also social. For this reason, the Gay Civil Rights Movement has achieved a diversity at the grassroots level by creating literally thousands of gay groups across the country covering every issue, every profession, every situation, every body of government, and most local communities. The grassroots approach puts a strong base in place, and has proved quite effective at reaching the majority of America's private and social institutions.

To add efficiency to this effectiveness, there are some national organizations which serve to coordinate and assist the grassroots efforts. Some of these organizations, like the National Gay Rights Advocates and the Lambda Legal Defense and Education Fund, provide the financial and legal resources necessary for reform through the courts. They assist with legal research, provide expert legal assistance, and publish scholarly criticism of judicial decisions. These activities help the courts focus on the precise issues and relevant considerations, assuring a more informed and fair decision in each case. Other organizations, like the Gay and Lesbian Alliance Against Defamation (GLAAD), serve as watchdogs on the media, calling attention to inaccuracies when they occur. And other organizations, like the National Gay Lesbian Task Force, lobby the various institutions of state and federal government, and work with the national media. There are even gay political action committees, such as the Human Rights Campaign Fund, which also operate as lobbyists.

Education is still a major goal of the Gay Civil Rights Movement. Each case, each event, and each situation serves to educate judges, attorneys, administrators, and appointed or elected officials. The media attention these activities receive serves to educate the general public as well. Win, lose, or draw, the story gets out. And when the story is fully understood, gay people have faith that a majority of Americans will support gay civil rights. It is the gay minority's only hope.

Queers as Peers?

Injustice anywhere is a threat to liberty everywhere. *Martin Luther King, Jr.*

When struggling against an oppressive majority, minority groups generally have a greater appreciation of each others' needs. Gay civil rights leaders have therefore formed coalitions with other minorities, most notably black people and women. The similarities are different with each. While the oppression of women is more economic, the oppression of gay people is more social. Black people also suffer from both, but are somewhat protected from discrimination by the 1964 Civil Rights Act. But neither of these minorities, their gay members included, really enjoys full and equal civil rights. Both understand oppression and the need to struggle for civil rights. As a result, members of any minority group are generally less prejudiced and more supportive of civil rights for other disenfranchised groups. Gay people have also formed a coalition with the sexual liberation movement, as heterosexual men and women are coming out of a "closet" of their own with respect to freedom of sexual expression.

261

Although gay people have much in common with these other minorities, one critical difference remains: Gay people have the "luxury" of hiding their minority status to maintain certain privileges. This "invisibility" is both an asset and a liability. Black people and women are quite easily recognized as such, and therefore have nothing to lose by publicly calling for equal civil rights. Some gay people have literally everything to lose. Another disadvantage for gay people is that a gay identity may cause the withdrawal of support from friends and family. This is rarely the case for black people and women.

To help achieve this solidarity, gay people have actively supported other minorities. In fact, many white gay men have become ardent black civil rights activists and feminists. But gay people were not always immediately embraced in return. Acceptance gradually did come as the other minorities recognized the hypocrisy of simultaneously protesting and practicing discrimination. The National Organization for Women serves as a good example.

The National Organization for Women (NOW) was formed in 1966 to fight sexism. Because lesbians are doubly oppressed as (1) gay and (2) women, their rebellion is doubly strong. A politically active lesbian is, of necessity, a feminist. The converse, however, is untrue. Many lesbian feminists joined NOW, not as lesbians, but as feminists. Their sexual orientation was really irrelevant to the cause. But their support was not exactly welcomed. Many of the individuals who opposed equal rights for women attempted to discredit NOW by making an association of feminism with lesbianism. The fact women wanted more independence from the male of the species was construed to mean that women wanted nothing to do with men, which some uninformed individuals considered the essence of lesbianism. Society allowed that tactic to work, at least for a while. Still, lesbians continued to support NOW even though they did not share the exact same issues with straight women. All women were oppressed economically, but straight women had to deal with their marital relationships and were interested in the issues of contraception, abortion, and child care. Lesbians were interested mostly in economic equality, with no male "other half" to bring home half or more of the bacon. In 1971 at its national conference, a resolution was finally passed stating: "That NOW recognizes the double oppression of women who are lesbians . . . [and] that NOW acknowledge[s] the oppression of lesbians as a legitimate concern of feminism." In 1986 NOW even addressed the predominantly gay male issue of AIDS by passing a resolution calling for more research and recognition of the civil rights of people with AIDS.

But acceptance from other minority groups only is insufficient. Until the rest of society, the majority, is ready to accept queers as peers, the struggle for gay civil rights will continue. And until then, so will the injustice.

Justice Delayed is Justice Denied

The worst sin towards our fellow creatures has not been to hate them but to be indifferent to them: that's the essence of inhumanity.
George Bernard Shaw

Drs. Martin S. Weinberg and Colin J. Williams from the Institute for Sex Research pointed out the essence of civil rights reform: "Research on racial minorities has shown that one of the more effective ways to make societal reactions less negative is to change the institutions that sustain discrimination. When this is done, a change in individuals' attitudes often follows. Therefore, those aspects of social organization that support the moral meanings of homosexuality as sinful, immoral, dangerous, perverted, revolting, or sick should be a primary target for social change."

Virtually every social institution has homophobic policies or practices. These actions not only reinforce society's homophobia, but cause tremendous hardship for millions of Americans in the process. This is why justice delayed is justice denied.

Some of the same individuals and organizations which work to prevent other minorities from sharing equal rights also oppose gay civil rights. Many have even recently tried to undo some of the gains made by black people and women. Traditionally, the bigoted individuals, mostly men, have been referred to as WASPs: White Anglo-Saxon Protestants. A correction to this classification and its spelling is in order. These prejudiced people are WHASPs: White *Heterosexual* Anglo-Saxon Protestants. The WHASPs began diminishing in number and strength when prejudice was exposed as the grossly unfair and destructive force it is. So bigotry is just no longer fashionable. But homophobia was out of sight, out of mind when all this occurred. Indeed, support for gay civil rights is noticeably absent in the dominant culture. This support cannot be expected from the bigoted WHASPs, but it can and *should* be expected from a majority of the majority.

There still remain a number of reasons why this support does not exist. To begin, *everyone,* gay or straight, suffers from homophobia to some degree. Each gay individual is, in effect, forced to confront his or her own homophobia. Most straight people, however, have yet to confront theirs. Recent polls have shown that straight men and women who know openly gay people are far more likely to support gay civil rights. This is because having gay friends or relatives serves as a catalyst to learn the truth about homosexuality. Of course, everyone certainly has several gay acquaintances. But less than twenty percent of straight people know which of their friends and relatives are gay. For the other eighty percent, homosexuality remains an abstract issue; gay civil rights is an even more abstract issue.

Because their own civil rights can be taken for granted, gay civil rights seems like "special" treatment to many in this "eighty percent" majority. Others feel it is necessary to "like" homosexuality to support equal civil rights. This is not true; it is only necessary to *dislike* the suffering gay people experience every day that they continue to be op-

263

pressed. Still others claim that when people "choose" homosexuality, they forfeit civil rights. There is a double fallacy here. One is that gay people do not choose to be gay. But what if they did? What if homosexuality really were a choice, like religion or political party affiliation? This is the second fallacy. Such choices do not preclude equality. That might be the case in the Soviet Union, but it should never be true in a free society. Maybe others may fear "guilt" by association. Owing to the fact that straight people have not historically supported gay civil rights, very few seem willing to jeopardize their "heterosexual credentials" in this way. It is terribly ironic that many straight people are reluctant to support gay civil rights because, if they are suspected of being gay, they might be subjected to the very same discrimination they help perpetuate with their apathy. All of these so-called reasons are individually and collectively inadequate.

In many ways, Americans have lost sight of the documented rights in the Constitution. Civil rights are granted by the government, but we are the government. Therefore, civil rights are really granted by society's consent. The official rights provided by legislation and judicial interpretation serve as indicators of society's attitudes. Richard Mohr, in *Gays/Justice: A Study of Ethics, Society, and Law,* observed: "For its [society's] treatment of gays is a grand scale rationalization and moral sleight-of-hand. The problem is not that society's usual standards of evidence and procedure in coming to judgments of social policy have been misapplied to gays, rather when it comes to gays, the standards themselves have simply been ruled out of court and disregarded in favor of mechanisms that encourage unexamined fear and hatred." So without a spirit of liberty, the Constitution is just a piece of paper. Judge Learned Hand put it this way: "Liberty lies in the hearts of men and women; when it dies there, no Constitution, no law, no court can save it." In essence, there is really a great deal of truth to the adage "might makes right." The majority has made homosexuality "wrong" and the same majority has exclusive power to make it right.

The gay minority needs straight allies in its struggle for equal civil rights. Straight people outnumber their gay friends and relatives nine to one. Gay people cannot solve the problem without them. The "black problem" was really white racism, making it impossible for black people to eliminate racial prejudice alone. So Dr. Martin Luther King's message wasn't "black" at all, it was *American.* Well, the "homosexual problem" is heterosexual homophobia. And gay people cannot eliminate this form of prejudice alone either. The gay minority is not asking the straight population to *lead* the struggle for gay civil rights, but it is counting on their *support.* There is something in this for them too, because gay issues are really everyone's issues. As President John F. Kennedy noted, "In giving rights to others which belong to them, we give rights to ourselves and to our country." Think of gay civil rights as a thermometer used to measure the degree of oppression in the United States. You can help turn down the temperature by not practicing discrimination yourself, and by confronting those individuals or institutions which do. Remember, until you become part of the solution, you will remain part of the problem, for Harold Stassen was indeed correct: "Those who feed the flames of intolerance, set fire to their own house."

If it were not for the fact the United States is the most humane nation in the history of humanity, the problems discussed in this section would make life in the United States unbearable for gay people. As a society, we must be very fortunate to have both the time and "need" to worry about something as harmless as homosexuality. Some Americans will fight hard to preserve individual rights threatened by acts of aggression or oppressive governments in other countries, while simultaneously acting to deny these same rights to millions of Americans.

It has been said that someone who is both young and conservative has no heart; while someone who is both old and liberal has no brain. FDR said: "A conservative is a man with two perfectly good legs, who has never learned to walk." The principle of liberty cannot give anyone unrestricted liberty; it must be compatible with a system of liberty for all. And liberty is everything. As Lord Acton put it: "Liberty is not a means to a higher political end. It is itself the highest political end." Gay civil rights are not only what justice permits; liberty and equality for America's gay men and lesbians are what justice requires. For the truth is: It is right that makes might—eventually. And as Woodrow Wilson said, "I would rather fail in a cause that someday will triumph than triumph in a cause that someday will fail."

Section VI:

Family and Friends

Chapter 15

Growing Up Gay

From childhood's hour I have not been
As others were—I have not seen
As others saw.

Edgar Allan Poe

I grew up to be one of "those" people others warned me about when I was young. I first became aware of my own homosexual feelings when I was five years old, although I did not know at the time what sexuality was all about. I did, however, know enough to realize same-sex attractions were not expected. Like most young children, I "fooled around" with my friends. It was not quite sex; it was just, well, fooling around. I remember one of my brothers got caught fooling around with a girl in the front seat of Dad's car. He was scolded but not really punished. That story about George Washington and the cherry tree had a profound effect on me, so I told Dad what *I* had done. He thanked me for telling him and said, "Of course, you know that's wrong." I said, "Sure," but I was *not* really sure what he meant by "wrong" or specifically what I had done that was wrong. In any event, it was the beginning of an entire childhood of guilt and shame about sex in general, and homosexuality in particular.

I would eventually learn a number of horrible things about homosexuality. I would become confused and alone. I would learn to deny, then lie about my true feelings. I would also learn how to participate in my own persecution by laughing at the faggot jokes and even telling a few myself. My experience is shared by most gay men and lesbians growing up in the United States.

Homosexuality is not an easy hand to be dealt. I remained a virgin until I was nineteen years old, when I had my first homosexual, truly sexual experience. I waited so long because I was afraid to be one of "them." I finally admitted being gay, or came out, when I was twenty-six. Then and only then did I learn how wrong everyone else had been about homosexuality being "wrong." I also learned to be honest about who I was, even in the face of oppression and rejection. I learned that I am entitled to my civil rights and to the pursuit of my own happiness. Best of all, I learned how to love. For me, it was a happy ending. I realized I was born homosexual, but I had to become gay—a process that took twenty-one years. I wish I could have my childhood back, though. I missed so much happiness. Somehow it just doesn't seem fair.

This section gets personal by addressing how and why gay people come out, or announce their homosexuality, and how friends and family members can "deal with it" afterwards. With the understanding of homosexuality and homophobia provided in the first five sections, the straight readers are now in a better position to appreciate what it is like to be gay. As a straight person, the only way you can do this is from a "gay perspective." To gain this perspective, it is important to start from the beginning, with an appreciation of what being a gay child is like. So imagine that you too have your childhood back. But this time you are growing up gay.

Born Again — Gay

The difference between a childhood and a boyhood must be this: our childhood is what we alone have had; our boyhood is what any boy in our environment would have had. *John Updike*

Gay and straight children both learn guilt and shame regarding their anatomies and sexual desires in general. This is the first lesson in sexual behavior conditioning. These same feelings apply to any sexual expression, whether it conforms to social standards or not. The conditioning begins when children start to inquire about their genitals. (It is necessary that I approach this nostalgic journey from a male perspective. After all, I was born this way.) Most parents, at least in the "old" days, could not bring themselves to say the P-word (*penis*). Instead, we were taught to call it a *pee-pee* or something like that. My favorite is "down there" as in, "Don't play with yourself 'own there."

As a young child, you are expected *not* to like members of the opposite sex. Later, as an adolescent, you are expected to have an "interest" in the opposite sex, but not to do anything about it sexually for years. Lust is bad, you are told. Sex is only for marriage — heterosexual, of course. These anxieties about sex are very real for boys and girls.

The first formal exposure to the concept of homosexuality is usually through vicious jokes or snide remarks. This normally occurs before a child is ten years old. Adults and childhood peers, who learn from adults, make these remarks. Most people would not think of referring to black people as niggers, especially in the presence of black people. But some still refer to gay people as faggots and dykes regularly. This is done unknowingly in front of gay people, and also in front of the friends and family members of gay people. The offenders either don't know their comments are in poor taste, or they just don't care. Of course, the worst comments come from the family, because you always hurt the ones you love.

269

The Family

Unlike most minorities, gay children are not raised in the tradition of their subculture. Dr. Bruce Voeller provides an excellent summary of what you would experience as a gay child:

> Nowhere has the hostility to homosexuality been more frightening to large numbers of gay men and lesbians than in their own families, forcing them to feel like minority group members in their own homes. A black child growing up in a white neighborhood or a Jewish, Catholic, or Mormon child in nonminority areas may have problems with bigoted neighbors, peers, and teachers. But he or she does not usually face these same bigotries at home. There a refuge of sorts exists, where it is not necessary to fear attacks on the issue of race or faith. There a person need not defend, explain, apologize for, or hide minority status. There one finds others who share the status, and, at least in good families, share the cultural experience of handling internal and external oppression.
>
> But the young gay person is usually sharply separated from this kind of sharing and mutual support. The last place most gays wish their secret to be known is in their own families. The fear by teenagers of being thrown out of their homes if their feelings are discovered is intense, and, as those who counsel in gay groups well know, too often this fear is well founded rather than paranoid. Even if one is not disinherited or ejected, the ostracism, ridicule, rejection and unpleasantness visited upon a young gay individual by parents and siblings is much feared and is one of the things giving deepest concern to lesbians and gay men. Unwittingly, parents and siblings intensify this fear every time they talk about "tomboys" or "sissies" or make a "fag or dyke" joke.

Because homosexuality is so foreign to most straight people, the vast majority of parents never even consider that one or more of *their* children might be gay. Ideally, all parents would inform their children that gay people are basically just like straight people, and that homophobia is a form of prejudice. This would help open the closet door for gay children, while closing the door on homophobia. Most parents, however, still believe that homosexuality is caused by "dominant" mothers and "weak" fathers. Certainly, no parent is going to think she or he is that way. Homosexuality happens to other people's children, not theirs. For this reason, if a child happens to mention experiencing "those" feelings, parents simply discount them. "That's normal. Don't worry about it. You'll grow out of it. Now go out and play."

As a gay child you continue to experience "those" feelings you cannot understand — feelings that are apparently normal but are somehow evil. Yet no one seems to be very concerned. No wonder you are confused. Finally, you get your chance. A friend invites you over to spend the night. You fool around. It wasn't really sex; it was more like wrestling, but it was great. The following morning your friend refuses to talk about it. You seem to have enjoyed it much more than he did. "Why is that?" you wonder. Your friend feels ashamed. The shame is contagious. You keep fooling around for a while until your friend loses interest. He is apparently growing out of it, whatever "it" is. Finally, he declines your offers to fool around anymore. "Maybe it is a phase," you think. Since you are still going through your *phase*, you try to find another "friend." When you make your suggestion, he calls you a faggot. You will remember that word. You are not quite sure what a faggot is, but you think it has something to do with terrible people who corrupt children. You think, "Why did he call me that? My other friend didn't think I was a faggot. I guess all my friends are getting interested in girls. I'll probably be outgrowing my 'fooling around' phase soon too. Because I don't want my friends to think I'm a faggot, I'll just 'wait it out' until I start getting interested in girls."

The Peer Group

While peer group acceptance is very important throughout life, it is valued most during youth — especially between the ages of eleven and seventeen years. Adolescence is tough enough on kids. Being gay makes it much more painful. During this period, conformity brings acceptance; differences, especially those which are stigmatized, bring alienation. So children are constantly trying to be like their peers. Boys are expected to be "boys" and girls are expected to be "girls." Parents and teachers, all appearing to be straight, serve as behavior-forming and opinion-shaping role models. The early years of adolescence are also when children, gay or straight, *really* learn homophobia, even though this conditioning actually began in early childhood. They don't know what homophobia is yet, and may not even hear the word mentioned, but they learn it just the same. There are a number of other very important things that happen at this age as well.

Adolescent children are sexual beings. This is simply a fact. Studies show that identification of feelings as being homosexual in nature occurs around the age of thirteen for most gay children. In other words, when ninety percent of all children are old enough to recognize *their* own heterosexuality, ten percent of their peers are old enough to recognize their own homosexuality. According to the Institute for Sex Research, "By the time boys and girls reach adolescence, their sexual preference is likely to be already determined, even though they may not yet have become sexually very active." The words *sexual orientation* and *homosexuality* are likely in a child's vocabulary, but the concepts will not be fully understood until much later.

Teenagers are supposed to be *hetero*sexual, they just aren't supposed to be hetero*sexual*. Initially, homosexual erotic feelings are denied, serving only for fantasies and frustration. The first homosexual sexual "experience" is usually a fantasy during masturbation. The first actual homosexual sexual experience normally occurs around sixteen years of age. This is also the average age for a straight child's first experience with heterosexual intercourse. Approximately eighty percent of all teenage boys and seventy percent of all teenage girls experiment with sexuality. The same percentage of sexual participation, not too surprisingly, applies

271

to homosexual children as well. The gay teenager feels guilt, not just for being sexual, but for being homosexual.

Throughout this critical period, gay adolescents are led to believe there is something extremely abnormal and terribly wrong about what they feel and possibly do. Even if a teenager regularly engages in homosexual sexual activity, it is very rare for either boys or girls at this age to identify as gay. This marks the beginning of denial. It is also rare for the participants of this "forbidden" activity to discuss it themselves, even in private. Yet their straight peers seem to have no problem talking about *their* sexual adventures. When none exist, the stories are frequently fabricated. Being a virgin is just not "cool" for boys. Girls, on the other hand, are not expected to talk about their sexual adventures, even though at least some of them must be having sex or the straight boys wouldn't be able to brag so much.

Imagine what it would be like. You are still going through your "phase" while all your peers seem to have outgrown theirs. You get the feeling that if you don't like *their* kind of sex, there must be something wrong with you. Although their kind of sex is not very appealing, you try it anyway. Most gay adolescents at least experiment with heterosexual dating and sexuality, only to discover it's not that enjoyable — for them. But as a child growing up gay, you would still brag anyway. Now you feel really different, and begin to wonder if there actually is something wrong with you. You have heard that word again. Maybe that is what's wrong with you: You're a faggot. "But that's impossible," you think. Faggots are older men who molest little children, getting them to become faggots too. That has never happened to you, so there is no way you could be a faggot. "Damn, I wish I'd outgrow this phase. Why won't these feelings go away?"

"Official" Information

Unfortunately, the next exposure to homosexuality is "official." It arrives disguised as a sex education course. Nearly all sex education courses and textbooks either fail to address homosexuality entirely, or they do it poorly. Here is where most children, gay or straight, learn about the homosexual "problem." The day finally arrives when homosexuality is discussed. That's right, it's "sexual perversion day." Homosexuality is presented as a disease or some other abnormality. Everyone snickers. Ten minutes later, the teacher brings up the next topic: pedophilia.

This knowledge is a "license to kill" for some of the less compassionate young men. They now know "officially" what a faggot is. For them everyone becomes a faggot, just as when they learned to use a hammer, everything became a nail. Some boys and young men physically assault "suspected" faggots to help establish their own masculinity. They are invariably bigger or stronger or more numerous. Some people must have a warped sense of values to view this kind of victory as being meaningful in any way. Physical aggression should prove only that the aggressor is socially incompetent. Yet this kind of behavior continues to occur

272

with predictable regularity, causing both physical and emotional damage. These same bullies will later put down any girl they suspect is a lesbian, apparently because they have no use for a girl who cannot serve their sexual "needs."

Most of this victimization is verbal. Nearly every boy, straight or gay, at some time or another is called a faggot or a "queer" or a "fairy" — for any reason or no reason at all. The straight child will be offended but can shrug it off. The gay child is struck with horror. Imagine how you might react. "Does it show? Is it true? I don't act like a faggot. I'd better try harder to hide my true feelings." You are starting to learn how to pass — a very valuable lesson. You might even victimize a few faggots yourself to gain the "respect" of your peers. You begin to experience constant anxiety because, by this time, you are starting to think your feelings are more than just a phase.

In an attempt to learn more, you desperately search for information on homosexuality. Any books which are available in your school library are about the same as the textbook in your sex education class. All of them are approved by the board of education or the community, so you might as well look elsewhere. You could go to the public library, but you certainly would not want to get caught reading a book on homosexuality. What would people think? Then you discover Dr. Reuben's book, *Everthing you always wanted to know about sex* . . . It has a chapter on "Male Homosexuality." Perfect. If you get caught, you can pretend you are reading it for the chapters on "Sexual Intercourse" and "Birth Control." A "stud" like you would not want to "knock up some chick." In shock, you put down the book after reading "your" chapter and think, "This is even worse than I thought."

Occasionally, you are able to read something in the newspaper about homosexuality. As usual, the story is about some problem, normally an arrest. In fact, the only "gay" role models are likely to be the flamboyant stereotypes offered by the media. *All* "normal" people appear to be heterosexual. Finally, there is some "good" news: A lesbian won a lawsuit to regain her job. A judge declared her sexual orientation was okay. But the next day you read about "moral outrage" from the respected members of your community. The politicians are going to fight these "militant deviants" with all their power. You wonder why everyone gets so upset. What are all these "threats" they keep talking about? Then someone mentions arrests, catching you totally by surprise, because you had no idea it was *illegal* too!

The flurry of activity does not go unnoticed by your church. On the following Sunday there is a sermon about the "sin against nature," immorality, abomination, Sodom and Gomorrah, fire and brimstone, and homosexuality. "Sin against nature" sounds terrible, but not nearly as bad as "fire and brimstone." Possibly some members of your church are getting together to assist the politicians in their fight against these "militant deviants." Now you must add eternal damnation to your growing list of youthful worries.

So far the only information you have has come from jokes, vicious comments from others, awareness of stereotypes, and school discussions about this "problem." You know that you could wind up in jail, and that you're going straight to hell when you die. Oh yes, you also have your feelings of anxiety, guilt, and shame.

Feeling Alone

You feel utterly alone. There appears to be no one who is able to help, not parents, ministers, doctors, teachers, or trusted friends. Many have already made their negative views known. Maybe you can work up the courage to seek help. You decide to go to the minister. "Oh, you're not gay. You come from a loving family and a good home. You go to church regularly. You're a good student. Oh no, you're not gay."

What a relief! But the feelings have not gone away. You decide not to go back to your minister for advice, because he or she might start to believe you really are gay. You are totally unaware of the helpful resources in the gay community or that such a thing as a gay community even exists. Even if you know your town has a gay neighborhood, your parents likely warned you about what would happen if you wandered into "that" section of town. So you are reluctant, more like scared, to go there. The feelings of loneliness build.

Next you start to doubt the validity of your homosexual feelings. Eventually you begin to distrust or invalidate, then deny all your other feelings as well. You become angry, then deny the validity of your anger. You feel hurt, but cannot identify the cause. The confusion adds to your loneliness. Self-respect becomes difficult if not impossible. The entire situation is demoralizing. The doubt, denials, sacrifices, lies, anxiety, fears, confusion, and feelings of inferiority and worthlessness begin to take their toll. Suicide may seem to be the only way out of your homosexual "problem."At least, that's what they do in the movies.

The concept of homosexuality begins to be more fully understood, at least in a stereotypical way, around the age of sixteen or seventeen. But the stereotypical "description" of homosexuality doesn't fit. For example, I thought I was the only gay person, like me, in the world — or at least in my small home town, which was my world at the time. I remember this one boy in my high school who everyone thought was gay. I never met him, but I even remember his name. I'll call him John, to protect his privacy. John had a small build, platinum blonde hair, which looked dyed, and a fairly "deviant" look owing to his recessed eyes. All three characteristics were probably natural for John, as people have very little control over these things. Anyway, the effect was to make poor John look like the stereotypical faggot. For this reason, he was ostracized by nearly everyone in my high school who knew him or simply knew of him. I felt sorry for John. Yet at the same time I almost envied him for his ability to be himself. Now I wish I had gotten to know John. He was probably a fine person. But I was not "like" John, or at least I didn't want to be. Maybe I just didn't want to suffer the way John suffered. So I kept my distance, thinking I couldn't afford the association. As a result, I continued to feel alone and confused.

Imagine how you would handle the situation. You know you are different and that this difference is "bad," but you still can't understand quite why. Why is it bad to be yourself? Why do people hate you, when they don't even know you? You know you should keep your feelings secret, but how do you if you are or aren't gay? Is what you hear all around you, about homosexuality being a disease or a crime or a sin, really true? If it is, can you be "cured"? Where could you go for help? Do you even dare? No, you deny it. You resist, but your denial just isn't working. The feelings won't go away, yet you can't identify with the stereotypes either. You're just not *that* disgusting. Maybe you aren't really gay. Maybe it *is* just a phase. So you try to "hold out" a little longer. You try your best to be the ideal person everyone expects you to be. Because your feelings constantly conflict with what appears to be universal expectations, you begin to hide any and all behavior which might lead others to suspect your "possible" homosexuality. This is a critical point in your life. The denial starts to break down, while passing skills are acquired. You either withdraw or put up a front, pretending to be someone or something you aren't.

The Tears of a Clown

Like the overweight child who becomes jolly, you might become your high school's "class clown." It is better to have your friends laugh *with* you because you're funny, than *at* you because you're gay. Maybe instead, you bury yourself in your studies, or some sport or other activity. "I don't have time for girls." You might even retreat into a protective shell. It works. You gain acceptance through this false identity. Society is not concerned that you're miserable on the inside, as long as you're straight on the outside. This survival technique becomes valuable. Passing is painful, but not as painful as *not* passing.

Finally, you make it through high school. At this point all young people, straight and gay, face the big life decision of continuing school or starting work. Remember, you still sincerely believe that you're really straight at this age. On the average, most gay people do not acknowledge their homosexuality, adopting a gay identity, until around nineteen or twenty years of age. You can't imagine becoming a hairdresser or an interior decorator. You might consider the military: "That'll make a man out of me." Whether you go to college or start to work, you sense things aren't going to change much. Well, at least you know how to pass.

You have also reached your "sexual peak" at this age, and that's a shame because you have no idea how or where to meet people "like you." You are afraid to go to the gay community, partially because you don't really believe you are gay, and partially because, if you really aren't, you certainly don't want to be "recruited" or molested. After all, Dr. Reuben and others warned you what might happen. So you look for a sex-substitute to fill this void in your life. According to the categories from the Institute for Sex Research, if you aren't currently Asexual, you're likely to be Dysfunctional. In either case, you're still very homophobic, although you don't yet know what homophobia is. In your old or new circle of friends, most of them are probably straight. You reinforce each other's homophobia regularly with jokes and comments. Maybe you suspect, or more likely hope, that some of your friends might be "like you." But you're not quite sure how to broach the subject. If they really are like you, then they're being careful to protect their image as well. What if one of your friends approaches you sexually? You think, "Is it a joke? If it is, the joke will be on me. He told that faggot joke the other day. He probably really hates faggots. Maybe he's afraid *I'm* gay and he's just 'testing' me. I better call *him* a faggot instead."

Eventually, you will have an opportunity to engage in same-sex sexual activity. Although it is very enjoyable, the experience is encumbered by feelings of guilt and shame. Because you still identify as straight, you make up any excuse to explain your "strange" behavior. Just about any excuse will do. You claim that you had the "male" role, or that "it's only for now," or that your partner is a "special" friend. You might even label your actions an "experiment." Maybe you claim it was a "favor" for him, or an "accident." In any case, *you* are "innocent." Possibly it was "just physical." There was no emotion, you were just horny and it was this quickest and easiest "outlet." Perhaps you were drunk and he "took advantage" of you. Of course, you're not actually mad at him, so you get drunk again. Regardless of the excuse, you still feel you're just not sufficiently disgusting to really be gay. You are now fully aware of the gay community, but continue to avoid it just the same. What you don't know is that you are also avoiding the help it could provide. So you remain trapped in your own little world.

A Life of Denials, Lies and Sacrifices

We lie loudest when we lie to ourselves. *Eric Hoffer*

Growing up gay in America is not a whole lot of fun. Dr. Eli Coleman described the experience very well in his article "Developmental Stages of the Coming Out Process": "Minimally, the child feels 'different,' alienated, and alone. As they grow up, many such children develop low self-esteem. If acknowledged, same-sex feelings would mean rejection and ridicule; consequently, individuals protect themselves from awareness through defenses, such as denial, repression, reaction formation, sublimation, and rationalization. These defenses keep the individuals, their families, and society from experiencing the crisis that would occur if the issue of homosexuality were confronted directly."

In his book *The Gay Mystique,* Peter Fisher summarized growing up gay quite eloquently:

Inch by inch I had given in for years, stifling a feeling here, holding back a word there. I expected less, but that did not mean that life could not be happy. If you did not expect too much, I thought, you were not disappointed when you did not get too much. I never expected to be able to live the same life that heterosexuals led, so I felt no real anger or pain when day after day I held myself back from doing things they were entitled to do, hid the feelings they were entitled to express. Slowly, effortlessly, comfortably, I sacrificed a little part of myself each day, never realizing how much I had lost.

If I had to make these sacrifices all at once, I might have rebelled. If someone had told me that I would have no right to love, to feel, to take pleasure in my own body, it would have seemed monstrous. If someone had told me that I would have to hide, lie, and dissemble for the rest of my life, I might have resisted. If someone had told me that if I broke the rules which they had set I could be locked up, beaten, brainwashed, spit on, called names, and subjected to indignities for the rest of my life, I might have fought to the death to defend myself.

But nobody told me.

It is easy to remain in the closet. You become your own jailer, your own cop. The better you get at hiding, the less you feel your restrictions. At the beginning, society knocks you down for breaking the rules. Soon you learn not to break them, and life becomes easy in comparison.

Does this sound like paranoia? Maybe. But psychologists have an interesting observation about paranoia: Being paranoid does not necessarily mean that the world is *not* out to get you! When gay people are young, no one tells them it is normal to be gay for ten percent of the population. No one tells them they can be gay and still be good citizens or Christians or Jews. No one tells gay people they can love and be loved. No one tells them they can find happiness being gay. No one tells gay people they can have rewarding careers like straight people do. No one tells them any of this. In our "Jack and Jill" society, gay people must learn all of this on their own. These lessons do not come quickly; nor do they come easily. And they only come when gay people come out.

Chapter 16:

Coming Out

Such is the irresistible nature of truth that all it asks, and all it wants, is the liberty of appearing. *Thomas Paine*

Coming out of the closet" is essentially the personal acceptance of homosexuality through the adoption of a gay identity. A valid identity exists when there is agreement between what a person *feels* he or she is and what he or she *claims* to be. It involves the sharing of certain attributes with a particular community of others. In *Behind Ghetto Walls: Black Families in a Federal Slum,* Lee Rainwater explained, "A valid identity is one in which the individual finds congruence between who he feels he is, who he announces himself to be, and where he feels society places him." How *society* views homosexuality is the single most significant influence on an individual's decision to adopt a gay identity. Society's misunderstanding of homosexuality, and the resulting unfavorable view of gay people, creates some interesting effects.

The term *coming out* is regularly used and misused. There are actually two types or stages of coming out. They tend to occur in succession, but depending on an individual's unique circumstances, may occur simultaneously or in reverse order. The first type or stage of coming out is generally the *personal* acceptance of homosexuality, whether or not that realization is welcomed. This involves adopting a gay identity. In effect, the individual is saying, "Yes, I *am* gay." But adopting a gay identity is not necessarily accompanied by a change in behavior. Some identify as gay before having a single homosexual sexual experience. Conversely, others have years of same-sex sexual experimentation before identifying as gay. Coming out to oneself marks the beginning of the end to a life of denials. It is a recognition that gay people are *entitled* to be gay. For most gay men and lesbians, adopting a gay identity occurs around the age of twenty.

The second type or stage of coming out is informing straight friends and family members of this gay identity. It too is a very difficult step, for it exposes the individual to the possibility of ridicule and scorn. Some writers discuss a third type of coming out which is said to exist after coming out to the self and before coming out to family and friends. This is coming out to others who are gay. Yet for various reasons, it is virtually nonexistent in practice. The very definition of coming out to the self is to identify with the gay minority. Coming out to other gay people is simply an integral part of that identity.

This "ability" to come out makes the gay minority unique. For example, black children recognize, or more likely are told very young in life, they are black. It is therefore unnecessary to "come out" to friends and family. Of course, the majority of black people could not pass as white, even if they cared to for whatever reason. So the ability to come out for gay people is actually more of a necessity in a world where everyone is assumed to be heterosexual.

For homosexual adolescents and young adults, their "problem" remains unresolved as they struggle to comprehend something even the experts don't quite yet understand. Each individual must therefore devise his or her own strategy to deal with homosexual feelings and homophobia, internal and external, on a daily basis. The "problem" of homosexuality can only be resolved by coming out. The *real* problem, then, is that of adopting a gay identity, which is thought instead to *create* a problem — making the "problem" of homosexuality a real "Catch 22" dilemma. Given the complexity of the situation, it is not uncommon to become preoccupied with this "problem" of problems.

Straight children, on the other hand, can simply accept the common. There is a wealth of information, in propagandist proportions, about the joys of heterosexuality throughout our society. Heterosexuality is affirmed constantly — almost relentlessly. There is *nothing* a straight child experiences which even comes close to the torment caused by coming to terms with homosexuality. Gay children must have the courage and the strength to explore "unacceptable" feelings, risking the rejection a gay identity will certainly bring. While straight teenagers are learning how to date and establish relationships, the nonstraight teenager is learning how to hide feelings and make excuses. This is the reason behind the emotional immaturity discussed in Chapter 4. Basically, the gay teenager first must learn how to survive — alone.

In his book *The Best Little Boy in the World,* John Reid described the feeling of being alone in the closet: "I felt a little like the character in one of those totalitarian stories — *1984* or *Animal Farm* or *The Grand Inquisitor* or *We* — the character they have somehow forgotten to brainwash, the one for whom ignorance is somehow *not* bliss. There must be at least a few others out there like you whom they have also missed, who have the same odd ideas. But spies and informers are everywhere, so in order to keep from having your brain amputated, you act and talk exactly as though you were like everyone else. But you desperately want to find your fellow oddballs. How do you find them? How do you communicate in a way only they will understand? If you tell the wrong man, you are zapped."

The Chicken or the Egg?

> Resolve to be thyself: and know, that he
> Who finds himself, loses his misery.
>
> Matthew Arnold

Through social conditioning, all people are taught the horrible stereotypes about homosexuality, resulting in internalized homophobia for the one in ten destined to identify as gay later in life. The *internalized* homophobia leaves just two possible *first* steps in the process of coming out: Either accept the *negative* identity which society defines for homosexuality, or somehow acquire a *positive* understanding of homosexuality. The latter approach makes adopting a gay identity relatively easy. But the reinforcing experiences, which help lead to a positive understanding of homosexuality, are prevented by the self-denial of internalized homophobia. So which comes first: the chicken or the egg?

The first step depends on a conundrum of circumstances for each individual. Coming out can be a revelation, but it is normally an evolution. Conditions which might accelerate the process include an open mind, liberal peers and family, access to accurate information, the existence of a local gay community, or knowing an openly gay person.

Sometimes an event occurs which helps the individual come out. This might mean "getting caught" by a parent or a friend while engaging in same-sex sexual activity. It might be a suicide attempt. It could even be something as simple as being called a faggot or dyke, and taking it seriously. On the other hand, these apparent "catalysts" could have just the opposite effect. When an individual is labeled gay by anyone else, this can evoke a reaction of denial and resistance. External labeling therefore might tend to impede self-identity. Everything depends on the individual and his or her personality and circumstances. Normally, though, the first step is without the help of others.

AIDS has undoubtedly had some effect on coming out as well, although I am unaware of any studies which quantify this influence. With increasing knowledge in the scientific community and more education on safer sexual practices, this influence is bound to be minimal. Some men may not come out during the AIDS crisis, but their homosexual feelings will not go away.

Coming out can occur in the early teens or as late as retirement. Most gay people come out between the late teens and early thirties. Again, the average age is nineteen or twenty.

This chicken-and-egg dilemma has caused the gay community to offer educational services to help the one-in-ten learn the truth about homosexuality. Gay switchboards provide accurate information on homosexuality, offer referrals to counseling and other services, and maintain a calendar of activities in the local gay community. Switchboards are usually listed in the white pages of the telephone book under *Gay* something-or-other. In extremely homophobic communities, the listing can be found under the names *Lambda* or *One* to avoid receiving harassing phone calls. A Metropolitan Community Church, other religious organizations, or even a local chapter of Parents and Friends of Lesbians and Gays can also be helpful.

This brings up an interesting phenomenon. Extremely homophobic people label this assistance "recruiting." They don't see it as one generation of gay people trying to spare another unnecessary suffering. Instead they claim the gay community is turning "straight" people gay. In response to this purported threat, the homophobes try to make it as difficult as possible for anyone to obtain accurate information on homosexuality. The effect of their actions is to do the greatest possible harm to the "straight" people they are ostensibly trying to protect. Such actions go well beyond simple ignorance and irony. The ultimate form of oppression is when people cannot even admit they are being oppressed. This is why gay people who have made it "out" feel so liberated.

For example, one young woman felt she "was the only girl who had the sex desire for [other] women." Years later, after meeting other women who had similar feelings, she commented, "How much suffering would have been saved me . . . if I had known earlier." Such stories are typical for gay and lesbian youth. What's so remarkable about this one is that the young woman made these comments over one hundred years ago! How many more generations of gay youth will continue to suffer from the "big lie"? Coming out remains a turning point for nearly all gay people. It means that for the *first* time in a gay person's life, the individual has the chance to learn the truth about homosexuality.

The Truth at Last!

The truth is its own reward. *Plato*

The institutions and the resources of the gay community offer, almost exclusively, the only real opportunity in our society to learn the truth about homosexuality. Most school or public libraries either do not stock books on homosexuality or have books that are inaccurate. Straight peers, parents, and preachers are generally unreliable sources of information. The homophobic critics who claim the gay community is biased apparently fail to recognize the extent of censoring and propaganda in their own actions.

For most gay people, the first formal exposure to the truth about homosexuality is their first visit to a gay bar. This is a profound event in the life of a gay person, and many individuals even associate the experience with coming out. It is significant in itself because it is a way of "publicly" declaring the adoption of a gay identity. It is substantially more significant, though, as a learning opportunity. This single event can divide a gay person's life into "before" and "after."

As my own experience is fairly typical, I will share it with you. My catalyst for coming out was when I nearly committed suicide at the age of twenty-six. I had experimented sexually with both men and women. The heterosexual variety was unfulfilling for me, almost boring. The homosexual variety was wonderful, but I always felt tremendous guilt and shame afterwards. My torment was caused by my (then) stereotypi-

281

cal view of homosexuality and my refusal to admit I was one of "them."
So I sat in bed alone with my homosexual thoughts and my gun, having
reached the conclusion there was but one way to get those thoughts out
of my head. Yet I couldn't just end my life without making a statement,
and I couldn't make a statement without destroying my mother and
hurting everyone else who loved me. (Being gay is full of dilemmas.)
They loved me even though they didn't know the *real* me. Then it dawned
on me: Even I didn't know the real me — and I vowed to discover who
that was. Recognizing that I probably was homosexual, I decided to be
gay, *without* guilt or shame, as a three-month experiment. If I did not
like "being gay" after that, I would go back to "being straight."

The only information I had at the time was the stereotypes. I had
no idea there was a gay community in Indianapolis, although I had heard
people talk, quite repulsively, of a cruising area in one of the city's
parks. So I got in my car and drove down there — not once, but at least
twenty times. I just drove by, never stopped. I was afraid of being arrested or getting a sexually transmitted disease. Time was running out
and my experiment had not even begun.

"Plan B" was either to get my hair done or to have my house redeco-
rated. (Again, all I knew was the stereotypes.) As luck would have it, I
was having dinner with a male friend one night. Our waiter was gay
and apparently thought we were a gay couple. My friend is straight and
felt deeply offended. I pretended I was offended, too, but remained very
friendly to our waiter. I paid for dinner, leaving a generous tip, and told
my friend I was going to stay for a drink at the bar. He left. When our
waiter got off duty, I bought him a drink. We talked a while, nothing
"official" yet, when he said he was tired of being there. I suggested we
go to my house for a "drink." He accepted. Picking up a man in a straight
place is risky, but desperate situations call for desperate measures.

My experiment was working. That night was the first time in my
life I enjoyed gay sex without feeling guilt or shame afterwards. I was
not ready to admit I was one of "them" just yet, but "they" did not seem
quite as bad as the stereotypes claimed.

My new friend introduced me to another gay waiter who invited
me to go to "the bar." Reluctantly, I accepted. I was to meet him at the
same restaurant when he got off duty on Saturday night. Around 8:00
that evening, I began to get nervous, almost scared. I had heard horrible
things about gay bars. I envisioned a dimly lit, smoke-filled room, crowded
with sleazy men groping each other. After all, this *is* the stereotype for
a gay bar. My heart started pounding and I actually began to sweat. I
had a few drinks to relax, got dressed, and went over to the restaurant
to meet my new friend. I was visibly nervous, so he suggested we wait
a while. Finally, he recommended we drive downtown in separate cars
and we left.

I had never been to "that" part of town before. I began worrying
that my car might be vandalized and wondering if I might get attacked
by some teenage fag-bashers. My thoughts quickly returned to the imminent visit to "the bar."

When we met at the entrance, I noticed some young men, probably not old enough to go inside, just hanging around. I was shaking. My friend told me there was no reason to worry. He was so kind and patient, yet I kept thinking he was trying to "recruit" me. They asked for proof of my age at the door, which I thought was nice (since I was twenty-six at the time), then we paid our cover charge and went in. I was shocked! There were hundreds of men and women, just like you and me, talking, laughing, and dancing (men with men and women with women, of course). All were having a genuinely good time.

I was instantly relieved to realize that "they" are not bizarre, deranged, or disgusting — "we" are normal. Where others claimed there was misery, I knew *I* would find happiness. Simultaneously, I was overcome by anger at the society and the so-called experts who had misled me, *lied* to me my entire life. They caused so much unnecessary suffering — and to think I nearly took my own life.

Coming out is usually a long and arduous process. Adopting a gay identity involves a transformation of the individual's very meaning of homosexuality. Meeting other gay people, who also do not conform to the stereotypes, validates and strengthens the gay identity by enabling the individual to challenge the "straight" image of homosexuality. In other words, identifying as gay becomes socially acceptable, even if only in the gay community, promoting feelings of self-worth and self-esteem. Years can pass in the process. The closet "mentality," or internalized homophobia, stays with most gay people for quite some time after coming out. The emotional immaturity still exists from denying so many feelings for so many years. It will take many more years to completely eliminate the internalized homophobia and to get back in touch with all the lost feelings. The process may be difficult, but the rewards are abundant. In fact, even in sorrow there is an element of joy. John Reid describes his mixed emotions after losing love: "Now I had had my Summer of '42. Now, crushed by Freddie, it was apparent that I was as feeling as anyone else. Sad as it had been, it was a relief to know the songs were written for me, too. I was no longer left out of the stream of common experience, no longer the superfluous man."

Identifying as gay, more often than not, does have an effect on lifestyle. Recall the discussion of "Gay Lifestyles" from Chapter 4. The Institute for Sex Research defined five categories. Asexuality is characteristic of denial. The torment during the transition from "straight" to gay is demonstrated by Dysfunctionality. These are the "Troubled" categories. After accepting a gay identity, the individual normally becomes Functional. This is when the process of unlearning internalized homophobia begins and emotional maturity develops. After a while, the majority of gay people "settle down" in relationships, either Open-coupled or Close-coupled.

In his book *Living Gay*, Don Clark makes an enlightening analogy. Picture a closet door as a dam and the closet itself as the resulting reservoir. The dam represents the denial of feelings; the water being held back represents life's experiences. Each gay man and lesbian builds a dam of a different size and strength. Of course, society helps in both the construction and maintenance of these dams. Coming out destroys the dam, ending a life of denials. The life experiences rush out, almost uncontrollably. What results is a river — life at last. For those who come out, life is no longer a destination, it is a journey down the river. They have no idea where the trip will lead, but they are on their way at last. So in a way, a gay person's life is both damned and dammed. Coming out is indeed very liberating.

Coming Out to Straight Friends and Family Members

Friends are to be feared, not so much for what they make us do as for what they keep us from doing. *Henrik Ibsen*

Coming out to the self is one thing. Coming out to others is quite another. Only a minority of gay people inform straight friends and family members of their homosexuality. This passing as straight is not really a lie of commission; it is a lie of omission. Everyone is assumed to be straight. Gay people pass whenever they do not correct this assumption about themselves or even encourage it to continue. Lovers become roommates; dates become outings; boyfriends or girlfriends become "just friends." The first "lie" begins a pattern of deception.

Gay people "lie" when they take a friend of the opposite sex to a social function, rather than taking the one they love. They "lie" when someone tries to "fix them up" with a date of the opposite sex and they accept. Gay people "lie" when they laugh at the faggot jokes and when they fail to point out homophobia in others. When a person is living a lie, he or she is also living with the anxiety of having that lie discovered. So gay people are forced to engineer situations where their sexuality is unlikely to become an issue. This creates a lack of personal integrity as the "lies" continue to reinforce the illegitimacy of their very existence.

About the only time gay people don't "lie" is when they are with each other or with straight people who know their secret. But not too many straight people know. According to the Institute for Sex Research, approximately sixty percent of gay people conceal their homosexuality from straight friends and family, over seventy-five percent do so from employers and co-workers, and nearly eighty-five percent do so from neighbors and distant relatives.

Gay people offer many reasons for not coming out to straight acquaintances. Here are some of the more typical ones. "It's none of their business" or "They couldn't handle it right now" or "It would be an intrusion into their lives." Some gay people claim, "If they ask, I'll tell them," knowing full well that very few, if any, straight people will ever ask such a question directly. Of course, gay people conveniently interpret "Are you seeing anyone?" as meaning "Are you dating a member of the opposite sex?" and answer, "No I'm not," quite "truthfully." Others claim, "They already know." Well, if they already know, there should be no problem talking about it. "But they don't want to talk about it." If that were also true then *they* must be saying the same thing about their gay friends and relatives. The theme is identical in all of these excuses: *They* are the reason; *they* are to blame. Gay people claim they are somehow protecting others, when in fact, they are really protecting themselves. The individual thinks, "What *they* don't know won't hurt me." Unfortunately, this is true.

Most straight people, around eighty percent, simply do not understand homosexuality. Worse than this, they actually misunderstand homosexuality. There is an incredible chasm between the real meaning of being gay and the "straight" image of homosexuality. Gay people know if they come out they will be judged, at least initially, on the basis of the stereotypes rather than on their own merits as individuals. This situation could last indefinitely. Do most straight people think homosexuality is "good"? No, they think it's "bad." The difference is a matter of degree. The announcement of homosexuality is invariably received as bad news. This reaction brings opprobrium to gay people. Depending on the situation and the individuals involved, the news could also bring oppression. The fear of opprobrium and oppression motivates gay people to conceal their sexuality. So they remain in the closet.

Now comes the dilemma: Remaining in the closet is contradicted by a simultaneous desire to be accepted as a gay person. Passing as straight drives a wedge into friendships and family relationships. A straight person can share the intimacies of his or her life, while most gay people feel the need to remain aloof and evasive about theirs. The wedge is driven in little by little, a bit further each time the "What's-new?-Oh-not-much" question and answer game is played. Gay people would like to share the blessings and burdens of being gay, but they know others will not understand. They desperately want others to know about their lives. Yet whenever anyone asks, "Why aren't you married?" the question is interpreted: "Why isn't your life complete? Why aren't you happy like I am?" Gay people want to say they *are* happy, but they cannot say *why*. The foot is on the brake and the accelerator at the same time.

Damned if You Do; Damned if You Don't

All truths that are kept silent become poisonous. *Nietzsche*

Dr. Bruce Voeller describes the feeling: "The instant we are honest and forthright about ourselves, we face intense *open* discrimination in our jobs, homes, and lives. As long as we are hypocritical, hide, lie, and pretend, the world likes us, but we are *quietly* ostracized through our awareness of what would be done to us if we were otherwise."

The workplace serves as a good example of this dilemma. The problems caused by homophobia at work were discussed in Chapter 12. Here is a look at what it is like to be in the closet at the office. Passing as straight usually begins during the job interview. If an employment offer is made and accepted, the new gay employee wisely decides to make a good impression *before* coming out. Socializing with co-workers will necessitate "lies" of both omission and commission. After a period of working hard and befriending others, the good impression is established. In fact, the impression is so good, the gay employee is eligible for a promotion. Not wanting to jeopardize a lucrative career at this point, a gay man or lesbian might wait a little longer before announcing the news.

A sense of humor helps. For example, a gay person might be asked, "When are you going to get married?" An answer like, "The second — the second I have to and not a moment earlier" avoids the issue. Sometimes the humor is not so obvious. A work associate of mine once accused me of having an interest in an attractive woman at the office. I responded, "There are two reasons that's not true: She's a married woman." He didn't get it.

Eventually, the success and habit of passing becomes self-perpetuating. The deception may have reached the point of no return, making passing the path of least resistance — or so it seems. If gay people come out now, they need to explain why they waited. Others may ask, "Didn't you trust your work associates? Are you ashamed? What else aren't you telling us?" Many jobs today require selling ideas to co-workers. Have gay people just ruined their credibility? It is almost as if gay people need to choose between their success and their sexuality.

A different form of discrimination can be experienced by the openly gay person at work. Fellow gay employees may feel it necessary to discontinue any association for fear that *their* secret will be discovered. In effect, then, closeted gay people may avoid openly gay people for the very same reasons straight people do.

Knowledge is power. Coming out at work or elsewhere creates an opportunity for alienation or discrimination or both. Even if most co-workers do nothing, for example, it only takes one to cause significant problems. And the office is not exactly void of chronically homophobic individuals. So it is not a matter of expecting problems or not, it is a matter of degree. There *will* be problems. And most perfectly legal, leaving no remedy or recourse. Because gay people have virtually no enduring civil rights, their only real defense against discrimination remains passing as straight.

Another fundamental problem of coming out is that most straight people view it still as "flaunting." This is clearly a matter of personal perception, but that makes it no less of a real concern. To even suggest that straight people should similarly conceal their heterosexuality would be unthinkable. Yet most straight people do not consider this to be a double standard. It actually goes well beyond a double standard, though, becoming an oppressive "mind-your-manners" mentality. This mentality surfaces after coming out in the form of a higher set of standards for gay people: Homosexuality is all right as long as it's invisible. The situation was expressed eloquently by Peter Fisher in his book *The Gay Mystique:*

> The "good" homosexual is the gay equivalent of an Uncle Tom. He is supposed to be serious and reticent about his homosexuality. If it comes up as a topic of discussion, he is expected to deal with it in intellectual rather than emotional terms, speak in a sociological vein about the many problems faced by homosexuals. He should be understanding about the hostility he encounters from many straights —

286

after all, they really can't help it, you know, they were brought up that way and they don't know any better. He should never reveal the measure of anger he sometimes feels.

The "good" homosexual is a heterosexual homosexual. He may wear a sign around his neck stating "I am a homosexual," but he should look, act, think, and feel no differently than a straight person would. He should not be an embarrassment. His straight friends should never have to feel uncomfortable about introducing him to people whose respect they want to keep. He should be a tribute to their liberalism, not to their unconventionality.

Actually, the "good" homosexual should not even really be a heterosexual homosexual. Heterosexuals are all too open about their sexuality, and the "good" homosexual should avoid giving any hint that he has a sex life. He must be sexually neutral.

Just as there are potential costs of coming out, there are clearly costs associated with being closeted. The fear of external oppression often obscures the extent of one's current internal repression and the suffering it brings. But adapting to an environment is frequently easier than changing it. So gay people usually make some sacrifices and settle for less. They may become angry when someone they know makes a homophobic comment, yet they remain silent or even agree. This introduces an entirely new type of shame: the shame for lacking the courage to speak out. The situation is all very frustrating.

For homosexuality, the alternative to *dis*closure is enclosure. Gay people build a protective shell around themselves to keep out society's homophobia. But that is not the only thing kept from their lives. To have access to a gay community and achieve some degree of anonymity, many gay people move away from home. They make a new home, with fewer and shorter visits back to their previous home. Visits from family and friends may be discouraged, as these might be awkward. In preparing for straight guests, gay people must hide everything that could represent homosexuality. Of course, when a gay couple lives in a one-bedroom apartment, the situation is hopeless. If they cannot "pull off" the visit properly, their secret will be discovered. This shell becomes an affront to personal integrity, leading to near isolation from family members and straight friends. The energy consumed in this "straight charade" is enormous.

The dilemma must be considered from the perspective of straight acquaintances as well. The life of a gay friend or relative is a mystery to them. They must wonder why the individual doesn't talk about his or her activities, friends, and "love life." To them, here is a person who only works, eats, and sleeps. This odd behavior does not go unnoticed. Maybe they think they caused this apparent alienation. Until they find out their friend or family member is gay, they are quite likely to think something is terribly wrong.

Coming out can, and usually does, improve friendships and family relationships — eventually. The openness brings everyone closer together, providing an opportunity for total communication and mutual support. But it still can be a long and painful wait.

Damned if you do; damned if you don't. This dilemma causes gay people to lead "two lives": one in the dominant society and another in the gay community, thereby striking a balance between passing and "flaunting."

To Be or Not To Be

A man cannot be comfortable without his own approval. *Mark Twain*

To be or not to be "out" is the second most difficult decision, next to identifying as gay, that a gay person will make concerning homosexuality. Years can be spent in agonizing consideration and preparation. These years of anguish and anxiety begin to take their toll — gradually, but effectively. When the burden of secrecy becomes intolerable, the sense of isolation and hypocrisy too oppressive, one is compelled to act. But when? That question introduces the final consideration, in addition to the trade-offs outlined above, which must be taken into account: the individual's degree of internalized homophobia. In fact, this is *the* most significant influence.

It is unlikely that a gay person's straight friends and family members will overcome their homophobia *first,* clearing the path for instant acceptance. The oppression caused by society's general homophobia is decreasing but remains very strong. On the other hand, a gay individual's feelings of opprobrium, caused by his or her internalized homophobia, change much more rapidly.

When most gay people first identify as gay, they have a high degree of internalized homophobia. Although they accept the fact they are gay, they still feel homosexuality is "bad" or unfortunate to some extent. Gay people simply expect their friends and family members will feel the same way. Basically, then, as long as a gay person feels homosexuality is "bad" or unfortunate, he or she will *not* come out to family and friends.

Time passes. The individual meets other gay people. He or she gets involved in the gay community and starts to learn the truth about homosexuality. By doing this, internalized homophobia begins to diminish gradually. Gay people start to learn that gay is not "bad" or unfortunate, it's what they make it. So they start to make it "good." At first, being gay is just okay. Gay people no longer deny their ability to love and be loved, but they still accept the limitations society places on their existence as sacrifices which must be made. Then it gets better. Gay people ignore some of the limitations, sacrificing less. Eventually, the individual realizes: "Hey, I'm just as good as anyone else. In fact, I'm better! I've made a good life for myself despite all the obstacles placed in my path, and I'm proud of that! World, if you're not ashamed of your homophobia, then don't expect me to be ashamed of my homosexuality." When a gay person reaches this point, he or she is ready to come out openly. No longer will he or she be deterred by the "I-hope-they-won't-mind" mentality.

Since coming out is an irreversible event, burning the bridge to a heterosexual charade, this gay pride must be tempered by the reality of each individual's circumstances. Owing to the myriad personalities and situations involved, most gay people strike a balance between being openly gay and passing as straight. Not everyone comes out, and those who do, come out only to certain people. The fact that ten percent of the population is gay is irrelevant to the individual who must devise his or her own strategy for coping with being out on a daily basis: "Under what circumstances do I conceal my homosexuality? How far should I go in attempting to pass as straight? Who can and who cannot be trusted to know that I'm gay? Who already knows? Should I simply tell everyone? What would happen if the 'wrong person' found out?" The process of coming out can create a labyrinth of situations that require constant attention and management. There is clearly an element of risk, but risk is the price gay people must pay in seeking true acceptance.

Coming out, therefore, is not just an incident; it is a continual and often complex process. For this reason, many gay people adopt a strategy. Since honesty is the best policy, the simplest strategy is a nonchalant one where gay people treat their sexuality just as straight people treat theirs. This involves never making an issue of being gay, but never passing either. All it requires is being natural. When someone asks, "What did you do this weekend?" the openly gay person can answer, "I went camping with my lover." If others have a problem with that, it's *their* problem. While this strategy works well for all new acquaintances and maybe even some old ones, it will not work for those who have already been "fooled." They must be told.

Telling the Family

Telling the family is among the more difficult steps in the coming out process. Every gay person has many straight friends and acquaintances who, if any demonstrate extreme homophobia after being told, can be replaced by new, less prejudiced friends and acquaintances. Gay people can get new apartments and even new jobs. But each gay person has only one family. On the average, it takes four years after adopting a gay identity for most gay people to reduce their internalized homophobia sufficiently to come out to the family. Because this is so difficult, for both gay people and their families, the rest of this book primarily focuses on the family. Most of the discussion will be useful in other situations as well.

Once a gay person feels comfortable enough to disclose openly his or her homosexuality, the next step seems almost contradictory. It involves preparing for rejection, or "contingency planning" as some would call it. Although rejection is recognized by the gay individual as being both uninformed and unfair, a negative reaction can and does result in over half of all such situations. An argument may result. Physical violence is rare, but does occur. There are countless stories of children being disowned and evicted from their parents' homes, unable to provide for themselves. For this reason, gay children should be especially cautious about coming out to parents.

Wes Muchmore and William Hansen, authors of two books for gay men, have offered an interesting observation about parents' reactions to a child's homosexuality: "Children generally suppose parental love to be unconditional. Fiends on death row get visits from their mothers, who emerge in tears, telling the press their Igor is really a good boy and didn't mean to hurt all those blind schoolchildren he bludgeoned to death ... The gay son who reveals his way of life to his parents, however, is testing severely the limits of their love, and often they fail the exam." A most hateful reaction was told by Dr. Howard Brown in his book *Familiar Faces, Hidden Lives*. The story is about a twenty-two-year-old man who informed his parents of his homosexuality. The mother put her hand on her son's shoulder and said, "I've only made one mistake in my life. Twenty-two years ago, I should have had an abortion." Her arrogance was only surpassed by her insensitivity. Fortunately, the man was prepared for it, but the form of this rejection must have left a permanent scar on his heart.

Preparing for rejection involves physical and emotional support. In the normal course of events, both forms are already in place. Most gay people do not identify as gay until the late teens or early twenties. On the average, four more years pass before families are told. By this time, most gay people are working and can provide their own physical support. Sufficient time has also passed to learn about the resources of the gay community and to establish many gay friendships, both of which help provide emotional support. This "support system" may not be needed, but it should be in place just in case.

Of course, many parents will respond to the news, "So what? We've known all along." Most reactions are between the extremes of this immediate acceptance and instant rejection. Just as it takes time for gay people to adjust to being gay, it takes time for their families to adjust to knowing a child or sibling is gay. Announcing the news is only the beginning. What follows is a process of education and understanding, leading to acceptance. Those who truly love and respect a gay person will eventually accept the individual for who he or she really is. If they cannot, their love and respect was actually lost a long time ago. As Andre Gide said, "I would rather be hated for what I am than loved for what I am not."

Life is a series of choices. Each choice presents a host of new ones and precludes numerous others. When the choice to conceal homosexuality prevents a gay person from being close to friends and family, he or she must choose to come out. Since coming out is really inevitable, then, it is actually more a matter of timing. But when? When the individual is ready When he or she is self-accepting and self-sufficient — and not a moment before.

The Moment of Truth

The remainder of this chapter is for gay readers, but straight readers are encouraged to follow along. Presented here are a number of suggestions about coming out to your family. No general suggestion is ever universally applicable as people and circumstances vary greatly. You must use your own best judgment in your own situation.

Before you come out, listen carefully for any clues to what sort of reaction you might experience. Possibly, you will be able to "test the waters" by first dropping hints. In anticipation of the moment of truth, rehearse your mental script of exactly what you will say. It is impossible to predict anyone's reaction, so prepare for several possible ones — hostile, okay, or "so what?" — by role-playing with gay friends. They can give you both practice and constructive criticism. Also, prepare answers to the general or personal questions that might be asked. Locate educational materials and support organizations which will be helpful during the "aftermath."

A good way to experiment is to come out casually to total strangers. You can do this with the person sitting next to you on an airplane, the checkout clerk at a store, standing in a line somewhere, or any other anonymous setting. This will give you valuable practice and confidence, and your actions will help educate others in society.

Here is an example. I was at a florist shop the other day buying roses for Leonard. His mom was joining us for dinner, so the roses were actually for the table. Instead of commenting on the weather, the girl at the counter made casual conversation by asking, "Are these for your girlfriend?" (She must have noticed I wasn't wearing a wedding ring or she would have asked if they were for my wife.) I answered, "No, they're for my lover. *He* likes roses." What was her response? "Oh, you're not gay." We bantered back and forth in the usual "Yes-I-am-Oh-no-you're-not" routine, when I said: "Really, I *am* gay. Ten percent of the population is. But I'm not offended. Your reaction is quite normal. Gay people don't usually say they're gay because some individuals are terribly prejudiced. And you can't tell by looking either, because gay people are basically just like straight people . . ."

(In fact, straight readers could try this experiment. "No way!" you say. Go on, try it. Oliver Wendell Holmes said, "A moment's insight is sometimes worth a life's experience." It will give you some startling insight into how our society views homosexuality and gay people. If just the thought of doing this makes you uncomfortable, imagine what it must be like to feel this way several times each and every day.)

You will need to make a special announcement about being gay. Unless you are particularly skillful, homosexuality is a difficult subject to "work in" to an everyday discussion. You should also not disclose the news during an argument over some other topic. Your homosexuality is not a weapon to help you get something through guilt. If you do this accidentally or already did this inadvertently during an argument, apologize immediately.

The perfect moment will never come, so waiting for it should not serve as an excuse. Here are some ideas on how to set the stage for your announcement. Try to hold the first conversation in person if at all possible. That will enable you to see, not just hear, the reaction. One-on-one is best with friends, but you may choose to tell both parents at the same time. Select a private setting where you can be alone, with-

291

out interruption, so both or all of you can express any emotions experienced. But do not stage a major event; it will seem like a "sales job." Don't beat around the bush, either. Get to the point. A long introduction is usually the sign of some great tragedy. Remember, being gay is no big deal. Choose a good time, one which is unencumbered by current sorrows or joys. The worst time to come out is when you need emotional support, such as when losing a lover. Get over your hurt first, using your support system. If you live away from your family, a personal meeting may only be possible during a holiday visit. Do not choose actual day of the the holiday. Hold your conversation before, if it is a short visit, or after, if several days are still available for questions and continued discussion. But keep in mind, the longer you wait the more difficult it will be. The morning is the best time of day, giving you the rest of the day to talk about it. Too much talk on the first day, however, may be inappropriate. The news needs to "sink in" before other information can be absorbed. Disclose your homosexuality in a simple, matter-of-fact fashion. Do not apologize or display any sense of shame, guilt, or tragedy. That will only elicit a similar reaction because emotions are contagious. Again, this is *not* bad news, so be positive.

If you cannot tell your remote family members or friends in person, then hold the conversation by phone. If you want to come out, but cannot seem to work up the courage to do it in person, then write a nice long letter full of information; your words will likely be read several times as you will not be there to answer any initial questions. Follow up your letter with a phone call after a few days to ask how *they* feel. Above all, *never* have someone else convey the news on your behalf. That implies shame and fails to set the stage for open and constructive dialogue.

You will need to initiate the conversation. If you are still at a loss for words, here is a good example of coming out to parents: "Mom, Dad, I love you and I've always tried to be open and honest with you. But I've kept something a secret from you because I thought you might be hurt. Now I want you to know. I'm gay." Now, that wasn't so bad was it? Then immediately say, "I know you don't want to believe it. Before you say anything, though, there are three other things I want you to know. First, you did not cause my homosexuality. Second, there is nothing which can or should be done to change it. Third, I'm very happy. I've learned to accept being gay and I want you to accept it too. If you want to talk about it, I'll be happy to answer any of your questions. If you'd rather be alone with your thoughts for a while, I'll understand. Even though I've deceived you about my sexuality for years, I want to be completely honest with you now. I also want you to be completely honest with me. Let me know your true feelings. This is all I want from you for now. Everything else will come with time. You probably know very little about homosexuality. I hope you'll be willing to learn. I'm certainly willing to help. I love you and I know you love me. We'll work it out." If you don't like the above style, at least find some way of expressing the three points mentioned and emphasize you are telling them you are gay because you love them, not because you want to hurt them.

It is not important to have a flawless performance. Coming out is not an act in a play being viewed by a paying audience; it's real life. Mistakes will not assure rejection just as perfection will not assure acceptance. In all your words only one, *gay*, will be remembered the most. Everything else will be eclipsed by its significance. Even if you just blurt it out, "I have something to tell you — I'm gay," at least you've said it. Then you can compose your thoughts and continue. Sure, you'll be nervous. But the world will not come to an end; the sun will rise and set again, and you'll be able to appreciate each day a little more.

Remember, you get to choose the time, the place, and the tone of the conversation. You get to practice, possibly spending years in preparation. Just because *you* are ready to make the announcement, does not mean *they* are ready to receive it. You are going to catch them off guard with some pretty substantial news. The very nature of the situation seems to demand a reaction; the conversation may appear confrontational, especially if you are noticeably nervous. Try to relax so they can relax. Their reaction, in all probability, will be based on the stereotypes. You must be understanding. Nearly everyone can recall making homophobic statements. Parents may feel they were inadequate as role models. The guilt others feel could surface as a defensive reaction. The fear of saying the wrong thing might keep them from saying anything. Coming out is an inherently awkward situation. It will be *your* responsibility to keep it productive.

Now What?

Here are some suggestions to help you handle the variety of possible reactions to your announcement. Again, only you can decide how to manage your own situation.

Do not expect immediate acceptance. Any problems you experience will likely be temporary. It probably took you years to accept your own homosexuality. With your help it won't take your parents that long, but it will take time. Be patient.

Act as if nothing has changed. Be yourself, but be aware. Everything you say and do, for a while at least, will be considered in the context of your homosexuality.

Be suspicious if you get no reaction. Almost no one is neutral on this topic. No reaction is normally a symptom of some problem. This is not to say that a reaction must be negative; many people, parents included, already accept gay people and should tell you so. If you get zilch, ask why. They may have some hidden fears or anxieties. Your parents need to acknowledge and accept, not deny, their own feelings. You know all too well what it is like to deny feelings. Let them know that negative reactions are quite normal — initially. If they simply don't want to talk about it immediately or can't deal with it rationally at first, then back off. But don't give up. Periodically and casually bring up something about being gay. If they are ready to talk about it, they will. If not, drop it again. Later will be soon enough to resume your discussions. If after several attempts there seems to be no interest, then ask why and insist on an answer. Something may be bothering them, but their silence is certainly bothering you. You have a right to know where you stand.

Express your own feelings. If you are angry or disappointed, say so. On the other hand, if you are pleased with their reaction, let them know that too. In any event, keep the dialogue constructive. You can express emotions without getting emotional. Understand that your parents will almost certainly blame themselves for your homosexuality. Because they are also likely to think that being gay is "bad," they will possibly believe you feel resentful toward *them*. Emphasize this is *not* the case and that, like always, you love them.

Offer assistance. Volunteer as a resource for information. Make it known that questions are welcomed. If no questions are forthcoming after a while, guess which ones might be of interest and answer them anyway. The stereotypes are a good place to start. Give them a copy of this book or others to read. Write a personal note inside the cover. Help them locate resources like Parents and Friends of Lesbians and Gays. If your parents want counseling, assist them in finding a minister or therapist who will be truly helpful. Tell them when there is going to be a show on TV or an article in a magazine covering homosexuality or gay issues. Keep them informed.

Parents may not care much about homosexuality in general, but they may want to know a great deal about you and how you live as a gay man or lesbian. Tell them how normal your life really is. What is ordinary to you may be interesting news to them. Feel free to tell them as much or as little as you want. You have a right to your privacy, but they have an equal right to their curiosity and concern. On the other hand, if you're telling too much, you'll be informed verbally or through body language.

Try not to be offended by questions, requests, or statements of concern. Some typical questions include: "Are you sure?" or "How long have you been 'that way?'" or "Have you considered the consequences?" All of these questions are totally innocent and equally insulting. But each is also an opportunity to educate. Stereotypical knowledge may be all they have. At least you are still communicating. If you consider any question to be too personal, simply answer it in a general way when possible. Otherwise, politely state the question was too personal. For example, my mother asked me, "What do you do in bed?" I was sure she meant, "What do gay men do in bed?" So I answered her *real* question.

Recognize that your parents will likely offer "help." After all, that's their job. They may feel they have failed you in some way and want to make up for that now. They may even think you have made a poor "choice" because *you* do not understand homosexuality like *they* understand homosexuality. This "help" will probably come in the form of suggesting "professional assistance." Simply explain that you are well-adjusted and perfectly happy just the way you are. There is no need for any help, because there is no problem for you. Tell them the help they can offer is to accept you, even be proud of you just the way you are. If, on the other hand, *they* are having a problem, you might suggest various means of help already mentioned.

Do not act defensively. No parents ever approve of everything their children do. Remember, you are not seeking approval for what you do, you are seeking acceptance for who you are. Do not apologize for telling them you are gay. Do not apologize for being gay. Do not apologize for living gay. If you are a man, your parents may be concerned about your health. You should be too. Tell them you practice safer sex and, because of your precautions, they have no need to worry. Your parents may even try to relate everything they do not like about your life to your homosexuality. Point out that this is either a double standard or an unrealistic standard and, that either way, the judgment is unfounded.

Never respond to the hurt or any anger you experience with attempts to hurt them or with your anger in return. This is *not* a battle. If you must take a few lumps to assure that a tense situation doesn't escalate, then by all means do so. If you feel that an argument is imminent, simply excuse yourself, leaving the door open for constructive dialogue at some later time. If you don't, you run the risk of saying or being told something both of you might later regret. Simply say, "Well, we seem to disagree here and we're making no progress. Why don't we each just think about this some more and come back to it later?"

If that doesn't work, be more assertive: "I want to work this out as much as you do, but I will *not* argue. If we can't carry on a productive conversation any longer, then we should just stop right here." If you honestly think the situation is impossible, then walk away. You apparently have nothing to gain by continuing. But if the situation is not impossible, do not make it so. Also, if your emotions get the better of you and you say something out of line, apologize immediately and sincerely. I am reminded of the response Archie Bunker, from the TV show *All in the Family,* gave to a challenge of his attempt at revenge. He said, "What's wrong with revenge? It's the perfect way to get even." Your goal should not be to get "even" in this way. You want to be accepted as an equal; that does not mean being "even." Your gay pride should serve as a tool to build relationships, not destroy them.

Try to comply with any reasonable requests — at least for a while. This will give others time to adjust at their own pace without feeling pressured. Typical requests include not telling other relatives or family friends, not "flaunting" your homosexuality, or agreeing to read a book *they* have on the subject. Try to understand *why* the request is being made so you can help them deal with the underlying feelings or beliefs. For example, the book they give you may be full of misinformation. Read it and point out its fallacies. This is an opportunity to educate. You should also respect any rules that people establish for conduct in their homes, no matter how unfair or unnecessary they seem. These rules typically cover displays of affection or sleeping arrangements with your lover. It's their home; it's their rules. Your only choice is whether or not you wish to be their guest.

Do not make deals. "All right, I'll do this . . ., if you'll do that . . ." You are already honoring all reasonable requests and hopefully making only reasonable requests in return. There is, therefore, no need to deal. You need to educate, not compromise. If you cannot reach agreement on an issue, simply agree to disagree.

Tell the entire family. This includes both parents, if your parents are still together, and all your brothers and sisters. Telling only one parent could make the news a lonely burden and might actually do more harm than good in the long run. Allow your family to at least have each other for emotional support. Also, because secrets destroy mutual trust, telling only one parent might harm their relationship. You may want to tell each parent separately. That's different. If so, tell whichever one you think will be the most understanding first. That will help give you confidence and provide some support when you inform the other. Of course, the reaction of the first parent may be negative. That is unfortunate, but you still need to go through with coming out unless you have been asked, "Please don't tell your father (or mother)." Honor this request, but only for a short while. You have worked up the courage to go this far, so don't stop now. Honesty is still the best policy.

If you have brothers or sisters, it may be best to tell them first. Younger people are generally more accepting of homosexuality. Even if they're too young, under the age of twelve or so, to understand sexuality, they can still understand love. Siblings do not share the same expectations or feelings of guilt that parents normally have. Again, this will not only give you a chance to practice, but can provide a base of support.

If you don't have siblings to provide support for your parents, you might consider telling one of their friends, or your pastor or rabbi. That will give them an outside resource to discuss their feelings. This also brings up another important consideration. If you're an only child, *you* are the "only chance" your mother and father have to be grandparents. Do *not* let this deter you from telling them. It is unfair to let them hang on to this false hope. Do not feel guilty, either. Just as you might be circumstantially denied the joys of having children, they might be denied the pleasure of having grandchildren. It could hurt them just as it hurts you, but they, too, will adjust. With no one to "blame" for this situation, there should be no guilt by anyone.

If you are married, get divorced. This is the only fair and responsible thing to do for both you and your husband or wife. "Fooling around" on the side will only cause more anxiety and grief for both of you. Once you recognize and accept your homosexuality, you have an obligation to share this information with your spouse. Otherwise, your spouse is likely to believe he or she is somehow causing the apparent indifference in your relationship.

There are two points which are important here. First, you should let your straight spouse (or boyfriend or girlfriend) know that he or she neither contributed to nor caused your homosexuality through some inadequacy. Second, his or her hurt and anger, while natural reactions initially, are unfair and unnecessary if prolonged. You never intended to hurt anyone. In all probability, you made a sincere effort to make the relationship work for a number of reasons. Any deception is simply inherent to the situation.

The best thing to do at this time is for both of you to move forward. If you must look back, look back at the good. Surely your years together were not without plenty of good times and love. Life goes on, and a grudge is a heavy load for the journey ahead. Guilt and bitter feelings are inevitable. They should be experienced, but not endured. You did what you had to do, both in entering and in ending the relationship.

For the gay man or lesbian leaving a marriage, coming out is extremely difficult. Unlike gay relationships, marriages are well-known to all friends and relatives. When one ends, it is necessary to explain "what went wrong." If you don't wish to come out openly like this just yet, try to agree with your spouse on some story to tell your families and mutual friends. The good-old-reliable "We just drifted apart" is not really a lie and probably won't be questioned further by others. But do not be deterred if such an agreement cannot be reached.

If you have children, psychologists generally concur that they should be informed about your homosexuality — regardless of their age. It is possible to inform very young children in ways appropriate for their age and maturity. Coming out to children can circumvent or begin to reverse their homophobic conditioning. A child may not understand homosexuality any more than he or she "understands" being black or Jewish or a member of any other minority for that matter. But children can understand love. Eventually, your children will find out one way or another. The sooner they do, the better for everyone involved.

Let your children know homosexuality is not contagious or hereditary (even though someday science may discover it is indeed hereditary). Most children will not know the other theories even exist, and they know they will not be "recruited" either. Teasing from peers may become an issue (homophobia has many victims), but the effects are not necessarily negative. Reinforce in your children a belief in mutual respect for others, especially those who are different in some way.

Finally, join one of the numerous support groups for gay parents. Most of these offer an auxiliary support group for children as well. Groups like this can be very helpful in dealing with your situation.

If your lover will be meeting your family, discuss it with him or her first. Share your mutual anxieties and expectations. Your lover will likely want to make a good first impression and may be a bit nervous. So will your family. Tell your family some information about your lover, and vice versa, before everyone meets. This should help "break the ice" and promote some casual conversation. Obviously, everyone should just be natural.

"In-laws" have a long-standing reputation for thinking no one is good enough for *their* children. They are proud of you and want the best for you. So maybe they'll be a little critical. But some parents have actually "blamed" their child's homosexuality on the lover. Explain to them before you get together that this is not the case, and get their agreement. You are in love because you are gay, not gay because you are in love. As long as they keep the proper perspective, everything should be all right. If the first meeting doesn't go well, solve any problems before you get together again. But do get together again.

If your coming out experience deteriorates completely, don't blame either your homosexuality or your honesty as the cause. The cause is homophobia. Never forget that. Some parents do react negatively. You have hopefully prepared for and can handle this reaction. Again, if you are even partially at fault for something said, apologize immediately and sincerely. Of course, you also have the right to expect an apology if you were treated unfairly. If the door was closed and a continued relationship is still important to you, don't give up just yet. Make contact again in a few months. If you have had to move out of your parents' home, write or call immediately to inform them of your new address and phone number. Let them know you are all right. Ask how they are doing, and express hope that someday you will be able to make amends.

Conclude each conversation with your parents, good or bad, by keeping the door open for continued and constructive dialogue. End your initial conversation by reiterating the three points mentioned above: They did not cause your homosexuality; it cannot and should not be changed; and you are happy. Then a few days later, stop by or call to see how *they* are feeling.

A joy shared is twice the joy; a sorrow shared is half the sorrow. Coming out shares both the joys and sorrows of being gay—for you. You are accustomed to dealing with homosexuality; straight people are not. Initially, the news may present some problems for them before everyone can live happily ever after.

Chapter 17

A Happy Ending?

You're either part of the problem or part of the solution.
Eldridge Cleaver

Will there be a happy ending to the millions of personal coming out stories? The answer depends on the reaction of straight friends and family members. Therefore, this final chapter is for straight readers. You are probably reading this book because someone you know has already told you he or she is gay. You may be a little confused right now. Your emotions are myriad and intense. You aren't quite sure how to react. What do you say? What do you do? How will you deal with this?

Presented here are a number of thoughts and suggestions about dealing with your own feelings after learning that someone you love is gay. While these ideas are directed especially to parents, most of them will work for the friends, relatives, and other family members of gay people as well. Again, these suggestions have been accumulated over the years from many different sources, and no general suggestion is ever universally applicable. So use your own best judgment in your own situation.

People find out someone they love is gay in a number of different ways. Maybe you found out through a mutual friend, another son or daughter, a spouse, a mother or father, a teacher, or possibly the police. Parents of a friend of mine found out when they saw their son at a gay pride rally on TV! I even read of one family where the mother had already figured out her son was gay and told *him*. He accepted the news very well. It is likely, though, that you were told directly by your gay friend or family member. You should be flattered. It means you are trusted, respected, and loved. In any event, now you know. Maybe this is not the best news you could get, but it is certainly not the worst. Keep this thought in mind: Homosexuality is *not* a tragedy; it's what *you* make it.

Your initial reaction may be one of shock, disbelief, guilt, denial, anger, fear, hurt, grief, shame, inadequacy, tension, worry, anxiety, panic, disgust, confusion, and on and on. It may all seem like a bad dream. The news can be devastating to some parents. Expectations may have been shattered. "Why does this need to happen? How could I have not known? What if other people find out?" Just as most gay people have felt alone, most parents of gay children feel their circumstance is so unique that no assistance is available. You have no similar experience to guide your thinking. Your life may seem as if it will never be the same again, yet the world appears to go on as if nothing had changed. Really, not much has changed. You may experience any or all of the above emotions, but four of them are the most common: guilt, grief, shame, and confusion.

Guilt

Guilt generally results from feeling embarrassed about your initial reaction, homophobic comments you may have made before finding out, or something you think you may have done to "cause" the homosexuality. Maybe your guilt is a a combination of all three. Relax. None of these reasons should make you feel guilty.

If you reacted less than admirably, that's all right. You didn't "blow it." Sticks and stones can break bones and words can hurt, too, but words can be taken back. A negative reaction is not uncommon, nor was it entirely unexpected. You likely were caught totally by surprise. Just like all gay people before indentifying as gay, you probably have only a stereotypical understanding of homosexuality. There is no reason to feel guilty. If you said something you regret now, a simple and sincere apology will suffice. Then stop worrying about it. Time heals all wounds. Besides, your guilt will only get in the way. Your long-term reaction is what really matters. Because gay people need all the allies they can get, no gay man or lesbian can afford to reject acceptance *whenever* it comes. So a gay person is unlikely to hold a grudge, especially against someone he or she loves.

Do not feel any guilt for any other things you may have said or done in the past. Remember, *everyone* suffers from homophobia to some extent. A homophobic comment can occur without thinking, and usually does. Everyone, you are included, has made homophobic comments on occasion. Nearly all parents warn their children about sexual abuse from adults. Part of this warning includes watching out for "those" people. Children need to be warned about pedophiles. Your only mistake may have been equating pedophilia with homosexuality. And everyone, gay people included, has told, or at least laughed at, faggot jokes. Maybe you have even laughed at gay people. The gay community is not without its "humorous" members. Finally, everyone has expressed his or her less-than-positive opinion on some gay civil rights issue or made some derogatory comment about the "militants" in the Gay Civil Rights Movement. Leave the past in the past—just learn from it. If you really want to apologize for earlier comments, go ahead, but it's not necessary.

You may also be concerned that you will make some homophobic comments again. Don't worry—you will. So what? If you worry about it, you'll be on pins and needles, and that won't do anybody any good. When I first got involved with the Gay Civil Rights Movement, I had the opportunity to work closely with a number of lesbians. I soon learned how sexist I really was. It was clearly a revelation, for I sincerely thought I had worked through all my prejudices. Believe me, they were quick to point out the errors in my thinking. But at the same time, they were sincerely appreciative of my willingness to learn. Our friendships actually improved in the process. If offense is not meant by your comments, offense will not be taken. Just be on guard for symptoms of your own homophobia, especially because prejudice can be subtle at times. If you slip and make an offensive statement, simply say, "Oh, I'm sorry. My homophobia is showing again." Then get on with it.

There is nothing quite like the guilt some parents can inflict upon themselves. It is truly amazing. Most parents use guilt as a means of controlling behavior. The problem with guilt as a means of "motivation," however, is its tendency to boomerang. But this feeling is somewhat different than guilt. At least with real, honest-to-goodness guilt, you know what you did wrong. Now you don't. Initially this reaction is normal, but don't carry it to your grave. Finding out your child is gay does not make you a retroactive failure as a parent who is unfit to continue in that capacity. You are needed now, just as much as ever, maybe even a little more in certain ways. While you are undoubtedly disappointed, do not feel that you have in *any* way contributed to the homosexual sexual orientation. In the quest to determine what caused a child's homosexuality to develop, parents will look for patterns of behavior or even isolated incidents. You may try to evaluate your worth as a role model. You search for what you did "right" with your straight children and what you did "wrong" with your gay child. Don't bother. Even the experts aren't sure yet what factor or factors determine sexual orientation. If the cause is indeed genetic, and in all probability it is, don't blame yourself for sexual orientation any more than you blame yourself for the color of your children's eyes. You can't exactly control your genes. Whether you blame yourself or your spouse, tension will surface between the two of you once the "blame game" is started. Please don't torture yourself in this way.

Parents, all too frequently, try to blame themselves for anything and everything they don't like about their children. No child is perfect; no parent is perfect. But there is absolutely *nothing* you did or could have done, either maliciously or negligently, that would have made *any* difference. There is no fault, so there is no blame. Therefore, there should be no guilt. Guilt means there is something wrong, and as long as you continue to feel this way, you will never be able to accept homosexuality or your gay child. If you are a real glutton for guilt, you might even feel badly because you were unable to recognize your child's homosexuality in time to offer support. Forget about it. You did the best you could with the information you had at the time. Of course, if you still want to accept *all* the blame for centuries of misunderstanding and homophobic oppression, that is your prerogative.

Grief

In *Parents of the Homosexual*, David and Shirley Switzer compare learning of a child's homosexuality to the feelings of grief which accompany the death of a loved one. This is not the case for all parents, but it is for many. The questions which are symptomatic of this feeling are,

301

"Why? Why *our* child? Why *us?*" The news seems so tragic. It's almost as if there is a "different" child taking the place of your child. Well, something *is* different; something *has* been lost. That "something" is *your* expectations: your image of your child. This is the loss. This is the tragedy.

Parents make an incredible investment in their children. You made and may even continue to make countless personal sacrifices for your children. Many parents actually begin to see their identity mainly *as* parents. There are numerous expectations, shared and private. These expectations never include homosexuality. Even if you might have suspected your child is gay, you likely hoped and prayed it wasn't true. Parents are accustomed to deciding what is good and bad for their children. You want your children to have more and better. Homosexuality itself is neither of these. It is just as bad or as good as you choose to make it. Some of the disappointment may never go away. But keep this thought in mind: When others do not meet *your* expectations, it is not *their* problem. So keep your expectations high, just different. Remember, your children, gay or straight, are not responsible for making *your* life complete, just as you are not fully responsible for making their lives complete. All you can do is love each other. While you may have lost a "part" of your child, don't risk losing the rest.

Shame

If you think homosexuality is "bad," and you are likely to believe it is at this time, then you are experiencing shame. Your family name has been disgraced. Your association with a gay person could ruin your reputation. If this is true, then you are creating a problem where none should exist. The shame you are feeling is understandable. The part about you creating a problem is serious, though, because you are. Your shame sends the implicit message: There is something wrong with being gay.

You need to recognize that your shame is not caused by someone else's homosexuality. It is caused instead by homophobia — the very same homophobia you help perpetuate by your shame. Because you know everyone is homophobic, you correctly assess that others will think less of you for having gay friends or relatives. In effect, you have just become a victim of this type of prejudice too. Welcome aboard. You may not experience the oppression, but now you at least know what the opprobrium feels like.

Confusion

Even if you feel no guilt about anything; even if you have experienced no grief over some "loss;" even if you are completely unashamed, you are undoubtedly confused at this time. This is actually a special kind of confusion, so the psychologists have a term for it. They call it *cognitive dissonance*. Cognitive dissonance is an internal conflict caused by some apparent contradiction. In other words, one plus one equals something other than two. To eliminate the contradiction, something must "give." What "gives" is either behavior or attitudes; normally, it's attitudes.

Here's what is happening. You have been conditioned all of your life to think homosexuality is "bad." But now you find out someone you know, someone you thought was "good," is gay. In effect, you may have previously disliked gay people, only to discover you have actually loved one all along. On the other hand, maybe you thought homosexuality was okay, but now realize it's only okay for *other* parents' children. In either event, there is a conflict and you are confused.

You have basically three choices at this point. First, you can discontinue the association with the gay person. This eliminates the conflict by completely ignoring the situation. One parent of a gay son described the problem like this: "I guess I could have said, 'Get out of my life and don't ever come back.' And he could have agreed. But he wouldn't have been out of my life." This first approach only works for ostriches, not for people. So it is not really a viable alternative.

Your next choice is to change your opinion about your gay friend or relative. To do this, you admit you have been "fooled," and that the "good" person is actually "bad." You can then build on this approach by trying to change the new "bad" person into the old "good" person — again. This, of course, would be accomplished through a conversion to heterosexuality, which is "good." By now, the futility of this choice should be obvious.

Your final choice is to change your attitude or beliefs about homosexuality. These are your choices; anything else is just a variation or a combination of the three.

No Easy Answer

For every complex problem, there is a solution that's simple, straightforward — and wrong. *H. L. Mencken*

Before deciding how you are going to react, take some time to put things in perspective. Remember, when you discover someone is gay, he or she is still the same person as before. The only thing that has changed is your knowledge of an existing situation. Except for that, the situation itself has not changed. The way the two of you related before is the way you can continue to relate. The values you shared before, you will continue to share. The interests you had in common, you will continue to have in common. This "different" person is actually the same person, minus *your* expectations. Possibly you are thinking, "How could I have not known something so fundamental?" Then you think, "What else don't I know?" So far, so good. But then you think that everything else you don't know is bad and *this* is where your homophobia takes over your reasoning. What you are actually doing, whether you consciously recognize it or not, is assuming all the stereotypes are accurate. When you believe the stereotypes, your natural reaction will be to offer "help" to end the tragedy. The obvious form of this "help" is to change gay people to be like *you*. You are "normal." You are "good." Your motives are admirable. It is your assumptions which are flawed.

It is natural for you to use your life as a frame of reference, or perspective, from which to view others. Your own heterosexuality probably brings you much happiness. That is wonderful. Gay people are very happy for other's happiness. But *your* form of happiness is not *their* form of happiness. You may not like homosexuality. Homosexuality would not bring you much happiness. You might even think that you would be quite miserable being gay. You only feel this way because you are straight. The fact that something is not "good" for you does not make it "bad" for someone else.

This is going to be especially difficult for parents to accept. Parents, you have already had your chance to significantly influence your children's development. And you have probably done a fine job. The very fact you have been told this news demonstrates your child's love and respect for you. Parents have many responsibilities for their children. You provide the basic physical needs of food, clothing, and shelter. You teach values and develop character. You provide comfort and advice. In total, you teach your children how to fly from the nest and live independently of your care. But your responsibility has never — doesn't now and never will — include the determination *or the redirection* of sexual orientation in your children. Any previous attempts at such were obviously as futile and harmful as any current attempts will surely be. You must recognize that the real reason for wanting to "change" gay people is your happiness, not theirs.

Gay people don't come out to seek this form of "help" anyway. They have already been damaged enough by too many would-be helpers. Gay people eventually give up any hope for "change" and learn to accept their homosexuality *long* before you find out about it. Help is not what gay people need; help is not what they want.

What Do Gay People Want from You?

In a word, gay people want acceptance. Acceptance means giving up the hope that a "cure" is possible or even desirable. It means realizing that all people really are born equal and that heterosexuality is not inherently superior to homosexuality. The dictionary provides a very appropriate definition for acceptance: "To regard as proper, normal or inevitable." Homosexuality is all three. Acceptance means respecting gay people and granting them the dignity they deserve. Finally, it means love. It's that simple — nothing more, but absolutely nothing less.

Conversely, there are a few things, in addition to "help," which acceptance is *not*. It is not approval of homosexuality. And when acceptance is conditional, it is really approval in disguise that shows up in statements like: "It's okay if you're gay as long as you don't . . . or only if you . . ." Naturally, you do not approve of everything everyone else does. If you disapprove of something specific a gay person does, simply be specific and keep homophobia out of the picture.

Acceptance may include empathy, possibly even sympathy, but it does not include pity. Sure, it's not easy being gay. But gay people take great pride in their accomplishments, and pity undermines that pride.

Along these same lines, gay people do not want their friends and families to worry. Yes, there are problems, but worrying won't help anyone. Worry is interest paid on a debt yet made. But some parents love to worry. They are probably the same ones who experience tremendous guilt. (When it rains, it pours.) Voice your own fears and concerns. If you don't share a fear or concern expressed by your spouse, say so and why. If both of you worry about the same thing, then share your concern with your son or daughter. Instead of worrying, channel your energy constructively into your relationship.

For all practical purposes, acceptance means one more thing: replacing society's stereotypical image of homosexuality with one of gay reality. This is the *only* way to resolve the conflict you are now experiencing. And the only way to do that is to unlearn your own homophobia. This is what anyone, gay or straight, has had to do in accepting homosexuality. The unlearning process will require some effort on your part, for homophobia runs deep and surfaces easily. But have confidence. You can do it if you try. You aren't the first person to unlearn homophobia, and you won't be the last. You're just next.

Whatever you decide to do at this point, do not claim that you will *never* change your views on homosexuality. In the first place, people should rarely say "never." It is such a permanent word. We all, more times than not, end up eating it. Second, you are hopefully open-minded enough to *want* to learn, regardless of where your new knowledge may lead you. As your knowledge of homosexuality changes, your beliefs may change as well. The word *never* is not so much a description as it is a prescription. If you close yourself off in this fashion, you risk alienating the person who respected and trusted you enough to say, "I'm gay and I want you to accept me for who I am." If you have already proclaimed your views are cast in concrete, forget about it and start unlearning your own homophobia.

Unlearning Your Own Homophobia

You have learnt something. That always feels at first as if you had lost something. *George Bernard Shaw*

Be patient with yourself. It will take a while to unlearn a lifetime of homophobic conditioning. This is quite normal and there is no real hurry. Different people learn at different rates. Unlearn your homophobia at your own rate.

But don't just sit there — react. React honestly in either a positive or negative way. Don't attempt to hide or deny your real feelings; that will do neither of you any good. Your feelings are respected and they *are* important. State your beliefs even when you feel uninformed on a subject. If you want, ask if you have ever offended unknowingly. This will allow you to "bury the hatchet" and get on with your relationship. If you still

305

feel uncomfortable discussing homosexuality, that indicates you are keeping your feelings to yourself. Let them out.

While you are reacting to the news, try to behave as though nothing had changed. If you normally hug, hug. If you normally dine together, dine together. If you normally discuss politics, discuss politics. You can even tell gay jokes, as long as they are in good taste and there is no malicious intent. Be careful that you are laughing with gay people, though, and not at them. Of course, the jokes should be funny too. A straight person who feels comfortable enough telling gay jokes usually accepts homosexuality very well. Make sure this is *your* reason for doing it.

Read and ask questions. Be honest about your ignorance and express a willingness to learn. Your curiosity is natural and questions will be welcomed. Do not ask questions which are too personal, however. As a rule, anything you would not also ask of another straight person is probably too personal. Everyone, including sons and daughters, has a right to privacy. If you are not quite sure, ask anyway. If the subject is off-limits, you will be told so. The only dumb question is the one which isn't asked.

Probe more for feelings than for behavior, as you will be able to gain a better understanding of the individual through his or her feelings. Your gay friend or family member will not know all the answers. No one does. But he or she is certainly a willing resource for *reliable* information. Being "personally involved" does not disqualify a person from being trusted. You are probably a reliable resource for information on heterosexuality. Your knowledge and experience is just as valuable as a gay person's is. Besides, friendship and love require a reciprocity of trust and respect. If someone has trusted you enough to tell you he or she is gay, you can trust that person to give you the truth about homosexuality.

There may be no truly objective observers of this subject, but get the facts any way you can. Read this book again; you might learn a great deal more the second time through. Read other books and articles. If you feel uncomfortable going to your local library, go to one in a nearby town. The bibliography at the end of this book contains a list of other books on homosexuality.

When you ask questions, use words like *gay* and *lesbian* even if this is awkward at first. Eventually, the g-word and the l-word will become comfortable additions to your vocabulary. Avoid using these words, along with "homosexual," as nouns. For example ask, "When did you first realize you're gay?" instead of, "How long have you been a homosexual?" or "When did you first realize you were 'one?'" Refer to a lover as a lover, not as just a friend. Better yet, refer to him or her by name. Ask, "How long have you and John been lovers?" instead of, "How long have you and your 'friend' been living together?" Questions can be loaded with judgment. Make yours neutral.

Obviously, after you ask a question, listen. And listen *to* the answer given, not *for* the one you want. This "selective" listening is not even listening; it's censoring.

Seek help. This is especially important for parents. Gay people do not unlearn homophobia alone, so neither should you. Support is available both from within and outside the family. This could be a spouse, a trusted friend, a professional counselor, a minister, the parents of your gay child's friends, or a group like Parents and Friends of Lesbians and Gays. Try not to feel embarrassed or ashamed for seeking support. You will not be putting a burden on someone unless you make your needs burdensome. Others may feel sorry for you, but this is not unlike *your* initial reaction. A friend may not know what to say, but can still provide moral support and serve as a "sounding board" for you to sort through your own thoughts. If your friend is not understanding, seek help elsewhere. You have your own needs at this time.

Your son or daughter can help you locate many of these resources. The local college with a gay organization or a gay switchboard should be willing and able to offer referrals. If resources like these do not already exist in your own town, consider traveling to a larger city nearby. Other parents of gay children could be located by contacting the ministers in your community's churches. If you are still going through a "shame phase," call around anonymously until you locate a minister who can and will help. Then you can identify yourself and set up a meeting. In addition to seeking help, you may also want to offer help to your spouse or other children. It is not necessary to unlearn *all* of your own homophobia before you can genuinely help others.

One of the best organizations available is Parents and Friends of Lesbians and Gays (PFLAG). There are chapters in most larger cities throughout the United States. These local groups generally meet once a month in homes, churches, or community centers. PFLAG offers a valuable service, and gay people genuinely appreciate its work. In fact, the two groups which receive the most enthusiastic welcome in Gay Freedom Day parades are People With AIDS and PFLAG. If a local chapter doesn't already exist, you may want to consider forming one. Probably by the time you are ready to do this, though, you won't need the support — but others certainly will. Why not help them and establish a few new friendships in the process?

Meet other gay people. This is one of the best ways to unlearn the stereotypes. You can do this by meeting the friends of any gay person you know. He or she is really an example of gay people in America, not an exception. Frank Kameny was a prominent gay civil rights leader during the Gay Liberation Movement. His mother was asked, "What happened to make you change your mind about your son?" She responded:

> I started to listen to him. Your best education is your own child.
> I wanted to know what kind of life he led. I especially wanted to find out what kind of friends he had. I know about people. I can judge what kind of character a person has. You don't need to be a psychiatrist to do that. So I met his friends, and I talked with them a lot. I made sure that Frank brought them over to my house whenever he could so they would feel comfortable with me.

Do you know what I found out? I found out they were nice people. They were all educated people like him, and they were good friends for him, the kind of friends I would have liked Frank to have no matter what he was. And Frank was the same son I had always known and loved. My son was nothing like what the psychiatrists had said he was.

Get Involved. You might be concerned about the oppression gay people face in our society. Instead of just worrying about it, get involved. Whenever you are presented with a chance to effect change, do it. This might include voting in favor of gay civil rights issues, writing your elected representatives in government to encourage such legislation, and merely calling attention to any expressions of homophobia you witness. You might even get involved in local or national gay groups; one need not be gay to belong or contribute. Your support will be sincerely appreciated and there is something in it for you as well. Your involvement will have the same therapeutic effect for you as it does for gay people. Being able to say, "My child (friend, brother, sister, relative) is gay and I'm proud" is powerful medicine.

Sarah Montgomery, cofounder of Parents and Friends of Lesbians and Gays, told her son, "Charlie, you've been through an awful lot without me beside you, and since you're out in the open now, I'll never be a closet mother." Even after her son Charlie and his lover John committed suicide, Sarah continued marching in Gay Freedom Day parades, carrying a sign which read: "I Will Not Be a Closet Mother." Sarah very successfully unlearned her homophobia.

Try not to give advice or make unreasonable requests. Even though your opinion is respected, your requests may not be — especially if they're unreasonable. The most common requests include not "flaunting" homosexuality or not telling others. Understand that both imply shame. Such requests may force gay people to choose between what is best for themselves and respecting your wishes. The choice may not be an easy one, and it may not be the one you want. Growing up homosexual in a homophobic culture destroys an individual's sense of self-worth. Gradually, after coming out, gay people replace the internal homophobia with a rebuilt self-image that is healthy and positive. But the self-esteem that accompanies this gay pride can be fragile at times, especially when the sacrifices required to accommodate external homophobia serve as daily reminders that gay people are still second-class citizens. So carefully consider all your requests before making them known. Above all, avoid "emotional blackmail" by not making your love or friendship conditional. Love and friendship are not weapons — and self-worth is not negotiable.

Judge not. Judgment is an inevitable outcome of any human interaction. But you should *never* (this is one of those rare occasions the word is appropriate) judge *any* person based on stereotypes. Gay people simply want you to consider their homosexuality as just another dimension of their lives, not as the very definition of their existence. Although any individual can identify with many different groups, no single group can give anyone his or her total identity. Be careful also not to start interpreting everything in terms of homosexuality. If you do, you'll only be repeating the same mistakes made by so many zealous psychiatrists in the past.

Because no one approves of *everything* someone else does, you will probably form some negative opinions about how your gay friend or relative has implemented his or her sexual orientation. Of course, he or she will undoubtedly do the same of you. After all, judgment is a two-way street. The only difference is that most gay people, having adopted the philosophy of live-and-let-live, are unlikely to say anything to you. It's your life, not theirs. And as long as you aren't hurting anybody by what you do, there is no reason to comment. However, if you feel you must say something, say it. And if you do, once is enough. Avoid launching a barrage of criticism and focus exclusively on the specific issue at hand. Try to understand, from a *gay* perspective, why this behavior exists. Respect the individual's right not to accept your advice and, instead, question your reasons. You might just be wrong.

Make reasonable rules. You definitely have the right to make the rules in your own home. But your gay acquaintances have every right to decline to visit under conditions which are unfair or too restrictive. A good rule of thumb is not to establish any rules for gay visitors that you would not establish for straight visitors. In other words, avoid double standards. For example, if a straight couple, staying overnight, is permitted to sleep together, then a gay couple should also be. The issue of marriage is irrelevant, for gay people are not permitted to marry. The fact a gay relationship is not "official" in the eyes of the state or the church makes it no less real. Gay lovers display affection just as straight couples do. They hug. They kiss. They hold hands. If you are bothered by seeing gay people do these things while you do them or never notice when other straight people do, then you have a double standard. Recognize this as your problem and try not to make it someone else's.

Welcome lovers as you would a spouse. When you don't, you force a tough decision that is just asking for trouble. Meeting a lover is no more difficult than you choose to make it. The lover is likely to be as nervous as you are. Relax and just be yourself. If the first meeting doesn't go well, you'll surely have another chance to get together. In the meantime, address whatever problems occurred. When you phone and the lover answers, talk. Even if your conversation is only small-talk, it can help build big rapport. Lovers are just as important to gay people as spouses are to straight people. Show some interest.

It is entirely possible, homosexuality *completely* aside, that you genuinely do not like the lover as a person. Lovers are people and some people are real losers. While it's unfortunate, it happens in many relationships, gay and straight, and is not unlike a straight man or woman you know who married the "wrong" person. Love can be blind. If your loved one is romantically impaired in this fashion and you feel compelled to say something, by all means do so. After all, what are friends and family for? Before you do, though, be absolutely certain your opinion is not influenced by homophobia.

Resist anger. This is because, in addition to being denied feelings of love, gay people have also repressed feelings of anger. This all-too-human emotion may have been dammed up for years and could release as a flood of ire directed at you. The situation is unfortunate, but try not to take it personally. You are likely being viewed merely as a "representative" of oppression. Remember, when gay people are ready to come out to family and friends, they have lowered their internalized homophobia enough to develop a strong sense of gay pride. The anger is legitimate and well-earned, even if it isn't well-directed. Sometimes, though, a gay son or daughter unconsciously desires a confrontation with parents in order to clarify his or her "position." In fact, the repressed anger may have served as the impetus to come out. If this is the case, try to understand. But you have every right to expect an apology for such behavior.

There are a number of actions which hold the potential of setting off an argument and should therefore be avoided. One is unrelenting offers of "help." Sometimes these offers are disguised as discussions on the difficulties of being gay, as if this "revelation" might alter the "choice." Gay people already realize it's not easy being gay in the United States. They do not need others to "rub it in" by reminding them. Another is discrimination in the form of double standards. Still another is being judged on the basis of the stereotypes. All of these actions imply a lack of understanding and possibly an unwillingness to learn. Your gay friends and family members will hopefully be patient while you unlearn your homophobia, but the process does have its frustrating moments.

Nothing evokes anger as much as a patronizing or condescending statement. Quite frankly, gay people are sick and tired of being second-class citizens, especially in their own circle of friends and within their own families. So whatever you do, please try to avoid saying anything like, "Of course, we'll always love you no matter *what*." No one wants love or respect "in spite of . . ." Even a statement like, "I respect the fact this is your choice," shows no understanding and really means, "I question your wisdom — how could you possibly choose such a terrible lifestyle?"

Of course, parents feel anger for a number of reasons too. Maybe you are angry with your son or daughter for "causing" a problem in *your* life. "I never raised you like this! How could this happen to *me*?" If you have just now found out, you might feel deceived, partly by your child and partly by your own assumptions. "Why did you wait so long to tell me?" Maybe you have always known, but are angry you were told for now you must deal with it. "What you do is *your* business, not mine." Possibly you have become frustrated trying to offer "help." "He (or she) doesn't care what I think!" You may also be tempted to blame any family problems on homosexuality. Don't. The root of all evil in this arena is homophobia — period. If you are angry, try to determine exactly why before attempting to deal with the situation. Otherwise, it might make matters worse.

In dealing with anger, be honest with your feelings, but express your anger calmly. Do not let your anger build up inside, for when it erupts, as it will, neither of you will benefit. Obviously, don't say something you could regret later. If a tense situation begins to escalate, back away. Swallow your pride as a dose of medicine, not for you, but for your relationship. In the long run, this action will be appreciated for the truly selfless sacrifice it is.

Do not discriminate against gay people in anything you do. This not only applies to the openly gay people you know, but to all the other gay people you know, but don't know they are gay. Remember, gay people are everywhere, including your workplace, your church, your health club, your social service organization — everywhere. Speak up and help others unlearn their homophobia too.

Your Opportunity to "Come Out"

Straight people who know and love gay people have their own version of "coming out." You might not be ready for this quite yet, but hopefully someday you will. Because our society still "blames" homosexuality on Mom and Dad, this derivative of coming out is especially difficult for parents. In her book *Coming Out to Parents,* Mary Borhek described her thoughts in this regard: "What will *my* parents, my brothers and sisters, my other relatives, my friends, my minister or priest or rabbi, my co-workers think about me? They'll think I was a bad parent, that I did something wrong raising my child. They'll think there is something wrong with my marriage, that it's a failure."

Some of your friends or relatives *will* make homophobic comments. How will you react? Are you offending the gay people you know by *not* saying something? When someone asks, "So, has your son gotten married yet?" are you really going to answer, "Well he has, almost, his lover is a very nice man"? It gets worse. Because homosexuality is so much a part of gay people's lives, they frequently move to cities where there is a prominent gay community. You are not going to change your life in this fashion. The extreme homophobia gay people often leave behind remains for their families and friends. For this reason, it may be even *more* difficult for you to "come out."

So, what are you going to do? Just like gay people, you are going to "pass" as someone who has no gay friends or family members, at least for a while. And just like gay people, you will need to learn the truth about homosexuality first. Prior to that day, there is something you can do as a compromise which will not compromise your secret.

It is entirely possible to confront homophobia in a general way. You are not likely to be suspected of being black, unless you are black, because you have black friends or defend black civil rights. When you hear a homophobic comment, simply say something like, "Hey Herb, your prejudice is showing." If people ask why *you* are defending gay people, just point out that those in our nation, including you, believe in liberty and justice for *all.* As you become more sure of the facts, you need not be intimidated by the ignorance of others. Inform Herb that ten percent of the population is gay, and the fact he may not "like" homosexuality is not a good enough reason to deny the civil rights of twenty-four million Americans.

In fact, you might even try this experiment. Pick some "harmless" nongay minority group for which you have negative feelings. They might be of a particular national origin, political philosophy, or religion. Choose labor unions or management, transvestites, radicals, or even the Soviets. Choose your least favorite group and then defend them. Yes, defend their opinions and their right to hold and express those opinions. No "good" group is all good and no "bad" group is all bad. You might be surprised at how easy this is to do. There are very good reasons people feel or act the way they do. You could find that the people who actually share your *real* opinions may back down when someone challenges them. Hate is a difficult emotion to defend. Their response may be, "Well, I don't really hate them, I just wish they wouldn't . . ." (By the way, this is a good experiment for gay people to try as well, for no one is immune from prejudice.)

Telling Others

There still remains the immediate concern of telling others. You may want this news kept secret from *all* your friends and relatives for a while. This is a reasonable request only until you have had a short period of time to adjust to the news yourself. You should realize, though, that any desire to keep this a secret implies shame. On the other hand, there is no need to make an issue *all* the time of someone being gay. Of course, the presence of a lover may make the issue a difficult one to avoid. Should you pretend the lover is just a friend, or should any introductions acknowledge the significance of the relationship? This apparent dilemma can be resolved quite easily. Together, you and your gay friend or family member can discuss which mutual acquaintances should and should not be told — and how. You should also discuss how to handle general situations which might arise. But recognize that gay people have the right to inform whomever they feel is important to their well-being. Conversely, owing to the possibility of discrimination, gay people also may have a need to continue keeping their homosexuality secret from certain individuals. For these reasons, if agreement on exactly who else gets told cannot be reached, the gay person's rights and needs should prevail.

Unless your son or daughter specifically requests that you keep this news to yourself, do not keep it from your spouse or the rest of your family. You will not be "protecting" anyone — at least for long. Keeping it a secret is not easy nor is it wise. The truth will eventually come out. If you delay, you will start to wonder *when* you should say something. When you finally do, the fact you waited so long will become an issue. Mothers are more likely to be told first, because moms are generally more sympathetic. If this request *does* come from your son or daughter, honor it. Otherwise you will destroy the confidence you currently have with your child. Then work it out. Simply explain to your son or daughter that your marriage is built on mutual respect and trust. The request for secrecy is asking you to violate this important premise. Your child should understand.

312

Sometimes external circumstances may force you to "come out." Maybe your son was arrested for solicitation and the event was reported in the local newspaper. Maybe your daughter is a lesbian feminist who appeared on TV. My family was forced to "come out" with the publishing of this book. It is tough having to deal with it when you aren't quite ready. Maybe you think you will never be ready. Don't wait. Start now.

In his book *The Church and the Homosexual,* Father John McNeill told the following story: "I shall never forget the grief of a young man who, because he loved his parents very much and wished to spare them the grief of learning of his condition, had chosen to live in a distant city, when he received the following revelation at his father's funeral: before his death his father confided to a friend that he could not understand why his son had moved away, and felt that perhaps his son did not appreciate how much he loved him."

My dad died when I was only nine years old. Like most children at that age, I took my parents for granted. "Everyone has parents," I thought. Then, Dad was gone. I would never see him again. I had to learn the hard way to be grateful for everything I have.

We all feel sorry for someone who has no shoes, until we meet someone who has no feet. So whenever you feel like you have no shoes, be grateful for your feet. Be grateful you have your family and your friends, and count all your blessings one by one. Homophobia has already taken too great a toll. Don't let anything you have or anything you are be its next victim.

At a meeting of Parents and Friends of Lesbians and Gays, a mother casually commented, "Our children sure are lucky to have parents like us." She was right. We are *all* very lucky to have each other — today.

The Gay Nineties

Children of the future age,
Reading this indignant page,
Know that in a former time,
Love, sweet love, was thought a crime.
            From "Little Girl Lost," William Blake

What about tomorrow? Will the situation for gay men and lesbians in our country improve? Undoubtedly it will.

Someday our nation will look back on the oppression of the gay minority in much the same way that we now view slavery. We will be at least embarrassed, and more likely ashamed, that we, as a nation, could treat people that way. How could we, such a civilized society, not have known better?

How soon will that day come? In the 1990s perhaps? Maybe, with your help. And how will we know when it's finally here?

AIDS will have a cure. There will be no need for a term like "fag-bashing" because such behavior will have ceased to exist. Sodomy laws will disappear. In fact, the very concept of "Gay Civil Rights" will become meaningless because discrimination based on sexual orientation will be illegal at all levels of government and in private enterprise. Even the military will honor its gay men and lesbian personnel.

"When was Gay Freedom Day?" will become a trivia question as gay people begin celebrating their full freedom on the Fourth of July with everyone else. The 1990 census, hopefully as a sign of a kinder and gentler nation, has a new category of "unmarried partner" right along with the usual choices of married or single.

In a little town in the Midwest, a high school teacher will ask, "Are there any gay people in this class?" and four of her students will proudly raise their hands. Commercial advertisements will prominently display gay couples, providing role models for America's gay youth. A female priest will preside over the marriage of two gay men. And no one will even notice when two lesbians walk down the street hand-in-hand or when two men kiss goodbye at the airport. But if anyone does notice, they'll say, "How nice. Look at those two who are so much in love." Homosexuality will become as transparent as heterosexuality is today

315

and the need for a gay community will fade away as gay men and lesbians are welcomed into the dominant society.

And finally, when that day comes, this book will be a relic of the past you can donate to some museum. Until then, I hope the understanding of homosexuality provided on these pages helps make your life a little better.

Notes

Introduction

Page

1 "There is probably . . .": Weltge 1975, p. 3.
4 Origin of words homosexual and heterosexual: Laure 1983, p. 129; DeCecco 1985 *Gay Personality*, p. 35; Rofes 1984, p. 3.
7 "An important lesson . . .": Bell and Weinberg 1978, p. 218.

Chapter 1

11 Controversy surrounding the publication of Kinsey's book: Weinberg 1976, p. 16; Tripp 1975, p. 218–225.
12 "The Institute for Sex Research bibliography . . .": Weinberg and Williams 1974, p. 4.
Freud quote: Bayer 1981, p. 21.
"We assume that . . .": McNeill 1976, p. 129.
13 Example of bias on research: DeCecco 1985, *Bashers, Baiters*, p. 9.
"The obvious explanation . . .": Scanzoni and Ramey 1980, p. 81–82.
14 "I myself feel terribly remote . . .": Koertge 1981, p. 76.
15 Sexuality in prisons: Scanzoni and Ramey 1980, p. 56–57.
"Another obvious and understandable finding . . .": Bell and Weinberg 1978, p. 128.
16 "If my concept of homosexuality . . .": Weltge 1975, p. 13.
"When the heterosexual . . .": Weltge 1975, p. 17.
"If we assume that homosexuality . . .": Bieber 1962, p. 305.
Tripp quote: Tripp 1975, p. 228.
Tissot reference: Szasz 1977, p. 183.
17 Other evils believed to be caused by masturbation: Szasz 1977, p. 180–206; Silverstein 1977, p. 162–163; Nelson 1978, p. 169; Bullough and Bullough 1977, p. 55–73.
"In my opinion . . .": Szasz 1977, p. 186.
"Of all the vices . . .": Szasz 1977, p. 186–187.
18 *Boy Scout Handbook* and the US Navy references: Szasz 1977, p. 201.
American Handbook of Psychiatry reference: Szasz 1977, p. 202.
Diagnostic and Statistical Manual, Mental Disorders reference: Silverstein 1977, p. 177.
19–21
Freud's theories: DeCecco and Shively 1984, p. 68; Doyle 1983, p. 123–124; Ruse 1988, p. 65, 71; Bell, Weinberg, and Hammersmith 1981, p. 64; Hart and Richardson 1981, p. 31.

22   Kinsey's methodology: Weinberg 1976, p. 34–56.
"These figures are . . .": Kinsey, Pomeroy, and Martin 1948, p. 625.
Institute for Sex Research study: Levine 1979, p. 26.

22–23
"Males do not . . .": Kinsey, Pomeroy, and Martin 1948, p. 639.

23   Kinsey's findings: Kinsey, Pomeroy, and Martin 1948, p. 650–651.
Blumenfeld and Raymond 1988, p. 79.
1970 Kinsey Institute study: Fumento 1990, p. 203.
Statistics on American hobbies: Kirk and Madsen 1989, p. 15.

24   "The opinion that . . .": Kinsey, Pomeroy, and Martin 1948, p. 660.

25   "In the final analysis . . .": Bayer 1981, p. 164.
"It is my belief that . . .": DeCecco 1985 *Gay Personality*, p. 33.

26–27
American Psychiatric Association references: Brown 1976, p, 201, 205, 208;
Troiden 1988, p. 64; Bayer 1981, p. 3, 40, 101–154; Silverstein 1977, p.
182–183; DeCecco 1985 *Gay Personality*, p. 11.

27   DSM-III: DeCecco 1985 *Gay Personality*, p. 13, 21.

28   American Psychological Association position: Silverstein 1977, p. 183.

29   "Our findings indicate . . .": Bell, Weinberg, and Hammersmith 1981,
p. 184, 191.
"The theory that . . .": Weinberg 1972, p. 26.

29–30
"The dominant-mother theory . . .": Tripp 1975, p. 73.

30   Institute for Sex Research study: Levine 1979, p. 29.

Chapter 2

33   "Poor Miss Right! . . .": Weinberg 1972, p. 53.

34   Two example studies: DeCecco and Shively 1984, p. 12.

34–35
Hormonal development: Doyle 1983, p. 50–61, 250; Ruse 1988, p. 84–129;
Hart and Richardson 1981, p. 16; Masters and Johnson 1979, p. 410–411.

35–36
Genetic determination: Bell, Weinberg, and Hammersmith 1981, p. 212–
220; DeCecco and Shively 1984, p. 162; Weinberg and Williams 1974,
p. 7, 8; Koertge 1981, p. 17, 18.

36   "To grow up . . .": Nungesser 1983, p. 27.

36–37
"Cure" techniques: Marmor 1980, p. 342; Tripp 1975, p. 240–242.

37   "One must remember . . .": DeCecco and Shively 1984, p. 75.
"It is a heartless hypocrisy . . .": Szasz 1977, p. 168.

37–38
"Not infrequently . . .": Tripp 1975, p. 230.

38   "Paul spent almost seven years . . .": Hall 1985, p. 30–31.
Weinberg example: Raymond and Noguera 1979, p. 129.

39   "A New York psychiatrist . . .": Tripp 1975, p. 236–237.

40   "In the seventeenth century . . .": Silverstein 1977, p. 177.

40–42
Lesbian/Gay Affirmative Therapy: Bell and Weinberg 1978, p. 339; Brown 1976, p. 214; Hall 1985, p. 97; Hart and Richardson 1981, p. 42; Jay and Young 1979, p. 772; Masters and Johnson 1979, p. 334; Spada 1979, p. 297; Tripp 1975, p. 239, 255–257; Weinberg and Williams 1974, p. 150, 161, 186.

41 "If a homosexual . . .": Bayer 1981, p. 172.
"It would appear . . .": Bell and Weinberg 1978, p. 216.

42–43
"For many years . . .": Masters and Johnson 1979, p. 3.

Chapter 3

46–47.
"The process of generalizing . . .": Nungesser 1983, p. 38–39.

47–48.
"A belief system is . . .": Nungesser 1983, p. 31, 41–42.

48 "The homosexual stereotype . . .": Silverstein 1977, p. 153.

49–50
"To most Americans . . ." Levine 1979, p. 1–2.

50–52
Studies about gay people being identified easily: Levine 1979, p. 7, 26; Back 1985, p. 194.
Studies about passing as straight: Bell and Weinberg 1978, p. 295–297; Weinberg and Williams 1974, p. 105; Jay and Young 1979, p. 68, 141; Levine 1979, 32.

53 Institute for Sex Research study: Levine 1979, p. 26.

55 Institute for Sex Research study: Levine 1979, p. 24, 26.

55–56
Statistics and issues on child molestation: Gearhart and Johnson 1974, p. 262, 263; Levine 1979, p. 9; Berzon 1979, p. 7; Curry and Clifford 1986, p. 129; Fisher 1972, p. 168.

56 Racist beliefs about rape: D'Emilio and Freedman 1988, p. 217–221, 297.
Institute for Sex Research study: Levine 1979, p. 29.

57 Institute for Sex Research study: Weltge 1975, p. 107.

58 Institute for Sex Research study: Levine 1979, p. 26.

61–62
Transvestism and transsexuality: Jay and Young 1979, p. 575; Kleinberg 1980, p. 174–190.

62–64
Sexual practices of gay men and lesbians: Marmor 1980, p. 238; Kinsey, Pomeroy, and Martin 1948, p. 371; Nelson 1978, p. 176; Jay and Young 1979, p.544; Spada 1979, p.126; Masters and Johnson 1979, p. 65, 124–125.

65 Myth of gay unhappiness: Hart and Richardson 1981, p. 42; Spada 1979, p. 310; Bell and Weinberg 1978, p. 432; Hall 1985, p. 19; Rofes 1984, p. 73–74.

66 Myth of gay lonliness: Bell and Weinberg 1978, p. 178.
"We find no age-related differences . . .": Weinberg and Williams 1974, p. 217.

Chapter 4

68 "Our hope is that . . .": Bell and Weinberg 1978, p. 23.

69 "The Dysfunctionals . . .": Bell and Weinberg 1978, p. 225–226.

70–71
Studies of cruising activity: Marmor 1980, p. 270; Scanzoni and Ramey 1980, p. 105; Brown 1976, p. 109.

72 "Sexual contacts during this period . . ." Weltge 1975, p. 19.

72–73
Studies of sexual and related behavior: Mendola 1980, p. 41; Weinberg 1976, p. 175; Weinberg and Williams 1974, p. 111–112; Doyle 1983, p. 254–255; Jay and Young 1979, p. 161.

74–76
Studies of relationships: McWhirter and Mattison 1984, p. 149; Spada 1979, p. 197; Jay and Young 1979, p. 171; Mendola 1980, p. 68, 112; Kleinberg 1980, p. 126.

76 "Same sex couples? . . .": Berzon 1979, p. 30.
"The interesting thing . . .": Borhek 1979, p. 148–149.

Chapter 5

80–81
Institute for Sex Research study: Levine 1979, p. 27.

82–83
Gay bars: Levine 1979, p. 286; Weinberg and Williams 1974, p. 112.

83–84
Gay bathhouses: Bell and Weinberg 1978, p. 413.

85 "Probably our most salient finding . . .": Weinberg and Williams 1974, p. 276.

85–86
Rochlin's "Heterosexual Questionnaire": Back 1985, p. 188–190.

Chapter 6

90 Statistics on masturbation: Levine 1979, p. 20; Kinsey, Pomeroy, and Martin 1948, p. 499.

92–93
Studies on homosexuality as a threat to society: Levine 1979, p. 24; Weinberg and Williams 1974, p. 19–21, 98; Nungesser 1983, p. 98–99.

93 "If all persons . . .": Kinsey, Pomeroy, and Martin 1948, p. 666.
APA Task Force position: Gomez, et al 1984, p. 160.

94 Study of homophobia in men and women: DeCecco 1985, *Bashers, Baiters*, p. 75, 77.

95 Study of effect same-sex relationships have on marriages: Knutson 1980, p. 60–61.

96–98
History of nature: Ruse 1988, p. 179–180; Knutson 1980, p. 45; McNeill 1976, p. 90–91; Boswell 1980, p. 303–334.

100 Studies on sexual behavior in animals: Bayer 1981, p. 47; Tripp 1975, p. 12–14, 23.

102 "The only unnatural sex act . . .": Doyle 1983, p. 241.

104 "The reason is that . . .": Weltge 1975, p. 45.

107–108
Reaction formation: Weinberg 1972, p. 12; DeCecco 1985, *Bashers, Baiters*, p. 10–11; Ruse 1988, p. 60.

109 Statistics on the extent of homophobia: Levine 1979, p. 32–33; DeCecco 1985, *Bashers, Baiters*, p. 2; Gonsiorek 1985, p. 26; Bayer 1981, p. 167; Doyle 1983, p. 244.

Chapter 7

110 Formation of homophobic attitudes: Schulenburg 1985, p. 24.

112–113
Journalism experiment: Alyson, et al 1982, p. 30.

117 Surveys of psychology textbooks: Bayer 1981, p. 192; Hall 1985, p. 21–22. National Opinion Research Center poll: Kirk and Madsen 1989, p. 75.

119–120
Studies of sex education in schools: Levine 1979, p. 33–35; DeCecco 1982, p. 98; D'Emilio and Freedman 1988, p. 341.

Chapter 8

123 "Which of us knows . . .": Bauman 1981, p. 199.

125 "It is taken for granted . . .": Bell and Weinberg 1978, p. 121–122. "Every choice . . ." Weinberg 1972, p. 75.

126–127
"No one knew why . . .": Clark 1979, p. 179–180.

127 "It is fun but barren . . .": Rofes 1984, p. 43.

128 Characterization of the most homophobic individuals: DeCecco 1985, *Bashers, Baiters*, p. 6–7, 69–70; Levine 1979, p. 33; Nungesser 1983, p. 109.

130 "This century's most extreme . . .": Licata and Petersen 1985, p. 141.

135–136
"I am seething . . .": Back 1985, p. 84–85.

136 Weinberg quotes: Weinberg 1972, p. 1, 21.

Chapter 9

138 "There were about 200 people there . . .": Pennington 1978, p. 37–38.

141–142
"This situation appears . . .": Mickelsen and Mickelsen 1982, p. 54.

142–143
"It is not readily apparent . . .": Boswell 1980, p. 335.

155–156
"The land of the Sodomites . . .": McNeill 1976, p. 72–73. Fairchild and Hayward 1979, p. 161.

Chapter 10

164 "It is clearly . . .": Bailey 1975, p. viii. Rapid spread of sodomy laws: Boswell 1980, p. 292–295.

165 "But what next? . . .": Boswell 1980, p. 280.

166 "The widely held belief . . .": Boswell 1980, p. 286.
"For if the just Lord will punish . . .": Boswell 1980, p. 294.
"Although we are reluctant . . .": Boswell 1980, p. 288.
Ancient sodomy law: Boswell 1980, p. 283–289.

167–168
Salem witch-hunts: Szasz 1977, p. 300.
Sodomy laws in colonial America: Knutson 1980, p. 35.

168 "Moreover, whatever its effect . . .": Boswell 1980, p. 302.

171–172
"For thousands of years . . .": McNeill 1976, p. 50.

172 "I have not carried . . .": Bailey 1975, p. viii.

174 "The ethicist cannot . . .": Curran 1972, p. 194.
"The Church is discredited . . .": Bailey 1975, p. ix.

175 "What is served . . .": Weltge 1975, p. 61.

176 "One of the most popular errors . . .": Batchelor 1980, p. 76.
"Does the logic . . .": Batchelor 1980, p. 72.
" 'God is love' — so runs the argument . . .": Batchelor 1980, p. 75–76.

177 Institute for Sex Research study: Levine 1979, p. 21.

Chapter 11

180 Survey in Great Britain: McNeill 1976, p. 153–154.
Institute for Sex Research findings: Weinberg and Williams 1974, p. 256.

181 "When social structures . . .": McNeill 1976, p. 189.
Curran reference: Curran 1974, p. 126–132.
Nungesser quote: Nungesser 1983, p. 46.

182 "Moral theology must be open . . .": Curran 1979, p. 69.

183 "Except for the fact . . .": Weltge 1975, p. 13.

184 Perry quotations: Borhek 1979, p. 105; McNeill 1976, p. 173.
Metropolitan Community Church history: Fairchild and Hayward 1979, p. 176.

186 "Church assemblies may . . .": Batchelor 1980, p. 208.
"The time has surely come . . .": Spong 1988, p. 199.

186–187
History of marriages: Nelson 1978, p. 132; Greenberg 1988, p. 305; Spong 1988, p. 236–237.

187 "There must be . . .": Curran 1979, p. 71.

188 "The most prominent feature . . .": Bailey 1975, p. 155.

189 "They stand inside your church . . .": Scanzoni and Ramey 1980, p. 42.

Chapter 12

192 "In our American culture . . .": Weinberg and Williams 1974, p. 17.
"It is difficult for those . . .": Weltge 1975, p. 4.
Ford and Beach study: Bullough 1979, p. 60.

194 "That intense rage . . .": Schoenberg, Goldberg, and Shore 1985, p. 102.

195 Statistics on homophobic violence: Schoenberg, Goldberg, and Shore 1985, p. 93; Gonsiorek 1985, p. 147; Goodman 1983, p. 13.

196 Male-male rape statistics: Schoenberg, Goldberg, and Shore 1985, p. 94.
197 Saghir and Robins study: Brown 1976, p. 225.
"At the time of the assault . . .": Gonsiorek 1985, p. 150–151.
199 "By their very existence . . .": Fisher 1972, p. 135–136.
200–201
Solicitation laws: Kirk and Madsen 1989, p. 69; Knutson 1980, p. 108; Weltge 1975, p. 93.
201 "Four years ago . . .": Back 1985, p. 91.
202 Example court case: Knutson 1980, p. 14.
"Private personal acts . . .": Knutson 1980, p. 29.
202–203
Organizations opposing sodomy laws: Berzon 1979, p. 5; McNeill 1976, p. 158.
204–205
Institute for Sex Research studies: Levine 1979, p. 23–24.
205 How to Tell a Businessman from a Businesswoman: Doyle 1983, p. 154.
206 Institute for Sex Research study: Levine 1979, p. 24.
American Federation of Teachers: Fairchild and Hayward 1979, p. 98.
207 "Armies cannot be maintained . . .": Knutson 1980, p. 121–122.
"An officer or senior enlisted person . . .": *Beller v. Middendorf,* US Court of Appeals, Ninth Circuit, October 23, 1980.
The Case Against Army Segregation: Knutson 1980, p. 117.
208–209
Navy regulations: Knutson 1980, p. 117–128; Mohr 1988, p. 194–195.
209 Army regulations: Knutson 1980, p. 142.
209–210
"If *individual* homosexual women or men . . .": Bayer 1981, p. 160.
210 Exclusionary reasons offered: Knutson 1980, p. 131–140.
DIS Manual for Personnel Security Investigations: High Tech Gays v. Defense Industrial Security Clearance Office, US District Court, Northern California, August 19, 1987.
Institute for Sex Research study: Levine 1979, p. 24.
FBI and Defense Intelligence Agency testimony: Mohr 1988, p. 198–199.
210–211 "Of course, any homosexual . . .": Knutson 1980, p. 136.
211 "It is not irrational . . .": Mohr 1988, p. 210.
212 Institute for Sex Research study: Weinberg and Williams 1974, p. 105.
213 Civil Services Reform Act of 1978: Knutson 1980, p. 28.
216 Studies on incidence of marriage: Gonsiorek 1985, p. 93; Mendola 1980, p. 88; Bell and Weinberg 1978, p. 374; Rofes 1984, p. 22.
217 "If you have decided . . .": Schulenburg 1985, p. 107.
217 "If defendant retains custody . . .": Schulenburg 1985, p. 124.
218 California State University study: Nungesser 1983, p. 102.
219 APA and NASW positions: Schulenburg 1985, p. 99.
221–222
INS policies and practices: Marmor 1980, p. 210–211; Knutson 1980, p. 79–86.
222 Oregon study: Fairchild and Hayward 1979, p. 105.

Chapter 13

239 "The bitter truth . . .": Shilts 1987, p. xxii.

Chapter 14

243 "As an invisible minority . . .": Mohr 1988, p. 187.
243 Organizations supporting amendment of the 1964 Civil Rights Act: Marotta 1981, p. 325.
248 *The Advocate* survey: Levine 1979, p. 137.
249 Rehnquist quote: Knutson 1980, p. 150.
"It has been the unscientific inclusion . . .": Bayer 1981, p. 144.
256 Homophile organization statistics: Weltge 1975, p. 119.
Russo reference: Levine 1979, p. 205–210.
262 National Organization for Women position: Marotta 1981, p. 287.
263 "Research on racial minorities . . .": Weinberg and Williams 1974, p. 279.
264 "For its treatment of gays . . .": Mohr 1988, p. 26–27.

Chapter 15

270 "Nowhere has the hostility . . .": Marmor 1980, p. 239.
217 Studies of adolescent sexuality: Spada 1979, p. 23, 31, 325.
"By the time . . .": Bell, Weinberg, and Hammersmith 1981, p. 186.
276 "Minimally, the child feels . . .": Gonsiorek 1985, p. 33.
276–277
"Inch by inch . . .": Fisher 1972, p. 246.
278–279
Process of adopting a gay identity: DeCecco and Shively 1984, p. 55; Batchelor 1980, p. 33–34; Gonsiorek 1985, p. 36; DeCecco 1982, p. 50.
279 "I felt a little like . . .": Reid 1978, p. 64.

Chapter 16

280 Studies about coming out: Levine 1979, p. 107; DeCecco 1982, p. 50.
281 Example coming out story: D'Emilio and Freedman 1988, p. 228.
283 "Now I had had . . .": Reid 1978, p. 143.
284 Institute for Sex Research study: Bell and Weinberg 1978, p. 295–300.
"The instant we are honest . . .": Marmor 1980, p. 241.
286–287
"The 'good' homosexual . . .": Fisher 1972, p. 122.
289 Reduction in internalized homophobia: DeCecco 1982, p. 50.
290 "Children generally . . .": Muchmore and Hansen 1982, p. 26–27.
Brown story: Brown 1976, p. 81.

Chapter 17

307–308 "I started to listen . . .": Silverstein 1977, p. 122.
311 "What will *my* parents . . .": Borhek 1983, p. 128.
313 "I shall never forget . . .": McNeill 1976, p. 182–183.

Bibliography

Books

Albert, Paul, Leonard Graff, and Benjamin Schatz. 1988. *AIDS Practice Manual: A Legal and Educational Guide*. San Francisco: NGRA and National Lawyers Guild AIDS Network.

Altman, Dennis. 1987. *AIDS in the Mind of America*. Garden City, NY: Anchor Books.

———. 1979. *Coming Out in the Seventies*. Boston: Alyson Publications.

———. 1971. *Homosexual: Oppression and Liberation*. New York: Avon Books.

———. 1982. *The Homosexualization of America*. New York: St. Martin's Press.

Alyson, Sasha, et al. 1982. Talk Back. Boston: Alyson Publications.

———. 1988. *You Can Do Something About AIDS*. Boston: Alyson Publications.

———. 1981. *Young, Gay and Proud*. Boston: Alyson Publications.

Back, Gloria Guss. 1985. *Are You Still My Mother?* New York: Warner Books.

Bailey, Derrick Sherwin. 1975. *Homosexuality and the Western Christian Tradition*. Hamden, CT: The Shoe String Books, Inc.

Batchelor, Edward. 1980. *Homosexuality and Ethics*. New York: The Pilgrim Press.

Bauman, Robert. 1986. *The Gentleman from Maryland*. New York: Arbor House.

Bayer, Ronald. 1981. *Homosexuality and American Psychiatry*. New York: Basic Books.

Bell, Alan P., Martin S. Weinberg, and Sue Kiefer Hammersmith. 1981. *Sexual Preference, Its Development in Men and Women*. Bloomington: Indiana University Press.

———, and Martin S. Weinberg. 1978. *Homosexualities*. New York: Simon & Schuster.

Berzon, Betty. 1979. *Positively Gay*. Millbrae, CA: Celestial Arts.

Bieber, Irving. 1962. *Homosexuality*. New York: Basic Books.

Blackwood, Evelyn. 1986. *The Many Faces of Homosexuality*. New York: Harrington Park Press.

Blumenfeld, Warren J., and Diane Raymond. 1988. *Looking at Gay and Lesbian Life*. Boston: Beacon Press.

Borhek, Mary V. 1983. *Coming Out to Parents*. New York: The Pilgrim Press.

———. 1979. *My Son Eric*. New York: The Pilgrim Press.

Boswell, John. 1980. *Christianity, Social Tolerance and Homosexuality*. Chicago: The University of Chicago Press.

Brown, Howard. 1976. *Familiar Faces; Hidden Lives: The Story of Homosexual Men in America Today*. New York: Harcourt Brace Jovanovich, Inc.

Bullough, Vern L. 1979. *Homosexuality: A History*. New York: The New American Library, Inc.

Bullough, Vern, and Bonnie Bullough. 1977. *Sin, Sickness, and Sanity*. New York: The New American Library, Inc.

Castelli, Jim. 1988. *A Plea for Common Sense: Resolving the Clash Between*

325

Religion and Politics. New York: Harper & Row.

Chesebro, James W. 1981. *GaySpeak: Gay Male and Lesbian Communication.* New York: The Pilgrim Press.

Clark, Donald H. 1988. *As We Are.* Boston: Alyson Publications.

――――. 1979. *Living Gay.* Millbrae, CA: Celestial Arts.

――――. 1977. *Loving Someone Gay.* New York: The New American Library, Inc.

Coleman, Eli. 1988. *Integrated Identity for Gay Men and Lesbians.* New York: Harrington Park Press.

Colombo, Furio. 1984. *God in America: Religion and Politics in the United States.* New York: Columbia University Press.

Cox, Allen. 1982. *The Cox Report on the American Corporation.* New York: Delacorte Press.

Curran, Charles E. 1972. *Catholic Moral Theology in Dialogue.* Notre Dame, IN: University of Notre Dame Press.

――――. 1982. *Moral Theology: A Continuing Journey.* Notre Dame, IN: University of Notre Dame Press.

――――. 1974. *New Perspectives in Moral Theology.* Notre Dame, IN: University of Notre Dame Press.

――――. 1979. *Transition and Tradition in Moral Theology.* Notre Dame, IN: University of Notre Dame Press.

Curry, Hayden, and Denis Clifford. 1986. *A Legal Guide for Lesbian and Gay Couples.* Berkeley: Nolo Press.

D'Emilio, John, and Estelle B. Freedman. 1988. *Intimate Matters: A History of Sexualtiy in America.* New York: Harper & Row.

Davidson, Alex. 1970. *The Returns of Love: A Contemporary Christian View of Homosexuality.* Downers Grove: InterVarsity Press.

Day, David. 1987. *Things They Never Told You in Sunday School.* Austin: Liberty Press.

DeCecco, John P., ed. 1985. *Bashers, Baiters and Bigots: Homophobia in American Society.* New York: Harrington Park Press.

――――. 1984. *Controversy Over the Bisexual and Homosexual Identities: Commentaries and Reactions.* New York: The Haworth Press.

――――, ed. 1985. *Gay Personality and Sexual Labeling.* New York: Harrington Park Press.

――――. 1982. *Journal of Homosexuality,* Volume 8, Number 1. New York: The Haworth Press.

DeCecco, John P., and Michael G. Shively. 1984. *Origins of Sexuality and Homosexuality.* New York: Harrington Park Press.

Doyle, James. 1983. *The Male Experience.* Dubuque: William C. Brown Company.

Dyer, Richard. 1980. *Gays and Film.* London: British Film Institute.

Fairchild, Betty. 1982. *Parents of Gays.* Washington DC: Lambda Rising.

Fairchild, Betty, and Nancy Hayward. 1979. *Now That You Know: What Every Parent Should Know About Homosexuality.* New York: Harcourt Brace Jovanovich, Inc.

Falwell, Jerry. 1984. *Wisdom for Living.* Wheaton, IL: Victor Books.

Fisher, Peter. 1972. *The Gay Mystique.* Briarcliff Manor: Stein & Day.

Fricke, Aaron. 1981. *Reflections of a Rock Lobster.* Boston: Alyson Publications.

Friedman, Richard C. 1988. *Male Homosexuality.* New Haven: Yale University Press.

Fumento, Michael. 1990. *The Myth of Heterosexual AIDS.* New York: Basic Books.

Gomez, Jose, et al. 1984. *Demystifying Homosexuality: A Teaching Guide about Lesbians and Gay Men.* New York: Irvington Press.

Gonsiorek, John C. 1985. *Homosexuality and Psychotherapy.* New York: The Haworth Press.

Goodman, Gerre, et al. 1983. *No Turning Back*. *Philadelphia:* New Society Publishers.

Greenberg, David F. 1988. *The Construction of Homosexuality*. Chicago: University of Chicago Press.

Griffin, Carolyn Welch, et al. 1986. *Beyond Acceptance*. Englewood Cliffs, NJ: Prentice-Hall.

Hall, Marny. 1985. *The Lavender Couch*. Boston: Alyson Publications.

Hanckel, Frances, and John Cunningham. 1979. *A Way of Love, A Way of Life*. New York: Lothrop, Lee and Shepard Books.

Hanscombe, Gillian E., and Martin Humphries. 1987. *Heterosexuality*. London: GMP Publishers, Ltd.

Hart, John, and Diane Richardson. 1981. *The Theory and Practice of Homosexuality*. London: Routledge, Boston, and Henley.

Heger, Heinz. 1980. *The Men with the Pink Triangle*. Boston: Alyson Publications.

Heron, Ann. 1983. *One Teenager in Ten*. Boston: Alyson Publications.

Horner, Tom. 1978. *Jonathan Loved David*. Philadelphia: The Westminster Press.

Hunt, Morton. 1987. *Gay: What Teenagers Should Know About Homosexuality and the AIDS Crisis*. New York: Farrar, Straus, Giroux.

Isay, Richard A. 1989. *Being Homosexual: Gay Men and Their Development*. New York: Farrar, Straus, Giroux.

Jay, Karla, and Allen Young. 1979. *The Gay Report*. New York: Summit Books.

Johnston, Maury. 1983. *Gays Under Grace*. Nashville: Winston-Derek Publishers.

Katz, Jonathan. 1976. *Gay American History*. New York: Avon Books.

Kinsey, Alfred C., Wardell B. Pomeroy, and Clyde E. Martin. 1948. *Sexual Behavior in the Human Male*. Philadelphia: W. B. Saunders Company.

Kirk, Marshall and Hunter Madsen. 1989. *After the Ball*. New York: Doubleday.

Kleinberg, Seymor. 1980. *Alienated Affections: Being Gay in America*. New York: St. Martin's Press.

Knutson, Donald C. 1980. *Homosexuality and the Law*. New York: The Haworth Press.

Koertge, Noretta. 1981. *Nature and Causes of Homosexuality: A Philosophic and Scientific Inquiry*. New York: The Haworth Press.

Krieger, Nancy, and Rose Appleman. 1986. *The Politics of AIDS*. Oakland: Frontline Pamphlets.

LaHaye, Tim. 1983. *What Everyone Should Know About Homosexuality*. Wheaton, IL: Living Books.

Laure, Gerald. 1983. *Sex and the Bible*. Buffalo: Prometheus Books.

Levine, Martin. 1979. *Gay Men: The Sociology of Male Homosexuality*. New York: Harper & Row.

Lewes, Kenneth. 1988. *The Psychoanalytic Theory of Male Homosexuality*. New York: Simon & Schuster.

Licata, Salvatore J., and Robert P. Petersen. 1985. *The Gay Past*. New York: Harrington Park Press.

Loovis, David. 1977. *Straight Answers About Homosexuality for Straight Readers*. New York: Harper & Row.

Marmor, Judd. 1980. *Homosexual Behavior*. New York: Basic Books.

Marotta, Tobby. 1981. *The Politics of Homosexuality*. Boston: Houghton Mifflin Company.

Martinelli, Leonard J. 1987. *When Someone You Know Has AIDS*. New York: Crown Publishers.

Masters, William, and Virginia Johnson. 1979. *Homosexuality in Perspective*. Boston: Little, Brown and Company.

McNaught, Brian. 1988. *On Being Gay*. New York: St. Martin's Press.

McNeill, John S. J. 1976. *The Church and the Homosexual*. Kansas City, MO: Sheed, Andrews and McNeill.

McWhirter, David P., and Andrew M. Mattison. 1984. *The Male Couple*. Englewood Cliffs, NJ: Prentice-Hall.

Mellor, Enid B. 1972. *The Making of the Old Testament*. Cambridge (England): University Printing House.

Mendola, Mary. 1980. *The Mendola Report: A Look at Gay Couples*. New York: Crown Publishers.

Mickelsen, A. Beverly, and Alvera M. Mickelsen. 1982. *Understanding Scripture*. Ventura, CA: Regal Books.

Mickley, Richard R. 1976. *Christian Sexuality: A Reflection on Being Christian and Sexual*. Los Angeles: The Universal Fellowship Press.

Mohr, Richard D. 1988. *Gays/Justice: A Study of Ethics, Society and Law*. New York: Columbia University Press.

Muchmore, Wes, and William Hansen. 1986. *Coming Along Fine*. Boston: Alyson Publications.

———. 1982. *Coming Out Right*. Boston: Alyson Publications.

Murray, Stephen O. 1984. *Social Theory, Homosexual Realities*. New York: Gay Academic Union.

Nelson, James B. 1978. *Embodiment: An Approach to Sexuality and Christian Theology*. Minneapolis: Augsburg Publishing House.

Nungesser, Lon G. 1983. *Homosexual Acts, Actors and Identities*. New York: Praeger Publishers.

Patton, Cindy. 1985. *Sex and Germs*. Boston: South End Press.

Payne, Leanne. 1985. *The Healing of the Homosexual*. Westchester, IL: Crossway Books.

Pennington, Sylvia. 1978. *But Lord, They're Gay*. Hawthorne, CA: Lambda Christian Fellowship.

———. 1985. *Good News for Modern Gays*. Hawthorne, CA: Lambda Christian Fellowship.

Perry, Troy. 1972. *The Lord is my Shepherd and He Knows I'm Gay*. Los Angeles: Nash Publishing.

Pharr, Suzanne. 1988. *Homophobia: A Weapon of Sexism*. Little Rock: Chardon Press.

Reid, John. 1978. *The Best Little Boy in the World*. Toronto: Random House.

Richmond, Len, and Gary Noguera. 1979. *The New Gay Liberation Book*. Palo Alto: Ramparts Press.

Rofes, Eric. 1984. *I Thought People Like That Killed Themselves*. San Francisco: Grey Fox Press.

Ruse, Michael. 1988. *Homosexuality: A Philosophical Inquiry*. Oxford: Basil Blackwell, Ltd.

Scanzoni, Letha, and Virginia Ramey. 1980. *Is the Homosexual My Neighbor?* New York: Harper & Row.

Schoenberg, Robert, Richard S. Goldberg, and David A. Shore. 1985. *With Compassion Toward Some: Homosexuality and Social Work in America*. New York: Harrington Park Press.

Schulenburg, Joy. 1985. *Gay Parenting*. Garden City, NJ: Anchor Press.

Scroggs, Robin. 1983. *The New Testament and Homosexuality*. Philadelphia: Fortress Press.

Shilts, Randy. 1987. *And the Band Played On*. New York: St. Martin's Press.

Silverstein, Charles. 1977. *A Family Matter: A Parent's Guide to Homosexuality*. New York: McGraw-Hill.

Spada, James. 1979. *The Spada Report*. New York: Signet.

Spong, John Shelby. 1988. *Living in Sin?* San Francisco: Harper & Row.

Stoddard, Thomas B., et al. 1983. *The Rights of Gay People*. New York: Bantam Books, Inc.

Switzer, David K., and Shirley Switzer. 1980. *Parents of the Homosexual*. Philadelphia: The Westminster Press.

Szasz, Thomas S. 1977. *The Manufacture of Madness*. New York: Harper & Row.

Taylor, C. Rattray. 1965. *Sexual Inversion: The Multiple Roots of Homosexuality*. San Francisco: Glide Publications.

Thompson, Mark. 1987. *Gay Spirit*. New York: St. Martin's Press.

Tripp, C. A. 1975. *The Homosexual Matrix*. New York: The New American Library, Inc.

Troiden, Richard R. 1988. *Gay and Lesbian Identity: A Sociological Analysis*. Dix Hills, NY: General Hall.

Uhrig, Larry J. 1986. *Sex Positive*. Boston: Alyson Publications.

Vida, Ginny. 1978. *Our Right to Love*. Englewood Cliffs, NJ: Prentice-Hall.

Warnken, Jeannette Kennedy. 1983. *Judge Not*. Binghampton, NY: Vail-Ballou Press.

Weeks, Jeffrey. 1985. *Sexuality and its Discontents*. London: Routledge & Kegan Paul.

Weinberg, George. 1972. *Society and the Healthy Homosexual*. New York: St. Martin's Press.

Weinberg, Martin S. 1976. *Sex Research Studies from the Kinsey Institute*. New York: Oxford University Press.

Weinberg, Martin S. and Alan P. Bell. 1972. *Homosexuality: An Annotated Bibliography*. New York: Harper & Row.

Weinberg, Martin S. and Colin J. Williams. 1974. *Male Homosexuals: Their Problems and Adaptations*. New York: Oxford University Press.

Weltge, Ralph W. 1975. *The Same Sex*. Philadelphia: The Pilgrim Press.

Magazines and Newspapers

The following sources were used for information on current events:

> The Advocate
> Newsweek
> OutLook
> OutWeek
> San Jose Mercury News
> US News & World Report
> The Washington Blade

Miscellaneous

Publications by the following organizations were used for additional information on current events:

> American Civil Liberties Union
> Lambda Institute
> National Gay & Lesbian Task Force
> National Gay Rights Advocates
> People for the American Way

Index